Manaus

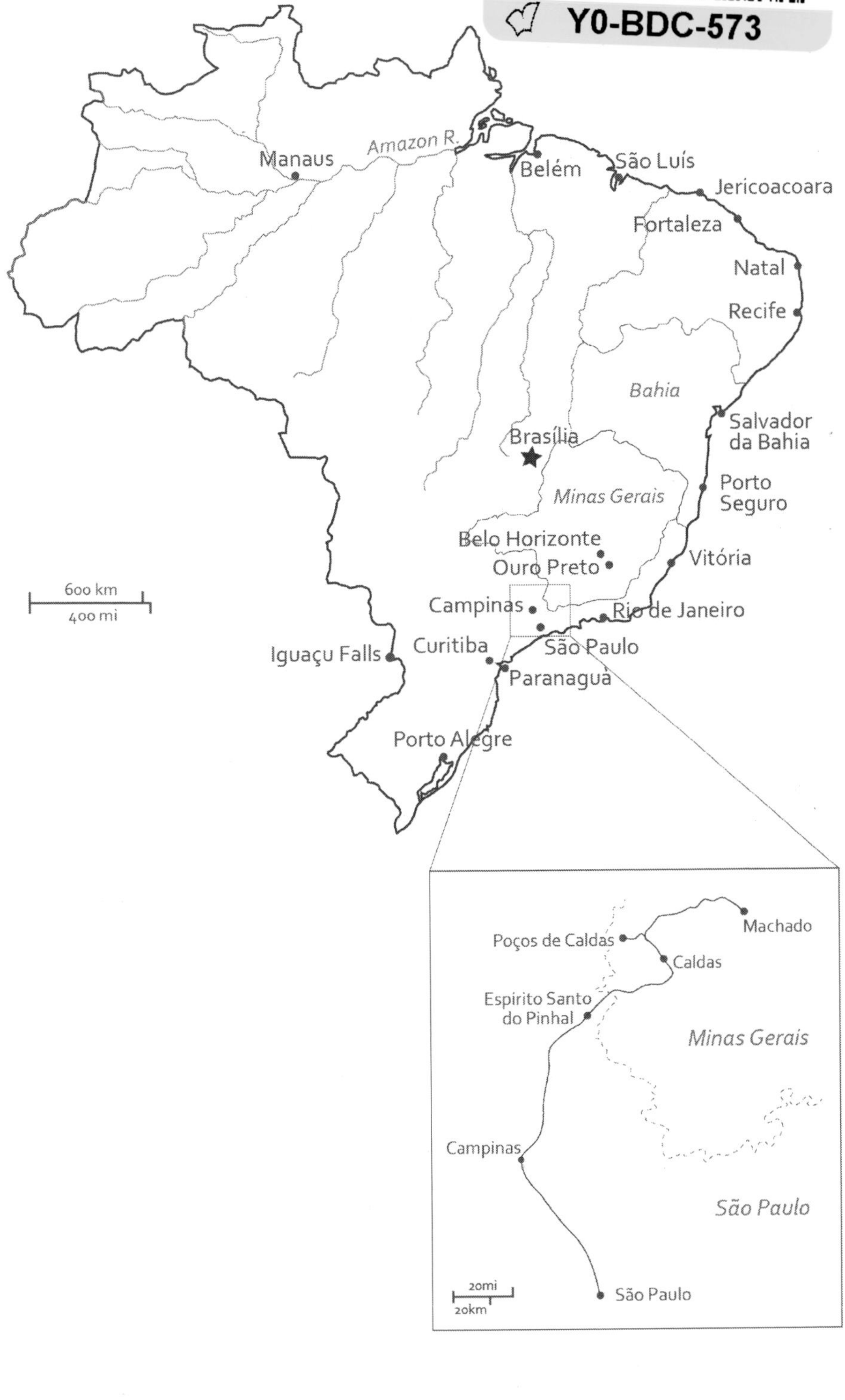

*Amazon R.*

Belém

São Luís

Jericoacoara

Fortaleza

Natal

Recife

*Bahia*

Brasília

Salvador
da Bahia

*Minas Gerais*

Porto
Seguro

Belo Horizonte

Ouro Preto

Vitória

600 km

400 mi

Campinas

Rio de Janeiro

Iguaçu Falls

Curitiba

São Paulo

Paranaguá

Porto Alegre

Poços de Caldas

Machado

Caldas

Espirito Santo
do Pinhal

*Minas Gerais*

Campinas

*São Paulo*

20mi

20km

São Paulo

# *SAUDADES*—Brazilian Family Memories from Monarchy to Millennium

*Saudades* are lovely poignant sweet tender emotional collages of thoughts, dreams, desires, sounds and smells that comprise and awaken the memory of something far away in time or space, that just might return.

Annita Clark-Weaver

*[handwritten inscription:]* fr Judith - dear friend and inspiration, with love, Annita

People and places in this book are perceived through the myopic eyes of the author, who hopes her accounts will not be found offensive to anyone.

*SAUDADES* — Brazilian Family Memories
from Monarchy to Millennium
Annita Clark-Weaver
www.saudadesbook.com

Published by Trumpet Vine Press
1143 Camilia Street, Berkeley CA 94702 United States

Layout by Together Editing & Design, Inc.
www.togetherediting.com

ISBN-10: 0615936431
Printed in the United States of America

First Edition: December 2013
9 8 7 6 5 4 3 2 1 .

In memory of my dear Vovó, Chiquita Pereira de Moraes Clark, I dedicate this book to all present and future descendants of Manuel Pereira de Moraes and Maria Ovídia Pereira de Camargo; especially to Troy Forester Pappas, my dearly beloved grandson, from his Vovó.

# Contents

# About the Text

My Brazilian grandmother's *Reminiscências* came to me written on four tablets of airline stationery, unorganized and incomplete, with some obvious gaps in the narrative and page numbers. She wrote in English, her second language, with many Portuguese words and phrases. Later I received hundreds of loose pages, letters, newspaper clippings, calendar pages, and miscellaneous writings, most in her handwriting (though a few were typed), some in English, some in Portuguese, almost all yellow and brittle with age.

Although she certainly intended for them to be read, and she must have wanted them transcribed, there are no known typed copies, except for thirty-five pages titled *Reminiscências* (Reminiscences) which were evidently transcribed from the tablets.

I have organized her papers into chapters, named them, edited out parts of limited interest, and changed her grammar and syntax when necessary for clarity, but it is still my grandmother's story, told in her words.

In São Paulo, my second cousin Yedda gave me the narrative *her* grandmother, my grandmother's sister Cacilda, had written in 1951 of *her* childhood in Caldas, Minas Gerais, Brazil. This *História Veradeira* (A True Story) as she called it, was especially important to me because it answered some of the questions I had while reading my own grandmother's story. I have translated some of this account that my Great Aunt Tia Cacilda wrote for her great-grandchildren, and I have incorporated parts of it into my grandmother's narrative.

My grandmother, Vovó as we called her, has given us very little from 1883–1889, between her fifteenth and twenty-first years, when she was a student in a boarding school in São Paulo. Accounts of these years must be in the missing pages of the tablets, page 106–152. During this period her mother died. I assume Vovó did write about these important years in a young woman's life. I have used my imagination, based on facts I know to be true from genealogical data from several family sources, to chronicle these events, and filled in the blanks just a little from my imagination in this part of the story only.

*Saudades* is an interweaving of two distinct memoirs; it is primarily my grandmother's story; written in her words, containing many Portuguese words and phrases. Throughout the book, these chapters are prefaced with a fountain pen icon, and are shown in serif font. Chapters in my voice are written in the present tense in sans-serif font. They relate to my experiences in Brazil; and form a frame for the unfolding of Vovó's narrative. These chapters are prefaced with a suitcase icon.

This is a very large family, and to help the reader, I have included an index of names with reference numbers to genealogy charts. Because first or nicknames are often used without surnames, the index is alphabetical by first or nicknames, (in parentheses) rather than last names. My grandmother's names are in bold print. A map of Brazil is included to show places important to the stories, and to indicate our travels there.

One further complication: between the years 1915 and 1943 Brazil and Portugal simplified the spelling of Portuguese in order to make it more phonetic. The orthography used by my grandmother is for the most part, but not consistently, the older one, while I have used the current system. This accounts for spelling discrepancies in the text. This should only concern readers who notice and are bothered by Portuguese spelling inconsistencies!

# Prologue

I have been reading old letters....I must not say too much here, but this much I will send to you, my grandchildren, from one of them, written when your grandfather was away from home. Deep waters again...but I love to go down this big ocean of the past and rescue those precious pearls...

–Chiquita to her grandchildren

I found the enclosed clipping here on my desk yesterday. I think you have seen it before, but I send it to you just the same. How much the first stanza is like our case, isn't it, precious darling? Myron

–Myron to Chiquita, April 2, 1913

## FATE

Two shall be born the whole wide world apart,
And speak in different tongues and have no thought
Each of the other's being, and no heed;
And these o'er unknown seas to unknown lands
Shall cross, escaping wreck, defying death,
And all unconsciously shape every act
And bend each wandering step to this one end,—
That, one day, out of darkness, they shall meet
And read life's meaning in each other's eyes.

And two shall walk some narrow way of life
So nearly side by side, that should one turn
Ever so little space to left or right
They needs must stand acknowledged face to face
And yet, with wistful eyes that never meet,
With groping hands that never clasp, and lips
Calling in vain to ears that never hear,
They seek each other all their weary days
And die unsatisfied—and this is Fate!

–Susan Marr Spalding,
In "Wings of Icarus"[1]

---

1. This poem was included in a letter from Myron to Chiquita. Susan Marr Spalding, "Fate," in *The Wings of Icarus* (Boston: Roberts Brothers, 1892), 14–15. You can view the book at http://archive.org/details/wingsoficarus00spal.

# Preface

If you ask people what they think is the most melodic word in the English language, they will usually say, "dawn" or "lullaby," or something equally poetic, but my Brazilian friend Sima used to say she thought the most beautiful English word was "garbage," and she said it softly and dramatically as if it were a term of affection. "So much more beautiful than its Portuguese equivalent, *lixo*, (pronounced lee' shu: 'which smells bad')," she said. Well, sound and meaning are different things, but they do get mixed up. To me, the most beautiful Portuguese word is "*janela*" (pronounced zha ne' la) which means window.

A long time ago, when Dom Pedro Segundo was Emperor of Brazil, a little girl looked out the back windows of her house at the mountains which surrounded her small town in the interior of Brazil, and imagined crossing those mountains to discover people and places beyond her own. Her dream was fulfilled; she lived in the United States and Portugal and met people rich and famous, humble and unsung. This is her story. Woven into the fabric are my recollections of the influences of Brazilian culture in my life, and my desire to experience the magic of Brazil firsthand; to feel for myself the rhythm of my grandmother's and my father's native land.

My paternal grandmother, Francisca Pereira de Moraes Clark, called Chiquita by all but her children and grandchildren, was born on June 2, 1868 in Caldas, a tiny village in the state of Minas Gerais, in Brazil. *Mineiros*, natives of her state, are known in Brazil as storytellers. My *Mineira* grandmother was no exception. On March 21, 1930, while visiting her youngest son George, my father-to-be, who was then twenty-seven years old and unmarried, she began writing her stories for her grandchildren. She had nine at the time; there were eventually eighteen of us.

Half a century after she began writing her *Reminiscências*, as she called them, when she and all her children and even some of her grandchildren were dead, these pages came to me—a precious legacy from the Great Beyond. Perhaps I valued them even more because she had told me many of the stories before—about her birth (as told to her by her cousin Severo, who was sent to fetch the midwife), about seeing the Emperor Dom Pedro II of Brazil when his train passed through a nearby town, and about her father, the town pharmacist, his visits to the sick with the doctor (and sometimes without), and his hunting trips with his favorite horse, Condor. She had told me about her mother and her conversion from Catholicism to Protestantism by traveling evangelists, about her seven sisters and one brother, about her family's slaves, Eva and her son João. But many of the stories were new to me; they were my *janelas* through which I could see and enter my grandmother's world.

When I received Vovó's *Reminiscências* (*vovó* is Portuguese for granny), I had already made several trips to Brazil, lured by my father's unrequited longing to return to his native land. I had learned to speak Portuguese, had lived and worked in Rio and Vitória and had met and become friends with many Brazilian second cousins in Rio and São Paulo. Now, after reading my grandmother's story I was eager to return, this time to trace her footsteps in Caldas. Here I found more storytellers, mostly elderly women whose memories of the old days were intact from much repeating. I stayed there for months, surrounded by friendly ghosts.

Vovó wrote about her ability to invoke the past through music, familiar places, photographs, and words. In working with her reminiscences and visiting Caldas, Rio, São Paulo, Lisbon, and Coimbra, I also often had the feeling I was entering her past. So I give you two narratives: my grandmother's story and an account of my search for my Brazilian roots through her memory. In a sense, we are both finding ourselves as Brazilians. I, as a North American of Brazilian descent and Vovó, whose Brazilian identity was brought into sharp focus by her marriage to an American and her life in other countries.

My experiences in Brazil have taught me something about how the cultures of family, community, and nations intertwine to shape our identities. I have learned how the attempt to bridge two very different cultures enables one to separate cultural identity from the more essential personal identity, and to see one's native culture in a fresh way. I also have learned how family bonds can transcend culture and experience— even (to some degree) language.

Culture that is too familiar is invisible; we can't separate the view from the filter. When I am in Brazil every day is an adventure: there is excitement, joy, and beauty. I want to live with that sense of adventure wherever I am, but the familiarity of my native culture makes awareness and discovery more difficult in the United States. I recognize the culture of my birth family in the families of my Brazilian relatives, and this makes bridging the gap between the two cultures very moving, and relatively easy. But always there are differences that I don't fully understand, and places where I move with some hesitation and insecurity. Like Vovó, sometimes I feel I don't belong in either culture—there is a quiet loneliness in my cultural duality. I hope that readers unfamiliar with Brazil's history and culture will get a sense of the vastness, the diversity, the beauty of the country, and of the unbridled joy and humor of Brazilians.

This is a love story—love between a man and a woman, love of nature, of beauty, of family, and love of country. In this time of calls to patriotism, I would like people to ask themselves what it is about their country that they truly love and value. The story is also about slavery: how the legacy lasts and how people deal with the shame and guilt.

Most of all this is a story about strong women: my grandmother, her sisters, her mother, and her grandmother, who lived in a very patriarchal society. It is a family saga, a weaving of memories that began with my grandmother's great-grandfather, who was born in 1789 in the backlands of Brazil. It is particularly the story of my grandmother and me—two women of different eras and cultures whose lives and countries overlapped, and who loved and honored their parents and grandparents, their contemporaries and descendants, the beauty of nature and of simple pleasures, enough to leave more than photographs—enough to set down their memories and feelings about the events and landscapes of their lives. With the gift of my grandmother's memoirs as a guide, I traveled through the windows of space and time, and came to find my Brazilian heart.

# I. Girlhood

My Brazilian grandmother—Vovó to her grandchildren, Chiquita to her family and friends—was born Francisca Pereira de Moraes in Caldas, Minas Gerais, Brazil in 1868. She was sixty-three when I was born in 1931. Our lives overlapped by thirty-one years; we both became bi-lingual and, to some extent, bi-cultural. Although she spent much more time in the United States than I have spent in Brazil, we both came to feel at home in both countries. We lived for a while under the same roof in Athens, Ohio, and at my Uncle Neco's house in Rio de Janeiro.

Until the middle of the eighteenth century, the area around Vovó's town was occupied by peaceful indigenous people known as the Caiapó.[1] Her village, originally called the *Arraial de Nossa Senhora do Rio Verde das Caldas* (Hamlet of Our Lady of Green River Hot Springs) was founded in 1806 by Antônio Gomes de Freitas, a Portuguese native, who came to Brazil in search of gold, and failed to find it.[2] In 1833, the year of her father's birth, the population of Caldas was 5,320; by 1842, near the time of her mother's birth, it had risen to 12,845. According to the testimony given in 1920 by an old black woman of Caldas, Esperança, when she was said to be 114 years old, "I was already biggish when the two first aligned houses in this city were built." One was the house of Pedro Antônio da Silva, Vovó's great-grandfather.[3]

In 1868, the year Vovó was born, Brazil was engaged in a bloody boundary war with Paraguay.[4] It was a rural economy dominated by an aristocracy of landowners (*fazendeiros*) who held great political and social power.

---

1. The information about early residents of Caldas came from a wonderful book given to me by my friend Mailde Jerónimo Tripoli: Reynaldo de Pimenta, *O Povoamento do Planalto da Pedra Branca* (The Population of the White Rock Plateau).
2. Pimenta, *O Povoamento do Planalto da Pedra Branca*, 141.
3. Ibid., 155.
4. In spite of a history of conflict over boundaries, Brazil, Argentina, and Uruguay joined forces in 1865 in what was then called the War of the Triple Alliance to defeat the Paraguayan dictator, Francisco Solano López. The war lasted five years, and all armies suffered huge losses from heat, fever, and insects in tropical swamps and forests; López was defeated mainly by disease and starvation. Old men, boys, women, and girls took the places of the soldiers as they perished. At the end of the war, Paraguay was practically annihilated and women over age fifteen outnumbered the men by more than four to one. Haring, *Empire in Brazil*, 78–83.

Coffee had replaced sugar as the main export of Brazil, and the principal regions for coffee growing were southern Minas Gerais and the valley of the Paraiba, in the province of São Paulo. The slave trade had been abolished in 1854, but slavery was still legal and the economy of the entire country depended upon the unpaid labor of slaves. The *fazendeiros* and their sons, educated in the professions, "monopolized politics; dominating the parliaments, the ministries, in general all positions of authority, and affecting the stability of institutions by their unquestioned dominion."[5]

Although we don't know why or when Vovó's ancestors came to Brazil, they were established in Minas by 1763, towards the end of the "gold cycle" and the beginning of the "pastoral cycle." Based on the surname *Pereira* (pear tree), they were probably descendents of Sephardim Jews. By 1868, when Vovó was born, Brazil was a monarchy ruled by Dom Pedro II. His grandfather, Dom João, had become the first Emperor of Brazil and Portugal in 1807, when Napoleon's armies sent the royal court fleeing from Lisbon to Rio, and Rio de Janeiro temporarily became the capital of the Portuguese Empire.

When Dom João reluctantly returned to Portugal in 1821, he left his son, Dom Pedro, in his place as regent, and Dom Pedro promptly declared Brazil independent from Portugal. The United States, under President Monroe, was the first country to recognize the new Empire and Dom Pedro as the "Constitutional Emperor and Perpetual Defender of Brazil." He ruled for nine years, until 1831, when because of many economic and political pressures, he abdicated in favor of his son Dom Pedro II, then five years old. He thought that Pedro, being a native Brazilian, would be more acceptable to his subjects than a Portuguese ruler.

Brazil was ruled first by a board of three regents and then, in 1834, by a single regent chosen by Parliament. In 1841 Dom Pedro II, at age fourteen, was crowned Emperor. He ruled for forty-nine years and was a scholar and a patron of science. He was beloved by his people for his human qualities of honesty, tolerance, and public spirit.[6]

---

5. Buarque de Holanda, *Raízes do Brasil*, 89–90.
6. Background information on the Portuguese/Brazilian royal family was largely obtained from my reading of Haring, *Empire in Brazil*.

Although I was born when my native land was suffering its greatest economic depression, my first decade of life in Athens, Ohio, a small college town nestled in the foothills of the Allegheny Mountains, was a happy time, with my sisters, parents and maternal grandmother, Nanny. Neighborhood kids of all ages played together outside in the long twilight of summer—games we learned from older kids and games we made up. In winters we bundled up in caps and mittens, leggings and galoshes, and made snow angels and snow ice cream, and whizzed downhill on our sleds. Sometimes Vovó visited, and that was a special treat.

# 1. A *Gringa* in Brazil

 *Caldas, Minas Gerais, Brazil, November 13, 1984*

I am always the only person on the bus with a suitcase—a big one—amidst the bundles, cans of milk, sacks of rice—and in the aisle this time, a box full of puppies. My suitcase embarrasses me; it telegraphs *gringa* (foreigner). I am tall, fifty-three, and traveling alone. The suitcase and I both stand out. My grandmother's memoirs, written on tablets of browned and brittle airline stationery, were way too fragile and too precious to bring with me, so I packed the tapes I had made from them, and a few typewritten pages I had transcribed. My suitcase also carries a family tree (tracing my Brazilian roots back to an ancestor named Joaquim Bueno de Camargo, who lived from 1763 to 1868), a typewriter, and a tape recorder, in case I meet someone with stories.

I've been traveling by bus through Minas Gerais, the interior heartland of Brazil, for a couple of weeks, after a month in Rio and three weeks flying around the country on a Brazil Air-Pass. Now I'm alone in a dream world, with no one to interrupt my perceptions—not thinking much about anything, just observing—but I'm getting more and more excited as we near Caldas, the birthplace of my *Vovó* (for *avó*, grandmother), Francisca Pereira de Moraes Clark.

Now on the final leg of my journey, I feel that peculiar combination of excitement and calm satisfaction that one has when going home after a long absence. While I wait for the bus, I meet Denise, a friendly young woman with a pretty face, rosy cheeks, full red lips, and laughing eyes, who reminds me of someone I know back home. She is returning to Caldas from the neighboring town of Poços de Caldas and is curious about me. Caldas is not on the tourist circuit, and in this part of Brazil, it is not common to see women traveling alone unless, like her, they are just taking a short shopping trip. We sit together on the bus going in a meandering way (the only way) towards Caldas, and talk about my mission.

I tell her the story of my grandmother's reminiscences while watching for some of the landmarks Vovó described—the *pinheiros*[7] and *Pedra Branca*, or White Rock, the peak of a mountain which my grandmother once imagined was a ship on the far sea. Denise points it out. I explain that I want to see the place of my grandmother's birth, and possibly find people still living there who might remember her. And I tell her about João, the slave. She tells me she will help me, and other people will too, and after a trip of about half an hour, which is plenty of time to get acquainted, we arrive in Caldas, where she helps me get the one taxi to the one hotel, where I have a reservation.

I can hardly believe I am in Caldas! It is like walking into the past. Vovó called it a poetical little town—it is a lovely town of stucco buildings with thick walls and red tile roofs, winding and undulating streets, bright flowers, and trees in many shades of green. All around are the mountains Vovó wrote of as the limits to her world, and in the middle of town, the *praça*, or plaza—a long, wide garden encircled by streets of *parelelepípido*, or stone paving blocks, and anchored by a church at either end. Through the windows of my mind I can see the old *largo* (public square) of one hundred years ago, muddy and corrugated, carved by the hooves of cattle and goats. I envision the church as it was then, with the cemetery behind, and in the *largo* the huge black cross hung with those instruments of torture which one occasionally still sees in rural Brazil. Today, the *praça* invites strollers to its fountain and stone benches, but in my grandmother's day it was a fearful place, dominated by the towering cross. Old houses and stores, most of them looking like the photo I have of Vovó's house, face the streets on the two sides of the *praça*, which lies on a ridge. From both sides of this long flat *praça*, perpendicular streets descend precipitously.

There are television antennas on some of the houses, and rock and roll may be blaring in the street, but in my mind's eye, the *praça* is still the largo that was my grandmother's Camp of Action, with the scary cross and the *chafariz*, the faucet where the slaves pumped water for cooking, washing, and bathing while telling each other their stories. I feel as if I have just stepped out of a time machine. It is a gentle place, and I can feel Vovó's presence here.

---

7. Paraná pine, Brazilian pine or candelabra tree.

I am excited and filled with quiet anticipation. Something wonderful is waiting for me here.

# 2. Wings of Memory

To have lots to do and not to have time to perform all the duties that are thrown upon one's shoulders is not the hardest thing. The hardest thing is to have twelve hours at your disposal in a small town where you are a stranger, and the company of the only person who is attached to you by blood is available for only a few minutes at night. After your eyes are tired from mending, knitting, reading, or writing letters to your family scattered in different cities in two different countries, if you have seen more than six decades pass over your head and you are five thousand miles away from the land that you call home, you can't help turning your thoughts to the days of your youth and try to live again those happy times which are buried in the past.

This is what I am doing seated in my room beside two corner windows in the house of my youngest son, George. One window opens almost over the beautiful Ohio River, and through the other I am watching the river crawl along the hills of West Virginia until it disappears in a curve where a wee island divides its waters in two streams. I am remembering.

I remember one night when I was visiting at the home of my eldest son, Orton. I was seated by a big fire in the grate, my grandchildren crawling all over me asking me to tell them a true story. I told them some very interesting incidents in the life of a little boy and seeing how thrilled they were with my true story, I disclosed the fact that the little boy was their father. The thought came to me; why not make use of some of these long hours to gather the fragments of my life, scattered in several corners of the globe and leave them to my grandchildren?

Perhaps some day my grandchildren will be interested to know that their Vovó burned her hair many times when she was a little girl while crocheting or studying her lessons by the flickering light of a candle made by her own mother; and then she lived long enough to read by an electric lamp, listening to music programs brought from other countries by the radio!

So, on the wings of my memory let us fly to my little town, Caldas, in the state of Minas Gerais, in the interior of Brazil, and see what is going on in one of the back rooms overlooking lovely country scenery, in one of the houses on the Rua Conde d'Eu.

> *Can't you see something sticking up far, far away where the earth touches the sky? That is the end of the world and those things are ships on the sea. I wish I could go there and sail away in one of them. It must take a long time to get there on horseback.*

Rigged up in one of my mother's dresses which swept the floor, with a small pillow fixed up as a baby in my arms, that is how I used to talk with some imaginary visitor who was present always when I played *faz de conta* (make believe) in this back room in one of the wings of our house. I would point through the window that opened to rolling country spreading out for miles and miles through stretches of green pastures where horses and cattle could be seen grazing, and areas of darker green formed by little woods where small streams would provide a drink to the thirsty animals. Further on, little forests of *pinheiros* marched up the mountainside with their branches stretched out on the top of each trunk like an umbrella.

My imagination was very fertile and the subject of the conversations that I had with these imaginary friends was always about some far-away country, which in my mind was located on the other side of the *serra* (mountains) that walled one side of the little town of my birth.

## *Wooster, Ohio, July 1934*

I did not get very far with this story, for I began my roaming again, visiting children in both hemispheres. Finally I decided to find a parking place where I could extend my stay without being afraid of becoming a nuisance. I chose Wooster, Ohio, the place where I last kept house, where my daughter Ruth lives, and where I have many friends.

The first night when I got up to see how far my friend, the moon, had gone in her night-traveling through the sky, and not being able to find her from my bedroom, I sneaked into my little living room, almost afraid that somebody would see me. Turning on the light, I looked at pictures of my children, some when they were babies and again with their babies in their arms. They seemed to say to me: "Go back to bed, Mother!"

And now I am ready to dig into the Past.

# 3. The House on Bever Street

 *Berkeley, California, April 18, 1981*

It's my birthday; I'm fifty, and feeling sad. My mother died in February in my hometown (Athens, Ohio), and I have just returned to Berkeley. The phone rings; it's my cousin Sylvia. She is excited and talks very fast in her musical, high-pitched voice. She tells me she is in Wooster to sell the family home, since her mother, my father's sister Ruth, is not going to be able to return from the nursing home.

"Oh, Neech," she says to me, "You'll never believe it—I was in the bedroom Vovy used to have when she stayed here—you remember?—the one to the left at the top of the stairs. I was just going through everything, deciding what to keep and what to give away; throwing stuff out—lots of stuff—you know this house. At any rate, what I'm getting at is—in the top drawer of the curly maple bureau there were three old tablets with pictures of airplanes on the covers. Well, there they were, the paper all browned and brittle—pages and pages in Vovy's handwriting, in English, although there are a lot of Portuguese words. I really don't know what all they contain; they're hard to read and I don't have time to do it now anyway, it's such a huge job to clear out this house. Oh—there are some loose pages too—all in her handwriting, and thirty-five typewritten pages—I don't know who did that—about her life in Caldas."

Listening to Sylvia, sharing her excitement, I am transported back in time thirty-five or forty years ago to that large old house, elegant and chaotic at the same time, on the corner of Bever and Spring Streets in Wooster, Ohio, where my sister Jan and I used to visit in the summers. In my mind's eye, I enter the front door, past the vestibule (it's the only house I had ever been in that had a vestibule) with its walk-in coat closet filled with assorted coats, umbrellas, and boots, through the entry room, remembering the wide staircase, fronted by a wooden bench with a hinged top, hiding unknown-but-possibly-accessible-contents. I walk into the dark living room with its heavy furniture, including a grand piano in front of the windows facing the street. The quiet darkness of the room envelops me, and the sudden brightness of the glassed-in sun porch next to it draws me into the slanted rays of dusty sunlight. I hear my cousin Marquita singing as Aunt Ruth accompanies her on the piano, "Believe Me, If All Those Endearing Young Charms." I see the two families, Spencers and Clarks, when we were young, playing charades in front of the big stone fireplace in the living room.

I hear Uncle Warren summoning us girls to the corner of the living room beside the floor-to-ceiling bookcases flanking the French doors leading to the dining room. He sits in his favorite chair, fills his pipe, and reads a didactic Victorian novel called *Rosamond*, drawing out the words while drawing on his pipe. We groan—we have heard it so many times we have almost memorized it—Rosamond mustn't climb trees like her brothers because she might get her pretty dress dirty. It is boring, yet funny the way he reads it; we're cringing, begging him to stop, and not wanting it to end.

When he tires of this, we play a game Uncle Warren makes up using old studio photographs he inherited from his grandparents. He calls the game "Ancestors." He deals out the cards, and there is some sort of rummy-like play, combined with poker-like hierarchy. The suits are features like "beards", "sideburns", "button shoes", "feathered hats", "silly dogs", etc. We sort of make up the game as we go along.

Then, in my imagination, I enter the dining room filled with summer evening light, and see Uncle Warren riding on a broomstick around the table—because the carving knife is too dull for the roast! He then returns to the carving, which he manages successfully, saying something like, "You see, girls, it always works—when you are stuck, you just have to ride on a broomstick!" We hoot hysterically. Aunt Ruth just sighs, probably thinking that her dinner is getting cold.

Uncle Warren isn't always directing our activities on Bever Street, though; the house itself holds secrets to explore—a clothes chute that runs from attic to basement we can use to pass notes to each other, and a dumbwaiter connecting the attic to the kitchen, big enough for us to ride in one at a time as the others all pull on the cord. It comes down fast and bounces as it goes up. Deliciously scary, fun.

In those days, Aunt Ruth was delicate and affectionate. She was tall and willowy with a Modigliani face and a sweet, wistful expression. She seemed fragile, somehow, and I didn't want to see her unhappy. She was a beauty, and all the family—Uncle Warren, my father, my aunts and uncles—talked about the hearts she had broken when she was young. Sylvia told me she had had thirteen proposals of marriage, and was engaged three times.

All these memories are flashing dreamlike through my mind's eye as Sylvia talks about the tablets. And then we wonder together—how long has it been since Vovó tucked her life away in the chest of drawers? After our grandfather's death, did Vovó cart her tablets from house to house as she divided her time among her six children? Did anyone—our parents or aunts and uncles—know of them? Sylvia tries, but can't remember the last time Vovó might have been in that house before she died at Uncle Henry's. Has no one opened the drawer in the nineteen years since her death? Or was Aunt Ruth perhaps planning to do something with the tablets, and either got discouraged or forgot about them? And most important to both of us, were there more tablets waiting to be discovered?

So from then on, as she wades through the flotsam and jetsam of the decades in that house, Sylvia looks for more tablets, for old brittle pages, for that venerable handwriting, but finds nothing more. When she visits her mother in the rest home, Sylvia tells her about the tablets; Aunt Ruth seems neither surprised nor curious.

Back home in Rhode Island, Sylvia calls again to tell me she has copied the typewritten pages and sent them around to her cousins, including me; but there is no way to copy the tablets and, she advises me, it will take her a while to read them. After reading the thirty-five typewritten pages, I am very eager to see the tablets, and I call her to offer to transcribe them for the family. Sylvia promises to send them to me as soon as she has read them.

I am beginning to sense that these tablets will have an effect on my life, but I will have to see them before I can understand the excitement beginning to stir my dreaming. Eventually, after a very long gestation, my grandmother would come alive again, and speak through me.

# 4. Caldas in the Moonlight of Memory

"You were born, *prima* (cousin), on a most beautiful moonlit night. I shall never forget, because I was sent to call the midwife, and I was scared to death to pass so late at night by the church behind which some important people were buried. Not one soul was about in the long, wide *largo* with the moon shining bright above the big black cross in front of the church, with the ladder and the tools which were used to torture our Savior hanging from its arms! Not a light shining in the long row of white houses on both sides of the *largo*. What a silence! I could hear my footsteps and the thump, thump, thump of my heart! But I never saw a more beautiful night than that of the second of June, 1868!"

Thus my cousin Severo, who lived with my family when I was born, used to talk to me every time we saw each other when I was young, and again when I couldn't call myself that any more. His father was a pharmacist, and my father as a young man had worked for this uncle. My father also became a pharmacist and Severo worked for him after he grew up. I liked to hear him tell about that lovely night because there was nothing else worthy of remembrance about the event. Wasn't I the fifth girl who had arrived under that roof when my mother was only going to be twenty-four years old the very next day?

Well, I don't remember that night, but I do remember those following it a few years later, when my mother with all the children would go to our grandmother's and I would sneak into one of the beds and, at the time to go home, play possum to be left there. I couldn't forget either those nights when the mothers of the town called on their intimate friends, taking all the children with them. It was not uncommon for two or three families with five or more children each to be gathered in the same place and oh! What glorious times we had playing hide and seek and other games! These calls were almost always made on moonlight nights because no small town in those days had any other light than that furnished by

"Front of house where I was born in 1868. Henry took this in 1920."

the kind old moon. It was rather dangerous to go through that spacious *largo* on dark nights as you might fall on top of something, and the next second you would find out you were riding a cow! Stumbling over a cow was not a rare occurrence, and caused much jeering in some families. That *largo* was our Camp of Action. Right in the middle of the huge *largo*, there was a fountain. It was a public place with faucets for the people to obtain water, because there was no piped water in those days. Around the fountain we played happily, inventing games. Unhappily, there is a time to laugh and a time to cry.

We had strict rules about how far we could go, which were strictly broken or we would not have had any fun. Children had no privileges in those days: they were thought to be creatures who were always doing what they ought not to do. When they were found out, there were not many George Washingtons around those regions to tell the truth, because they were afraid of the rod. I am going to give a personal illustration—my father had in his pharmacy a medicine so good we would wish to be sick all the time—if we could take that instead of castor oil! It tasted just like plum jam, oh so good! The can of *tamarindo* constituted a big temptation to us children. So whenever we had a good opportunity to help ourselves to

The largo in 1875. Photo of painting in the courthouse in Caldas.

the delicious jam, we did.

One night that opportunity came to me, so using my hand as a spoon I grabbed as much as I could hold, and went to a dark room. There, standing on a trunk by an open window where I could dispose of the seeds, I was devouring my prey as quickly as possible. Suddenly I heard voices; a family was calling and my father was bringing them to the place where intimate friends were entertained—the dining room, that was right by the room where I was hiding. My father saw me there.

He came to me, closed the door, and asked what I was doing there in the dark. "Nothing, nothing and nothing" was my answer. Then he took the nearest object he could lay his hand on, which was a shoe, and using this as a reinforcement to his questions he succeeded in getting from me that I was eating sugar; then he said to me that if I had told him that before he would not have punished me. I don't know really which was worse—the humiliation or the spanking!

In my childhood there were many imaginary things that made a child's life full of apprehensions. Tales to scare you told by slaves—your own or those of your friends—and conversations you heard and didn't understand and wouldn't dream of questioning your parents about. As a child there was nothing that scared me more than to hear that there was a *Negro fugido*, a runaway slave, in the neighborhood. If you did this-or-that a *Negro fugido* would surely catch you. We never heard this from our parents, though. There was an old colored fellow, a freed slave, who killed his wife and was in prison for that, yet he could do errands at night. He was a cobbler, and used to come to our house after nine o'clock. Well, you can imagine how we children feared that fellow.

My mother and other mothers used to go for a walk sometimes after dinner in the country near the *campo santo* (cemetery). Behind this a man had been hung for murder. We children used to go ahead of our mothers, running and playing, but just as soon as we began to get near that place we would slow down—we were forever fearing ghosts. We didn't have the courage to get some information on these things from our parents. I was a child when a child was to be seen and not heard, but an old person had to be respected and treated by children with some benevolence. I wonder if that is why I love to be heard so much now! Believe me, today is certainly an age when a child is to be heard, and everything done to make the child's life pleasant and free of fear. As for old people, sometimes they are treated as Private Nuisance No.1!

We had two slaves: a woman and her son, Eva and João, because we had to have help, as the duties were many and machines were not available then. Think for a minute of the duties of a household in those days. The rice that we used twice a day had to be taken from the husks; the sugar had to be refined, and coffee roasted and pounded. We helped our mother many times to make candles and soap. It was a profitable way to get rid of the great quantity of ashes that came out of those gigantic places for cooking and what was left from the fat you fried. There was the washing and the ironing to be done. We each ironed our own clothes, and my older sister ironed my father's stiff shirts and collars. A certain class of woman did the washing—no lady did this job. So our clothes, like those of our friends, were taken to a river or spring to be washed by those women. And what about the cooking! From those clumsy brick and mud stoves where logs were burned came the most delicious dishes!

One of the jobs that you and I would think the slaves would hate was carrying the water from the public *chafariz* on their heads in cans that once brought kerosene or in barrels which came filled with wine from Portugal. But the slaves liked that. No wonder, poor souls; wasn't it at this place that the older ones had a chance to talk about their troubles with the other slaves that they met there, and the young, while the crystalline water was filling their cans, were pouring their very prohibited love into the ears of the other sex? It was there too that their masters were discussed and quarrels were fomented!

Taking care of the horses was another job for the slaves. Most everybody had to have horses—they were the cars of those days. My father was very proud of his horses, especially Condor, who had the reputation of not consenting to anybody but a woman on his back. The fact was, that being a very spirited and impetuous horse, the minute he heard or felt the spurs and the whip of the man on his back he did everything to knock him down, and ordinarily he did. João accompanied my father on hunting trips to take care of the horses, as the men could not enter on horseback those wild woods 2100 feet above the town, which was itself about 3600 feet above sea level. The horses had to be left outside of the woods. Few people had the courage to penetrate those forests at that time. But what a view one had from the peak of Pedra Branca! It was superb! One could see on clear days the land of three states.[8]

As I look back to injustices which were done to the slaves, even what my own family and my own self thought they ought to do, I cannot understand how God permitted such injustice! Later in school, when I was in contact with a much purer Christianity, I realized their rights and wrote to my father asking him to give Saturday to them as was done by some, so that they could make a little money for themselves. And he did.

There were many laws suggested by the Abolitionists, the breach of which made slaves free. Once, as my father exercised the position of Judge of the Peace, there were eleven slaves who became free because of their masters' breaking some of those laws. He was the one to sign the letter of freedom, and after the ceremony all those present—the ex-slaves, and the band of the city—accompanied my father home. Not understanding what made those slaves free I gave all the honor to my

---

8. Minas Gerães, São Paulo, and Guanabara, now the state of Rio de Janeiro.

father, and how proud I was! Yet I did not stop to think why he didn't free his own: he did a little later, not forced by law.

We have been very fortunate in my country that changes that cost rivers of bloodshed to the United States were accomplished without the sacrifices of lives. Slavery in Brazil was abolished by decree of Princess Isabel who was reigning while Don Pedro II was in Europe, on the 13th of May, 1888, and the Republic was proclaimed in 1889 with no bloodshed.

As in my imagination I look back to the days of the candle and the spinning wheel, I see seated at it my grandmother who became a grandmother a few days before she was thirty. There she is changing those fluffy strips of cotton that had been through the teasel into the thread that she was going to make into cloth for towels and bedding on the clumsy old loom! I see my own mother with a baby in her arms at fifteen. As I think of them now, I can't help but realize that they were wonderful women for that age. How much schooling do you think they had? I cannot tell you, except that it was very little, but this I can say: they knew all about the Reign of Terror and the fall of the Bastille; about Marie Antoinette, and Anne Boleyn; about the Rothschilds and Napoleon, without having George Arliss[9] to bring these gentlemen to them. They read the works of Victor Hugo and Alexandre Dumas, and Don Quixote de la Mancha was familiar to them.

My grandmother being so young, it was not a hard thing for her to have the grandchildren around so much, and I loved to go there. I remember one day when it was pouring rain, I wanted to go there, and as it was quite far away and I knew that my mother would not let me go if I asked, I decided to go without asking. I hunted for an umbrella and started walking bare-foot in the water that ran in the middle of the street.

The rain was falling heavily and half-way there I met an old colored woman, a friend of the family, who immediately saw that I was going without permission, so she told me a story of a little girl who on a day like that ran away from her mother and a wind blew and carried her away

---

9. George Arliss, 1868–1946. British-born American actor who played many historical characters, including Nathan Rothschild in *House of Rothschild* in 1934.

with the umbrella and they never heard of her again. I was having quite a time to hold the umbrella, but to go back was dangerous, so, scared to death and seeing visions of a bad little girl like myself disappearing in the clouds above me, I finally arrived at my grandmother's. She of course admired my courage and my love for her, and my mother would not punish me, as she was afraid to hurt my grandmother's feelings. So that was that.

I think my grandmother was an unusual character, and I might say, a heroine, too. Her father was an honest man but of a very strong will. There were three sisters; she was the youngest. When the oldest reached the marriage age at fourteen, her bridegroom was introduced to her and, as she refused to accept him, her father convinced her with the rod. She didn't live very long, and she left a baby daughter to be raised by her parents.

The second, in words of today, eloped, but in the judgment of those days, she committed a great crime to run away to marry the man she cared for. My grandmother faced her fate at fourteen and, submissive, married the man chosen by her parents to be her husband rather than have the humiliating experience of her older sister or follow the disgraceful behavior of the other one. She had a very large family, her three younger children being about the same age as my mother's three older ones. Four of them are living yet.

My mother was beautiful, helpful, hard working, and above all, kind. Many times she gathered to her house the poor vagrants of the streets and offered them a bath, clean clothes, and food. She took sick people who lived in the corners of the town and walked them to the hospital. I remember well when I was young seeing her on a street behind our house accompanied by some people who were carrying a poor sick woman to *Santa Casa* (the hospital) on an improvised hammock!

My father's grandfather, João Sabino Pereira, was the first pharmacist in Caldas. I don't remember anything about him, but my father's pharmacy was called the *Farmácia do Cervo* (Deer Pharmacy). It had a stag painted in oil opposite the door. It was richly equipped, with everything necessary to function well. It had electric batteries, *alambiques* (stills), and fine

1870. Chiquita on father's lap, her mother pregnant with Ophida.

copper equipment to vaporize mineral waters. And it was beautiful! How I remember the bottles filled with liquids of different colors and the rows of lovely French porcelain jars, white with blue and blue with white. The best ones were in white and gold with the names of the contents in Latin. Just behind this, he had his laboratory, where the medicines were made and where my father had his office. And there, at night, after the labors of the day, he would do his bookkeeping. When it came time for us to go to bed, we would go to him to say good-night in the following way: "*Sua benção, Papai!*" to which he would answer, "*Deus te abençôe, minha filha.*" (Your blessing, Daddy; God bless you, my daughter.) Don't you think that was a beautiful custom?

My father was also proud of being a good hunter. He had a shotgun with two chambers, which was rare at that time. He made the cartridges and gunpowder himself with much diligence. He had his own little machine to turn the edges of the shells after they were filled with the powder, lead, and plugs. He had whistles of bamboo and *taquara* (a variety of small bamboo) to imitate the chirping of the birds, and a cartridge belt that he wore when he went hunting. He had a beautiful macramé bag, made by my mother, to carry the birds, which he brought already prepared so that they would not spoil, and a mattress stuffed with cotton to sleep on in the forest, because sometimes he stayed there a few days. He also carried a couple of rolls of black wax, covering a wick made of strings of cotton to serve as a candle. This wax was rolled from the center out, making a curl just like snakes make, with the end raised to be lit. It really looked like a rattlesnake ready to spring.

My father spent nights there in order to hunt that precious bird called *macuco*[10] that one could only hunt at night. It was abundant in the forests where there were jaguars, but was very difficult to catch, and my father used to brag to his hunting friends whom he considered to be less skillful, saying, "I'm going to get a *macuco* for dinner tomorrow." And he would bring it! My mother cooked it in a delicious way, with milk, but oh, how we hated to pull those feathers, without even boiling water to make the job easier!

Caldas means hot springs, and there are, at a distance of half a league from the town, springs of sulfurous water, which today are well-known and prescribed for diseases of the stomach. My father discovered and began the improvement of these waters in Pocinhos do Rio Verde, but he died before the completion of this spa which is now visited by people from many places, especially Rio and São Paulo.

---

10. The Solitary Tinamou (*Tinamus solitarius*). Taylor, s.v. "macuco," *A Portuguese-English Dictionary*, 397.

My father built a rustic house there where he took the family for a week of great activity, when the men were trying to divert the Rio Verde, which passed through that place, from its bed. One day during that week they had a *mutirão*, a neighborly gathering for work. When there was a big job to do in rural areas, it was customary to invite workers of the area to gather together, and in one day, to work without remuneration, except for a party for all. My mother made many sweets, including the traditional sweet rice, and many tasty delicacies for the workers. As it was impossible to have a table big enough for so many people, they stretched cloths on the grass and served lunch there. The women piled *farinha* (ground flour of the manioc root) in long mounds at intervals on the cloths. We spent a happy week there, returning in a carriage with wooden wheels pulled by six pairs of oxen.

It was in this town that the sun—whose rays seem more brilliant because of the altitude, freshness of climate, and purity of the air—shone for the first time for my dear mother and sisters, and it was there that my dear father spent all his youth. There I had the good fortune to be born, and to spend all my infancy surrounded by the loving care of my parents. Mountains, offering beautiful panoramas on all sides, surround my village. The climate is cool and mild, the air pure and healthy. Pedra Branca, two and a half leagues away, is a giant of stone, and from its peak one can see, way down below, a white spot in the middle of green fields—Caldas, the cradle of my dear and always-missed mother.

Many years after I had seen some of the world's wonders, like Niagara Falls, the skyscrapers of New York (the Singer Sewing Machine and Woolworth buildings), Westminster Abbey, St. Paul's Cathedral, Napoleon's Tomb, and the Monastery of Batalha, I went back to my little town of Caldas. I had not been there for sixteen years. To my great delight everything was just as it had been in my childhood, and in my mother's and grandmother's.

# 5. Vovó

I was born on April 18, 1931 in Youngstown, Ohio. My father had just lost his job. Unlike my Brazilian grandmother, I was born in a hospital—and no one noted the phase of the moon. I was born into a world of electricity, cars, telephones, and airplanes—although no one in my family or anyone we knew had ever been in an airplane. All of these modern inventions were unknown when Vovó, my father's mother, was born.

She was in Wooster, Ohio when I was born. She wrote, in a letter I still have:

> *Dear little Annita,*
>
> *We are so very very glad that you are safely here and that your dear Mama pulled through all right. We do welcome you to our family circle which is growing very rapidly.*
>
> *It is the beginning of what I hope will prove to be a long long journey and that your pathway will be covered of the most beautiful and fragrant flowers. Wishing you all sorts of happiness I am your Vovó.*

Soon after my birth, Daddy was offered a job at Ohio University as Assistant Professor of Civil Engineering, and we moved to Athens, Ohio. Nanny came with us. She's my mother's mother.

I'm ten now; my sisters Jan and Sydney are nine and five. They were born here in this hilly college town in southeastern Ohio. Vovó is staying with us. Most of the time she lives in Brazil, but she has two daughters, my Aunts Ruth and Argy, and two sons, my father and Uncle Orton, living in the States, so she comes here every three or four years on a big ship and then visits each family for a month or two. She doesn't have her own home; she just lives out of a suitcase. She stays most of the time in Rio with Uncle Neco; I suppose that's where she feels most at home. Uncle

Henry lives in Buenos Aires. She visits his family too. She doesn't like to be alone; she wants to be with family.

She speaks English well, but with a very strong accent, which is musical and amusing. Her tongue is seldom at rest, and she always has a strong opinion about every subject. She and Daddy speak Portuguese; I love to hear the rhythm of it, even though I can't understand the words.

Vovó likes attention, but she can also busy herself with reading, writing letters, needlework, and church activities. Her bony brown fingers are always busy knitting, crocheting, or embroidering. I am amazed that she can do it without looking; she says she could do it in her sleep. She tried to teach me once, but I don't have the patience. She embroiders handkerchiefs, pillowcases, hand towels, and she crochets afghans. She is making one for me with, as she says, "all the colors of the Brazilian sunset."

She is tiny for a grownup—my size—and ancient. She stands very straight, like she's stretching her delicate bones to hold them erect. Her face is strong, with high cheekbones and caved-in cheeks, a prominent Portuguese nose, and a low-toned gravelly voice that is surprising in such a small woman.

She wears her hair in a twisted bun at the back of her head, secured with large white bone pins. Sometimes at night, when we see her in her bare feet and long white nightgown, her hair is loose, lying lightly on her back and reaching to her tiny waist; silvery white like the ropes of *gargalhadas*, a Brazilian candy we make at Christmas.

Her eyes are black, and always sparkly. Her brown, wrinkled face reminds me of a walnut; I think she's beautiful. She always wears dresses with small floral prints, black on white, or white on black. I don't know if that's because she's a widow, or she just doesn't want to wear colors. The scent of lavender flows around her like a cape, and lingers in her room. She cackles and calls herself "lavender and old face."

We girls play Go Fish, Parcheesi, and Chinese Checkers with her, and she teaches us how to play in Portuguese. She never gets cross with us about

Vovó—isn't she marvelous?

anything. She likes to play the piano, a tune she calls "Sans Souci," and a little waltz. Sometimes she gets up from the piano and dances, a shawl around her shoulders, looking so dainty and demure, her tiny feet in their laced-up shiny black shoes moving gracefully.

She tells us about the days when she was a little girl in Caldas, deep in the interior of Brazil. She laughs a lot, and is always saying, "What a co-eeencidence!" about things we usually don't see as anything especially unusual. Mother rolls her eyes; she has heard her stories many times before. So have we, but I never get tired of hearing them again.

Mother and Daddy are both heavy Camel smokers, and we all know Vovó disapproves of smoking and of drinking—which they do sometimes—and even the penny-ante poker that they play every Saturday night; but she prides herself in minding her own business, and her business is her past.

She's always talking about her *Moço Louro* (young blond man) and how when she arrives at the Pearly Gates, St. Peter will tell her she is too old for him. Then she cackles.

Vovó is an optimist, always saying, "You know, I really think the world is getting better," rolling the "r" and stretching the vowels. Nanny lives in Athens and is always near. She is a regular part of our lives, but Vovó comes from far away; her visits are rare and short, and very special to me.

Now she says as she twirls her forefinger around her ear that she is *caducanda* (which Daddy tells us means weak-minded), and doesn't seem to know what she wants. For instance, when we ask her if she would like to go for a ride, she says, "Deceesions, deceesions, deceesions!" Then we just say, "Come on, Vovy, we're going for a ride now." She loves to ride through the rolling hills of southeastern Ohio, especially now in the fall when the brilliant leaves display their glory before giving way to winter. Perhaps their colors remind her of the Brazilian sunset that she is crocheting into my afghan.

## Berkeley, California, 1962

Vovó was visiting Daddy and Mother in Athens when Daddy suddenly collapsed as they were cuddling on the davenport and was rushed to the hospital. Later Vovó told me they had looked so happy she had wanted to leave them alone, and had gone up to her room.

My sister Jan was married with two sons, living in Ohio; she got there first when she heard about Daddy's collapse. I was married, living in San Francisco and pregnant with my first child, Andrea. Sydney was also in California, teaching kindergarten in Carmel. She and I got a plane to Cincinnati and took the train to Athens. There was patchy snow on the soggy, brown ground, and all I saw from the window of the train were graveyards. We went directly to the hospital, and got there in time to each be pulled inside the oxygen tent for a last kiss from Daddy, and for me, a pat on the tummy; a blessing for the grandchild he would never see.

Vovó, then in her nineties, could not comprehend it. Aunt Argy came for the funeral, and took Vovó back to Columbus with her, where I visited before returning home. It was the last time I saw her. Vovó died in her sleep at Uncle Henry's in 1962, six days after her ninety-fourth birthday.

# 6. Our Swedish Neighbors

I sometimes wonder if the two Swedish neighbors who lived on either side of our house were not the cause of my imagination and dreams to turn to ships and far, far away countries where funny people lived. Our neighbor André Frederick Raguel,[11] an old bachelor, a physician and a botanist, came to our dear old town with only one lung. The region was noted for the number of people who arrived with tuberculosis and returned to their homes cured, and others who decided to move there. The dry, temperate climate evidently suited Dr. Raguel, as he lived there for thirty years and made a fortune practicing in the surrounding area of 50 to 80 leagues (150-240 miles), getting around on horseback.

The doctor must have been about eighty when I was old enough to remember him. He was a queer, tall, old man who went out dressed as if he were a clown. We children kind of feared him and the grownups respected him. As I think back, I guess they feared him too, because he always told them the truth. His clothes, always too big for him, must have been in fashion some eighty years before he landed in Brazil. When he called on his patients, a very few privileged ones at that time, or when he went to his *chácara* (a little country place), he would wear two or three coats of different sizes and colors that he would dispose of one at a time according to the temperature he would meet on his errands. He wore a big handkerchief tied under his chin under his straw hat and another in front of his mouth, which was tied at the back of his head, and long boots or *polainas*, which reached above his knees.

Gabriel, a faithful, young, coal-black, and very bright slave accompanied him to his *chácara* with big tin cans hanging from his back along with some implements to gather wildflowers and plants which Dr. André studied, classified, and dried on special racks made for that purpose, and

---

11. Dr. Anders Fredrik Regnell, 1807–1884. Pimenta, *O Povoamento do Planalo da Pedra Branca*, 260–61.

then sent to his country. Anybody who discovered in their garden a plant or a flower that they did not recognize brought him the specimen. To the people around there, he was Einstein. He discovered a parasite which bears his name.

Dr. André's clinic extended to very distant towns. He saw the rich people in their homes, but those who could not pay much brought information about the sick person left at home and paid for the prescription. He often took my father with him or sent him to see patients and then inform him of their symptoms and condition. Sometimes people came to my father and told him that they had been to get Dr. André to see somebody and he had said: "*Vai busca Mané Pereira, elle pode faz como eu.*" Very, very poor Portuguese, worse than my English! I will translate: "Go find Manny Pereira, he can do just as well as I." In his last year he sent my father almost all the time, except only in very special cases when he went like a scarecrow on horseback right through the town. His prescription, no matter where the sick person was, had to come to my father's pharmacy, as he didn't trust any other pharmacist.

In this way, my father learned much about doctoring, although he did not care to be a physician. He had to be, though, especially to those who couldn't pay the doctor. Sometimes payment was tendered in strange ways. Many years after my parents and three of my sisters were resting in the little cemetery on the outskirts of the town, I spent a few months in the town with my children. One night somebody knocked at the door. It was an old, old, colored fellow. He said to me; "I live in the country and I heard that you were a daughter of Senhor Manuel Pereira." Taking off his hat in an attitude of respect and looking towards the starry sky, he said, "Whom may the good Lord have in His glory—he was the father of the poor. I brought you this little present." I rejoice that I am a daughter of the father of the poor. There, all prepared for roasting, was a whole pork ham and tenderloin! I had many more assurances of his charities then but I mention this because I was sure that the old fellow was giving with sacrifice.

Dr. André died a few months after my mother died. She never had any other physician. His tombstone came from Sweden, and its inscription is in Latin. Dr. André's fame was international. Two Swedish scientists

Vovó and Eduardo Westin, at his *chacra*, c. 1908

visited him in my time; one of them, Dr. Mosin, must have been of some importance, as he was one of the twenty guests at a banquet given in honor of the Emperor of Brazil, Dom Pedro II, in Stockholm. I cannot swear that this is true but I heard it, and even if I was not more than ten or twelve years old then, it is printed or carved somewhere in my mind.

Dr. Mosin became quite friendly with my father and, knowing that my father was the best hunter in that neighborhood, Dr. Mosin joined him on some of his hunting expeditions. Well, once when they came back they surprised us with the kind of game they brought. Monkeys! After they were skinned, an operation performed by Dr. Mosin, they could well be called "Babies from the Woods"—such was the resemblance of the game to human beings. Our naturalist assured my father that the meat of this kind of monkey was a very savory dish. So they banqueted on the dear little creatures! It gives me the creeps!

Senhor Augusto was the other neighbor and an intimate friend of the family. He was a nephew of the first Swedish Consul.[12] He married the

---

12. Lourenço Westin, 1787–1846. Pimenta, *O Povoamento do Planalo da Pedra Branca*, 258–59.

daughter of a prominent wealthy farmer. He used to call me *"arrepiada,"* which means "terrified"—I suppose he meant "terror" just as you say to a child "naughty girl." Was I that? Well, I was named after my grandmother—Francisca, and the saying goes that everybody who bears that name has a bad temper just as you say about red-headed people. So if you did not have a temper they surely created one for you. But I guess they didn't have to do that for me—I had one all right. Senhor Augusto Westin had many children. Most of them are dead now, but one of those living (Eduardo, married to Maria Ignez), a friend of mine, will appear in this narrative later on.

# 7. Conversion

My great-grandfather, Pedro Antônio da Silva, was born in Lavras, Minas Gerais, in 1789, the son of Simão Antônio da Silva Teixeira, who was the founder of the city of São Simão, in the state of São Paulo. I do not know any other facts about my mother's great-grandfather, but I do remember *my* great-grandfather.

Everyone called him Padrinho (Godfather). In my earliest memories he was over eighty. We children thought he was a very queer person and our attitude of respect toward him was nothing but fear. I never saw him without his rosary in one hand and a cane in the other. When there were no customers in his grocery store, he was passing his beads and murmuring a prayer. But if anything went wrong with his slaves, right in between the beads, his vocabulary was not worthy of being mentioned here.

When we came to his house we had to repeat something after my mother at the door of the grocery if he was there and he most always was. I never got all the words she said and those that he answered until after I was grown up. The passwords were these: "*Louvado seja Nosso Senhor Jesus Cristo*" ("Praised be our Lord Jesus Christ"—said very rapidly) to which he answered, "*Para sempre seja louvado*" (He shall be praised forever).

His house was built on the corner of a street right in front of the lot as most of them were and many are even now, and only a door, the entrance to a little chapel, separated it from the next house, which belonged to his daughter—my grandmother. This chapel belonged to my great-grandfather, and there were images of several saints. On each of their feast days the chapel would be open for anybody to worship, to go in and say their prayers.

The house had three doors—two belonged to the grocery, and the other was the entrance to a narrow hall where there was a door at the left to the parlor, modestly furnished and with pictures of saints around the wall. Two windows faced the street—not glass windows, but shutters made of crisscross wood so that you could see from inside what was going on outside without being seen. They were called *rótulas*. They had wood trimming in the top and were very pretty. To enter the dining room there was a short dark corridor, separated from the first one by a heavy door that was always closed. The furniture of this room consisted of a rustic table and two benches on each side of the table, one of them next to the wall. Fortunate were those who sat on this one as the wall gave some support to their backs. This room was not used much.

There were little frames all around the wall with pictures in relief—white on a black background, of scenes of the life of Christ. At Lent, the family, children and grandchildren, would gather there to sing, and the children would do the *Via Sacra* (Stations of the Cross) on their knees. I remember one of my aunts talking about one of those nights of worship. She and one of my sisters who was about her age had to kiss the floor at a certain stage of the *Via Sacra*. Well, they did it but with one hand flat between their lips and the floor, which was very dirty. Even as young as I was, I can testify that they were right.

I guess I was too young to do the *Via Sacra*, but I remember a certain Good Friday, one of the most celebrated feast days there. I was awakened at midnight and dressed up, together with two of my sisters, as little angels, even to the wings fastened on our backs, to take part in the procession of the *Senhor Morte*, the Dead Christ. My mother, a very devout Catholic, had promised to send three angels to accompany the procession of the burial of our Lord after the crucifixion. My disposition after being awakened like that was very far from that of an angel! They had a representation of Judas and of the Roman soldiers, which were bad enough to scare anyone, and the body of Christ with features that were far from attractive, carried along in a coffin through the streets of the town.

I remember to this day, though I was only about six or seven years of age then, how perfectly scared I was all through the ceremony. I was so frightened that I did my best to keep away from the terrible-looking thing! There was a compensation to this sacrifice; every angel received a large cornucopia full of the finest French bon-bons. I remember also at another time waking up at night in the midst of a thunderstorm and seeing my mother burn some palm leaves that had been blessed by the priest as a protection against lightning.

In Padrinho's house, there was another corridor with doors to sleeping rooms and then to another room that had one step up to the kitchen. This seemed to be the brightest spot, and the dirtiest, too, of the house. If all the doors of the corridors were open, one could see from the street clear up into the kitchen with its big mud stove and Josephina, the slave, cooking. My great-grandfather's wife, Siá[13] Tereza, stayed most of the time in this kitchen, I presume because it was the warmest room. I remember her by the spinning wheel or scolding Josephina.

They ate most of the time here in the kitchen on an improvised table made of some stools shoved together. Siá Tereza always sat by the window, so this table was fixed in front of her. On top of that they put a home-spun tablecloth. I must add that this was always very clean. There was always plenty of tasty food. When the meal was over Padrinho would rise, and everybody who was there did the same and with his hands in an attitude of prayer he would thank God for the meal. After my immediate family had become converted to Protestantism, we did not join in making the sign of the cross. But my little sister, Manoelita, who was about three then, would stand by him and do everything he did. How the poor old man loved that! Padrinho died in 1879, ninety years old. They made such a fuss over death in that little town! All the relatives tried to face it with the dying person.

In 1873 an epidemic of smallpox infested the town, and it marked a period in its otherwise very uneventful history. When people talked about things that had happened they always said, "This happened before or after the plague." The epidemic caused quite a panic in the town. As my father was the only pharmacist in the town, the bottles came from the sick rooms to be refilled and so were washed in our own kitchen. This constituted quite a danger to us. Everybody that could leave the town, left; and some of us children were taken to the farm of a *fazendeiro*. My mother had a baby and so could not leave town. I was a little over five

---

13. Short for *Sinhá*, a corruption of *Senhora*.

years old and although I was delighted with the idea to go somewhere, it did not take long for me to imitate the calves when they bawled for their mothers, only I did the bawling at night and they did it in the morning about milking time. To this day when I hear cows and calves bawling, a feeling of homesickness comes to me.

The priest of the town, Padre Francisco de Paula Trinidade, was a very charitable man so his home became a hospital for the poor people. As the old Swedish Dr. André was the only physician in the town, my father was called to perform the duties of a doctor many times, and with Dr. André's assistance, he became quite skillful, but his patients were those who could not pay. To this hospital he went every day, taking only the precaution of wearing linen clothes when he went there. We were all vaccinated—seven of us then.

My grandfather died of smallpox in 1873, causing a great change in my grandmother's life. She had to take a position to teach the three R's to the children of wealthy coffee farmers. These big plantation owners were very well-educated men; most of them graduated from the law schools. They had grand times between the farm and the Court, as the capital was called in those days. Prominent men from the *Corte* visited the *fazendeiros* for hunting, and ordinarily each meal was a banquet. On the *fazenda* the slaves moved to the harsh voice of the *feitor* (overseer) who was always a heartless man. Although she herself had slaves, she saw many injustices practiced with these. Perhaps she then had the opportunity to realize that she once had been hard on them also.

Since in each region most of the *fazendeiros* were blood-related—this to keep the money and the plantation in the same family—usually the children from other farms came to the most prosperous one for schooling, so my grandmother had a regular school. She took two of her younger daughters, who helped her. Many prominent men in the state of Minas Gerais learned to read and write with her. And so my grandmother lived on a *fazenda* near Machado, three days away, and I could no longer walk to her house in the rain, or play possum to sleep in her bed.

In the 1870s, three young Portuguese men were sent to the interior of Brazil to preach the Gospel. They were among the missionaries of the Presbyterian Board of Foreign Missions, under whom they had studied for the ministry. My mother and grandmother, who were then devout Catholics but at the same time very independent in their beliefs, began to go to hear about the so-called new religion. They were also reading books concerning Martin Luther's life and conversion, which had been translated into Portuguese. Although the priest, who was a good friend of theirs, admonished them against the heresy, they were converted and united with the little church.

I was about ten when my parents made their profession of faith and we were all baptized; nine of us, for the second time. We had been baptized in infancy by the Catholic priest. After the service in a large room at the house of the minister, I went to the home of a friend of mine whose family had been converted much longer than mine. She told me the story of Joseph sold by his brothers, of Pharaoh, Moses and the plagues, of Daniel and Esther. I was thrilled and going home I read them again, as I had asked her to mark the places in my Bible. We all read the Bible, and I well remember my mother teaching an old woman to read for that very purpose. The cross was abolished from the homes of the new converts, as well as images of the saints.

But alas, this new religion deprived us of the few amusements we had, for Sundays in South America are the days chosen for all sorts of diversions, and as the Latin peoples are inclined to be fanatic or extremists in everything, the new converts were very strict in their new ideas. If we went to a dance after a wedding on Saturday we had to leave at midnight, and we didn't like that. Besides, all the literature given us to read then consisted of stories of persecuted Christians and their final death as martyrs; such deaths were not very appealing to us children! And those stories became very real to us when we heard that some of our relatives in other places were being persecuted and their lives threatened. Bibles taken from itinerant booksellers who traveled from town to town on foot were being burned by the roadside.

About that time some Catholic missionaries were going around the country visiting those places where the Protestants were located, and arousing the ignorant people against the new converts. Some of these missionaries came to our town, and after their sermons in their church a mob was formed and went around the streets crying out: "Away with the Protestants; kill them!" We children were quite excited, but my father said, "Don't worry; they will not touch us, for they need me more than I need them." My father had the only drugstore in the place, and every one of those in the mob was in some way indebted to him. The very next day several men came to our house to say that they were not in the crowd.

But as I look back now I can see that there was intolerance on both sides. The earlier missionaries, and more so our Brazilian ministers, emphasized too much the errors of the predominant church. Fortunately this aggressive way is something of the past, and we are not called Protestants, protesting against the form of worship of the dominant church, but *Evangélicos*.

Before our conversion, we went to the public schools, which were united with and sometimes ruled by the church. We had to learn everything by heart even though we didn't know what those definitions meant. We said the multiplication table all together, loud as a chant, moving together backward and forward. Everybody was happy then, because this meant that school would be out soon, but I cannot forget an unhappy incident between the teacher and me.

Before dismissing the children, the teacher required us to repeat out loud the *Ave Maria*, and make the sign of the cross over the face and body, repeating certain words. Well, not being taught that at home, and knowing that my parents didn't believe in that, I didn't follow the teacher, but mumbled something passing my hands over my face and body—in other words, just playing, but I didn't get by very long. One day she called me to the front and told me to make the sign of the cross repeating those words and as I could not, she got the *palmatória* and punished me right there! The *palmatória* was an object as necessary to those schools as a clock and was used quite a bit, but that was my only experience. This instrument consisted of a round, one inch-thick piece of wood with five small holes and a handle, which was used for striking the palm of your hand. My father took me from the school after that. The pastor of our little Protestant church was responsible for the theological preparation of a young man who was studying for the ministry. Before there were seminaries this was done in Brazil; and these young men were examined by the Presbytery. Thus Senhor Caetaninho, who needed funds, became our private teacher.

We had a music and piano teacher also, and it was in this subject that we put most of our efforts. If you wanted to be somebody around there you had to play the piano. From the time I was old enough to play, we had a piano. Ours came to Caldas from the piano store in the big city of São Paulo. It took one day by train and eight days in a ten- or twelve-oxen cart through bumpy roads over hills and valleys! We had delightful hours of music in the evenings among our friends. At home, we played two hands, four hands, and six hands. We sang some, and my older sister and I sang *duettos*.

Things moved very slowly in that little town in the line of amusement. Occasionally when somebody got married, we had a big ball that was quite formal, and we had informal ones on birthdays. The *quadrilhas* (square dances) were called in French; music was furnished by the city band. It was very important in those days to have a *salão* (a big parlor) in your house and I well remember the three largest ones in that town. They could dance five or six couples at the head of the room, called the *cabeceiras*, and eight or ten at the sides, called *laterais*. What a thrill to dance to the music of a band!

It was so graceful. You had to be very insensitive not to feel it. We danced those *quadrilhas* as enthusiastically and gracefully as if they were military affairs. Between the *quadrillas*, they waltzed or danced the polka. I never was good at them; there were always only a few couples for these dances. You had to know them or you would expose yourself to ridicule. These balls were big occasions for you to be face-to-face with your beau, if you had one, and it gave you an opportunity to get one if you didn't.

The second *quadrilha* was supposed to be of the *namorados* (sweethearts). At this time the parents could find out who was your beau. There was one part of the *quadrilha* that we loved: the grand promenade when the caller clapped his hands, and the *cavalheiros*—the men in the dance were always called *cavalheiros* and the women *damas*— were supposed to move to the next *dama*. The caller would keep on clapping his hands until they got back to their original partners. Well, if you had a *namorado* (boyfriend) he had to pass by you some time during the promenade, and then he just stuck to you and did not pay any attention to the call, as long as he could throw smoke in the eyes of the parents who ordinarily were right there on the spot. These were really the only times for a touchable flirtation.

When I was about thirteen, there were sometimes not enough young men to go around, and some of us *meninas*—not young ladies yet—would be wallflowers. Then my father, together with some other fathers, would come to our rescue, much to our displeasure, for I would much rather sit than dance with my father. In those days there was no intimacy between parents and children. The respect we had for them was wrapped up in fear, especially toward our fathers. A young lady at twenty-five was an old maid, so at fourteen you had a permanent beau. If it were arranged by your parents it was all right, but if Cupid alone had anything to do with the affair— look out for trouble. You were supposed to stick to one: tryouts were bad behavior!

My beau was the brother of my dearest friend Mariquinha Lobo. There were five brothers and Mariquinha. They had a coffee plantation and raised cattle. The mother, a widow then, came from a family of rather well-to-do farmers and lived in town, having married a Portuguese merchant. The boys now took care of the farm except for Christiano, who stayed home with his mother. The others came to town when there was something going on, or sometimes on Sundays. This Christiano was a fine fellow, very different from his brothers and from the fellows of the town. He was such a gentle fellow; the name fitted him perfectly. But it was Joãosinho who captured my heart. Mariquinha spent a day and a night in our home nearly every other week and on the weeks she did not come, I went to hers. It was not only her friendship that made this day a great one for me, but the possibility of sometimes seeing her brother Joãosinho on these occasions.

# 8. Gargalhadas

 *Athens, Ohio, 1943*

My father is way different from all my friends' fathers. Maybe because he was born in Rio de Janeiro. I know Rio is a wonderful place from the way his eyes shine when he talks about it. He spent his childhood outdoors, running around barefoot among the other wild creatures in the virgin paradise that was Copacabana in the first decade of the century. He was my age, twelve, when the family left to live in Portugal. He speaks of Portugal sometimes too, but not like he talks of Rio.

English is his second language, and Portuguese, I know, is the language of his heart. I don't hear it very often, because he is the only one in town who speaks it, but when Vovó, or one of my aunts or uncles is visiting, they fall into it, and it is like listening to music, the soft roundness of vowels, the percussion of the consonants, the crescendos of inflection, and the nasal sounds like the plucking of guitar strings. He sings to us sometimes in Portuguese, and has taught us a few words and phrases that are part of our everyday life. Someone, maybe Aunt Argy, gave him a painting of Rio's bay and mountains. It hangs over the mantel in our living room. I love to feast my eyes on it, and let my imagination take me into it. The painting's soft blues, greens, and browns of the distant view dissolve as I gaze, shifting into red rhythms, warm breezes in palm trees, the smell of salt air off the waves as they splash on the sand, leaving lacy patterns of foam. As long as I can remember, I have longed to see Brazil for myself.

Mother was an only child. She never talks about her childhood. I know she once had a father, but I don't know what became of him. Mother and Daddy are very happy together, but there is a sadness in her eyes that makes me sad, too. I asked Mother about her father, and she told me crossly that she didn't remember him. It's as if she didn't have a history until she met my father. They met on the evening of Daddy's arrival in Wellsville, Ohio, to work for the Pennsylvania Railroad. It was a fairy-tale romance; she was twenty-one years old and engaged to someone else when he entered the bank where she worked. He swept her off her feet and to the altar in less than two months. Nanny wasn't very happy about her marrying a foreigner, even if he was a United States citizen.

They are complete opposites. He is tall, slim, has dark skin, black eyes, curly black hair, and is very energetic. He takes stairs two-at-a-time, and when we walk together, I have to run to keep up with his wide stride. My mother is very pretty; she has bobbed blond hair, blue eyes, and fair skin. She looks athletic with her lean, boyish figure and small bones. Everyone thinks they are a good-looking pair. They are opposites on the inside, too. Daddy is always confident—his voice is calm, strong, firm, and gentle—while Mother often looks worried, and sometimes her voice sounds mad.

They are a couple of lovebirds; they never argue, like some people's parents. Whatever Daddy decides to do—roller-skating, poker, ceramics—Mother joins in enthusiastically. They sing together in the Gilbert and Sullivan troupe at Ohio University. Daddy always has a leading role; Mother is a fairy, a bridesmaid, a schoolgirl, a rapturous maiden, a lovesick peasant girl or a sister/cousin/aunt in the chorus.

Daddy takes us for walks in the woods and he can identify all the birds by their songs. He shows us nests and burrows, and knows the names of all the animals they belong to, even the insects. He knows so much about nature! It is really fun to go to the woods with him. Sometimes at night he sets up his transit (a surveying instrument) and we look through it at the moon and the stars and planets. Last summer we went to Cherry Grove beach in South Carolina, where we three saw the ocean for the first time, we saw a huge horseshoe crab on the sand, and Daddy taught us how to swim in the waves. As we were leaving, I overheard someone say, "There goes a happy family." I guess we are.

Brazilian customs season our daily life like *sal e pimenta*. Daddy taught Mother to make Brazilian rice, which we have all the time. Occasionally, we have *feijoada*, the Brazilian national dish made of black beans, which are hard to find, and ham hocks, sausage, or whatever meat you have. Sometimes for dessert we have *doce de leite* (cooked sweetened milk), or *creme de abacate*, made by mashing avocados with sugar and lemon juice. Occasionally, when someone brings a can from Brazil, we have *goiabada*,

The way we were in 1940. Sydney on Mother's lap, Jan on Daddy's.

or guava paste, and cheese. Daddy says in Brazil they call it "*Romeu e Juliete*" because they are such a perfect pair. But the best dessert of all, and the most fun of all, comes from the yearly ritual of making the Brazilian candy we call *gargalhadas*.

Christmas at our house means decorating the tree, singing carols, and reading from the second chapter of Luke. And we always have a white Christmas, not because of the snow that sometimes blankets the Ohio farmland for miles around, but because of the snowy-white candy that comes from our kitchen and our hands. Neighborhood children often join us in the making of it.

*Gargalhadas* translates to "guffaws," or as, Daddy says, "horselaughs." I never understood this, as horses always seemed pretty sober to me. Daddy remembered making this candy as a child at Tia Noemi's house, and he got the recipe from her daughter, his cousin Francisca. We make it every year from a recipe written on a three-by-five card in spidery, sloping handwriting, with the measurement of sugar given in teacups. Every year we have the same debate about how many ounces there are in a teacup. Why we never write down what we do, I don't know.

There is a lot of preparation, and everyone participates. The ritual begins when Daddy takes three or four coconuts, a hammer, and a sanitized nail outside to the sidewalk. He makes a hole through the eye of each coconut large enough to pour out the thin milky liquid into a china bowl, and carefully saves it, as the recipe tells us, but then forgets to tell us what to do with it. Then he whacks the coconuts' hairy heads with a hammer like a caveman with his prey. With each blow, the sphere of the coconut falls into continents of various shapes. Back inside and seated around the kitchen table covered with shiny oilcloth, Jan, Syd, Mother, and I pry the coconut meat from the pieces of the tough outer shell with dull knives. Daddy supervises the process, helping when we need him.

The next step is to cut the pieces into strips small enough to be fed to the meat grinder, but first we have to remove the brown papery inner skin with sharp paring knives and vegetable peelers, being careful to get every bit of dark color off the snowy white coconut. Now the pieces are ready to be washed and patted dry. This is Syd's job; she's too little for the knife. Next we all take turns grinding the pristine pieces in a hand-cranked meat grinder clamped to the kitchen table. We each get our turn at the handle, being very careful not to let our fingers get pulled into the grinding gears. When all is ready, Daddy spreads some of the fluffy, slightly moist, ground coconut on a clean dishtowel and rolls the towel lengthwise, twisting it at the ends like a firecracker. Then we have to decide what to do with the reserved coconut milk. Sometimes we just drink it, sometimes we add it to the large cooking pot.

While we three watch breathlessly, Daddy holds the rolled package with its precious contents over the pan while Mother pours boiling water on the bundle and the clear water filters through on the other side, blue-white as milk from a cow's teat. When it stops dripping, Daddy starts wringing the hot cloth, twisting it until nothing is left inside but dry pulp, which we throw away, because now all the flavor is in the liquid in the pan; the remains look and taste dry, like cotton. He does this many times, until all the ground coconut is discarded, and his hands are lobster-red from the hot water.

Up to this point, we are very sober and serious, but now we three sisters are getting excited. The pot goes to the stove, sugar is measured and added, and Mother stirs the mixture with a wooden spoon over low heat until all the sugar is dissolved. Meanwhile, Daddy goes upstairs for the marble slab from Mother's dresser and carries it to the kitchen table, where Nanny cleans and butters it lightly. The steam rising to the ceiling from the boiling water fills the kitchen air with the humidity of the tropics.

The recipe says the mixture should be cooked until it is "not too hard, not too soft." When it starts to boil, we spoon it, a dollop at a time, into a glass of cold water. We all gather around the glass, watching each drop sink to the bottom, waiting to see if the next will form the little ball that means it's ready to pour. Finally, when we all agree it is ready, Daddy carries the heavy pot to the table, where he quickly pours it out onto the prepared marble slab.

The cooked coconut juice is hot, viscous, translucent, and yellowish when it goes on the slab. We watch and touch it lightly as it begins to cool, resembling a sheet of celluloid. The trick is to pick it up at just the right time. When you can wrinkle the surface with your finger, and when you push it and it doesn't flow back, but stays all wrinkly (like Nanny's face), and it is cool enough to hold, then it is ready to pull. If we wait too long, no pulling will be possible. We wait, shifting from foot to foot, poking and pushing, until we all agree that it's ready.

Now the fun begins; timing is everything. We lightly butter our hands so the goo won't stick—it always does anyway—and Daddy cuts the mixture into pieces, slides them from the marble, and gives us each a hunk to pull, sized according to our ages. We try to get it into a ball in our palms, so we can pull it between our hands, like an accordion, but it gets in-between our fingers and joins them together like a duck's foot. Our noses are sure to itch; Daddy instructs, "Keep it moving, keep it going!" If we are lucky, and manage to scrape the material from between our fingers, we find our separate fingers again and have control over the sticky stuff. We twist the stiffening and cooling mass into ropes, which we stretch as thin as our fingers. Gradually, it starts to get white and shiny, and we can transfer it from hand to hand and pull and stretch it out.

Everyone's mass is always at a different stage; we stand around the kitchen table watching and encouraging each other and squealing with excitement. Sydney plays with her allotment, getting it in her hair and on her clothes. Jan lovingly works hers like a sculptor, and I try to outdo them all in grand gestures. I pretend I'm a juggler, deftly manipulating the elastic slinky that I can twist and re-twist into whitening bands.

The taffy gets stiff but bendable, like wire cables, and we fling the middle of the string in the air like a jump rope, then bring the thicker, harder ends together with a clunking sound. We fold the stretched out parts and pull again, this time stretching the ends. It's sort of like making a cat's cradle; all the strands have to be worked in together. It's tricky to know when it's ready to put down on the slab; if we do it too soon, it will lose its ropy texture, flatten out on the cool slab, and sometimes even remain yellow and gummy, as it was before we started to pull.

Suddenly our hands get very hot. This is the signal to get it down on the marble quickly, before it cracks, hardens and turns into a fistful of gravelly coconut-sugar bits. If we are too slow, there is nothing to do but wait until all the heat goes out of it, then rub our hands together to get the crumbly pieces off our hot hands to the slab. Then it isn't pretty, but still delicious. Sometimes we pull until the mixture becomes stiff as steel, and our arms very tired, without getting to the crucial point. Then, after Daddy places his on the slab, he relieves us, one by one, pulling it until the heat is transferred to his strong hands.

More often than not, the results are less than perfect, but when we get it right, it looks beautiful, stretched on the slab in long ropes, silvery white, curving back and forth. As it cools further, it loses its luster, becoming creamy white, with fine tunnels of air. You bite into a soft, extremely sweet, coconutty chunk—delicious.

We wrap the results carefully in waxed paper, put them into a can with a tight-fitting lid, and share them with friends for Christmas. But the candy can't possibly taste as good to anyone who does not know the magic of making it. For me, the memory of the making of *gargalhadas* embodies the Brazilian character—sweetness and tenderness, love of family, love of ceremony, unbridled enthusiasm, uninhibited playfulness, and pleasure in the ridiculous.

# II. Leaving Home

Brazil's republican movement dates back to the ill-fated *Inconfidência Mineira* (Minas Conspiracy), which took place in Minas Gerais from 1788 to 1792.[14] Joaquim José da Silva Xavier, a dentist best known as *Tiradentes* (Toothpuller), was a leader in the unsuccessful attempt by a group of intellectuals—inspired by the North American example—to overthrow the monarchy and establish a republic. *Tiradentes* was betrayed by one of his followers and murdered in Ouro Preto, Minas Gerais on April 21, 1793.[15]

This was the era of two of my grandmother's great-great-grandfathers, Joaquim Bueno de Camargo, who according to family records lived from 1763 to 1868, and Simão Pedro Antônio da Silva Teixeira. His dates are unknown, but his son was born in 1789.

Further influenced by the French Revolution, the republican movement grew in the nineteenth century and was one of the factors in the 1831 abdication of Dom Pedro I in favor of his minor son, Pedro II. Toward the end of his reign, Dom Pedro II himself apparently believed that a republic was the ideal form of government, but he thought that because his subjects were largely illiterate, they were not ready for it.

The republican movement was also associated with the abolition of slavery. As early as 1840, Dom Pedro II—who had always been opposed to the idea of slavery—freed all his own slaves, but since Brazil's economy required a large unpaid labor force, he favored gradual abolition and did not want to move too far ahead of public opinion. Antislavery sentiments were increasing, but during the war against Paraguay the familiar argument of solidarity in time of war prevailed. Nevertheless, opposition to slavery was growing throughout the nation. In 1871 the "Law of Free Birth" was passed, making all slaves born thereafter free, though apprenticed to their mother's owner until the age of 21.

Seventeen years of parliamentary struggle followed, due to the strong

---

14. Most of the historical data in this section is based on my reading of Bello, *A History of Modern Brazil, 1889–1964*.

15. Haring, *Empire in Brazil*, 78–83.

opposition of the rural aristocracy. In 1887 the city of São Paulo, using funds raised by popular subscription, freed all the slaves within the city. Finally, on May 13, 1888, Princess Isabel, ruling as regent for her father, Dom Pedro II—who had gone to Europe for medical treatment—signed a bill freeing all slaves with no provision for compensation to the owners. Brazil became the last country in the new world to outlaw slavery. Crowds in the galleries shouted vivas and threw flowers down on the legislators, and eight days of festivities followed.

When Don Pedro II returned to Brazil he said the emancipation had given him the greatest happiness of his life, but the decree signed by his daughter made him very unpopular with landowners. This and other factors, including the growing republican movement, promoted the end of the empire. Dom Pedro II was forced into exile, although he was loved by his people, welcomed emancipation, and was sympathetic to republican principles.

On November 15, 1889, republicans seized the government and ordered the royal family to leave within twenty-four hours, and so on a rainy night the family—along with close friends who followed them into exile—were put aboard the steamer Alagoas, bound for Portugal, and banished from Pedro's beloved Brazil. The era of empire in the New World was ending.

Brazil's politics in the mid-twentieth century, when I first visited the country, were no less eventful. In the 1920s charges of corruption and graft had led to public unrest and the rise of military movements. In 1930 after a revolution following a presidential election, the army installed Getúlio Vargas as president of the provisional government. Vargas won the support of the urban masses by legalizing labor unions, creating a minimum wage and social security system, and instituting paid vacations, maternity leave, and medical assistance. He represented a complete break from the rural-controlled political machine, and became the most popular Brazilian leader since Dom Pedro II.

The new constitution, which provided for a limit of one four-year term of office, was drafted in 1934 and the interim presidency ended. Vargas was then elected president by Congress. But a year before the end of his term, Vargas, with the support of the military, closed Congress and replaced the Constitution with a document giving him dictatorial powers. He called his reign *O Estado Novo* (The New State).

As the Vargas dictatorship became more and more repressive, political opposition grew. The military, which had supported this move, became disillusioned and called for him to legalize opposition parties and to hold a presidential election in 1945. Instead, Vargas urged his supporters in the labor movement to unite with the communists. Facing this threat, the military overturned his government; but five years later, Vargas was returned to power—this time in a popular election. His victory did not end the opposition, however, and in 1954 the military gave him an ultimatum to resign or be overthrown.

Unwilling to accept either alternative, Getúlio Vargas took his life in the Presidental Palace in Rio to "depart from life to enter history."[16] The palace is now the Museum of the Republic. In the bedroom where the suicide took place, his pajama top, with a bullet hole in it, can still be seen.

The election of 1955 was one of extreme political tensions and a confusion of parties and candidates. The *Partido Social Democrático* (*PSD*; Social Democratic Party) nominated Juscelino Kubitcschek de Oliveira. The *Partido Trabalhista Brasileiro* (*PTB*; Labor Party) supported João Goulart, a former Vargas protégé who was regarded by many conservatives as pro-Communist. However, Goulart accepted the vice-presidential nomination of the *PSD*. Brazilians love nicknames: the candidates were known as Juscelino and Jango.

The election was held on October 3, 1955, when I was in Vitória. Juscelino Kubitschek was elected in the most honest and orderly elections the country had ever known. Not surprisingly, rumors of a *golpe*, or coup d'état, were rampant. These rumors provoked a "countercoup," and a state of martial law was declared from November 11, 1955 until January 31, 1956—the inauguration day of Juscelino and Jango.

Upon taking office, President Kubitschek began the implementation of his

16. Bello, *A History of Modern Brazil*, 322.

plan to move the capital from Rio to a new city to be built in the vast and largely unpopulated interior of Brazil, an idea that had been discussed since the days of the Empire. At the time it was thought that having the capital on the coast made it vulnerable to invasion. The intention was incorporated into the Constitution of 1891; a site was chosen in the remote and empty plateau of eastern Goiás. The motive at that time was to encourage a westward movement, as the great majority of Brazil's population lived along its long coast.

The winning design for the city—to be called Brasília—was in the shape of an airplane, with the government buildings located in the fuselage and the commercial and residential areas on the wings. Brasília became the capital in 1960, and the Three Powers of the Republic[17] simultaneously took their seats in the new city.

---

17. Executive, Legislative, and Judiciary.

# 9. Capivary

And now I want you to meet my hero: my father's cousin, and Severo's brother, Eduardo. He visited us several times on his vacations from São Paulo where he was studying for the ministry, and on one of his little visits on the way to see his mother, he said to me, "How would you like to go with me to see your godmother?" Only once since the smallpox epidemic when I was five had I crossed the outskirts of the town to visit some friends on their farm. The whole family had gone in a hide-covered cart with big solid wooden wheels pulled by eight or ten oxen with no springs to break the bumps. We stayed there a few days. I never could forget that bumpy trip—it left quite an impression on my young body. But here was a chance to go on horseback, just *me* alone with cousin Eduardo!

Of course I wanted to go, but knew my parents would not let me. All this was going on only in my mind and my inquiring eyes; my cousin read it all and said, "I tell you, before you go to bed tonight, get some of your clothes and hide them in the parlor near my room; get up very early tomorrow and we will start before they are up. I will put a pillow in front of me on my saddle and there you will be all fixed up." My, how great to go to San Antônio do Machado to see my godmother and perhaps my grandmother, as she lived in a *fazenda* around there. What an adventure!

That night I made a little bundle of my clothes, went to bed, and woke up next morning with the shouts and the laughter of my older sisters playing with the bundle of clothes and making fun of me for trying to run away with my cousin—and for being left behind. Well, I was just as good for work as my older sisters, everybody used to say. I could climb trees that they couldn't and run as fast as any of them, so although tears of disappointment were running fast, I settled my troubles with a good fight. But what disillusion and humiliation!

And now I want you to meet another cousin of my father's, a brother of Severo and Eduardo. You could not find anywhere more intelligent boys than these, or a more handsome fellow than Ernesto! There had been some trouble in their family between their father and mother, but they were bound to have an education and they did, through lots of hardship. A wealthy *fazendeiro* friend of my father sent him to a fine school in São Paulo. Ernesto put his feet in cold water to keep awake to study.

Ernesto was teaching French privately in the big city of São Paulo and it happened that one of his pupils was a very rich girl who fell in love with him. Whether he was in love with her I don't know. I guess he was, but I heard that the mother of the girl, a widow, made him understand that she would be very pleased to have him marry her daughter—so he did. His wife's family belonged to the aristocracy and so didn't do anything that could be called work, except fancy work. Jaiá, Ernesto's wife, did not even comb her own hair, and her clothes had to be laid out for her to put on. But although I think she was only sixteen or seventeen years old when she was married, she spoke French very well and could play the piano. In the United States, one cannot realize how helpless around the house a woman from the aristocracy in Portugal or Brazil could be in those days!

I don't know what happened —one can easily guess!—while the young couple was living with his wife's family, but Ernesto decided to take his wife and move far, far away in the interior of Minas where Severo and his parents lived. In Machado, the region where there were many wealthy farmers whom he knew and where my grandmother was teaching, he opened a boarding school, and most of the pupils were the children of *fazendeiros*. My cousin Ernesto took with him the two women servants who belonged to his wife. In fact one of them, Florência, had performed every duty that a mother is supposed to do for a child since the day his wife was born.

As converts to the Protestant faith, we could not go to the public schools in Caldas because Roman Catholicism was the state religion and the teaching of the Catholic faith was compulsory. For this reason my parents wanted to send us to a private school. Just as soon as cousin Ernesto had the school functioning, he wrote to my father to send some of the children, so the three oldest girls went. The oldest one, Maria, was going to teach.

My, how I envied my sisters when they were getting ready and when the day came. It was quite an undertaking. The place was twelve leagues[18] away through very poor roads made by the hooves of the horses and by the heavy wooden wheels of the oxen cart. It was quite a caravan: three *amazonas* (women on horseback), my father, a *camarada* (a man to wait on them on the road), and two burros to carry the *canastras*. These were big trunks for my sisters' clothes, constructed of hide with the hair on, and made especially to be carried on the backs of mules, one on each side. Then there was the man, then called a *cargueiro*—a mule driver—to take care of these mules.

Several months after my sisters had gone to the boarding school my mother decided to visit them and my grandmother, who was teaching in a nearby *fazenda*. Ernesto's mother, my godmother, was visiting us then, and she was going back home to Machado. She insisted that I go along, much to my delight. This time I didn't have to make plans or bundles. There were no inns or roadhouses so those who traveled stopped with the *fazendeiros*, who were always glad to have company that often would arrive in the middle of the night; even then, a warm supper would be provided. And listen, gas in those days did not yet run through pipes everywhere!

Now, looking through that back window of our house, I could imagine myself traveling in that lovely rolling country and disappearing far away in the horizon just as I had seen many men and women do on their horses. My father said to me, "I will take you if you will not be afraid to ride on the cute little mule I have just bought." Afraid? I did not know that word, I think, but if I did, I had enough courage to face anything in order to see the end of that road which disappeared there near the sky! So the day came when my traveling began. I was then ten years old. I hope I am not through yet, although I am now sixty-and-a-half years old.

That night our first stop was in Capivary, a big *fazenda* belonging to friends of my family. I shall never forget that event in my life although it seems that it happened centuries ago—the large one-floor house with its corral in the back, with cows, calves, chickens, and pigs. We were not expected, as there was no means of communication—we had mail

---

18. About 36 miles.

only once a week in our little town—but Brazilians are very hospitable people and we were friends. In fact two sons of this *fazendeira*, a widow, were godfathers of two of my sisters. Slave men came to help us off the horses, and lights like fireflies began to appear here and there on the porch and in the windows. Two ladies, mother and daughter, both widows, were at the door to receive us, calling my father and my mother by their names: Manoel Pereira and Maria Ovídia—a sign of intimate friends. A big warm and delicious supper was ready in a very short time. This family was famous for its culinary ability.

These two women were strong characters; they ran the big *fazenda*, and when they gave orders they were obeyed. Even a child could see that there was something unusual about them; something of distinction in their voices. The family was prominent; they had wealth in land and in human beings. Their ancestors were probably Portuguese aristocrats. They were used to entertaining high officials of the court of Dom Pedro II. Dona Ignez,[19] the daughter, had nine sons and daughters. Most of them were living on their own *fazendas* with children and grandchildren. Although some of the men graduated from the law schools, none of them did any work. They just saw that the *feitor* made the slaves work. In this *fazenda*, like in many large ones in Brazil, there was a chapel where Mass was read or sung by a priest who sometimes lived on the farm or came there on certain Sundays.

I was used to slaves; we had them, and so did our friends, but here they were swarming all over the place performing different duties. This place was a busy one, and believe me it was run with intelligence and order. Beside those who attended to the cooking and the housecleaning, there were those who were working with the cotton they raised for their own use. Children were taking the seeds out of it in a machine very much like a wringer. Two children faced each other: one putting the cotton with the seed in and turning a handle, and the other turning the handle on his side and getting the cotton without the seeds. This would have been fun if it hadn't been a job. Many women were then preparing the

---

19. Chiquita and her family visited Dona Maria and Dona Ignes, the daughter in our story, in 1878. Pimenta wrote: "Dona Ignes da Silva in 1889 was almost 100 years old and blind, but maintaining perfectly her intellectual faculties. At that time, she was matriarch of six generations." Pimenta, *O Povoamento do Planalto da Pedra Branca*, 257; her picture is on page 163.

cotton for the spinning wheel. From here it went to the old-fashioned loom. This material was for clothes and bedding for the slaves. From the backs of the sheep they made their blankets. Some of the men worked as carpenters and some were shoe and saddle makers. These shoes were for the masters to wear on the farm. The slaves, if they wore anything, wore sandals.

We always recognized the slaves that came from that plantation—Capivary—when they came to town on some errand; they were better dressed. Among them there were some who were more privileged because they deserved the confidence of their masters. I may say that these people were not too hard on their slaves. We stayed there two nights, as the ladies would not let us leave. The next day after a big meal we started again. I remember the meals here; they were real banquets, and not because they had guests, no.

We passed by the *senzala*, the slaves' place to sleep. They were two long rows of low shacks; one row for the men, the other for the women. This rule was not very strictly obeyed; the majority of the slaves were not married, but there were plenty of children among them. Nearby, groups of slaves were working in cornfields, patches of beans, sweet potatoes, etc., singing away their sorrows and afflictions while they worked with their hoes! That there was plenty of music in those creatures one could easily surmise by the harmony they carried in their *cantigas* (ballads, songs).

When we got near them they straightened up their bodies, which were bent over their hoes, and lifting their hats, they murmured a salutation, ordinarily *"Sua Bênção"* (your blessing). In this salutation one could hear that they accepted that they were inferior; that they had no will, no freedom, and that their bodies and perchance their souls belonged to their masters. Many times the slaves would run away and to subsist they had to steal and sometimes there were murderers among them. The *feitor*, generally a man with no heart, was going on horseback with a *relho* (a leatherstrap whip) from one group to another ready to strike if one of those human machines didn't please him. How little it was necessary! Many weird stories were told about these overseers in those days.

Many years ago, when I was in my fifties and a widow, this *fazenda* was in the hands of a grandson of the family, a great friend of mine who—with his family—occasionally spent some time there. While in Brazil I visited the place at their invitation, this time by automobile. It was not a very comfortable trip because the road was also still used by the heavy oxen carts with no springs, but what scenery! And the recollections when I got to the place! That enormous one-floored, whitewashed building, surrounded by several stalls and once full of living beings, was deserted now and falling to pieces. There was one wing that had been restored, where my friend and his family stayed. I had heard of the ghosts that swarmed the place—the cries of the slaves, the monotonous plaintive chant of the priests in the falling chapel—but I never thought of it during the day. Nature was so beautiful, so quiet, so peaceful; I was just remembering my first visit to the place.

My friend, who thought I was a remarkably courageous woman, had a good sense of humor and tried his best to scare me. He told me about the spooky things that people had seen around the place, probably adding quite a bit. The sun faded all these phantoms with its bright light, but when the shadows of the night came over the fields and the lonely deserted place became quieter than ever, it was hard to hide from him that I was not so sure about not believing in ghosts. My room was far from theirs and connected to the big *salão* where pictures of several generations of his ancestors still hung on the walls.

Oxen team, *fazenda* outbuildings, 1920.

I was ready to go to bed with the candle in my hands, so saying good night, my friend said to me, "Are you sure that you are not afraid to sleep there alone?" Oh, my reputation as a brave old lady was hanging from a cobweb! "Oh, sure, I am not afraid," I said. Not knowing what kind of ghost was coming to visit me that night, I did my best to fall into the arms of Morpheus the sooner the better, and I did, fortunately. I was awakened only at dawn by the songs of the birds and the call of the calves for their mothers.

On the third day we arrived at our destination; Santo Antônio de Machado. By that time all the lure of traveling had vanished from my mind because of what it had done to my body, and I had no peace thinking of our return home planned for a month later.

Cousin Severo, who told me that the moon led him quickly to the midwife's house the night I was born, was married to one of my mother's sisters and had a pharmacy of his own now in Machado, the same town where his brother, Ernesto, had the boarding school. Being related on both sides, we had a very happy stay with them.

I was very anxious to visit the *internato* (boarding school) and see my aristocratic cousin. Everything about her had, in my fertile imagination, excited my desire to see the big cities of the world. When the time came it was a great joy to me to find out that the girls there were very anxious to meet the fourth sister of the Pereiras. Soon Ernesto convinced my mother that I ought to stay in school too, so I was moved to the *internato* with my older sisters to my great delight, which did not last long after my parents left.

I was the youngest in the *internato* but a good deal more advanced than older girls, daughters of *fazendeiros*. Chiquita Oliveira, one of the *externa* (day students) in the school, though, was just as advanced as myself and we became great friends. We still are—perhaps because her grandfather, Augusto Westin, was one of the Swedish neighbors of ours, and from her mother's side, she was a great-granddaughter of the owners of Capivary.

# 10. Ernesto's *Internato*

 *Wooster, Ohio, 1943*

The boarding school in Machado was housed in a large, old, two-story building. Ernesto and his wife Jaiá and the girls lived on the second floor and the classes were also held there. His father and mother and the boys occupied the first floor. We all ate together in the same dining room. That home was enjoyed very much by the dwellers of the first and second floors because it answered two purposes: to feed the body and the soul. It didn't take long for Cupid to begin throwing his dangerous arrows at those innocent creatures who came there as students.

Windows in Brazil are made not only for airing and lighting the house but also for the dwellers to rest their elbows on when looking outside. At the *internato*, flirtation even in its most innocent form—looking at each other, not casually but with a motive—was prohibited. Well, the boys downstairs discovered a way to look at the girls who were at the upstairs windows without being noticed by their neighbors. They didn't have to turn their heads at all. They just held a little mirror and behold—there was the angel. But my old uncle and Ernesto's father, Tio Francisco, discovered the secret and was furious that such a crime would be performed under his roof, so he banned the use of such a dangerous instrument!

I must pay tribute to Florência, the colored woman, a former slave to whom freedom was given by her masters the day that Jaiá was born and who had taken charge of her since that day—and now was doing the same for Jaiá and Ernesto's baby, Julieta. Many times when Florência was too busy directing the cooking and the cleaning to take care of the baby, I was asked to do it. There were other little tasks around the house that I did for Jaiá so efficiently that she used to say—if jokingly, I didn't know— that she wanted me to marry her brother Geraldo who lived in São Paulo. He was about fifteen or sixteen then. Isn't it funny that in those days in my country we young people were not permitted to flirt or to talk about love, yet people were always planning to marry us off just as soon as we entered the teens? I knew she talked about me to Geraldo in her letters because there were always messages to me when he wrote. My imagination had strong wings and could fly high and far, so to marry a rich boy and to live in one of the largest cities in Brazil became a very pleasant dream to me.

I had not been at the *internato* a year when Ernesto's mother-in-law got sick, so he took his family and Flôrencia back to São Paulo, leaving my hero, cousin Eduardo, in charge of the school. In many ways he was a better educator than his brother. It was getting toward the end of the year and this meant oral exams. The parents of the pupils all came and the public was invited. If there ever was a crazy idea, this was one. The pupil was to exhibit on that day all he knew, answering the questions asked by examiners, who were invited by the director of the school. It was customary for the girls to wear a new dress on that occasion. This at least was a great consolation, yet I don't think it compensated for the agony we went through. Cousin Eduardo wanted to add charm to the occasion so he decided that some of the pupils would recite some poetry, and he chose a work about the lives of the Indians of Brazil.

By this time—almost a year since I had left home—all the fascination of traveling and of having an aristocratic cousin had vanished from my heart and my only desire was to go home just as quickly as possible. There was a new baby girl and I was eager to see her. My father arrived on the morning of the performance, having traveled all night on horseback. He brought *conduções* (conveyances) for us; four horses with outfits for women, and *camaradas* and mules to carry the *canastras*. I can't describe my joy at seeing my father. This was mixed with a kind of terror thinking about the barbarous performance before me, the oral exam.

My piece was the "Canto do Morte de Tupy,"[20] the death song of the warrior Tupy. It is a beautiful piece full of courage, sadness, and sentiment; yet not an appropriate piece at all for a girl eleven years old to recite. You know, it is a terrible thing to have to wait to do something you are afraid to do. When my time came I was in agony, and as I knew the

20. From "I-Juca Pirama," stanza 4, by Antônio Gonçalves Dias (1823–1864), a Brazilian Romantic poet. See Gonçalves Dias, *Últimos Cantos: Poesias*, 12–35.

piece well I went very fast. I must explain a little about the poem. This Tupy warrior (a fine tribe) fell prisoner to another tribe, and before being executed he had to tell something about his life.

Well, I went on very fast, hardly understanding the words which flew from my lips but when I got to the phrase, "My old father, blind, weak, and broken-hearted, was leaning upon me," I choked, and the tears came like a flood over my cheeks and, not being able to go on, I just put my head on the shoulder of somebody who was sitting behind me while one of my sisters was called for her piece that started like this: "Do not weep my son, do not weep. Life is a struggle which exalts the brave. To live is to fight," etc. Do you wonder that the outsiders thought it was meant to be like that? Even before my sister had started her piece my father was by my side, comforting me.

We started home the next day, my father on his horse Condor, who did not show any signs of having made a trip in one night that was usually done in two days. A wealthy *fazendeiro* saw him when he arrived and told him that whenever he wanted to sell that horse he would pay the price. Later on, when my father needed money, he sold Condor for less than what he would have gotten then from the *fazendeiro*. Yes, a family of nine children—eight girls and one boy—required lots of sacrifice in those days.

The first homecoming cannot be described. It was glorious. My mother was only thirty-five then but I thought of her as if she were older than I am now—seventy-five. All the beds had their best linen on, and the legs were well covered with starched frills. The cupboards were all full of the daintiest pastries. From the window in the back room I could see again the road stretching through the prairies and disappearing in little woods, to come into sight again far away near the horizon. But to me now it meant only the way that brought me home. Before the end of my vacation Jaiá wrote from São Paulo that she was not going back to the school, and since Eduardo, who was studying for the ministry, could not stay in charge—much to the disappointment of the parents (and to my delight), the school had to be closed.

The problem about our education had to be solved again. Dr. George

Chamberlain, an American missionary who traveled all over Brazil, arranged for my older sisters Maria, Josephina, and Lydia to attend the American Presbyterian Mission School in São Paulo, some 800 miles away. This was the school that later, under the direction of Dr. H. M. Lane, became the well-known Mackenzie College. We will meet Dr. Lane later on.

# 11. *Escola Americana*, São Paulo

 *Athens, Ohio, 1939*

In 1883, when I was fifteen years old, I said tender goodbyes to my mother, my sisters Offida, Cacilda, Manoelita, and Noemi—and my brother Argentino—to join my older sisters in the American School in São Paulo. My father and I, accompanied by pack animals and *camareiros*, traveled two days on horseback through the mountains to *Espírito Santo do Pinhal* (Holy Spirit of the Pines), where my father and I left the men and horses and traveled by railway to São Paulo. The Big City at last! It was the capital of the state of São Paulo, with a population of 60,000 souls!

My sister, Maria, whom we called Mariquinha, was now teaching in the American School in an old brick building on the corner of São João and Ipiranga. She and my sisters Josephina and Lydia were waiting for me, and it was a happy reunion. They had been away for four years, only returning to Caldas once a year for summer vacations in November and December, the rainy months. So it is that the sad and the sweet are always joined in my life: leaving some loved ones behind, reuniting with others; the ache of parting, the joy of reunion. This is what we mean when we say *"saudade."* There were more tears as we said goodbye to my father in São Paulo.

Mariquinha was twenty-four and Josephina nineteen, but it was Josephina who was the first to marry a few months after I came to the American School. Her husband was Manoel da Paixão, whom we called Mineco, a teacher at the school. On the 14th of July 1884, a year later, our dear mother died very suddenly when she was only forty years old. She left nine children and her husband inconsolable. After her burial, we did not return to the house for a week; everyone stayed in the houses of three friends. Mariquinha did not go back to the American School in São Paulo, but stayed in Caldas to take care of the ones who were still at home. My youngest sister, Noemi, was only six years old. A year later, my younger sister Offida was ill. Four months later, she was dead. She lived only 14 years! Death, always.

Dr. André died a few months after my mother, and shortly afterward, Dr. José de Aranjo Matto-Grosso, a *Baiano* (a native of the state of Bahia), came to the town to set up practice there. Within two years, he and Mariquinha were married. Two months after the wedding, Josephina and her family moved from São Paulo to Caldas, where Mineco made his living as a bookkeeper. By this time they had two sons, Minequinho and Armando. My father had also remarried and had a son, Manoel *segundo*. Lydia left the school also, returning to Caldas; she and Josephina took charge of the younger children. Now all of my family—father, sisters, brothers and two nephews—were back in Caldas; I was alone in São Paulo.

At about that time there was a grand celebration in [nearby] Poços de Caldas for the inauguration of the Mogyana Railroad. It was July, but I managed to get away from the school to visit my family. Poços was full of visitors because the Emperor Dom Pedro II and the Empress Dona Teresa were going to be there. Naturally, everyone wanted to see them. There wasn't a room in any of the hotels. Mariquinha and her husband rented a house there, and had food delivered from a hotel. There weren't any beds in the house, so we slept on mattresses on the floor. How wonderful it was to all be together again, and to have the opportunity to see the Emperor and Empress with her maid of honor! The Emperor Dom Pedro II walked through the streets, accompanied by the crowd, but the Empress rode in a carriage; she was lame.

Except for that event, I saw my family only once a year, on my summer vacations in December and January. If I was not too tired after those two days on horseback, that same night I had to play all my new pieces for my father. He loved music. On the visit after my last year as a student, he liked one of my new pieces, "Devil's March," so much that I was told— not asked—to play it five times that evening.

When I arrived home on vacation in November of 1888, I ought to have been able to drown in tears of contentment the immense longing that I had been carrying in my heart. Only those who have suffered the bitterness of finding themselves far from the parental home can imagine the joy in saying "I am home." But those days were short; vacation soon ended and I had to return to São Paulo, this time as a teacher in the school. The director realized that they needed to prepare their own teachers, so an educator was brought from Boston to teach a normal school—and I belonged to that first group of teachers.

My father's state of health had declined during my absence, and the certainty that his illness was not curable made the parting even more painful. On the day of my leaving, my father united everyone for a last lunch together. During the lunch little or nothing was said. Not being able to contain the ache that was in my heart, I got up from the table and went to release my feelings where no one could hear my sobs. The hour in which I had to say my last goodbyes to my sisters and brother was bathed in tears and suffocated by sighs, just as for the last time I asked for my father's blessing and received his last kiss. Had I known that only three months remained to him who was the best of fathers, I would have undoubtedly forgotten the duties that obliged me to leave.

Back at the school, one day when the church service was over and I was just leaving the room, Miss Kuhl put her arms around me and said, "Come with me, *minha filha*" (literally "my daughter", used here as a term of endearment), and there in the parlor Senhor Miguel, a messenger from Caldas, was waiting for me, holding a letter. The black stripe around the edge of the envelope revealed its contents. It was a brief letter from my sister Josephina's husband, Manoel da Paixão, written immediately after my father closed his eyes—never to open them again—on the 26th of April, 1889.

My brother-in-law promised to write again just as soon as possible with all the details about my father's last days. A few days later I received a ten-page letter in the most perfect small and even handwriting one could possibly have. That letter I keep among my few relics.

In it, he described my father's intense suffering, his heart trouble with the terrible shortness of breath; and the wonderful patience and strong faith in Christ and in the hereafter of a man who had lived a very unselfish life. As someone said at his funeral, "Who in Caldas can say that they don't owe him a favor?" In his last moments he, with a clear mind, said goodbye to them all, asked them to bring the grandchildren for him to kiss, and then sent a message of love to me, asking me to bear my sorrow courageously and saying that the sacrifice I was making would surely attract the sympathy of Dr. Lane, who he knew would be a second father to me. These were certainly prophetic words. Then Mineco's letter said he breathed comfortably for some ten minutes, and passed away with no effort.

Mineco also said that he reminded my father of the promise they had made to advise me to come when they thought the end was getting nearer, to which my father replied, "I don't think it is wise to do this, because she may not arrive here in time, and again, I may linger on, and she may have to go back to her duty, which will now mean so much more to her."

My father did not leave money, because he was not a person who would take the thing that meant bread, clothing, and shelter to many who came to him to relieve their suffering with medicine. There were several books with old charge accounts that would come to a good amount in those days. There were a few properties, animals, and pastures. There was the pharmacy, which was one of the best I have seen, even now. I do not want to leave an impression that my father was faultless. I wish I could, but he had a thorn in his flesh; yet his charity was much sharper than the thorn. But I am afraid I am wading in too-deep waters.

Let me move to some shallow places. I have to face some storms yet in my dive into the past; I still will have to lift to my lips a bitter cup. But before that, I am going to feast for awhile at the table of Cupid, with the sweetest nectar that this little gentleman has ever put before anybody.

The people who surrounded me at the school proved to be ones you love to have near when sorrow visits you. They couldn't have been more sympathetic. I didn't go back to school for a week, and when I took my place again the children showed their thoughtfulness by being very quiet and giving me less trouble than they ever did before, the dear souls. When I concentrate, I can hear in my classroom the voices of my students and see their faces right this minute.

That first homecoming after my father died was very sad. It was customary in Brazil then not to play or take part in any amusements or entertainment for one year after losing a parent. Of course you really didn't feel like it anyway, but even if you did, you would not dare to break this rule because public opinion was very strong. It was not because I was concerned about public opinion that I could not play my pieces for some time, but because it brought back memories of my father. I could almost hear him humming the tune. So that was the way I lived with the death of my father.

Dr. Lane found out that there were children yet at home to be educated, so before I went home for my vacation that November he had told me to be sure to bring them when I came back. Two of my younger sisters, Cacilda and Manoelita, and my brother Argentino—then fourteen—went back with me to the *Internato*, and I was now responsible for them, so my music was put away entirely. Sometimes my friends and colleagues insisted on my playing some special pieces, which I did. They loved them so much, and I myself loved to hear them once in a while.

In 1889, the same year that my father died, our country went through a great change. For some time there had been a strong republican movement in Brazil. Then the army and navy joined forces against the emperor. The day before the news of the revolt spread, I was going to the dentist for the first time. We young teachers did not go out alone, so one of my girlfriends went with me.

When we came out of the *bonde* (a streetcar pulled by mules) and arrived at the dentist's office on Rua da Imperatriz in São Paulo, we found the big wide door locked! Surprised, we looked around to see that everything was closed, and only then we realized that there was nobody around. Just when we were trying to find out why, somebody passed by almost at a run, stared at us, saying, "What are these two girls doing in the street, with the republican *golpe*?" (coup). We went immediately to the Largo da Sé and took the *bonde* back to the school. The governor of the state didn't give up his power as easily as Dom Pedro II, so the business houses, expecting a fight, had closed up.

Next morning, the papers (not all!) had, on the first page in big letters, *VIVA A REPÚBLICA!* All the teachers wrote *VIVA A REPÚBLICA!* on the blackboards in our rooms. One of my pupils, the son of one of the great republicans, said to me, "You are *vira casaca!*" (turncoat). I had said before that we ought to help the government always, and we had a good Emperor, but now I believed we ought to do our best to help those in power. And believe me, in the *Aula Intermediária*—where I taught three years—were the sons and daughters of Dr. Bernardino de Campos,[21] Dr. Campos Salles,[22] and others who were leaders in that city and have contributed to the betterment of Brazil as a republic. Of course there is always criticism, and it helps.

This incident reminds me of another, so here again I am tempted to mention a recent and very similar incident that happened to me two years ago, in November 1937 in Rio de Janeiro. As I left a bus which took me downtown to go to the dentist, which was right across from the Monroe Palace where Congress meets, I noticed that the palace was heavily guarded by cavalary, artillery, and infantry. I had not seen the papers so I wondered what it was all about, but I was much less scared now at seventy than I was in 1889 at twenty-one. It was another *golpe*. The soldiers were guarding the palace so that Congress could not meet; Getulio Vargas had declared himself a dictator. Having the good fortune to have most of my teeth yet brings me the thought that I might have to go to the dentist again and it gives me the creeps to think what form of government I will have to face in some future errand to the dentist!

---

21. Bernardino José de Campos was a governor of São Paulo and one of the founders of the São Paulo Republican Party (Bello, *A History of Modern Brazil*, 123, 140).

22. Manoel Ferraz de Campos Salles, an early leader of the Republican Party, became the fourth president of the Republic, serving from 1898 to 1902 (Bello, *A History of Modern Brazil*, 140, 162).

# 12. Rio, *A Cidade Maravilhosa*

 *Aboard the S.S. Brasil, February 1955*

My father is a happy man, but there has always been a longing in him to return to his native Brazil. This more-than-yearning is called *saudade* in Portuguese—an untranslatable word that Vovó called "that sadness that you love to feel." *Saudades* are poignant sweet/sad emotional collages of thoughts and dreams and sounds and smells that comprise and awaken the memory of something far away. I am sure my father has always had *saudades* for Brazil.

He left his beloved Rio at age eleven, and returned only once, just after graduating from college. After a short visit, he returned to the States to continue his education. Then came the Depression and, at the same time, marriage; soon he had a family to support.

Perhaps because he has not yet been able to go back, my father's longing has been imparted to me. I too seem to have always had this yearning to be in Rio; and now I want to discover for myself the land that calls me, before life's responsibilities overtake me. My dream is going to be realized, and my father can live it vicariously through me, until the day comes when he will have his own homecoming. At twenty-three, I quit my first job, put my life's savings into traveler's checks, get a passport and visa, and I pack my bags for Rio!

I have asked Pauline, a friend from work, to accompany me for the first phase of the trip. We are going to spend *Carnaval* in Rio, then travel by air to Montevideo, Buenos Aires, Santiago, and Lima. We find each other on the huge ship; it is freezing cold, so we can't stand on deck very long to watch as the *Brasil* slinks out of New York Harbor. We find our stateroom, which vibrates with the movement of the ship, and we try to contain our excitement. We are the only young single women in second class, so naturally we are seated at the Captain's table, an honor we don't appreciate because we'd rather be with people our own age. There aren't many—seven Mormon missionaries, off on their year of duty to convert Catholics in various Latin American countries, and Renato, a young Brazilian returning after study in the US.

It is beautiful and so peaceful to be on the ocean in our own world, without sight of land or any other ship and without news from the solid world. We see dolphins, flying fish, a peacock-blue sky full of fluffy cumulus clouds, and gorgeous, garish sunsets. We watch rain approaching from afar, and rainbows—one with its reflection making almost a complete circle. Then the surprise of the weedy Sargasso Sea, that warm current full of promises. Each day is warmer than the last as we follow the sun south. Our excitement grows with the temperature. Last night in the limpid sky, the Southern Cross made a quiet appearance among the radiant stars. It was much smaller than I had imagined, but magical somehow in its beauty. Renato pointed it out to me. There are the usual shipboard diversions, though they are new to us: shuffleboard and egg/spoon races, and a silly ceremony to mark the crossing of the equator. To earn my shellback (someone who has crossed the equator) certificate I am supposed to sit on a block of ice, be smeared with egg whites, wet spaghetti and tomato sauce, while people are stuffing ice in my bathing suit and taking my picture. Lots of people seem to find it amusing, so I put up with it for the sake of sport.

We also have a mini-*Carnaval* ball. The social director provides props—dresses and pants, hats and capes, from which we can choose to add to whatever we have with us to make costumes. The Mormon missionaries, Renato, Pauline, and I decide to dress as a group, and it is not hard to figure out what we will be. The Mormons are the Seven Dwarfs; Pauline volunteers to be the wicked stepmother; and I get to be Snow White, with Renato as my handsome Prince. Since we are the only group, we have no trouble winning the group prize

We stop for a day in Barbados and then Bahia, where the pulse of Africa is strong. With Renato as our guide, we ride the elevator to the upper, colonial part of the city where we watch street performers doing *capoeira*, a combination of dance and martial arts, accompanied by the *berimbao*, a string instrument made of a gourd. Capoeira was originally developed by slaves to disguise their battles from their masters, but is now an art form widely practiced in Bahia. We taste *acarajé*, a kind of croquette of cooked beans fried in *dendê* (palm) oil, highly spiced and served from carts by *Baianas*: stout, middle-aged Negro women in their long, crisp, white skirts and lacy blouses, turbans, and multicolored bead necklaces. For lunch, we feast on another Bahian specialty, *vatapá*, made of manioc flour and fish, also highly seasoned with unfamiliar spices.

As we near Rio, we begin to hear the *Carnaval* songs of 1955 on the radio. Renato learns them immediately and teaches me the words. Renato also is teaching me how to dance the samba the way Brazilians dance at *Carnaval*—everyone jumping with arms raised, keeping the syncopation going in the hips and shoulders. Nato and I stroll the deck at night, two friends, sweetly playing with young love. I am almost twenty-four; the age of my grandmother when she received her first kiss the night she got engaged. Renato's kiss under the Southern Cross is not my first; that happened eight or so years earlier on my front porch in Athens, Ohio—but oh so much more romantic!

Thirteen days after leaving New York, Pauline and I are up at seven to find we are already in Guanabara Bay. It is a breathtaking sight! We hurry breakfast and rush back on deck where we watch as the *Brasil* pulls in. A band is playing *Cidade Maravilhosa*, Rio's theme song, which begins: "Marvelous city, full of a thousand enchantments, heart of my Brazil"— I get goose pimples every time I hear it. People are shouting, waving, jumping, and crying with joy. How different Vovó's first trip on the ocean was from mine! She had to suffer three weeks of seasickness with three children; I had two weeks of luxury and beauty, with no responsibility. But the excitement she felt at seeing the United States must have been very like what I feel seeing Brazil with my own eyes. And from those two beginnings in opposite directions, each of us gained a country and a people. Like my grandmother, I belong to both.

I don't see Uncle Neco at first, but we share with Nato the excitement of seeing his family and friends, a small group of tiny people separating themselves from the rest of the crowd in order to be seen way below on the dock. Then I see Uncle Neco and my cousin Dolly with a man who turns out to be a *despachante*—one who knows how to get through red tape—who, I find, is there to help us through customs. I haven't seen any of them for five years, since their last visit to the States, when we had a family reunion in Athens at Christmas.

We drive through Copacabana to Uncle Neco's house in Leblon—a beautiful white stucco house where Aunt Ginger and my three year-old cousin Paulinho are waiting. Along the way, Uncle Neco shows us the beach in Leme where he and Daddy used to play and swim, where now we see children dancing to *Carnaval* music on the beach. He shows us the place where their house had stood, and where a skating rink used to be.

All of Rio is gearing up for *Carnaval*. The songs play incessantly on the radio; everyone knows them and has their favorites. My favorite translates something like this:

> *What God has given me, nobody can steal. Ha, ha, ha ha!*
> *Inspiration's no banana, which planted bears its fruit. Ha, ha, ha ha!*
> *If you have water, drink your water, see if you become accustomed,*
> *Every hunchback knows how to lie down...*

And so on, ending with this: *inspiration is not learned in school.*

People sing them as they dance down the streets, and on buses they beat the samba rhythm with their hands or feet, even dancing as they get on and off the buses. We can't believe our own eyes and ears—it is so startling and so freeing to the spirit to see adults playing with the spontaneity and joy of children, and everyone is caught up in it.

*Carnaval* has been going on since shortly after Christmas in the *favelas*, or shantytowns, and *escolas de samba* (samba schools—groups from different areas of Rio). There are many of these, each with their own songwriters and choreographers. There are also *blocos*, small neighborhood groups who march through the streets with their improvised rhythm sections. Anything can be percussive—pots and pans, tin cans and rocks, anything you can shake or whack.

We need costumes, and Aunt Ginger suggests we dress as Tyrolean boys, using our Bermuda shorts and knee-length socks. She makes pointy hats and suspenders for us. Renato comes for us at five, bringing his friends Paulo, Jorge, and Aluízio. They admire our costumes, and after an admonition from Uncle Neco about the dangers of getting separated in the crowd, they take us downtown on the *lotação*, a jitney which stops wherever you flag it. Aluízio is crazy about the United States; he thinks he knows all about it from Hollywood—which he pronounces "olly oo' gee." He is blond and blue-eyed, wears jeans—which are very difficult to get in Brazil—likes to lean on walls posing as James Dean, and is eager to improve his English.

We walk and dance all down the Avenida Rio Branco, where the action is. We join in with thousands of others behind the *escolas de samba*, dancing down the street, careful to hold hands whenever we find ourselves in a tight spot. Everyone's in costume: there are kings and queens; butchers, bakers, and candlestick makers; lions and tigers and bears; gods and goddesses; fairies and elves; circus acrobats and freaks; Minnie and Mickey Mice; Carmen Mirandas and Groucho Marxes; and many Brazilian politicians. Renato tells us the only costumes that are banned are those of police and clergy.

Streamers rain from the sky and people throw confetti and *serpentina*—rolled paper streamers—and spray each other with *lança perfume*, the perfumed ether in a gold canister that feels icy cold on our hot skin. Some people also spray their handkerchiefs, sniff the perfume, and get high on the ether. We buy our own cans but don't sniff; we know the danger of ether and we're already intoxicated with the whole scene. Suddenly, it is pouring, but that doesn't stop people from dancing and splashing in the streets. Most of the spectators, including us, run for cover, but the *escolas* strut down the street undaunted, their music defying the rain.

Besides *Carnaval*, there are the usual tourist sites to see—the views from *Corcovado*, the Hunchback Mountain, *Pão de Açúcar* (Sugar Loaf), the Tijuca forest, and the Jardim Botânico, the lush garden created in 1808 by then-Prince Regent Dom João VI with its *Palma Mater*, the mother of all the palm trees of its genus in Brazil. Uncle Neco and Aunt Ginger introduce us to all of these. Almost every day we walk a block to the Leblon beach, taking Paulinho with us, and occasionally we go to the movies with cousin Dolly.

One day, Aunt Ginger and Uncle Neco take me to meet Vovó's youngest sister, my great-aunt Tia Noemi, her husband Tio Henrique, and their daughters: Francisquinha, Vida, and Nina, and granddaughters Lia and Perla. They bring out loads of my baby pictures and one of the three of us sisters, framed! It is awkward; I'm not fluent in Portuguese and they speak no English, but I understand most of what is being said and hope I am successfully faking what I don't. Afterward, my mouth aches from so much forced smiling when I can't think of anything to say, and my head from the effort and self-judgments that come from the awareness that I am trying to participate in adult conversation with a child's vocabulary. Still I recognize something in look or gesture that is familiar and comforting; like lambs that know their mother, I know we belong to the same clan. It is a surprise to discover that while I'm struggling to learn their names and where they all fit into the family, they already know the names of my sisters and all fifteen cousins, and which of Vovó's six children they belong to. I'm learning how important the extended family is to Brazilians, including relatives they have never met and who have forgotten their Brazilian roots. It is very touching, and I'm a bit ashamed we in the States haven't kept up.

After a month in Rio, Pauline and I go to São Paulo where Vovó is visiting her other sister, Cacilda. All the rest are now dead. Tia Cacilda, also a widow, lives there with her daughters Cacildinha, very sweet and saintly, and Ondina, nice but very quiet. Tia Cacilda is a tall, bony, regal-looking woman. She's about my height—a head taller than Vovó—a peppy old lady with lots of sparkle who is very happy to meet me. The sisters are very comfortable with each other. Vovó is quite animated and keeps the conversation lively in both languages. She is very excited to see me, and delighted and surprised that I can speak some Portuguese. It is a pleasure to see the two sisters together and meet some of Tia Cacilda's grandchildren, my cousins Virginia, Yedda, and Marila, who brings me two beautiful orchids. They are all about my age. Later Yedda takes Pauline, Vovó, and me for a ride. Yedda, the youngest daughter of Daddy's first cousin Odila, is beautiful and effervescent—the most vivacious person I have ever met. She drives us madly around São Paulo, stopping everyone in their tracks, blowing kisses to the other drivers as she cuts in front of them. Just before we leave São Paulo, she takes us to her house at

Guarajá, an island off the coffee port of Santos, where we get another swim in the Atlantic.

After a week in São Paulo, Pauline and I swoop across South America, coming down for brief stops in Montevideo, Buenos Aires, and Santiago, then to Lima. On the flight from Santiago to Lima we see mighty Aconcagua, the tallest mountain peak in Latin America. Suddenly I hear Moussorgsky's *Night on Bald Mountain* in my head and feel the ghost of the terror I felt watching *Fantasia* when I was nine years old. In Lima, we look around a little and arrange a flight to Cuzco. It is a beautiful two-hour flight in a small plane through the snow-covered Andes. We are flying so high that we have to put oxygen tubes in our mouths. The plane corkscrews down to a Lilliputian field. We are warned to rest in our hotel room (which is freezing cold) until we are accustomed to the altitude. We ignore this, regret it, and return to the hotel breathless. Next day, we are up at five and after a quick breakfast, off to Machu Picchu.

It's a spectacular journey to the peak: first, a four-and-a-half hour ride from Cuzco by *ferrocarril*. This is a small bus-type vehicle, seating nine people and running on railroad tracks. It carries us through the narrow valley, lush with wild tropical vegetation. Huge bare rock cliffs rise from the valley bottom, and glacier-fed streams rush through the green valley right on the edge of the jungle that reaches far into Colombia and Brazil. Waterfalls cascade into the turbulent Urubamba River; snow-capped mountains loom in the distance, and all around are ancient Inca terraces and walls—the remains of a mighty civilization from over five hundred years ago, still used for growing crops. Then we transfer to a station wagon. It is a terrifying zigzag ride up the mountain on a narrow, one-way road without guardrails. We try not to look down into the valley as we leave the tropical rainforest and ascend into the cloud forest, and then to the peaks above the timberline.

Machu Picchu was once a complete city with houses, a palace for the Inca chief, terraces for farming, mausoleums for the important mummies and a cemetery for the others, a temple, an athletic field, irrigation canals, a jail, a place where criminals were tossed over the cliff—in short, everything a city needs! At nine-thirty we're walking around the ruins, fascinated by the remains of impossible structures of stone, smoothly cut and fitted together at the top of the mountain, bound together without any mortar. We are haunted by the ghosts of the Incas who lived there on the edge of the cliff, and warriors and virgins who may have been tossed over the edge in sacrifice to the Sun God. We walk around for about three hours, then have lunch at the little hotel—a delicious thick soup with eel and corn on the cob—and ride back to Cuzco, singing all the way.

Pauline and I part company in Lima, and any apprehension I may have had about being alone on this adventure soon dissipates as I discover that almost all the other passengers on the plane are members of a Brazilian soccer team returning to Rio, presumably from a game in Lima. Soccer, called *fútebol* in Brazil, is BIG, and these guys are heroes. There is a joke that the three most important things in Rio are *Carnaval, fútebol, e praia—Carnaval*, soccer, and the beach. I want to flirt but don't have the confidence, so I eavesdrop on their conversations while taking pictures out the window of the plane as we fly over the Peruvian desert, which looks from the air as the moon might appear through a high-powered telescope. We climb above the Andes again, and we fly over the turquoise waters of Lake Titicaca, the largest navigable lake in the world. Then my eyes follow our airplane's tiny shadow as it sweeps across the endless canopy of jungle beneath our wings.

The stewardesses are beginning to serve dinner as we approach Rio. Suddenly the athletes begin to pound out a samba rhythm on their food trays with their knives and forks, and to sing many *Carnaval* and other songs, and finally—as we come in sight of Guanabara Bay—*Cidade Maravilhosa*. Below me the lights of Rio stretch along Botofogo Bay. The lighted statue of Christ atop the darkness of Corcovado seems to float in the cloudless sky. It's like Christmas—Pão de Açúcar, with its necklace of lights, and beyond, the twinkling street and car lights along the shorelines of Copacabana, Ipanema, and Leblon. The view of Rio by night from the air is indeed marvelous—I have no words to express the thrill.

Before leaving Rio, I had done some preliminary job searching. I knew I wanted to stay in Rio for a couple of months at least, and Aunt Ginger had invited me to stay with them indefinitely; but now that I am back the problem of work is weighing on me. I am offered a part-time job at the *Instituto Brasil-Estados Unidos*, and I start teaching English in April to a class of fifth-year students studying *Huckleberry Finn*. Soon after, I am offered a full-time position and a year's contract at the *IBEU* center in Botofogo and I walk down to *Arpoador*, the Harpooner—my favorite beach—to make my decision.

It's a beautiful walk along the beaches of Leblon and Ipanema, and a beautiful day—clear, but a little cool. It is May now, and the sea is very rough. It is impossible to swim because the waves are enormous, splashing higher into the air than I have ever seen them and rattling all the windows of the houses along the Avenida. All through Ipanema and Copacabana the water is over the curb and into shops. In front of a toy store, grown men throw plastic fish into the mess and are fishing for them with lines and poles! Brazilians make a game of everything!

There is no beach at all at Arpoador; the waves are clear up to the seawall and splashing vertically into the air high up on the rocks that normally rise far above the pounding surf. I climb to the highest spot on the rocks to make my decision. There are only a handful of people; I stay there on my own for two hours. Around the corner to the north is the place called *Igrejinha* (Little Church) where once there was a little chapel for fishermen. The waves splash on the beach they call Devil's Cove, and in the distance, Pão de Açúcar stands, welcoming visitors to the Bay. On the open ocean the little islands with the lighthouse whose beams my father watched connect me to my roots. Standing there on the edge of the rock, I can feel the spray of the water splashing perhaps twenty feet in the air, and each time it shoots upward, I see for an instant a perfect rainbow.

To the south side of the rocks, the beaches of Arpoador, Ipanema, and Leblon hold memories of warm happy days, and towering at the end of them are the stately Gavea and Dois Irmãos mountains. Then I gaze at majestic Corcovado with its statue of Christ looking serenely down on one of the most beautiful places on earth, and I am once more keenly aware of the ever-presence of beauty and sadness in the nature of things. I am engulfed in a feeling of reverence that transcends human relationships, and yet I feel that if everyone could share this experience, there would be peace on earth. In that beautiful place, I decide to stay for a year in Rio.

I need a permanent visa in order to work full time in Brazil, and it involves a lot of Brazilian-style bureaucracy, impossible for me without a *despachante*. In addition to my classes at the *Instituto*, I'm giving private lessons to the Ambassador of Guatamala. After my lesson with him today, he offers me his chauffeured car to meet the *despachante*, so here I am—always a small-town girl no matter where I happen to be—being driven through the heart of Rio by a uniformed chauffeur in a limousine paid for by the people of Guatamala! This is not a scenario I could have dreamed up.

I get a permanent visa with the assistance of the *despachante*, who knows who and how much to bribe. My democratic sensibilities make me uncomfortable—people who have to do this on their own are bypassed— but there seems to be no other way for me to do it. I try to think of it as a form of tax on the wealthy. In two hours, I am registered at the American Embassy, fingerprinted, have made an appointment for a physical, and I have been given two other papers: I don't understand what they are, but it doesn't matter. On later appointments with my *despachante*, I get my signature authorized, and I have a physical exam and lab tests.

During this wonderful period of my life with my second family, I have learned Portuguese and something of the Brazilian way of looking at life. Vovó is staying with us now, and she waves to me from her room's little balcony as I head off to catch a *lotação*, a jitney that rushes down Avenida Ataulfo de Paiva and Visconde de Pirajá. They all have accepted me into their family, helped me with my adjustment problems, and listened to my daily adventures with amusement. Aunt Ginger says I am like Uncle Wiggly, always coming home with a story to tell. Because the culture is so new to me and so different, and because I am often alone, I pay attention to everything—listening in on conversations on the bus and observing what is happening on the streets. And instead of keeping to myself around strangers as I do at home, here I talk with my seatmates on the bus or anywhere—for the practice, even on the beach where I am sometimes approached by young men. Most of the time, they recognize me as a North American—there was one who wanted to practice his English, which consisted of an unusual line—"Hey, baby, okey dokey, damn your hide!" This did not start a romance, but entertained the family at dinner that night! Everything is interesting, and every day is an adventure. I have come to love Rio as my father did.

Yesterday at dinner, on my twenty-fourth birthday, Aunt Ginger gave me three *figas*, Afro-Brazilian talismans, and two very pretty small watercolors—one of Pão de Açúcar, the other of Corcovado. After dinner my father's cousin Manoelita came with her husband Carlos and their daughter, Emília, who is married and has two small sons. She brought me a pretty brooch. A little later Renato, Aluízio, and Jorge arrived; Renato with a nice red purse for me, and Aluízio with flowers. We all had ice cream and cake. A letter from my parents arrived on that very day. It was a wonderful birthday. I am richly blessed. I have the love of two families, and two lives in two countries.

Flying into Rio, 1955—Pão de Açucar—*que beleza!*

# 13. *O Moço Louro de Olhos Azuis*
## (Young Blond Man with Blue Eyes)

 *Wooster, Ohio, 1939*

In 1890 Dr. Chamberlain, the missionary who arranged for my sisters
and me to study at the American School in São Paulo, went back to the
United States for vacation. He was speaking at different colleges about
the young men of Brazil, and he emphasized the need of work like
the Young Men's Christian Association (YMCA) for them. Among the
students at Macalister College in St. Paul, Minnesota, there was one who
had worked during his vacations in the YMCA, and this was his last year
in college. After the meeting, this young man met the speaker, as he was
very much interested in his talk.

Subsequently he had an interview with Rev. Chamberlain and the result
was that in July 1891, on the boat Vigilance bound for Brazil, besides
Dr. Chamberlain, his family, and other missionaries, there was another
passenger: Myron Clark. Let us see what he writes to his family when he
sees land. One can hardly handle the little piece of a letter, as it is so dry
and old!

> *Dear ones at home, It really begins to seem as if I am far away from
> home! We crossed the equator at four AM and are going up the Amazon.
> As I rose this morning I saw from the porthole of my cabin for the first
> time far away on the horizon: Brazil—the land of my adoption! Shall
> I love it as now I know I love the land of my birth? The future will
> answer this!*

Myron went directly to São Paulo, the center of the Presbyterian Church
in Brazil. Well, that same night I met Mr. Clark, who had light hair
and blue eyes. We have many Valentinos and Navarros in Brazil, but
a gentleman with eyes of blue and hair of gold and a profile like this
Yankee—all North Americans in Brazil are Yankees—was a rare treat.
And what a profile! I think a nose has lots to do with the looks of a
person, and his was perfect. And now that I have outlined his looks and

my ideas of a handsome fellow, do you blame me if I fell in love with those eyes of *águamarinhas*, so liquid that I wished I could swim in them? I would not have minded being drowned in them in the effort to get to his heart. And what a chin! It was firm like that Rock of Gibraltar.

This young man contacted the Escola Americana, and Dr. Lane advised him to go to the village of Faxina[23] in the interior of the state of São Paulo, where he could not hear English, to live and study Portuguese with Prof. Rev. Benedito Ferraz, a Brazilian minister who was very intelligent and well prepared. Poor fellow! How he suffered those first six months! It took two days by train, and then three on horseback—and those beasts were not birds like our Condor, my father's horse! He never had been on a horse before. Can you imagine a boy who had never been on horseback, even for pleasure, making this trip? He had to stay in bed for a few days, sore, tired, and blistered with sunburn, almost wishing he were back in his country taking a Pullman car in New York for home. At that time the interior of São Paulo was called *sertão*—the backlands. In most of the houses in those days, there were no conveniences or comforts whatsoever; in fact there were not even boards on the floor, just plain hard dirt. Flies, fleas, bugs, and cockroaches had just as much right to the house as the family. That wasn't all; he suffered from another affliction— it was homesickness, lonesomeness. So, to learn the language as quickly as possible and to go back to civilization was his only ambition, and he did.

My cousin Eduardo Carlos Pereira, my hero, the one with whom I wanted to elope in order to visit my godmother when I was ten years old, was now pastor of the largest Presbyterian church in Brazil. Six months had elapsed since the American had come and disappeared, and one evening at church, Eduardo announced that Mr. Clark was going to tell the congregation something about the work he was interested in and hoped to organize here for the young men. We young teachers were talking excitedly. We giggled quite a bit when we heard this, and were very anxious to hear him and more yet, I guess, to see him again. When the day came for him to speak we were all there in a row, and believe me, I was very anxious for him because some of the girls were merciless when mistakes were made in our smooth *idioma* (language) and I was afraid he would be exposed to ridicule, daring to speak after only six months of

23. Now Itapeva.

study of the language! How many we knew that in two or more years couldn't say twelve words without making fifteen mistakes? We were amazed!

Eduardo introduced the young man and to the astonishment of the congregation, he spoke in very good Portuguese without any notes, and after his exposition, we were all full of admiration for the person, for his speech and his ideals! And what do you suppose he did right after the meeting? He came to us, shook hands with us all, and returned our compliments for his fine Portuguese with the most appropriate phrases! Everybody was surprised at his achievements in six months. We soon heard that he was speaking in other churches of different denominations and had rented some rooms where young men met to play games.

One day my friend Miss Nan, the matron of *Escola Americana*, told me that I ought to teach a class of boys in the Sunday school. I protested energetically saying that I was not prepared for that, but she convinced me that it was my duty to do it. I had never done any methodical study of the Bible. I had a good knowledge of its contents because when I was alone in school I was rather homesick and in order to be in daily communion with each other, my sisters and I agreed to start reading the Bible together, the same pages every day. We kept this up until we finished reading it.

My friend had noticed my religious inclination, so she did not give up until I said yes, and promised some instructions about the lessons on Saturdays. She loved me so and had such a nice opinion of me that I just had to do it, and so a great part of my Saturdays was spent in preparation for the lesson. I suffered this patiently and I certainly was rewarded for accepting this position of Sunday school teacher, because a few months after I took the class my cousin Eduardo, seeing how the *Moço Louro*[24] was

---

24. *O Moço Loiro* (*Louro* in the revised spelling) is the title of a novel published in 1845 by the Brazilian writer Joaquim Manoel de Macedo. It is the tale of a young man falsely accused of the robbery of a thirteenth-century gold cross belonging to his family. Berated by his grandmother, he runs away although he is in love with a cousin, Honorina. Years later, a mysterious man known only as the Moço Loiro (young blond man) appears, and courts Honorina, finally winning her love. Guess who? Although I don't recall Vovó ever telling us this story, she surely must have read the book, which is considered a classic of Brazilian literature, spanning the periods of romanticism and realism. In Brazil, blonds have a certain mystique, comparable to "tall, dark, and handsome" in American culture.

interested in the young people, invited him to be superintendent of the Sunday school. Oh, my lucky star! How I blessed that time I had thought was lost on those Saturdays!

The superintendent had to go to each class to take the attendance and the collection, so every Sunday we had a little personal talk in class. And there, in that country that I love so much, with the tendency being to keep young males and females away from each other, how precious to me were those minutes before the lesson and those afterward, and the times when he came for business to my class.

On Sunday afternoons we heard the American boys sing college songs in the Boarding School with the American teachers. They used to sing "Juanita," and I am sure that when the Moço Louro sang, "Say, darling say, when I'm far away," he was thinking of somebody in the States. Although we all could sing just as well as those teachers and, I know, much better than some of them, we were never invited to join them.

In fact, though, he seemed to prefer to speak to us than to the American teachers. And, my grandchildren, this would not do for many reasons! Things which were permitted in the United States in the 1880s were considered very improper in Brazil. And there were racial prejudices too; our race was considered inferior by citizens of the United States. During those years of studying and teaching at the American School, I was in contact with people whose standards for men and women were more alike. The wife expected of her husband what he expected of her. She was his companion, a beloved partner in the business of living, and not just a necessary thing, a housekeeper, a slave, or a loved pet. So down in the silent regions of my heart I admired these couples who came from *America do Norte*, because there was a better understanding between husband and wife.

Usually when a single young American man arrived in our community, he kept away from any recognition of Brazilian girls, going back to the USA for his equal. So of course Dr. Lane and the other Americans did not like what they called his boldness. The Americans were worrying that this young man might be doing just as was customary in his country; having a good time with us and then dropping us whenever he cared to, leaving maybe some broken hearts. They didn't know that we were having a good time also in this collective way. If someone were really wrapped up in the personality of this attractive young Yankee she would never admit it nor let anybody know it, in case he proved not to be what she thought he was. We were wise to it. But alas, the Americans were not the worst ones with whom we had to contend. There was prejudice in Brazil as well. Our Brazilian people would be merciless in their criticism of us if this Yankee, after being so lovable, all of a sudden would drop us for some American girl.

Now what would you think of me, dear ones, after I explain that in spite of all these warnings and circumstances, that I was letting myself be entangled tighter and tighter in the treacherous net woven around me by the merciless Cupid? Thinking that this secret I am telling you was hidden from everybody in my heart, I did not realize that my reputation was at stake. But what of it? Wasn't it worthwhile? What about the Moço Louro? He was not paying a bit more attention to me than to any of the other teachers! We all joked among ourselves that we were in love with him; being sure that it was just for fun, although I don't know how many of us were in earnest. I am responsible only for myself. The Moço Louro had two American friends, two brothers who came to Brazil to get a start in business. These two, along with a few Brazilian boys, organized a bunch of boys and according to a premeditated plan, we met with them in different places. Oh no! We never went two by two! They escorted us all together, which I preferred, because I didn't care to see the Moço Louro hooked to somebody else.

It was dangerous to be in couples; we might meet some unexpected acquaintances from either nationality, which were equally unwelcome and dangerous. I imagine you are wondering where we did meet. I had an aunt, and some of the teachers had married sisters or close friends who invited us on Friday nights. We played very innocent games. This became quite customary in the Protestant community in São Paulo. Most of us did not have homes in the big city, and parents would not do for that, anyway. If they were what people expected them to be, they would not be inviting a bunch of young men to their homes. It might look as if they were trying to find a market for their goods.

These parties were the most innocent gatherings anybody would wish
for their daughters, yet we, the teachers, were always afraid that we were
not doing the right thing, so we didn't tell the directors. We did not do
anything hidden; they could have found out if they had wanted, but we
were breaking the Brazilian traditions. So without being acquainted then
with Elizabeth Browning in *The Barretts of Wimpole Street*, your Vovó, my
grandchildren, did follow the advice Miss Barrett gave to her sister: "Be
wise, but don't do the wise thing always!"

The Big City of São Paulo lies in the beautiful valley of the Rio
Piratininga; in fact, Piratininga was the name of the city at the time of
the colonization. Just about this time, plans were being made for opening
an avenue where rich people could build their homes on one of the
highest spots overlooking the city. A streetcar line was built to take those
interested in scenery to the Avenida Paulista where in those days there
was only a small park with swings and a beer garden. This was just the
embryo of what is today a magnificent park with flowers and birds, pools
and cascades, arbors and a natural forest. The Avenida now is all built up
with palacetes (mansions) surrounded by lovely grounds.

On a holiday, the third anniversary of the Republic, a young Portuguese
man invited "the Bunch" and the Brazilian teachers, through my aunt, to
a picnic at the park. We joked a good deal about it, and in fact we were
a little uncharitable in our judgment because this young man was not
one of the Bunch and had nothing in common with us. My aunt was the
chaperone and you may have already guessed that she was just the kind
of chaperone you would like to have! We could do anything we pleased,
but custom was enough to make us behave properly. After we had fed
our eyes with the gorgeous view of the valley where the Tietê, like a
silver snake, was crawling along stretches of green land, the boys invited
us to the swings. In those days girls went to picnics dressed nicely in our
best, and the dresses went clear down to our feet. That night when we
went to bed we could not sleep. We were terribly ashamed—we were
thinking that they might have seen about one inch above our feet!

In those days ladies carried big fans in the summer months. The Moço
Louro wrote with pencil on the stick of my fan his name, and the date
of the picnic, and the place. The silk of the fan has long disappeared, but

I have carefully kept the wooden part as a souvenir, and the writing can still be read although very faded...*Avenida Paulista 15 de Novembro de 1892 Myron A. Clark.*

# 14. *Namorando*

 *Wooster, Ohio, January 27, 1935*

The beautiful banks of the Tieté River, where the Tropic of Capricorn is supposed to be, were also much sought for picnics. I had been on picnics with friends at that spot, but I had never seen the *Capricórnio*, the being who gives us the palm trees and the great variety of tropical fruits and flowers.

Once, on another outing arranged by my aunt, I well remember how we made little paper boats and cut little paper dolls. We placed in each boat a paper couple, and threw the little vessels in the water. We watched the fragile little rafts with their tiny passengers face the waves made by our big boat on the old River Tieté, to see which would stay afloat longest. I made two boats, putting myself and the Moço Louro in one, and my friend América and the Moço Louro in the other. The second one sank immediately, but the first stayed afloat as long as one could expect of such a ship facing such a surf. My boat won the race, but nobody suspected that one of the dolls was supposed to be the Moço Louro.

Vacation was getting near: it began in early December. Both my parents were dead then, and nobody from the family lived in my little hometown, so for the first time I was not to spend my vacation in Caldas. Instead, I would go to my oldest sister Mariquinha and her family who were now living in a small place, Caracol. To get there, my sisters and I had a day's journey by train and another on horseback. The night before we left, my aunt invited us, about four boys and four girls, for a *despedida* (a farewell party). After the party the boys took us home to the school, and said they were all going to the station to see us off in the morning: my two sisters, Cacilda and Manoelita, and me. I did not have many joyful expectations about this vacation except for the pleasure of seeing Mariquinha and my brother, Argentino, and sister Noemi, who lived with Mariquinha now. The place itself held no attraction for me, and besides, I was going to leave the Moço Louro for almost two months in the same city with some of the other teachers...Ai, ai, ai!

We had to be at the station about six in the morning. Just as I was going through a little garden, I saw a bed of forget-me-nots. I love blue flowers, so I gathered a little bouquet as I had done so many times and pinned them over my heart. This time, though, I was planning to put them in somebody's hands at the station, as I was almost sure then that I meant more to him than the others. The girls said to me: "I bet you are going to give them to him!" Of course I lied laughingly. Well, when we arrived at the station, everyone was there except the Moço Louro dos Olhos Azuis. Well, at first I thought he was just late, but when the first bell for the departure had rung, I thought he was not coming; that he did not care. The girls began to joke about my bouquet, and it did hurt.

Then at the gate of the platform the Moço Louro appeared, breathing heavily; seeing me at the window of the train, he ran directly to me, and I could see and so could all the others that he had made a great effort to get there before the train left. I had just time to remove the forget-me-nots, put them where they belonged, and shake hands; the train slowly started off, and I was quite happy. He had time to say that the alarm clock did not work, but afterward he found out that it was a trick of the two Hall boys who roomed with him.

The *vila* of Caracol—*vila* does not mean a house, but a village—was planted at the foot of a range of mountains of that name, the shape of which accounts for the name, which means snail. Although I say it was planted, it did not grow but remained very small and unimportant. It was the rainy season and, I presume on account of the mountains, the thunderstorms there were terrific. I believe that Brontes, Stereopes, and Arges[25] made their abode in that region. Besides there were many swamps at the foot of the *serras* (mountains), and as soon as the shadows of night fell over the place, the frogs started to tune their throats and the symphony began—the swamp symphony—*Marche Funebre*.

In the little old town where my sister and brother-in-law lived, people had to go to the post office for their mail. My brother Argentino went for the

---

25. In Greek mythology, Brontes, Stereopes, and Arges were the Cyclops; one-eyed giants. During the Titan war they crafted thunderbolts for Zeus.

mail and came home with a big smile all over his face, waving a letter and saying, "Your name and address are written by *machine!*" This had caused quite an excitement at the little post office in a small rented room. I knew immediately who had written it. My brother-in-law said, "Don't give it to her, Argentino; let her pay for it." The price was set and paid and the letter came into my possession. Oh, boy!

It began, "Dona Chiquita, dear friend, did you really expect to receive a letter from me so soon? It was only yesterday that you left and I feel almost ashamed to write so soon, but I am impelled to it by some kind of feeling I don't understand." There were five pages of very small and firm writing, and he ended it by saying, "If I cannot wait for an answer, I will write again. Let me give you the message that your flowers still breathe from a cup: 'Forget me not.'" I certainly had not said that to him but I had wished it with all my heart. Many other letters came and I still carry some pieces of those first ones—the ink he used was so strong that the writing tore the paper.

They came by every mail and as this was only every three days sometimes the mail brought more than one. Of course the postmaster had noticed that there was also a letter leaving Caracol by every mail to somebody who had the same name as the English manufacturer of the best kitchenware, the best thread, and the best shoes sold in Brazil. I did not realize how far my brother-in-law could carry his jokes, so though my letters were put away, they were not under key. One day at the table he recited some of their contents and of course he chose what I would not want repeated, because it was very private, but this was not all: the Moço Louro had ventured quite a bit of Portuguese in his letters, and as in matters of love you can't translate ways or words, once or twice he put it rather oddly. After that, I kept the letters in a safe place.

When the end of the vacation was drawing near, the Moço Louro asked my permission to come to meet me at the railroad terminal, *Espírito Santo do Pinhal* (Holy Spirit of the Pines), and make the return trip together to the Big City. It was a train trip of almost a whole day from São Paulo for him, and about half a day from Caracol on horseback to Pinhal, the town where we were going to meet again. Well, this meant breaking some of our rules concerning men and women, but what could I do? In that city lived an aunt of my father's and I knew that my old aunt would think this terrible. I would have to break the news to many relatives and many people who knew my family that this American was arriving there, and my sisters and I were going back to São Paulo with him. I would have to explain who this fellow was. I could not say he was my friend, because Brazilians do not admit friendship between men and women—and he was not my betrothed, so there you are! On the other hand, how could I explain to him that what he wanted to do was not right, or at least not the correct thing? I was guessing what the result of his trip was going to be, and after consulting with Cacilda, finally I told him to come. You know now that I was not always doing the conventional thing. We would arrive in the afternoon and he at night; he would go to the hotel, we to the home of a friend of our brother-in-law. In those days hotels were only for men.

His letter mentioned too that he was sure that São Paulo was not the place then for the organization of a YMCA, and as he had an invitation from a group of young men in Rio de Janeiro who were in favor of the organization of a YMCA, he was planning to move to that city just as soon as yellow fever began to decline; and ended the letter with this: "Have you ever been in Rio, Dona Chiquita? It is a beautiful city! Don't you think you would like to live there, Dona Chiquita, or are you such a *Paulista* that you could never live any where but in São Paulo?" I laughed a lot and answered that he was very mistaken, because I was a *Mineira* (a native of Minas Gerais), but that with the right company I would go to the heart of Africa. And the letters continued to come and also go, but not as frequently, because I was afraid; but in my imagination the croaking of the frogs now sounded like the Wedding March.

The day came when about the same time that the Moço Louro was taking the train for Pinhal, I was saying goodbye to my dear sister and her family, and to the *serras*, and saying thank you to the frogs for entertaining me for two months with the alluring Symphony of the Swamps, and all this time I was wondering why he wanted to see me before I arrived in the Big City to resume my duties! We had agreed that I would meet him at the station and he would go to the hotel from there, but being so nervous about it I had not really thought about how I would do it, but was just hoping it would work out.

As we had not met these relatives before, all the cousins and aunts were there to meet us soon after we arrived at the home of my brother-in-law's friend where we were staying, and after supper we all went to see my father's aunt. These relatives seemed to be fascinated with we three cousins; they wanted to escort us back to show us the little town by the light of the full moon. Arriving back at the house where we were staying, my cousins came in and stayed and stayed, and I could not go to the station. I realized that I had to say something about this young man as it was getting time for his train but I could not. I didn't know how to explain to my relatives and intimate friends of my brother-in-law, all of whom I was meeting for the first time, that a foreigner—a very attractive one—was coming just to go right back with us, my sisters and me! This was preposterous—it would furnish gossip for some time. My conscience accused me for having consented to his coming, but my heart felt happy at having done so.

I wasn't there; I was floating between that room and the station, hardly hearing what was being said, when all of a sudden the maid opened the door of the parlor and my Prince appeared, and I introduced Mr. Myron Clark! The house was full of relatives and friends when he appeared, and I presume if I hadn't been so up in the air, I would have noticed their astonishment. When I, very embarrassed, tried to explain why he was there—and to him, why I was not at the station—he, a little embarrassed, said that it was perfectly all right, because it was easy for him to find us since I had given him the name of the friend where we were staying. But the worst was yet to come!

About ten o'clock the cousins made a move to leave, which they finally did after exchanges of what you are supposed to say to relatives that you meet for the first time. My sisters went to bed but our hostess stayed right there, as it was not proper for a young man to be left alone with a young lady and in fact it would not be polite for the hostess to leave the room anyway. He waited and then he said that he would like to take me for a walk as there could not be more beautiful moonlight than the one over "The Pines." Now this was breaking all the rules, all good manners, and all the laws of decency! But wasn't I feeling that it was worthwhile to put my reputation at stake to hear what he said he wanted to tell me? Well, it was already at risk so I could face one more trouble. I was sure, though, or I would not have risked my reputation. So I explained American ways to my hostess and she tried her best to say that it was all right although it was written all over her face that what I was doing was terrible. I went upstairs and talked it over with my sister, too, but one person was troubling me more than anybody else, and condemning me more than anybody else, and I could not get rid of her: it was just me, myself. I never had been out alone with a young man at night, and I was going to be twenty-four in June. Then, what if I was mistaken about the motive of this trip of the Moço Louro to Espirito Santo do Pinhal?

We didn't know the area, but the moonlight was so bright that he could lead me outside the little town. The full moon was as beautiful as it was when it shone on that largo in Caldas on the night of the second of June, 1868, according to what my cousin Severo always told me. I don't know how long we walked until we got near a little creek, where we sat down, and there, with this Good Friend who saw me the night I arrived in this world as a witness—Miss Moon—we sealed the biggest, the nicest, the dearest contract I ever made with...oh, I am not going to tell, and I know that the Moon won't either! Nor am I going to tell everything that he said to me on that night, and that he always said when we were together, and in letters when apart.

We became engaged under the most perfect, beautiful moonlit night, on the 27th of January, 1893, in Espirito Santo do Pinhal, Estado de São Paulo. He put the engagement ring on my finger. His father had given it to him when he was twenty-one. It has never left my finger! To tell the truth the only thing I saw and remember from the time we left the house until we sat down by the creek at the outskirts of the town was my old friend the Moon! She was glorious! And with tenderness she enveloped us both in her soft pale robe, and with her blessing she said, "Take good care of my little girl, Moço Louro! I was present the night she was born and I was glad to hear her say yes to you....You'd better take her home now; it is after eleven." This was forty-two years ago, this very night of the 27th of January 1935. Yes, I do love this lady of the night and wherever I am when she is present, people call me to see her.

# 15. *Dona Professora*

 *Rio de Janeiro, September 13, 1955*

After my eight o'clock class at the *Instituto Brasil-Estados Unidos*, my boss calls me into her office and shuts the door. She asks, "How would you like to travel?" I respond that I always like to travel, and she tells me that the English Department at the University of Espírito Santo in Vitória needs a temporary English teacher. The U.S. Cultural Attaché in Rio has been asked for a recommendation for a substitute English teacher because the only English teacher at the University has just given birth to twins. She is also head of the English Department, and this will be my title as well. I could also teach at the *IBEU* there. Miss Adams tells me the job in Vitória is mine if I want it, but it is only for three months. I will lose my job in Rio, but it's a chance to go off on my own, to play an unknown role in an unfamiliar place. I am scared, but I am also intrigued by the opportunity to have a new adventure in an unknown place, to live with Brazilians, and to perfect my Portuguese. I can't resist an adventure like this! I think it over, talk it over with Aunt Ginger and Uncle Neco, and say yes.

Aunt Ginger accompanies me to the airport. It is a small airplane that makes the one-hour flight north along the coast to Vitória. From above, the city looks like a miniature Rio, with its bay and surrounding mountains. The American Embassy official in Rio explained that, as no respectable woman could live by herself, they had arranged for me to live with a family. I'm suddenly thinking weird thoughts like maybe this plane will plunge into the bay and I'll be out of this unknown scenario I got myself into, but I've got a role to play: I will just do it.

A small party including some future students representing the University and *IBEU* is at the airport to welcome and fetch me. In a caravan of three cars, they show me around Vitória, a lovely island city of hills and winding cobblestone streets and parks. Then they take me to the house where I am going to live, where I meet the de Paula family—Senhor José, a Baptist minister whom everyone in town calls *O Pastór* (the pastor);

his wife Dona Orlinda: daughter Ruth (a few years younger than I): their son Paulo's two small sons, Bobby and Junior (called Duna); and a maid, a young girl of fifteen or sixteen. They tell me that I met Paulo, Renato's friend, in Rio, and it is their daughter for whom I am substituting in the English Department. Then I am confused—is this just a social visit? Gradually, I piece together who they are, but I am so nervous and excited that I'm having trouble keeping up with what is going on. They show me a bedroom at the end of the hall in their seven-room apartment, bring my suitcases to it, and I finally understand that this is where I will live. I am going to share meals with them, too.

My head is spinning, everyone is talking at once, I can't keep up—it is all so new and unbelievable. I am in their hands, I know, and I can't imagine what my life here will be like. When I'm in a situation like this, where I understand generally what is happening, but I'm vague about the specifics, I just have to fake it to some degree; otherwise I am stalled and made more anxious by the difficulties. It is a childlike state of mind, where I just trust and accept what I do understand, and let the rest go. It's a little uncomfortable, but I have gotten used to it.

After a brief visit and a *cafezinho* (demitasse), we leave the de Paulas and are off in the caravan to the Ministério de Educação, the Department of Education, where Senhor José Leão is waiting for us. He tells me how happy they are to have me. Then, back in the cars, we are off to meet the governor of the state of Espírito Santo. I don't understand the reason for this, but as usual I just go along, trying to observe and understand as much as possible, curious about this new experience. The worst that could happen would be that I would behave inappropriately; that had happened before, and I learned that when you are a stranger in a strange land, people are tolerant—at least Brazilians are. On the way, I am reviewing in my mind the second-person-plural verb forms that are used exclusively for people of high rank. Because I have never used them, I don't know them very well. Now I will need them.

While this is going on in my head, my female students, who are about my age, are telling me that the governor has a young son who is single, and it is inevitable that we will fall in love, marry, and live happily ever after. Well, it would have made a nice parallel with Vovó's life, but it doesn't happen. After driving a long way to the governor's estate, we are informed that he is away, hunting. Although there were a couple more attempts by my sponsors, Cinderella never did meet the Prince.

That evening, I teach my first class—of five students! There are no texts, no library. I am completely on my own. My students at the University are only slightly younger than I. They have never had a North American teacher at the University, or at the *Instituto*, and are very curious about me. They want to learn how to speak English, so we talk. Later I get some copies of Huckleberry Finn. We read that, and talk about it.

Vitória is a lovely little town. It is actually about six times the size of Athens, Ohio (about 60,000), but has much of the same small-town atmosphere. The capital of the state of Espírito Santo, it is a major port for cargo ships. The city is on an island, a very hilly one, and has a lovely bay and mountains all around. There are lots of little islands in the bay. Narrow streets wind around the many hills and pleasant *praças* that offer benches in the midst of many-hued flowers. It is very quiet, quaint, clean, and beautiful. Everyone is very kind and considerate. I'm sure I will like it here. I am relaxing. Everything will be OK.

But I am in a funny position. It seems as if everyone in town knows about the arrival of the *professora americana*. When I speak English with my students on the street, everyone stares—people who can't speak or understand English come to my class just to see and hear me! As far as I know, I am the only native English-speaking person in the city. I am a curiosity not only for that reason, but also because I am a young woman alone, and tall. Teachers in Brazil are very much respected, and I am often greeted on the street by people I don't know saying "*Bom dia, Dona Professora*," ("Good morning, Miss Teacher") and then as they pass I sometimes hear, "*Puxa! Que moça alta!*" ("Wow! What a tall girl!") At times it seems that it is not my own life, because I am living in such a different world, but it is a beautiful and interesting world. Everyone is very *simpático* (likeable). I have the foreigner's freedom—neither I nor the people I meet have any expectations; it is all improvisation. Life should always be like this!

The *Instituto* gives a party in my honor. It is very nice but I'm not used to the attention—everyone crowds around me, pressing me with questions about life in the States and my life in particular, listening with delight to my English and with awe—or is it amusement?—to my Portuguese, and flooding me with compliments. This is typically Brazilian and I should be used to it now, but I'm not. The worst of it is that I just can't reciprocate. I'm afraid people think that I don't like it here, because I don't rave the way Brazilians do. I think that's one of the biggest differences between the personalities of Americans and Brazilians; our everyday language about feelings is bland, theirs is more poetic and sometimes flowery. As long as I am thinking in English, my translations are cool and flat. I have more than vocabulary and grammar to learn; I need to learn how to express my feelings without embarrassment. Later, though, I am introduced over the microphone to all the students, members, and guests, and one student who was chosen to welcome me says in very good English (laboriously prepared and memorized, I'm sure), "Miss Annita, we expected an American, but we did not expect anyone as nice as you." It was said very simply, very sincerely, and I was very touched.

My students are eager to practice speaking English outside of class, and they show me Vitória and its surroundings. Most are young women, from whom I am learning about relationships between young men and women in this part of Brazil; very different from Rio. Here the customs are very old fashioned and strict. Under no circumstances may a girl go out alone with a boy. A girl who doesn't have a *namorado* may go to the *praça* with another girl on certain nights of the week and walk around and around it. This is called *passeando*. As they walk around, they pass boys who are *passeando* in the opposite direction, and they meet or avoid each others' eyes.

If the eyes meet, the boys may walk with them or they may stop and talk. If one of the boys walks one of the girls home, and if she likes him, she asks him to come back later to meet her parents. If he hesitates or says "someday" then she knows he was just *passando tempo*, but if he accepts, then she tells her parents that she wants to *namorar*—and if they don't know him already, they check into his family, finding out what his father does, how much he makes, and everything possible about the son. If they approve, the boy comes to the girl's house to meet her parents, and from then on they are *namorados*.

This means that she must not, on penalty of immediate termination of the relationship without explanation, be seen with any other male with the exception of father and brothers—even if it's walking to the corner with a male cousin. She must obey all his wishes concerning her clothes, hair, and so forth. All of their courting must be carried on in the house with parents and family, or if they go out anywhere, they must be accompanied by at least one parent, sister, or friend. There must also be no physical contact between them except shaking hands, unless they become engaged, in which case they may hold hands, take walks together, and maybe even go to a movie alone, though they may never go anywhere in a car alone together. If they decide they don't like each other and want to break off the relationship, they do, but she must wait at least two months before she begins to *namorar* again, or everyone will think she "arranged" the second *namorado* when she was still *namorando* with the first. Of course, the boy may do as he pleases, although if he has too many *namoradas* in too short a time, he may eventually have difficulty getting parental approval. And this is 1955!

Tereza is the most advanced student, and I am often invited to her home, but my best friend is Moacyr, who always walks me home up the hill after evening classes. He is short, dark, and handsome—and more importantly, sweet, bright, and funny. We agree to spend half our time together speaking English, half Portuguese, so he has become my main teacher. But we have to be careful: I think these antiquated customs are ridiculous and want to ignore them, but I have to avoid gossip. Besides, he is my student, and I don't want anyone to accuse me of favoritism. So all of our meetings take place outside when it is not raining, mostly sitting on the rocks outside the Pastor's house.

I have students at the *IBEU* also, and one of them, José, a young man about seventeen or eighteen, has invited me to visit his family in the interior of the state. I don't know why he is inviting me, but the Pastor's family assures me it is all right, as long as I ask a friend to go with me. He wants me to see his village and, I suppose, to show this North American teacher to his family and the villagers. I know I am a rarity, but I am always surprised to be treated like a minor celebrity—or is this the way Brazilians show hospitality to all strangers?

José arrives at the house at five-thirty in the morning; we meet Lúcia, who is to accompany me. We are off first by bus to the mainland, and then to Fundão on the train. The tracks follow a river, and there are beautiful small mountains and woods, and a few cleared places. We are in the middle of the Atlantic rainforest, and José points out and identifies the trees—coffee, banana, *goiaba*, *manga*, *mamão* (guava, mango, papaya), and lots of sugar cane. At every village, people gather to watch the train go by or wave from their windows. Children are running around naked, chickens are walking in and out of houses, goats and horses are grazing in the streets.

When we arrive at Fundão there is a band playing and lots of people around. José explains that there is some kind of a *festa* (celebration)

People gathering to watch the train go by; town in Espírito Santo, 1955.

at the church that afternoon. José's father is there to meet us, and his mother and a sister of five or six years are waiting at his very modest home. The house has no running water, but it is very clean (José works during the day, studies at night at a junior college, and attends one of my morning classes. He is always well-dressed in clean clothes). They greet us warmly, offering Lúcia and me a bed, and suggest that we rest from the trip before going out to explore the village. We have coffee; then José shows us the village, which is quiet, primitive, and beautiful.

There are no paved streets, just one street with a hitching post at the center, near a stone monument of some sort and a huge mango tree. Except for the absence of the saloon with swinging doors, the town looks pretty much like the ghost town of a Hollywood western. We cross the tracks and a wooden bridge over a lovely singing stream, and we arrive at a farm where a man, smoking a flat reed, shows us his fruit trees— banana, guava, and lots of others. He climbs way up into a tree to get me a beautiful yellow flower that is blooming way at the top and hanging down. We end up at José's cousin's house which is much more elegant than his, having furniture and a tiny radio. The cousin picks some flowers for me from her garden, and shows us her chickens and an enormous pig that comes into the kitchen to be fed and entirely fills the room.

José's family is very gracious, providing a delicious meal of chicken stew, rice, beans, salad, beef, and beer, and afterward giving us guava and papaya paste and coffee. Then they bring out all their American magazines — *National Geographic*, *Holiday*, and one *Esquire*—and ask me to show them pictures of Ohio and to translate the ads. Then José and I converse in English for a while, with the family watching in wonder and amusement. They ask me about my country, and whether José is doing well. They are obviously very proud of him. His father gives Lúcia and me uncut garnets, presumably mined from the area. I am embarrassed— I should have brought something from my country for them. We return to Vitória at nine-thirty in the evening. It is raining, as is usual here in the spring.

While here, I am observing my first Brazilian election, following the suicide of the dictator Getúlio Vargas. Vargas had submitted his resignation under pressure from the military, in favor of his vice president, João Café Filho, and then shot himself in his bedroom at the presidential palace in Rio. As I understand it, Café Filho asked to be relieved of his duties as president because of "heart trouble"—no one believes he is really sick—and Carlos Luz, next in line according to the constitution, became president but was impeached three days later for being a *golpista*. This gives rise to many puns on his name, the best being, "*Coitado do Brasil, sem Café e sem Luz*" ("Poor Brazil, without coffee or light").

Among many candidates for president is a *Mineiro* (native of Minas Gerais), Juscelino Kubitschek, who is running on a coalition of the Social Democratic and Brazilian Labor parties with the backing of Vargas's supporters. We have to wait two weeks for the election results. In the end, Kubitschek wins with thirty-nine percent of the vote. An *estado de sítio* (state of siege) is declared. This is the counter-*golpe*—it is supposed to assure that Kubitschek will take office in January.

I really don't see much evidence of it here, except that every few minutes today there was an announcement on the radio preceded by a blast on a trumpet, but it's all a big confusion; no one seems to know what's going on. There are soldiers in twos on street corners, but people go about their business without seeming to take much notice.

We are in a state of siege for a month. They say that planes and ships are unable to leave Rio, and there is an American ship in the bay here now—stuck—because it can't proceed. If this lasts very long, I too will be stuck in Vitória, but I don't think it will. It is soon over and apparently forgotten.

It's December, and my time in Vitória is nearing an end. I leave Vitória with *saudades*, for I like the place and have many friends here, but my heart is beating double-time at the thought of getting back to Rio. My *Titia* (auntie) is waiting at Gavião for me, and I am soon at home. VoVó and Nilse, the maid, are astounded at my fluency in Portuguese. Everything looks so good! Paulinho is on the beach, and I run down without changing clothes and get a big hug from him even before he asks me if I have brought him anything.

My cousin Jim and his wife Nell have come from São Paulo for Christmas. Despite the fact that it is midsummer, we have a tree and celebrate just as in the Northern Hemisphere. After dinner we watch home movies of Jim and Nell's wedding and of the Christmas in Athens when three of Daddy's siblings—Uncle Neco, Uncle Henry, and Aunt Argy—and a bunch of us cousins were together. About ten that night we get a call from my parents in Athens, but it is disappointing. We can't understand much, and they can't either.

On New Year's Eve Uncle Neco, Aunt Ginger, Dolly and I are playing Hearts, but Dolly and I want to go to the beach to see a *Macumba* ceremony (a Brazilian variant of voodoo). I have been hearing about *Macumba* on the beach on New Year's Eve ever since I came to Rio. This is the special day of Iemanjá, the *orixá* (goddess) of the sea. I have seen *Macumba* offerings before, on the beach and on street corners—bottles of cachaça (a Brazilian rum made of sugar cane), cigars, candles, droopy flowers, occasionally a dead chicken; but I have never witnessed a ceremony. Dolly has seen the people gathered on the beach on other New Year's Eves, but has never watched the ceremonies. So, although it is raining, at about nine-thirty Uncle Neco takes us to the corner to see whether the festivities have started. The whole length of the beaches of Leblon and Ipanema are crowded with hundreds of people gathered in circles of twenty to thirty each. Every group has its own candles lit, which is all we can see from the street.

Dolly, who has said that she just wants to watch from the sidewalk, gets brave and asks her parents for permission to go on the beach. It is given, and we take off our shoes, join hands, and run towards the nearest group. We are just a little bit nervous, and agree to speak only Portuguese lest we be mistaken for *turistas*, who we feel would not be welcome. It is difficult to tell the *macumbistas* from spectators like ourselves, so we don't say much at all: we just watch in open-mouthed wonder.

Everyone is dressed in white, carrying candles. In every circle there are flowers, perfume, nail polish, lipsticks, and other offerings for Iemanjá. We approach one group, and stand in the back of the circle, where we can see the *pai de santo*, the shaman, wearing a chain around his neck from which hangs both a cross and an anchor. He is arranging things on a sheet spread out on the sand. It sort of gives the impression of a picnic. In the center is a big dish of the milky pink gelatin that Brazilians sometimes serve for dessert. All around the sides of the cloth, as if people were going to sit around it, are paper cups filled with different liquids. They are different colors, and I don't know what they are, except I can tell that one is beer. They probably also have wine and guaraná. There is also a cake of face soap (sort of spoiling the picnic effect, I think) and some other things I can't identify. There are lots of cut flowers, and we watch as the leader tries to make them stand up in the gelatin before we move on to the next group, where we hear singing.

Two women in a state of trance are dancing in the center of the circle, writhing as they and others sing. I have heard that this is done to call in the spirits and to get them to enter their bodies. The *pai do santo* is smoking a cigar, hopping, and chanting. Others join him in the circle; women twirling, chanting, in a trance, their bodies jerking and shaking. I have never seen anything like this before. I don't understand it, and because of that am frightened, but fascinated.

Suddenly a man in front of us throws up his hands, gives a blood-curdling scream, becomes absolutely rigid, and falls backward straight as a board. Dolly screams too and it gives me such a fright that I jump and bump heads with a man behind me. Everyone jumps backward, to avoid going down like dominoes. The blow hurts my head, so I imagine that the man I bumped is hurting too. I see him stagger, and although I feel guilty not staying to see if he is hurt, I am afraid, so I shout *"Desculpe!"* ("I'm sorry!") and grab Dolly's hand, and we run across the beach to the safety of the sidewalk, where Aunt Ginger and Uncle Neco are watching another group down on the beach. My rain hat flies off my head; I do not stop to find it. Uncle Neco and Aunt Ginger see us and say we look like a couple of witches, our raincoats trailing behind us as we run.

It is about eleven-thirty; we hear music getting louder as a procession approaches from the south, coming down the Avenida in front of our beach in Ipanema, with thousands of people on foot, and all the grandeur of the Roman Catholic Church. A worldwide Eucharistic Congress has been meeting in Rio, and this is the last procession of the Eucharistic year. An image of the Virgin is being carried on a coachlike platform resting on the shoulders of strong men. Some police or soldiers, all mounted on horses and dressed in elegant uniforms, ride in the procession and people are walking along, shooting off fireworks. It is dazzling in its solemnity, in spite of the rain that now comes down pretty fast. Meanwhile, still visible on the beach are the candles and white clothes of the *macumbistas*, whose rituals come to a climax at midnight.

We return home; I am filled with awe and amazement by the disparate demonstrations of faith we have witnessed. We continue our game of Hearts, and at midnight we open a bottle of champagne, toast the New Year of 1956, and when the bottle is empty, go to bed.

I don't have a job at the *IBEU* anymore, so I am teaching English for a while at the American High School in Gávea, giving daily private lessons to Jardel Filho—a handsome Brazilian movie star—and a woman who is going to the States with her husband, who has something to do with coffee. She lives in a penthouse apartment at the Copacabana Palace Hotel, and we have our daily lessons from five to seven on the balcony overlooking the beach and the swimming pool. As the sun sets behind us, we see pink sky over the ocean. Every day she orders lemonade for me. I can't believe I'm getting paid for this!

I want to stay longer in Brazil, but I also know that I want eventually to get married and have children. I have had a good look at relationships between Brazilian men and women and come to the conclusion that I am too independent to be a Brazilian wife. There is also the question of whether I can support myself in Brazil, so after much deliberation and soul-searching, I decide to return to the States.

Before leaving Rio, I get to enjoy another *Carnaval*. Aunt Ginger makes me a Grecian costume of white satin trimmed in gold braid. This time, although I am feeling pretty Brazilian, I am dating an American banker. After cocktail and dinner parties, we arrive at the Yacht Club Ball at midnight and dance all night, ending up tired and happy in a sidewalk café in Copacabana. As it begins to get light, someone begins tapping out a samba rhythm on the table with his silverware, and soon we and everyone else in the place join in and begin singing, as we watch the sun rise over the Atlantic.

# 16. *Noivos*

 *Petrópois, January 27, 1937*

When my Moço Louro and I left the little creek after his proposal, I said, "Goodness, where are we? I have no idea how to get back to the house." He said, "Never mind, you are with me, and I know the way." Yes, ever since then when I was with him I never paid any attention to the road; he seemed to enjoy my dependence on him! Yes, I was engaged to the Moço Louro this night forty-four years ago by a little creek where we gave and received our first kiss that sealed our pact of love.[26]

We found the lady of the house was up yet; she would not go to bed until I was in. I told her that we were engaged and this was the reason this young man came, as he wanted to be sure of that before I came back to the school. I don't need to say that there was no sleep for me that night. *Morpheu* again refused to lullaby me to dreamland, so I kept twisting around on my finger the wide ring the Moço Louro had had on his finger since he was twenty-one years old. That ring was not the official engagement ring nor the Brazilian style *aliança*[27]—those came later. Both my sisters and my brother rejoiced with me, as they liked him very much.

During the long day that followed, the railroad with necessary and unnecessary curves made me lose all my composure. Perhaps it was a good thing as the Moço Louro had the opportunity to see me at my worst— no sleep the night before and the food would not stay with me! Arriving in São Paulo, we went to tell my aunt that same night, and the next day to the home of Dr. Lane, to tell him, as I wanted to stop teaching and get ready. My Moço Louro didn't like the idea but he came. The quicker I got those two men to lose their prejudice toward each other the better. I did it that same night.

When we arrived at Dr. Lane's home he gave me a fatherly kiss. I was a

---

26. The title of this chapter, *Noivos*, means "An engaged couple."

27. An engagement or wedding ring, worn on the right hand on engagement and the left hand after marriage.

little uncomfortable because it seemed to me that my Moço Louro was not liking this coziness at all. Then, guessing right away what it was all about, said, "What does this mean?" My Moço Louro answered quickly, "I am going to take her away from you; we are engaged."

"Congratulations, but you are not going to marry right away?"

"Oh, yes, just as soon as you can spare her."

Then the dear old man said, "I will be the one to lead you to the altar, Chiquita, as your father." I said that I thought we would go to my sister's in Caracol and get married there, as my brother-in-law Dr. Matto-Grosso had always said he wanted to be the one to take me to the altar. "Oh, no, Chiquita, you must marry right here; you owe this to your friends in São Paulo and colleagues in the school who would like to be present, and I will be the one who will take you to the altar. Your brother-in-law can come here."

According to the Brazilian sentimental way, the thing for me to do would be to accept Mariquinha's invitation and go back to Caracol where her husband was a physician, and have my wedding there. But in the American practical way I accepted the very sincere invitation of my dear friends Dr. Lane and Miss Scott to stay and to have my wedding at the school to which I had been connected for eight years, studying and teaching.

The next thing to do was to let our friends know, and we chose the easiest and cheapest way—the next day was Sunday; we would go to church together and sit as far in front as we possibly could and let it work through the service. I am sure the majority of those people there knew the Sunday school superintendent and Dona Chiquita did not pay much attention to the sermon. Well it worked fine. When the service was over everybody congratulated us! This would not work in the United States.

A few days after we arrived in the Big City, the Moço Louro on one of his daily visits to me took from his pocket a wee box and from it he drew a lovely diamond ring that he put on my finger above the other one. My, what a surprise! Engraved inside was the date of our engagement and M and C in a monogram. He said to me, "Let us see how many sweet expressions we can make with these two letters besides what they stand for: Myron— Chiquita; *meu caro, minha cara*; mon chere, ma cherie; and again: Myron Clark and Chiquita Morães—my family name!" Do you think we were silly? We don't care—so that is that.

Your grandfather was invited to speak in other cities to the young men of different Protestant churches so now it was my privilege to receive letters—and I have them yet—from my fiancé from different places. In reading one of these now I find this at the end of it: "Good night darling. It is late and you must be *na terra dos sonhos* (in dreamland) where I will be too, pretty soon! I wish we could meet there." Yes, beloved, every night now for too many years when I go to dreamland, I am hoping to meet thee there, but that does not seem to be thy abode now. If we do meet, which happens very seldom, you are so different—it seems nothing is clear.

Through his letters I knew I was getting a treasure that night but it was only through those years of companionship that I realized the value of that treasure! And this is why my loss is so great. How many times in those days I wondered why my Father in Heaven had given me such great happiness when others close to me were so unhappy! And these days when I have been reading these precious letters that have turned so yellow because of the years that have rolled by, I am thrilled with what I read in them and at the same time my heart seems crushed with longings for him!

I had learned through his long missives that it was to serve his Master that the Moço Louro had left his family and his country. How happy I was that I had already accepted his Master as mine when I was in my teens. What an inspiration to be corresponding with a young man of such high ideals, I used to think, in those lonesome nights there in that little village! And that night by the little creek with the moon as a witness when he told me in words what he had hinted in letters I was perfectly sure I was going to be the happiest woman in the world. This assurance came to me because of my faith in the pure Christianity that he professed. I felt confident that he could help me in my shortcomings. He was like those Christians who had been around me since I had come to the American School—Dr. Chamberlain, Rev. Howard, Mr. Brown,

and others. How different he was from the young men I had known. This
does not mean that I had intimate young men friends, because no decent
or nice girl in my country was expected to go around with a boyfriend.
Through all those months of our engagement my happiness was perfect
knowing that I lived in that heart where my Master ruled.

Ours was a perpetual honeymoon. We many times talked about this
and wondered if the fact that we belonged to such different races made
us so deeply in love all through our married life. You American girls
begin to have a boyfriend when you are in high school and all through
your college days so there is no thrill when you become engaged; you
are already thoroughly acquainted with young men. I prefer our way. I
confess that we Latin Americans do not have many chances to know each
other before we settle down in married life, yet I think we stick to each
other "for better or for worse" more than Americans do. After all, isn't
Cupid supposed to be blind? Not having been so well informed about
married life as young people are today, I had many surprises, and I am
glad it was so.

But do not think, my grandchildren, that everything was rosy for your
Vovó during those three months of engagement, oh no! American
freedom and Brazilian strictness were always in conflict. Some of my
relatives thought I was smashing the rules of good behavior under my
feet when my *noivo* (fiancé) and I exchanged, as we met and as we said
goodbye, a very innocent kiss. When I suggested to my Moço Louro to
use this token of our pact, established for the first time that night by
the creek, only when there was no witness except the moon, he said,
"What is the matter with you? Are you losing your confidence in me?"
It was fortunate for us that Miss Scott, the *directora* (head mistress) of
the boarding school, had come to Brazil on the same boat that the Moço
Louro had. She had become quite attached to me, so she did not oppose
his very frequent visits to the school; in fact, she gave permission for us
to meet at her office.

Since then because of my dual nationality I am forever explaining to
Americans and again to Brazilians the whys of my ways. Living here in
the States, I find that I have not lost my Brazilian mannerisms, and when
I go back to Brazil, I realize how much I have acquired of the American

ones. My feelings have been deeply hurt sometimes because of this dualism, but it has been worthwhile because my privileges have surpassed my troubles. Yes, because once I possessed the greatest happiness, I am now paying the price with my deep sorrow and loneliness.

I am forgetting to mention the attitude of his family about his marrying a foreigner. They did not like the idea at all when he mentioned this possibility, but by the time of our engagement they were ready to welcome me into their family fold. Well, I didn't care, why should I when they were five thousand miles away from me? I did not know then that after all, this world is very small and that there were many surprises yet for this little dreamer to meet on that little speck on the map of the world! I continued to exercise my duties at the school until the end of March.

One day toward the end of February, Dr. Lane called to me and said very low; "Come to the office right after the dismissal. I want to speak to you." After school in his office he handed me a letter with a black edging, which came inside of one for him, and held me there with his arms around me. The letter was from my sister Josephina. Her husband Mineco had died very suddenly—sick and dead in three days—with yellow fever, which was very bad at Santos, the seaport where they were living at the time. She was left with four small children. Mineco was the one who was at my father's bedside when he died.

Dr. Lane had his arms around me trying to comfort me when my Moço Louro, who had been advised, appeared. Dr. Lane disappeared immediately. My Moço Louro was rather sore that he was not there before and that Dr. Lane was the first to comfort me, but that was not my fault and he apologized for his attitude. He was rather cross. I guess it was the old man's arm around me that made him sore. Such is life! While I was wrapped in happiness, unbearable sorrow came to my sister. Josephina was alone in Santos, so both Myron and Dr. Lane decided to go and bring her to the Big City. Dr. Lane insisted that he himself would go because it would be very dangerous for Myron to be exposed to yellow fever.

We had decided to be married on the 20th of April and leave the next morning for Rio, where Myron had been invited by different groups of young men and by pastors of different churches to come and organize the work for which he had been sent to Brazil by the International Committee of the YMCA. It had not been possible for him to do this work in São Paulo because of the dissention among the Protestants there. This engagement had caused quite a bit of excitement in the Protestant community where dissention prevailed between Brazilians and Americans of the Presbyterian Church. I was able to see how far the trouble had become personal on both sides. Some of our mutual friends were in hopes that this marriage might bring a better understanding between the two factions.

The plans began for the big event in which everybody of our acquaintance seemed to be interested. It was really big, as both of us had so many friends. The invitations were sent liberally to the churches and to the parents of my pupils, the father of one of them being the governor of the State of São Paulo, and many other prominent people who could afford to send their children to such an expensive private school as this. Dr. Lane and Miss Scott sent about eighty invitations for a reception at the school to more intimate friends. My colleagues made known to their pupils, and to those who had been mine, that flowers were needed— and they came in abundance from the lovely private gardens of the rich people.

The boys of the Bunch offered their services to help decorate the church and the schoolroom where the reception was to be held, which was a great opportunity for the boys and girls to have a delightful day together. Bouquets were placed among branches of *bambu* on a platform in front of the pulpit, and a large bowl of flowers decorated the place where we were going to stand. At seven o'clock the church, beautifully decorated with festoons and flowers in profusion, was packed to the limit. Many times I have heard people who were present at that wedding say that the church never looked as beautiful as that night of the 20th of April, 1893. In this temple, my memories went back much before 1893, to the time when as a student at the *Escola Americana* I came to worship with the good Miss Keuhl.

According to Brazilian matrimonial law, the arrangements for the marriage ceremony had been going on for a month already. Two witnesses that had known Myron for at least two years before he came to Brazil were required to swear that he was not married in the States. The Hall brothers did this. The older one was his very intimate friend and a fine Christian fellow who was Myron's best man. We were married by the Justice of the Peace in the morning at the office of the notary public whose daughter was a dear friend of mine. The notary public served drinks right after the ceremony to our amusement and confusion, and as a token of friendship to me there was no charge for his work.

I can't say that I can be precise about that day and night, but I remember that I walked up to the altar on the arm of my old friend and second father, Dr. Lane, with my brother-in-law Dr. Matto-Grosso the witness. A young German member of that church played the wedding march from Lohengrin. My good and dear friends, especially Miss Scott, América, and Júnia, who have long been sleeping in eternal rest, did everything to make the reception a pleasant celebration and it was, believe me.

In the dining room of the boarding school, refreshments and fine cakes were served. The bridal table was in the center under a canopy of bamboo; a big bell made of white dahlias, tied with bows of white ribbons, hung from it above the center of the table. Here my sister Cacilda, my brother-in-law Dr. Matto-Grosso, and Dr. Lane—among others—sat with us. There were nine smaller tables around this one where the other guests were served by the young teachers and by my sister Manoelita. When we left, these girls formed an alley through which we passed under a shower of rose petals. Oh, no, rice and old shoes are not used there.

The happy couple: Myron and Chiquita.

# III. Nurturing Family and Vocation

The politics and government in which Vovó raised her young family were complex and unstable. The first decree of the Provisional Government of Brazil stated that the nation's form of government would be a federal republic, and in 1890 the *Império do Brasil* was renamed the *Estados Unidos do Brasil*. Although achieved peacefully, the new republic did not get off to a smooth start.

Manoel Deodoro da Fonseca became the head of the Provisional Government, and in February of 1891, after much controversy, the Constituent Assembly elected him first President of the Republic by a small margin, and chose his rival, Floriano Peixoto, to be Vice President. This rivalry, and conflict between the executive and representative powers and between federal and state sympathies, sharpened during Fonseca's presidency. Under pressure he dissolved congress and declared a state of martial law, and in November, with the threat of civil war, he resigned in favor of Peixoto, who was president until 1894.

The peace following Peixoto's ascendancy to the presidency was also short-lived. Political rivalry and financial problems brought the country close to chaos and ruin, and in an attempt to consolidate his power, Peixoto, known as the "Iron Marshal," ousted all the state governors who had supported his predecessor, provoking violence in many parts of the country. A civil war exploded in the state of Rio Grande do Sul in 1893 and soon spread to Santa Catarina and Paraná.

At the same time, a naval revolt under the command of Admiral Custódio de Melo challenged the government with sixteen war vessels and eighteen merchant steamers and tugboats in Guanabara Bay at Rio de Janeiro. The admiral did not seem to have a clear idea of what he wanted, except to "restore the supremacy of the Constitution," which he claimed Peixoto had torn to pieces many times while praising it.[28] The United States sent a squadron of ships which proved decisive in ending the standoff in Guanabara Bay.[29]

---

28. Bello, *A History of Modern Brazil*, 122.

29. Bello, *A History of Modern Brazil*, 122.

It is not clear to me where the sympathies of my ancestors lay in those confusing times. I do know that Vovó's brother, Argentino, enlisted in the army during the naval revolt of 1893. Brazilians of that era may not have had clear ideological positions or party loyalties. They had hopes, as they do still, for the future, and for the most part they patiently went about their business in the midst of turmoil. After all, the verb *esperar* means both to hope and to wait.

Floriano Peixoto's successor was the first civilian president, Prudente José de Morais Barros. He was followed in 1898 by Manuel Ferraz de Campos Sales, then by Francisco de Paula Rodrigues Alves in 1902. This period was one of relative stability, during which large-scale public works addressed the unsanitary conditions of the capital. Brazilian cities, and Rio de Janeiro in particular, had a reputation for disease, including yellow fever, bubonic plague, cholera, smallpox, and malaria. Yellow fever had first appeared in Rio toward the end of 1849, probably imported from Africa. Science at that time was completely ignorant of its cause. Every summer the disease raged, especially among foreigners and provincials who were poorly acclimated. In 1904, based on research by Dr. Osvaldo Cruz, the Director of Public Health of the Federal District, a prophylactic campaign was begun. He and his assistants were ridiculed in the press as "mosquito swatters." [30]

In 1897, when Vovó visited the United States for the first time with her growing family, William McKinley was President. The following year the Spanish-American War began. It was called the "Splendid Little War," and the United States emerged from it as a great and global power with responsibility for the administration of the more than 7,000 islands that constituted the Philippines.[31]

---

30. Bello, *A History of Modern Brazil*, 180.

31. At the end of the Spanish American War John Hay, Secretary of State under McKinley, wrote to Theodore Roosevelt that it was a "Splendid Little War." See Freidel, *The Splendid Little War*.

# 17. *Ninho de Rosas*

*Columbus, Ohio, 1940*

After the wedding my new husband and I went to a hotel, and at daybreak we started our journey to Rio, the most beautiful city in the world. This would be our home, the land of our sweet dreams, but alas! of sorrows also.

When we left the church, the joy of my soul was quite a contrast with the soreness of my body. I had been hugged by more than 100 friends at the church and boarding school, and if you remember that the fashion for a girl in the early '90s required the smallest possible waistline (made by a certain torturesome garment), you ought not to be surprised that I was all in. It was a long and dusty trip. Railroad curves in Brazil then were no more than cuts and fillings, giving you the impression that you were on a merry-go-round. I had not been able to keep my food all day—I am sure I was not looking or feeling very romantic. I was wondering what my husband of 20 hours was thinking of his little wife when our train pulled in at the railroad station in Rio.

I saw Rio for the first time on the night that *cariocas* (residents of Rio) were commemorating the death of our great hero, Tiradentes. Here we were now by that sea of my dreams. I saw "*O Gigante de Pedra—Corcovado Chamado*"[32]—the words to a song my mother used to sing when I was very young—for the first time. Had the Greek gods known Corcovado, Tijuca, Gavéa, and Pão de Acuçar[33] they would not have lived on Mount Olympus!

Rev. and Mrs. Tucker and several other friends were at Central Station to welcome us into their midst. Several friends from different denominations of Protestant Churches in Rio had invited us to stay with them until we found out what part of that large city would be most

---

32. "The stone giant, called the hunchback."

33. Mountains around Rio: Corcovado, the Hunchback; Tijuca, the name of a large black-and-yellow bird; Gávea, hawk's nest; and Pão de Açúcar, Sugar Loaf.

convenient for my husband's work. Myron said we would divide the time among them until we were settled. We went first to the Tuckers, who lived right near the Methodist church in Catete (a section of Rio). We wanted to spend part of our honeymoon sightseeing in our capital, and the Tuckers' place was well situated for this. The Tuckers had some American and English boarders who were watching our behavior and were forever teasing us and joking and telling everybody about our behavior on our honeymoon. Later when we were settled very cozily in our home, they came to visit us many times and they joked and made fun of us right in our own home!

After a few days of sightseeing in the *Cidade Maravilhosa* (Rio's nickname, the Marvelous City), we met with Rev. James B. Rodgers, a Presbyterian minister, who told us that there was a very nice house for rent in Riachuelo (another district in Rio) and as they were anxious for us to live in that community, he advised us to see if the house suited us. So the Rodgerses took us to their place, which was very near the little chalet that was for rent. We liked the house immensely, so we took it.

The house was built right on the street as was customary there. It had three windows and a balcony to the street. Two windows belonged to the parlor and the other to a sleeping room. There was another sleeping room with a window to a terrace in the back of the house where a shower and other facilities were. The entrance was from the garden on one side of the house. The two windows of the dining room opened to the garden, which extended from the front of the house clear to the back. The kitchen was next to the dining room, with a door to the back part of the garden, where there were two or three fruit trees and a chicken coop.

There was no lawn, but there was a special delight—a big round flowerbed in the middle of the garden, another narrow bed along the high iron fence, and a border along the wall separating this place from next door were all planted with roses. I never had seen so many kinds of roses in one garden, and they were all blooming. Mrs. Rodgers immediately baptized the place with the poetical name *Ninho de Rosas*— Nest of Roses. The name fitted the place perfectly. Together with the blooms there were thorns that prickled our hearts that first year; but why linger in the clouds when sunshine is so near?

The Rodgerses and the Bragas, other friends whose children were grown, insisted that we board and stay with them until we had bought furniture and fixed the house with curtains and all. We had to be very careful with our pocketbook, and Mrs. Rodgers, being a very practical lady, helped us a good deal with her suggestions. She was an expert in planning, especially when there was not too much money. We had lots of fun buying what we needed most and sewing those curtains, and soon our pretty presents were in the second-hand china closet, and the kitchen things on the shelves; we moved to our nest, where I was going to cook our first dinner in our home.

My husband invited Senhor Camargo, his best Brazilian friend and one of the witnesses in our wedding, to come to spend the afternoon and eat our first meal at home with us. We planned to have an ordinary Brazilian dinner and for this we had to have soup, beans, rice, vegetable salad, and meat, which would be steak. This young man, although only about twenty-three or -four, was a widower and a father but the most jolly and witty person one ever heard of. He came to the house about one o'clock and we three started playing games (my husband had many)—Parcheesi, I think—and having loads of fun.

It required a long time to cook beans and meat for soup, so I went to the kitchen to start the fire with thick pieces of wood, which had been bought for that purpose. I had done some cooking at home on some special occasions when I was fifteen or sixteen, but the fire was made early in the morning by Eva, the slave, and kept burning all day. I piled the sticks on top of some paper and, forgetting the admonitions of my father about *never* using kerosene to make a fire, I took that liquid which Standard Oil has taken all over the world, and when the beans and the meat bone for the broth were all set on top of the stove in their respective pans and the wood well arranged in the stove, I poured the kerosene on it and, striking a match, I had a beautiful roaring fire!

I went back to my hubby, saying to the boys: "I don't know why people kick about building a fire; it is the easiest thing in the world," and so joined the boys in the game. It required at least two hours of boiling before I could add something else to the broth and the beans. One hour passed and I thought it would be a good idea to put more wood on the fire, so I went to the kitchen expecting to find everything boiling, and oh, what a disappointment! There was no vestige of fire in that stove, but a strong smell of kerosene. I decided to start again but this time, remembering my father's admonition, I did not use kerosene. I was a long time absent from my husband; he and his friend came to the kitchen to find out what was the matter.

They took the job from my hands, and with lots of jokes the two began to attempt to succeed where I had failed. We had no hatchet, so they gathered what wood they could find, which was very little, in the garden. Another hour passed and only smoke and bubbles of water from the wood came out of that stove and after several attempts with no result, at four o'clock my husband decided to go to Mrs. Rodgers and tell them that we would go there once more for dinner with them if they did not mind, and that we had a guest, too. To our surprise Mrs. Rodgers had made provisions for us that evening. She said she had heard of many failures before when a teacher cooked her first meal as a bride, and was not surprised at all by my failure! That was quite a comfort to me. I was so terribly ashamed that I did not want to tell any of my friends what happened although we three had lots of fun.

You, my granddaughters who are so well acquainted with Girl Scouts and Camp Fire Girls, may think that Vovó was very stupid not to know how to build a fire. No girl cared to learn how to do that—there was nothing special about it. It was done every morning at home by a servant. You didn't have to go to the woods for that.

My husband began then to visit the leaders of the different denominations, the pastors and the young men of different churches. Early in the morning, right after the first meal of the day that we call *café da manhã* (literally, morning coffee) my husband left our *Ninho de Rosas* and took the train to the city. He usually came home very late—about ten or even later—as it was in the evening that he did much of his work. I never knew the time of his returning until I heard his musical whistle when he was a few blocks from home. Even the neighbors learned what that whistle meant, and later our children also, and they never failed to run to meet their father before he reached the door. I learned the signal of his approach, and before he reached the last step to enter the house, he would kiss me, as there I would be just as tall as he was. When I said that I wished I were taller, he would say, "No, I want you just as you are." All through my married life, that whistle was the charm announcing the approach of my Enchanted Prince. There was something magic in it.

There was another Partner in this household of Clark and Company to whom we looked for advice and help. The family morning worship was established, and at night on our knees by our bed, each one alternately turned to this Partner, our Master, for guidance. Just about this time Rev. Rodgers, our intimate friend who had been conducting some missionary work in Riachuelo where we lived, organized a little church where we became members. My husband was elected an elder; he also served as superintendent of Sunday school and I taught a class.

Now that we were well settled in our *Ninho de Rosas*, many young men visited us on Sundays and stayed for tea. Among them were Mrs. Tuckers's boarders: dentists and businessmen—the ones who were forever joking and telling our friends about our bad behavior as newlyweds!

*Seu* (a corruption of *senhor*, or mister) Clark, as people called him here, began to hunt for a place to start the Y, and a few rooms were rented from the *typografia* (printers) on Rua da Assembléa, 96, *segundo andar* (second floor) and there the first YMCA was organized. These early days of the organization of the first Y in Brazil were busy ones, full of responsibilities, discouragements, and disappointments. Some of the Protestants could not see the need of such work among their young men; besides, this would take some of the money that otherwise would be spent on the Church. The Catholics saw in this work more Protestant propaganda and were right away ready to fight it. Those who called themselves free thinkers sympathized with the work because there would be a place where they could have some games without gambling being mixed with it, and the promise of a gymnastic class appealed to them also. These differing points of view prompted strong discussions such as we always had among our Protestant churches. Finally, it was decided that the members of the *Directoria* (Board of Directors) had to be Protestant.

Seu Clark gathered from the three groups: Protestant, Catholic, and free thinkers, those in favor of the YMCA, and after many hot discussions (some necessary and some not), the first Young Men's Christian Association in South America was founded on the Fourth of July, 1893, in three rooms on the Rua Sete de Setembro in Rio de Janeiro. What a coincidence this is! The street, Seventh of September, commemorates the date of the Independence of Brazil from Portugal, and the Y's founding was the Independence Day of the United States.

There were seventy-five founding members, if I remember right. It was called the *Associação Cristã de Moços*, or *ACM*. One room was for games, one for meetings, and one for a library, which consisted of a few religious magazines and one daily paper.

Sr. José Fernandes Braga, a prominent figure in Protestant circles who had joined the Protestant Church when a young man, was one of the principal contributors to this organization. He was a wealthy hat manufacturer, a capitalist and an industrialist. Senhor Braga, a Portuguese, his wife Dona Christina, and their five children lived very near us in a big *chácara* (country house) or villa, with all sorts of fruit trees. They were very rich, yet they always lived a very simple and quiet life except for taking every few years an extensive trip in Europe. Our friend the hat manufacturer belonged to an old family who had land. He was born in the old and very Catholic town of Braga, from which he got his last name, as did most of the Portuguese who went to Brazil.

With all these Protestant connections, that first YMCA was seen by those who had no religion as a religious institution, so they did not care to join it, and by the Catholics as *propaganda Protestante*, so they worked against it. Because of this very strong religious attitude the work developed very slowly and the support of it was in the hands of a few during the first years of its existence. As the members were mostly clerks in the different lines of business, a class for learning bookkeeping was organized in order that the young men might have an opportunity for better positions. When night classes were created and a *Departamento Phísico* (Physical Activities Department) was organized, the membership grew, as there were so many young men who could not get any education at all except at night classes.

But let us leave our Secretary with his hard tasks and problems and see what was happening in our beautiful capital.

# 18. The Yellow Lady

While Seu Clark was giving birth to the *ACM*, there was a revolution going on in Rio, which the history books call "*A Revolta de José Costódio de Mello.*" The city of Rio had been, since September of 1893, under an *estado de sítio* (state of siege). The navy revolted against the government, taking all the warships in port and keeping themselves at a safe distance from the many fortresses that face the narrow entrance to this marvelous bay. They threatened to bombard the city if the Governor didn't do something. Those who joined the revolt on land took part of the railway tracks connecting the interior of the country with the capital. Our *Ninho de Rosas* was near this section of the city.

All these months, while taking a ride on the streetcar along the seaside drive one could sometimes see the warships and the forts exchanging compliments with their cannons, but the bullets never reached their aim—purposely, it was said. You see, those behind those cannons on the ships and in the forts didn't want to fight. It was only those in the offices! The navy was revolting against the government of Floriano Peixoto, our second president since Brazil had become a Republic in 1889. My brother Argentino enlisted with the army and served at the fortresses of Santa Cruz and Praia de Fora.

There were rumors that the government had bought some armed ships from merchants in the United States to fight the rebel commanders of the navy who were blocking our spacious bay. Those in sympathy with the rebels called this commercial fleet, armed for war, the *Esquadra de Papelão* (the Cardboard Fleet). The arriving fleet and the forts on land were expected to blockade the revolutionary element, so we were looking for a bombardment. My people, the Brazilians, are full of fun even in crises. Sometimes they would say, "The *Esquadra de Papelão* arrived in *Mar de Hespanha* (Sea of Spain)," a city in the interior of Minas which has no sea or port at all!

Moreover, a revolt was not the only thing that clouded our happiness and alarmed us in those days. A more daring and merciless enemy was spreading its claws over Rio, grabbing hundreds of victims every week. The hot season was approaching and with it yellow fever, that terrible plague which devastated several cities of Brazil for many years. Records show that those days of February and March were worse than in any other year, before or after, in its history of devastation. Coming from a much cooler climate in the mountains, I suffered immensely with the heat. Foreigners and people from the interior were apparently especially chosen for her victims, which gave origin to the saying, "*Rio de Janeiro, açougue de mineiro e estrangeiro* (butcher of natives of Minas Gerais and of foreigners[34])." We both knew we were candidates for it, and so we lived in suspense!

Every night Myron came home with the news that some acquaintances of ours—friends, neighbors, or distant relatives—had died with the terrible disease, which took its victims so quickly! Before one heard they were sick, they were dead! You were not supposed to eat certain fruits as it was thought that they gave the fever. How little we knew then that the terrible disease entered the body through the skin and blood, and not through the stomach!

Our relatives from other cities and from the States urged us to leave the city, but this was impossible not only because Myron could not leave his work, but also because we were getting ready for a wonderful event in our lives: a baby, all our own, was coming to enrich our happy home. Myron's father, seeing by cablegrams that the disease was causing so many deaths among the foreigners, wrote commanding us to leave Rio immediately if we had not already done so. Letters came from other members of my husband's family in the USA, urging us to leave, and from my sisters also. Josephina, whose husband had died from that disease the year before, especially insisted that we leave Rio and go to the mountains. So there I was, facing the yellow fever, the terrific heat, and a bombardment at any time! My condition was aggravated because of the great joy that was coming to us; but we felt that it was our duty to stay. I lived in suspense

---

34. *Rio de Janeiro, açougue de mineiro e estrangeiro* is a common saying, of unknown origin. Diane Ackerman states in her book about the senses that "Yellow fever is said to smell of the butcher shop" (*A Natural History of the Senses*, 54).

and fear every hour, not knowing which of the two enemies was going to claim the life of my husband.

My husband had to be in the city, where stray bullets were constantly hitting buildings, and one did hit the *ACM* rooms. One day when the time had long passed for him to come back from work—remember, there were no telephones in those days—I began to worry and as the delay increased I began to be frantic. Not thinking about the consequences, I started to go downtown after him to find out what had happened, but couldn't get there because there was no transportation. The enemies' ships and the forts were exchanging shots.

My daring young man finally arrived home telling about his adventures. When the shooting began he and some other Americans had gone to the top of a well-known hill, *O Morro do Castello* (Castle Hill),[35] to see the bombardment. But when one of those bullets struck the hill, they ran down as fast as they could and headed for home. They had to wait for space on the streetcar pulled by mules—everyone was fleeing the city. It took hours to get home. Ordinarily I don't express my rage with tears but I did then, and it worked, all right. How sorry he was to have been tempted to fall in with such an adventure.

Rio, like all large seaports in those days, had quite a population of beachcombers: sailors who were left there by merchant boats, or who had escaped after being shanghaied and then subjected to tyranny on board. They surely were prey for the yellow fever. This prompted a Sailors' Mission in Rio. My husband was on the board of this mission. Sometimes he would send sailors to me to give them food or work as house cleaners or floor washers. These men made their scant living washing windows and scrubbing houses, a job in which they were experts. They were the best house-cleaners, on the very rare occasions when they were not drunk. I hired several of them in my young days in Rio.

When one expects a guest, one prepares for him; so when the time was nearing for the big arrival, I told my husband to bring a sailor to clean the *Ninho de Rosas* thoroughly. The sailor's name was George, I remember

---

35. The Morro do Castelo has since been leveled to make a strip of land along the bay, and skyscrapers are now in its place (Bello,. *A History of Modern Brazil*, 146–47).

very well. It seems to me that every detail that occurred at that time is carved on my mind! It was my first experience with sea labor, and he was marvelous! Every corner of the house was cleaned; by five o'clock in the afternoon the French doors were sparkling, the windows were shining, the walls, doors, shutters, and the floor were spotless as if they had been polished! We had no rugs—only the rich people could afford this luxury, and even then ordinarily only in the parlor, with small ones by their beds—but that floor was a beauty! The grain of the boards showed like a drawing.

Then George came to me and asked if he could take a shower and if I could give him an old shirt of my husband's, as the one he had on was not fit to wear any longer. What a shock—but I didn't let him see it. We had been married less than one year so my husband had no old shirt, and I didn't know what he would say, but then I remembered our partnership and that evening when my husband arrived home there was one less shirt in the drawer; I gave George the oldest I could find.

George took a shower and waited for supper in the garden, admiring the roses, with a smile that he wore the rest of the day. I remember so well how happy that young sailor looked. After dinner he left, wishing me happiness. George came many times to me with his troubles, and for food when he didn't have work. I had the opportunity to give work to several of those beachcombers on days when they were sober. One of them became quite devoted to me. He was known as Antônio Gibralter. He spoke a mixture of Spanish and English. Many times when he was penniless and not sober he came to our house. He never left hungry.

That evening my husband came home with the nurse, a German woman, Frau Geyer, who was engaged for the whole month of March. We never thought in Brazil in those days to go to a hospital for this event. Besides, the only hospital available was above our reach, or for the very poor, so we were doing it the Brazilian way. Even with all those evil forces around us, we were perfectly happy putting everything in order for the event. We believed in preparedness—everything was ready for the little baby. Every garment was finished and put away, together with the dainty gifts of lovely handmade sweaters, booties, etc. that came from my colleagues at the boarding school, in the right place, where hands could get to them even in the dark. And in the beautiful little basket trimmed in pink like some of our roses, the darling little first garment was carefully laid.

Two or three days later, on the 9th of March, my husband surprised me by coming home much earlier than usual, and bringing the cutest little French baby hairbrush with an iron back. As I greeted him at the door, I noticed that his eyes were a little red—he didn't seem very bright. I did not realize the Yellow Lady was knocking at our door! Then we went to the hammock, a hand-made present from the north of Brazil, and sat there very quietly. We were both afraid to say anything, because of what we were thinking! Finally I said, "You are looking somewhat sad, *meu amado*. What is the matter?"

"I am not feeling so well, but I have sent for the doctor already," he answered.

Just about that time I thought I saw Luiz Braga, a boy about fifteen from that beloved family, at the gate. It seemed to me as if he did not intend to be seen. I said, "There is Luiz," and my husband jumped and went to see him. My husband had already consulted the doctor, and there was no doubt that the symptoms were of yellow fever! He knew that Luiz had gone to get the first medicine, ordered by the doctor, that everybody takes who has symptoms of yellow fever. I was not supposed to know about his errand; Luiz had delivered the package of medicine to the maid. Many times after this prescription is taken the patient gets better and has only a slight case of the fever, so they were in hopes that this would be the case with my husband. The nurse took charge of him and that night he was a sick man.

The doctor didn't appear until he next morning. He was the physician for the American and English colony in Rio and one of the physicians for the *Hospital dos Estrangeiros*, so he was busy! He told me what I already suspected: the plague—yellow fever was a plague in those days—had entered our home and at a very bad time. "A bad case of yellow fever," he said. "And you," to me, "have to leave the house. Your baby is coming tomorrow, there will be no hope for you to survive in your condition if you get the fever!" I was furious, because we had expected him the day before, and said, "I will not leave my husband. The baby and I will both be in danger at the time of the confinement, so we will all three die together!"

I was thinking of the year before, when a missionary we knew was taken sick with yellow fever, died, and was buried while his wife was in the hospital to have a baby, and she never knew of it until it was safe for her to know. That day I received another letter from my sister Josephina in Santos, saying, "I don't see why you don't leave Rio; if I had a sister who had lost her husband as I did, I wouldn't stay in a place where that epidemic was raging as it is in Rio now." Myron was down with it already. It was thought then that cases of yellow fever could not be moved from one place to another, that that always meant death. I knew also that there was very little chance for a foreigner to recover from that disease, so I repeated that we all would die together.

That night, Saturday, our dear friend Mr. Rodgers came to our house and stayed there to help. He had had the fever before, and took charge of the situation; he was so full of sympathy and tact. Between three and four in the morning I told the nurse I was not feeling well but never connected what I felt with the coming event; I had no idea that the doctor had guessed so exactly! She got up immediately and was moving around fast, and so was Mr. Rodgers. I noticed that there was some consultation between them, but my heart was too full of my sick man to think of anything else.

I heard drawers, doors, and the gate being opened. Without my noticing, Frau Geyer had taken a sheet from a drawer, opened it on a table, put the basket with the first clothes and all in it. She took from the other drawers the things that had been laid out so carefully in the order that they were going to be needed, dumped them all together in the sheet, tied the four corners together, and sent it in a *tilbury*[36] to our friends who lived very near. There was no such thing as a taxi in those days. Locomotion was done by animal power.

---

36. A *tilbury* is a light, two-wheeled carriage without a top, named after its inventor, a nineteenth-century coach builder.

In an hour or so, at dawn, Rev. Rodgers came to me and said very tenderly, "Chiquita, you must go to your good friends the Bragas right away. They are ready for you. We have sent everything that is needed for you and the baby there, and I will promise to do everything for Myron, and I will not hide anything from you. He, too, wants you to go. You must go." What a friend! I got dressed. I didn't know what I was doing. I just did everything he told me without a word. Then I went to my beloved's bed, kissed him goodbye, taking his head in my arms, but I could see that already his mind was not all there. I didn't care at all if I got the fever. The first crisis was that day, and the second would be on the seventh day of the fever. After the seventh day, ordinarily the danger is over, but not until then.

Thus I left our *Ninho de Rosas*...I thought that it was for ever. I had no hope of my husband recovering from the dreadful disease. The Great Beyond seemed very, very near us, though life was only beginning. The Bragas lived just about two blocks from us in a big house with a lovely big garden. It was dark still when we crossed our lovely garden, our nest of roses. I heard little sounds like drops of water. There was dew on the grass; or were the roses weeping?

That morning, Senhor Braga, the dear old man, went to church and from there to the *Ninho de Rosas* to see my husband and he brought to me, written with pencil, a little message from my beloved, who was a bit out of his mind. It read, "*Coragem, minha amada. Estou aniooso pela bôa notícia. Tenho ânimo. Tudo irá bem. Teu marido.*" ("Courage, my love, I am anxious for good news. I am encouraged. Everything will be fine. Your husband.") The paper is right here with me. It is yellow, showing how far time has marched!

My doctor was also of the Strangers Hospital, which was full of yellow fever patients; so at the time I most needed him, he was not there. And so it came to pass that at noon on the 11th of March, 1894, a beautiful Sunday—while in a corner of the room my very dear friend Dona Christina Braga, a devoted Christian, fervently prayed out loud for me—the most beautiful baby girl was born, while that Beautiful City was threatened by the cannons of a rebellious navy, and her father was going through the first crisis of that terrible disease which marked one of the worst years on record.

We had decided before that if the baby were a girl, we would name her Ruth after Ruth in the Bible, who said: "Thy people shall be my people." Two hours after she was born everybody of the household, even the servants, including the gardener, came to see her and so did Mr. Rodgers, who carried the news to my very sick husband that his daughter Ruth was born.

I noticed quite a lot of moving around and also a lot of noise in that house, and in the streets the voices of excited people; so I asked the nurse the reason. She answered, "People are fleeing from the city because the ships the Brazilian government bought from the United States are arriving and the government has ordered the people who live near the sea to leave the city. A battle is expected between these ships and the fortress, together with the ships in the hands of the navy, and some bullets might go astray." So trains, electric cars, carriages, and tilburies were full of people fleeing to the suburbs. As the Bragas's church was near the General Headquarters and many of its members lived near the church, many came to the Braga home for shelter in case of bombardment. The hospitable Bragas had set up twenty extra beds for friends. So not only the seven members of the Braga family, but several of those who were there as refugees had been in my room to see the "little beauty."

Since the beginning of the world every first child is a prodigy and a beauty. Mr. Rodgers and the whole household of the Bragas, and the people who poured in all through the day, commented on her beauty, but I had hoped for blue eyes! The nurse, an old person, said she never saw a baby with such perfect features.

The day passed and so did the night, with no sound of bombardment. On the 12th, when the Cardboard Fleet entered the Bay, the ships and the fortresses that were in the hands of the rebels raised a white flag. The officers implicated in the revolt had left the boats in the hands of the sailors and lower officers and gone to a neighboring country. Thus ended the revolt, the first after the fall of the Empire, but not the last. It left lots of enmity between the two sides. The bitterness was even stronger in some of the southern states.

I lived in suspense there in that little room, anxiously waiting for the seventh day of Myron's fever to pass, and with it the crisis, and oh how slowly those seconds made minutes, and these formed the hours which made the days that brought the seventh, and the victory over death. The crisis was over! He lived! What I suffered in those sad days of separation is easier to imagine than to describe. Never had I been separated from my faithful husband. We always spoke about the happy day when we would have the good fortune to be blessed with a little being, and never for an instant had we thought it possible to be separated on this occasion.

On the 21st of March, my little daughter received a letter from her father brought by José Braga. I have it yet. The paper is yellow and spotted by tears of joy which I shed as I read it.

> *My dear daughter,*
>
> *You can't imagine how anxious I am to see you! I spend the days now thinking about you and your mother and waiting for the day when I will be able to go there to see you both. Just think! I have had a daughter for ten days and have not seen her yet. But I am very glad because they say that tomorrow, if God will permit, I can go to see you and your mother. Be a good girl and kiss your mother for your Papai.*

A few days later, I sat up for the first time to wait for my husband. My, how excited and thrilled I was when he slowly came through the door holding on to Mr. Rodgers's arm! He was so pale and thin! And his eyes were oh! so blue and melting in love! Our good friend Rodgers left the room and we were glad he did. With overflowing eyes we hugged and kissed each other, and with a choked voice, Myron spoke words of tenderness to his little daughter, kissing her interminably. The baby could not see the tears of happiness that we both shed! Then he said, "It is all over, darling!"

I am waiting to hear that again in that Hereafter where there will be no more separation! But there is a long string of tales to tell yet.

# 19. Maria Ovídia

Did you ever, my grandchildren, make a *cadeirinha* by holding your friend's arms, fists to elbows, to make a little chair in order to carry your playmates? Your Vovó as a child did that, and a week after Ruth was born, that was the way I traveled back to the *Ninho de Rosas*. Mr. Rodgers and Senhor Braga's gardener made a *cadeirinha* of their arms and in this way I went, with my arms around their necks. My how we laughed and had fun on the way home. How different from that night we fled through the garden! There was not a cloud in that blue sky for me that day.

Frau Geyer, the nurse, carried the baby home. Sweet perfume from the roses welcomed us at our gate. They were in their gala garments, and not weeping. Day by day your grandfather and I both grew stronger. When he was well enough, he went back to work where he realized how many friends he had already made in that city, and so did I.

We sailed along in calm waters for a while with a blue sky over our heads. But all of a sudden clouds were gathering on the horizon and it did not take long for us to realize that we were going to face a storm again. My sister Josephina, who had lost her husband with yellow fever not quite a year since, came to stay with us for a while on account of some plans of her own, and to bring one of her little girls for us to take care of as we had offered to do. She was Maria Ovídia, six years old. As soon as she arrived we noticed that Josephina was in very poor health. She consulted a physician, who declared she had quick consumption. The loss of her husband had been a terrible blow not only because he was a fine man and an affectionate husband, but now her four children under eleven years of age were dependent on her alone.

That same week, I woke up one night with a terrible headache and feeling as though I had been in a fight, as though every bone in my body were broken. At dawn the doctor came, and sure enough, Lady Yellow Fever was knocking at our door again. My baby, just a little over two months

old, was deprived on account of the fever of the food that nature
provides. My husband was very busy with his work, which had suffered
a good deal on account of the revolution and his sickness, and my poor
sister was unable to render any help.

I shall never forget what I suffered through those sick days. I felt as if
the *cachoeiras* (waterfalls) of Paulo Affonso, Niagara, and Victoria Nianza[37]
were roaring around my brains, yet I could not hear what was going on
around me. There were very few nurses available in those days. Ordinarily
we depended on members of the family or friends on these occasions;
they were instructed by the doctor what to do for the patient.

I was taking lots of quinine. I had not been able to sleep or even to close
my eyelids for over 48 hours! My husband was about to give me the last
dose of quinine prescribed by the doctor when Mr. Rodgers came to our
rescue again, saying: "She cannot stand any more of that." He was right;
I would have gone crazy with another dose I think. Instead they gave me
something to put me to sleep and after several hours, I awoke better. You
have the evidence that I pulled through not only at that time, but also in
other struggles, as I have a long tale to tell yet.

A few months later Josephina passed away very gently while I was
alone with her. I was holding her head on my lap to make her more
comfortable; my husband had gone for a *balão de oxigênio* (oxygen balloon)
to relieve her of lack of air. She left her four children, two boys and two
girls, orphans! Maria Ovídia, named after my mother, stayed with us. Poor
child! Everything was new around her, and we were almost strangers to
her. She was a beautiful child and exceedingly intelligent and attractive in
many ways.

I am sure, my grandchildren, that some day in your lives this unwelcome
visitor will knock at your doors to snatch from you some loved ones.
Remember then to open your heart to another who will be there to
comfort you if you will let Him.

We were all needing a change of climate after so much sickness and
extreme heat, so we accepted an invitation from my oldest sister,

---

37. Waterfalls of Paulo Afonso (on the São Francisco River, now dammed), Niagara, and
Victoria Nianza (Africa).

Mariquinha. She and her husband had moved from Caracol to Espírito Santo do Pinhal, where he was now practicing medicine. This would give Mariquinha an opportunity to get to know her brother-in-law, my husband. We were very glad, too, to be able to prove to our relatives and to the rest of the town that the daring *Norte Americano* was without reproach, and that their *patrícia* (compatriot) was the happiest little wife and mother, notwithstanding her daring adventure through those deserted lanes on that moonlight night in January when she got engaged. While we were there, this happy couple, together with the baby and Maria Ovídia, took a walk by daylight now to the little spot where their pact was made.

After we came back from that lovely visit with Mariquinha, my husband, who had to spend so much of his time every day in trains and streetcars, decided to move nearer his work. The place we found was right in the heart of the city, which was not then lovely and modern with its wide avenues, but a rather unhealthy place, visited by yellow fever and sometimes by the bubonic plague. We lived on the first floor of a two-story building on Rua Evarista da Veiga. Instead of a garden of roses, we had a small cemented place with a high stone wall separating us from an old convent.[38] The sun could not visit our abode except for a couple of hours in the morning. Our sleeping rooms opened to a damp, tiled patio and instead of roses, some little palm plants left by the last tenant grew in tubs.

On the second floor there was a boarding house for actors and actresses of very reproachful morals. They were not then glorified as they are today; in fact respectable people did not care to live in sections where they lived. Through the courtyard we heard their many quarrels, and from the windows looking onto this patio they tossed the stumps of their cigarettes, which sometimes landed on my head if I happened to be there watering the *palmerinhas*. So it was a little different from our *Ninho de Rosas*, but there was a great compensation: we had the pleasure of having the head of the family at the head of the table for every meal—and that was all we saw of him all through the day until eleven o'clock at night and later. The place was near a bathing beach which we took advantage

---

38. The convent of Santo Antônio, a 400-year-old Franciscan convent still in use today (with many renovations).

of when summer came.

When Ruth was thirteen months old, the services of Frau Geyer were required again. She told everybody who came to see the new baby that when the baby yelled Dona Chiquita gave a hearty laugh, Mr. Clark jumped and said "Hurray!", and the doctor said: "What a fine boy!" She always imitated your grandfather, jumping to illustrate her story. It struck me funny, the hurry of the boy to enter into this world, and he has always been like this—doing things quickly and unexpectedly. My husband wanted very much to have a boy to name after his father, Orton Skinner Clark.

How different the circumstances were from that first event! Orton was very healthy and for this reason very easy to raise. He liked pulling the blond hair of his sister, who suffered all with the most resignation because the baby was all to her! It was a beautiful picture to see her embracing him. But one can easily see that my burden then was not small! There was no gas stove, no electricity. We did have a young maid and a cook though.

Up to now, when my little daughter did not sleep with her bottle, she was rocked and put to sleep with lullabies, as I had rocked to sleep my brother Argentino and my sister Noemi when I was only twelve and thirteen years old, but Frau Geyer protested against this rocking business, so she put Ruth to bed with her bottle. Ruth, expecting to be rocked, protested too, in her own way, crying for over two hours. When I was ready to cry also and ask Frau Geyer for mercy, the poor baby dropped into a rather pitiful slumber with sighs and a broken heart! The next day she went through the same performance but dropped to sleep in less time. On the third night when she finished her bottle she was in dreamland already!

I had also mothered my sister Manoelita, seven years younger than myself, by lying with her in bed until she went to sleep. She called me *Madrinha*—Little Mother. Many times I crawled on all fours from her bedside; and just as I managed to get out of the room she would yelp: "*Madinha*" (baby talk for *Madrinha*), crying, and I had to go back, ready to cry also for losing so much of my time. Since I had started that habit my mother made me do it. Now I ask you, which method is better?

My niece Maria Ovídia was a great help in entertaining the children when she came home from school. She was an exceedingly beautiful and intelligent youngster, and didn't get spoiled even though she was told that frequently. When Maria Ovídia was thirteen or fourteen, we sent her to the American School where I had gone. Miss Scott, my friend and fellow traveler on the boat *Vigilança* in 1891, was so interested in her, noticing her extraordinary ability, that she arranged for some wealthy person to put her through college.

When Maria completed her studies, she taught in that school for several years, as I had done, until she got very weak. Needing a longer vacation than usual, she went to the summer resort near Caldas where we had seen the Emperor. Being so attractive, with an unusual education for a girl in those days, and an unsurpassed modesty, she immediately became the talk of the town, and Cupid became busy.

That summer resort had once been part of a large *fazenda* where hot springs and other mineral waters had been found—that was the reason for the name—*Poços de Caldas* (Hot Springs). A wealthy *fazendeiro* had given this land to the State and people had begun to come there to use the baths when there were only very primitive accommodations. My family used to go there in oxen carts with friends, taking everything we needed just for the fun of taking natural hot baths. Then people began to build hotels, and gambling dens, cabarets, and vice attracted more people there in the summer than the hot baths.

It happened that the youngest son of this *fazendeiro* was a handsome young man who had vast and varied experience with Cupid and with all the attractions of the town. Well, he fell completely under the charms of my niece, and she, who had many admirers with the same high Christian ideals as she had, was completely fascinated by him! Knowing that I was in the place of her mother, the young man, Affonso Junqueira, wrote to me asking permission to marry her, as was customary there. I knew his family and among them I had friends, but I was very much distressed, as I felt that her parents there in the great beyond were saying to me, "What would you say if she were your daughter?" After much thinking, I answered his letter saying that my niece had been taking care of herself for several years and although I preferred that she would marry some young man who professed the same religion we did, this was a question for her to decide herself. He didn't like this, but they were married.

Unfortunately he could not be faithful very long. Maria Ovídia faced problems that would wreck any married life, and yet she loved him dearly and was faithful until his death. She was admired not only by the citizens of Poços but also by her husband's family. Maria and Affonso had a daughter to whom he was very devoted. He was also a very charitable man, and I think charity covers a multitude of sins. He was very kind to me, in his queer way. I heard that he showed a Christian spirit before he departed from that flesh which he had served so faithfully.

I do not know how far I will go with these *reminiscências* so I do want to make a record here of a visit I made to Maria Ovídia at her coffee plantation a few years ago. Maria Ovídia taught for many years, sometimes because it was necessary and again because parents begged her to teach their children and they paid her well. But then it was necessary for her to move to the plantation to manage it. She was not teaching then. I had visited her several times in her town residence while her husband was still living, but not until my recent trip to Brazil had I been at the *fazenda*. I ought to leave this episode for the time when it happened, but I can't resist the temptation to make a note of it now. Who can count on the future? It may never come.

The big, square, one-story house where her husband, several of his brothers, his father and his grandfather had been born and had lived, had been built over 120 years ago. It was used now only to store things. It is interesting to think of the important guests who may have slept under that roof, because the Junqueiras were rich and the family goes back to colonial times. Maria Ovídia found here among other old papers a document, dated 1835, speaking of the land in the *capitania* of Minas Gerais given to Affonso's grandfather or great-grandfather by one of the kings of Portugal.

Maria Ovídia was living in a small, comfortable, and more recently built house near the old abandoned mansion. It had a bathroom with hot running water, a toilet inside the house, and electric lights. Not very far from the old building, vestiges of the huts where slaves had slept could be seen yet. She had food for her soul there too, as in her cozy little parlor was a piano, owing its presence there to the patience and strength of twelve or fourteen oxen. On another side of the room there were shelves with the works of Victor Hugo, Alexandre Dumas, Eugene Sue, Shakespeare, Dickens, Walter Scott, Mark Twain, Tolstoy, Cervantes, Hall Caine, Ralph Connor, Alexandre Herculano, Olavo Bilac, Jules Verne and many others,[39] prose and poetry, and she read them in the languages in which they were written.

While I stayed there, I took walks right after dinner, before the sun had completed its daily journey. I well remember one afternoon when I walked to the top of a hill where graceful tall *pinheiros* posed day and night for the birds to rest. I put on my high galoshes as a little protection against snakebites because I was always warned by Maria Ovídia to watch the path—such as there was —in order not to step on those venomous reptiles. Many times cows and calves scared me as I passed by them and they followed me with their big, inquiring eyes, but nobody ever suspected that I was afraid. The *colonos* (tenant farmers) thought I was a very courageous city woman.

I got there on the top of the hill in time to see the sun disappear behind some woods away on a far horizon, and almost immediately the full moon showed her plump face in the opposite direction. Then I dropped my eyes toward mother earth and there in front of a long row of the *colonos'* little houses all stuck together, children were playing; pigs, sheep, and chickens were running around, all seeming to be having a glorious time. The birds around me said goodbye to the day with their different songs and looked for shelter in the trees. The different shades of green, so fresh because of the abundant rain, led my eyes now to the coffee trees, now to the cornfields, now to the green pastures where a new highway snaked along a dense row of bamboo. I felt so small in front of

39. Between 1893 and 1930, Hall Caine was one of the most widely read of British authors. Ralph Connor was the pseudonym of Charles William Gordon, 1860–1937, a Presbyterian minister and Canadian writer. Before World War I, he was one of the world's best-selling authors. Portuguese poet and novelist Alexandre Herculano (1810–1877) was one of the great writers of the Romantic generation. Brazilian poet Olavo Braz Martins de Guimares Bilac lived from 1865 to 1918.

this calm and beautiful grandeur at my feet.

Above the low, tiled roofs, there was enough smoke for one to imagine a fire inside, and a tasty meal being prepared for the big family. Toward the rolling pasture, there was a bonfire, and around it a few men were resting near a long, hide-covered cart, and in a pasture nearby the oxen were enjoying their evening meal. I felt as if I were in a glorified place, and from the bottom of my soul came a prayer out loud which was more praise than petition. I wished then that, like Enoch as he walked with God, I would not ever have to go down among the living creatures. I was in ecstasy. Peace reigned there among men, beasts, and nature.

That night while I was reading the *Judeu Errante* (The Wandering Jew, by Eugene Sue) by kerosene lamp as I had done in my youth—there was electricity there, but it was not working—somebody in the colony was playing a guitar and singing some love song under only a bright moon's light.

I thank God I have so many beautiful scenes carved on the walls of my memory, representing pictures thousands of miles away and many decades ago, which I can get to in a twinkle of an eye.

# 20. Milestones

Now, where was I when I left the principal road of my story to go on a sidetrack, strolling around my niece's *fazenda*, listening to cows and calves at the *curral* (corral), the crickets and frogs in the brook, and the birds' symphony in the woods? Oh, yes, probably with Orton on my lap. But this is me all over. You'll have to get used to it.

Even if my oldest child was only thirteen months when Orton was born, the birth didn't seem as difficult for me as it had with Ruth because everything went on normally, and the suspense about yellow fever was over for a while. Orton grew fast and healthy, and the two were praised by everybody as the cutest and prettiest little children. They were the joy of the home—I think that children are for a couple what salt is for food.

Ruth and Orton played together, sometimes entertaining each other for hours. They were separated for many hours during the day because of the baby's sleeping, and upon meeting they always embraced each other with the greatest joy. Day by day, Ruth was becoming more womanly in the gentle, sweet way she conversed with her dolls and the pleasure with which she picked up the broom and swept the house.

Orton was very manly. The headquarters of the police force was a few blocks from us, so every morning a police detachment passed in front of our house, and he was always there to watch it. Later on, we moved nearer the presidential palace and we could hear a band and see the police guard in bright uniforms pass far away. One day when Orton was about three, he was playing with a boy a little older than himself and I heard him say to the boy, "Let us play that I am a battalion and you are the people who come to see the battalion march." Another time somebody asked him what he wanted to be when he was as big as his *papai*. "I want to be a coachman of a funeral carriage." "Why?" they asked. "Because I will drive four horses." A hearse was pulled by four horses covered with black robes and golden fringes! We will leave the battalion—or if you prefer, the four horses' driver—and see what his father was doing.

On occasions when he had to consult with one of the board members, Myron often had to walk to his office because many times there was no streetcar going in the right direction, and sometimes he had to make two or more trips before he could see him. The Bell Telephone Company had not reached us yet, except in public buildings and the Fire Department, and most of the time they were out of order. When you wanted to speak to somebody you had to go to his office or home. Myron Clark was very active and always walked very fast. Our friends used to joke that sometimes one would see far away in the narrow streets of old Rio a coat flying and only when it stopped in front of an office did one realize that it was Clark, stopping to ask for subscriptions for the *Associação Cristã de Moços!*

Seeing that Myron was exhausted with details that could be done less expensively by a young boy, I suggested that he ask permission from the *Directoria* to get an office boy like everyone else had for these errands; when the boy was not busy beating the streets, he could beat the dust from the furniture and do other little things around the office. With some reluctance, and under pressure from home, my husband engaged a boy, Ismael, who between errands moved the dust around with a feather broom. I wonder who invented this contraption? It was all I could do to convince my maid, when I had one, that a slightly damp cloth was the best thing to take the dust from the furniture, so I thought it was wise for me not to meddle with the office boy and let him play ball with the dust.

And the evening and the morning passed and the summer of 1896 came and found Myron very weak and badly needing rest in some cool place. As I mentioned before, Rio then was an unhealthy city visited every summer by yellow fever. A missionary couple that had been entertained in our home several times on their way to and from the States lived in Curitiba, Paraná, and we had had several invitations to visit them. My husband wrote to this couple and asked if they could board us for a while. They wrote back that they would be delighted to do so. Ruth was not quite two years old and Orton not quite one year. We also took Maria Ovídia, who was then ten or eleven years old.

Two other friends of mine, the American women who had been in charge of the American School when I first went there, now had a boarding school in Curitiba. Miss Kuhl had been the *Directora* when I first came to São Paulo and my place had always been by her side: at the table, in the church, and wherever we went as a school. They now reinforced our invitation to come to that delightfully cool climate.

My brother Argentino, who had enlisted with the army of Floriano Peixoto during the revolt of September 6th and served at the fortresses of Santa Cruz and Praia de Fora, was living with us then and Myron got him a job with an English firm, Watson Ritchie & Cia. He got very much interested in my husband's work and became quite active at the *ACM* rooms. I must introduce now too our friend Dominges A. de Silva Oliveira, who was a clerk at a Clarks' shoe store. He was quite a good friend of my brother's so we arranged for him to move to our place to be with my brother while we were away. They would both eat at the restaurant owned by a member of the *ACM*.

I was quite thrilled with the prospect of seeing nothing but water meeting the sky during our trip south. I was ready to drop after the preparations to leave, and was anxious to get on board to rest. Many of the young men, including my brother, came to see us off in little rowboats: we two, the two children, and my niece. Then the *Itaituba* raised anchor and out we went. It was my first experience in the Kingdom of Neptune.

The *Itaituba* was a very small boat that did not go too far from the coast. We had not even got through that lovely gateway made by Sugar Loaf and the Fortress of Santa Cruz, when I had to go to my cabin and I began to "feed the fishes." I thought that I was going to die, and how little I cared! I never left our cabin until three days later when we left the boat at Paranaguá! My poor husband had all the care of the babies. I am sure Columbus's men were not happier when the word "*terra*" passed among them than I was when we entered the port of Paranaguá, Paraná.

The trip by train, over and around the mountains to the capital, Curitiba, was magnificent. I think this narrow-gauge railroad is considered quite a piece of engineering. Gorgeous scenery was always before our eyes. All the vegetation and the trees were different from what we were used to.

Our friends, Miss Kuhl and Miss Dascomb, were at the station with a fine welcome, and soon we were settled in the home of the missionary couple who had invited us.

We had not been there very long when the two missionaries decided to visit their friends in the interior of the state, taking advantage of my husband's presence by asking him to fill the pulpit. Now, my grandchildren, this was one thing that I had to see all my married life: my husband would accept all requests to do this and that, outside of his strenuous work. God chose me to be Myron's wife knowing that I was not as good as he was, but I didn't know it then. So every Sunday my husband presented a fine new sermon, and I am not afraid to say that he was much complimented every time.

In the boarding school, Miss Kuhl and Miss Dascomb received us as if I were their own daughter. The children were also most welcomed at the school. These three children were just as pretty and bright as one could wish for and, indeed, were the center of attention.

We had a delightful time there for almost two months. I was well rested, and how I had enjoyed having my husband all day long. To have my husband around me was a treat always. When it was nearing the time for us to go home, my old teacher suggested that we leave my niece there until after we went to the States for home leave, which was due in a year. Both she and Miss Dascomb had known her parents very well—if you remember, Maria Ovídia's father, Mineco, a fine Christian man, had taught in the school in São Paulo when they were there, and her mother, Josephina, was a pupil until she was married. This offer was a surprise to us, but my husband thought it was the best thing we could do, as we could not take her to the States. I didn't want to consent to this at all but after studying the circumstances, I agreed with my husband. Poor child! It was very hard on her! It was also very hard for us to break the news to her and there were plenty of tears shed but she, in fact, was going to be looked after better than I could have done.

In those days the means of communication between states was limited; when it was time to return to Rio, we were surprised to find out that all the cabins in the small boats that made that trip had been sold out for months. During the revolt, government troops had been sent to the state of Paraná because there was more support for the uprising there, and now they and their families were being brought back to the North. We had to engage passage without cabins or beds or we would have had to wait two or three months. We could not do that, so we came on board the *Sirius* expecting to sleep on deck in our steamer chairs with children under two years of age! I think we put the children on the small lounging chair. Because of some trouble with the engines or machinery, the boat stopped at night, and in the daytime did not go very far from land. What a blessing, as then I could eat and sleep. One could hardly walk around, it was so crowded with troops and passengers; but you can stand things when you are young.

We left Curitiba for Paranaguá to receive just before sailing a cable from our friend Dominges saying that my brother Argentino had died on the 14th of March with yellow fever! What a blow! He was only nineteen years old. The death of my brother was a shock and a great sorrow, but I was so busy that I couldn't think very much about it. Then, too, when one is away it is hard to realize the sad truth.

We were back again at Rua Evaristo da Veiga. It was hard to come home and find the vacancy left by my brother. Again the harvester of lives was around my family. He had been buried on Sunday, March 15, in the cemetery of São Jõao Batista. There was nobody from his family around him when he was dying, but his boss—Mr. Sloan, who later was president of the Association—sent him to the best hospital in town and took care of all the expenses there, and of the funeral; he was surrounded by his friends until the grave claimed him. It was a sad homecoming, but when we heard how nice everybody had been to my brother, we were very thankful. Our friend Dominges, who had stayed with my brother at the hospital until he died, asked to live and board with us, and we consented.

We were greeted in Rio by our many friends; my husband was feeling better, and immediately he put his heart, mind, and soul into his work. The children grew strong and active and because of this there were cuts and bruises. Ruth fell when she was about eighteen months old and had a deep cut on her nose, near her forehead. When Orton was beginning to walk, he fell from a chair and broke some little bones in his arms.

So the evening and the morning passed and another summer came when I had to leave my husband to get stronger. That summer we decided that I would go with the children to Novo Friburgo for about two months to rest and get stronger in this summer resort in the Organ Mountains three hours from Rio, as we were expecting another visit from that Busy Bird, the stork. I have sweet letters from my husband written at this time. What a comfort they are from long, long ago!

The time for his furlough in the States was getting nearer so he was excited about it. He said that we were going to have many happy experiences, and added, "I know you are going to like my people and my country, but you may just as well be prepared for disappointments, also." I may say right now that my disappointments were very few compared with the joys and the surprises that this land of the brave and the free offered me! But I wondered what the reaction of his family towards this specimen from South America would be.

Other evenings and mornings passed and when Orton was two years and two months old, on the 18th of June, Frau Geyer and the same dear Dr. Henrique Baptista who presided at the second birth, were on hand. That night a dear little girl with coal-black eyes and a great abundance of black curly hair was born to us and we named her Argentina, after my brother Argentino. She was a very sweet baby. You see, they were coming fast.

I cannot go on with my story without saying something about our dear physician, Dr. Henrique Baptista. When our second child Orton came, the doctor who took care of me when I had yellow fever introduced us to Dr. Baptista, his old teacher, a professor of obstetrics and head physician at the maternity department of the medical school. He was the best obstetric physician in Rio. While he was waiting for Orton to be born, Dr. Baptista engaged in conversation with my husband about his work, a puzzle to him. He himself was a Positivist, a follower of Auguste Comte. His religion was to do all he could for the sake of humanity. Beyond the grave he could not see anything. All through the years of contact with him we saw that he really was interested in helping people.

He asked my husband how much rent he paid. Then he said, "There is some land by the sea outside of the bay which is being sold very reasonably and in very easy payments, considering that in the near future that place is bound to be the best and the healthiest residential part of Rio. Why don't you buy a lot to have a home some day?" He added, "Besides the tunnel that already connects this side of the city with that beach, there is a plan to cut another tunnel through these rolling hills, and then the land will be very expensive there. Now is the time to buy."

My husband said, "At present it is impossible." So that was that. As the doctor did not send any bill for some time, my husband went to see him, and he said, "I have my fees for rich people, but you live on a small salary so whatever you pay will be all right." When your grandfather handed him the money he put it in his pocket without even looking at it.

Now once again, while we were waiting for this little girl to arrive, after finding out that my husband had not looked into the matter of the property by the beach, the doctor advised him to make some sacrifice and buy a lot there while they were cheap. I loved that beach. We often had picnics there, alone and with the *ACM*. I began to dream of a home with the sea in front, the hills behind, and the blue sky above.

But we have to leave our dear Dr. Henrique Baptista until we need him again and get ready for my greatest adventure. I had other adventures in my married life, but this, being the first, was one never to be forgotten. Our much-needed vacation in the States was due in 1897. It was called a vacation but it was really a change of work with the pleasure of being in your own country. But for me, it would be different. I was going to leave my country and my people.

# 21. O Paíz dos Yankees

Just as soon as I was strong enough to move around I started the preparations for a trip on the ocean for twenty-one or twenty-two days with three children under three years and four months old. You can imagine what a job it was, getting the family ready to go, and our house and belongings ready to stay. There were no department stores in Rio; ready-made clothes were not available, except for very expensive French-made things that were out of our pocketbook's reach. Common folks like us paid to have clothes made, or made their own, but as all the material for clothing was imported, this was much more expensive in Brazil than in the States. My husband's father advised him not to buy anything except what was very, very necessary.

All the time we were getting ready I was wondering what my husband's people were going to think of me. But what a wonderful privilege to see *O Paíz dos Yankees*.[40] To a Brazilian, any American was a Yankee. Everybody in Brazil knew all that there was to know about Europe, and many of our friends had been there, but very few knew about this part of the New World. Hollywood, which furnishes more thrills to young people than any other place in the world, had probably been born but not christened yet. Instead, we had stereopticon views and later, when the cinema opened, it was Pathé, a French filmmaker. I thought Americans must be very good people because most Americans in Brazil were missionaries—people who made the sacrifice to come down to save us. Now I was going there, but my husband's people—that was the question.

My husband was busier than ever preparing to leave the work in the hands of a man who had no more to give to the Y than good intentions and what he had seen in four years. In addition to our preparations,

---

40. The Country of the Yankees. Chiquita refers here to the title of a Brazilian book published in 1884, by Adolfo Caminha.

before leaving I worked quite a bit on *kermesses*[41] to raise funds for a building for the *Associação*. These *kermisses* were very much in vogue in Brazil, as they were a good way to raise money and to bring people together, since women stayed at home so much. There was always plenty of good food to eat, hot and cold, so the families stayed from late in the afternoon until late at night. They always ended with an auction when things were sold for much more than they were worth.

When the day came to sail, I was anxious to get on board to rest. And on Saturday, the 31st of July, 1897, Myron Clark, who had come to Brazil alone in 1891, was sailing back to his country with his wife and three children, Ruth (three years, four months), Orton (two years, three months), and Argentina (one month and eleven days old). The boat was bigger than the one we took to Paraná, so my husband assured me that I was going to be all right.

It was a beautiful sunny day: After prolonged farewells with many tears, the *botafora*[42] was at 3 p.m. from Largo do Paço, in a steam launch offered by the *Directoria* and YMCA boys who came on board. There were prayers in our stateroom, and the boys and friends sang 'God be with you till we meet again,' in our cabin. We sailed at five. The ship was the *Nevelius* of the Lamport & Holt line, an English firm. The captain told us it had made its first trip to take the emperor of Brazil to the United States centennial in Philadelphia in 1876.

I never went below for my meals; they were brought up to me on deck. There I could keep the little food I took, but down in the cabin it was impossible! I got so discouraged that I began to think about the time I would have to come back, and I was feeling that I would much rather die than to go through what I was feeling then. The captain, an old widower, was very sympathetic and arranged for a steerage passenger, a German girl about seventeen or eighteen years old who was coming to the USA, to help me. She could not speak either Portuguese or English, but she got along fine with the children.

---

41. Of Belgian origin, a *kermesse* was originally a harvest mass followed by feasting, games, and dancing. The first *kermesse* in America took place in Rosier, Wisconsin, in 1858. The custom slowly died out in the United States after World War I. It was widely used in Brazil as a fundraiser for churches.

42. Send-off; literally, boat-away.

After a few days the waters began to look dark; we were nearing the Amazon. We saw lots of floating islands of seaweed. Finally, entering the harbor of New York at night, we saw the lights of the Brooklyn Bridge, Liberty Statue, ferryboats, excursions steamers, and tall buildings. I cannot describe my amazement! I was coming from Rio de Janeiro of the '90s that had not seen any improvements for several decades. There were no movies then as there are now to bring to you images of those skyscrapers, the suspended bridge, and the gallant French lady in bronze that became the American symbol of liberty. And to my delight, the minute I left Neptune's dominion I was my own master again.

You may be surprised, my grandchildren, to know that one of the things your Vovó enjoyed most in New York, and that you will never have the privilege to enjoy, was going up and down Fifth Avenue on the upper deck of the buses pulled then by three enormous, slim, and handsome horses. What powerful paws! Where have those horses' descendants gone? We took the two older children with us on that ride on the upper deck, and Orton was so impressed with those big horses that one of the first English sentences he was able to form came when he was saying his prayers that night. Kneeling down with his head on my lap, he said, "*Papai do Céu*, (Father in Heaven) bless *Papai*, bless *Mamãe*, and bless those horses because them are nice." He was two and a half.

We were about a week in New York and then two in Buffalo, the beautiful city where my beloved was born and lived until he was seventeen, and where he had many relatives and old friends. One of them, Uncle Henry, a bachelor brother of Myron's deceased mother, immediately made me feel at home. There was a G.A.R. (Grand Army of the Republic) reunion encampment in Buffalo then and so Myron's father, who was in the Civil War with the North, came from Minneapolis not only because of this reunion but also to meet us. He was a dear old man, and how moved he and my husband were when they saw each other!

He was delighted with the appearance of his grandchildren, but one could see his disappointment because he could not understand them and they could not understand him. As for myself, I had not made much use of the English language except when I was with somebody that spoke

English only. Our courting had been done mostly in Portuguese. Now I had to use English daily. The children were attracting the attention of everybody wherever we went: boarding houses, restaurants, homes, etc. Relatives and friends admired the lovely curly hair and beautiful black eyes of the children. People wanted to know what language they were speaking.

We arrived in this country at the time of the bicycle craze. I had seen men and women and boys and girls in New York riding them everywhere, the girls flying on wheels along the avenues with their skirts much above the limit line of decency for me. I was not shocked with this freedom I saw in New York, because they were just *people*, but here in Buffalo they were *my* folks. Of course, these Buffalo ladies were dressed in the only way possible to ride a bicycle: wide skirts way above their ankles. But, my grandchildren, if you could see a photograph of a group of us teachers taken before I married, you could understand my feelings then. You could see only the points of our shoes. Do you wonder that I was shocked? Yet the waist- and bust-lines of each of us are quite in evidence!

Everybody who knew my husband here before he went to Brazil came to see him and, I am sure, to see what his foreign wife looked like—Oh me, oh my! My grandchildren, it is hard for me to tell you my reaction to the following. Years ago in this country, there was much more restriction between boys and girls than now, yet not only all his cousins and his aunts but also all the girls with whom he was well acquainted, even some of those with whom he had had dates—although I don't think that is what they called it then—thought they had the right to kiss him! His kisses, which had been only mine for five years, now were distributed profusely—were *taken* is more accurate—among his many beautiful cousins and friends!

I, of course, was getting a double share from males and females, yet I felt as if he were slipping out of my grasp. I just wanted to pick him up, and my children, and go away to some desert island! In defense to my foolishness I'd like to say that it was all a matter of custom—but do not think that I let those around me see what was going on in my mind or heart. Oh no, I was trying all the time to win the friendship of my husband's relatives and friends, and I think I did. Before we left Buffalo, Uncle Henry said to me: "We loved you before we met you because you were Myron's wife; now we love you because of yourself." That made me feel at ease.

We left Buffalo on the train called the Nickel Plate for Chicago, and then to St. Paul, Minnesota. My sister-in-law Winnie was just as sweet as she could be to me, and sympathetic, as she herself had a baby boy, and another boy a little older than Ruth who was named after my husband. It did not take long for me to feel at home, and I could also see that Rob, her husband, was a jolly good fellow. He was always shooting jokes on me. One day when I was admiring the white squirrels going up the trees and running around the house unafraid, I told him how in Brazil we never saw them as they were rare—sometimes we had them in cages as pets. He turned to me very seriously and said: "You see, Chiquita, we never saw so many around here before, but since you came they are always around looking for something." Nuts of course, my little ones, if you can't see the joke! The only thing people here thought of when they heard the word Brazil was nuts. Then relatives and old friends of the family began to come to see the Brazilian nut. You see, I was a real curiosity!

One day a sister of the girl he left behind arrived on a bike, rigged in a very diminutive outfit. She jumped from it, rushed to my husband and planted a noisy kiss right on his lips! She was so tickled to see him. Poor man! He sure was embarrassed, not with the kiss but with what was going to be the outcome of it! He knew perfectly well the effect of that kiss on somebody's heart! Another day Rob said, "Now, Chiquita, I want you to meet one of Myron's girls, Louise—my, he was terribly in love with her." I tried to make him think that I could take the joke, but I was too green, and I know that he was reading in my eyes that I was jealous, and got a great kick out of that. Then I met the lovely blonde and saw her superiority in everything to me—I don't know anything about complexes, but the one I had began to work.

It seems to me that I must say something about my feelings then. Now that I was in the world to which he belonged before he was mine, I had a queer sensation. He was another person; not that he acted differently to me, mind you, but he really was not all mine. He was very happy in this world that he had left behind and which I didn't know. He had been away from home and from everybody he knew in this country for seven years and was now in seventh heaven! He had been the favorite of the family on both sides and after his experiences in another country, especially in South America, which was then less known here than Africa, and having pulled through yellow fever, he was now almost a hero. I felt that I had to get acquainted with this other personality! Oh, I was happy, but I was uneasy! Everything was different—homes, churches, persons, and customs. It was like a sweet dream and again it was like a nightmare. I loved his people—that I can assure you—but I felt terribly embarrassed near this girl. Rob did everything to throw us together whenever it was possible and would stay on one side and watch me.

And now that Jack Frost was beginning to paint the trees, they began to show off their colors according to their kind. This was a revelation to me. I thought the paintings I had seen in my country so exaggerated because the red, the yellow, and the brown were mixed with the green, but now here I was with a big living picture before my eyes! It is beautiful, but sad, too, because while the trees are changing color, they are losing their leaves, and when you are passing under the trees, you hear the crackling of their dying leaves. The wound in my heart was still open, and I could not think of my brother Argentino without my eyes filling with tears.

Then all of a sudden the trees were bare and on a moonlit night they made me think of ghosts—friendly ghosts! The trees here grew to be seen naked as well as robed, and they were just as beautiful one way as the other. Nature probably thought, "When the fall comes, the trees lose their leaves, so I will multiply their twigs ten times, twenty times, thirty until more than one hundred times." That is why even in the winter the trees are so graceful! Under the Southern Cross, in that giant of South America, Brazil is never disrobed—unless she is dying.

Coming from under the Southern Cross where it is warm, we had to do lots of shopping even for fall weather. Then we began to get ready for winter, and what a task! All the stores of the city knew that a lady from Brazil and her children were looking anxiously for the day when Lady Snow would make her appearance. My mother-in-law loved to tell the clerks in stores that I had never seen snow and that I had three children, the oldest not four yet. This was enough to make them stare at me. Also, I noticed that most everybody carried a smile on their countenances while I was talking—and yet I thought I spoke just like everybody else. Don't you know that a person who cannot carry a tune does not know it? Only lately I have found out that it is not my subject that amuses my listeners, but the way I deliver it—I didn't know I pronounced everything differently than they. The children and I were anxiously waiting for the snow and at last one day I was thrilled to see the air full of cotton flakes, or feathers!

On January 7, 1898, we were making final preparations for Myron's eastern trip. His headquarters were going to be New York City. Although he was supposed to be on furlough, my husband made frequent long trips to various cities to speak about Brazil in YMCA clubs, churches, etc. to raise money for the Rio Association. He would speak in the lobbies of buildings in which meetings were being held, showing pamphlets and slides, sometimes gathering a few pledges. When at home, he would be busy writing letters, reports, circulars, sermons and speeches. Myron had been away several times since we arrived in this country but only for days and a few weeks

I am very glad I didn't know how long this trip was going to be. One can stand troubles and sorrows so much better not knowing that they are coming to you, and that is true too with joy and pleasure—one enjoys them a good deal more when they come as a surprise, unexpectedly. I am not going to say much about myself who stayed behind, only that it was hard on his step-mother, as she had never had any children, and it was very hard on me too, as I had to get acquainted with the family and get used to American ways, and didn't have him around to smooth out differences. It was a long three months of longings and discouragement for both of us.

Finally, the day came when he arrived back in Minneapolis; it was on the 12th of April, after three months and four days apart. That month

Congress declared war against Spain, and everybody was wearing badges and buying perfumes and so on with this label: "Remember the Maine." Myron's brother Warren enlisted, and so did two cousins from St. Paul; they went to the Philippine Islands. Admiral Dewey defeated the Spanish fleet in Manila Bay on May 1st, and on the 4th of July we received the news of Cervera's[43] defeat outside the bay of Santiago de Cuba.

Now it was getting near the end of our vacation in the United States. Myron went on another speaking tour for a few weeks and I began the preparation for the long trip: sewing, calling on friends, etc. The vacation had been a very fine one, and I felt that I had gained many new friends and was looking toward my husband's people now as my own. Yet down in my heart I was glad that the time for us to go home and for him to belong just to me was getting nearer. After saying tearful goodbyes to more than sixty people in Minneapolis, and visiting relatives in Chicago and Buffalo on the way, we arrived in New York.

The next day we were on board the little boat *Galileo*. We were all seasick, I worse than anybody. My poor husband, having to take care of us all, got sick also. The captain came to our rescue again, bringing a girl from steerage who was willing to help if her mother could be with her too. Both came during the day; the mother helped with the baby, and the daughter flirted with the crew. The children once in a while had spells of sickness or some other trouble but one bright night we saw the Southern Cross for the first time, guiding us home.

After 22 very tiresome days on board, we approached the city of Rio. Only those who have been at sea for many days with no sight of land can have a faint idea of the thrill of the navigators of long ago who were in search of new discoveries, when the cry "Land! Land!" went from sailor to sailor! Before we had crossed the narrow entrance with the Sugar Loaf always at guard, we noticed a big launch coming in our direction. When it was getting nearer we noticed the leaders of the *ACM*, and friends and relatives waving their hankies; pretty soon, we could hear their voices.

This is my beautiful country! Thank God for it! How wonderful to arrive home, and home then meant the most beautiful city in the world—ours!

---

43. Admiral D. Pascual Cervera, 1839–1909.

# 22. Copacabana at the Turn of the Century

*Wooster, Ohio, 1940*

We came back to Rio at the foot of these beloved hills in 1898. Our very dear friends the Bragas met and took us to stay at their home until we found a suitable one. The very next day my husband saw the different members of the Board of Directors, Trustees and members of the *ACM*. Your grandfather was deep in his job even before we found our home, on Enrique de Sá, in Catete.[44] My niece Maria Ovídia, whom we had left in Paraná, was back home with us. She was then about ten years old and became a great help to me, playing with the children and doing things for me.

The *ACM* had its own building before we left for the States. A half-built building whose owners had gone bankrupt went to auction and two well-to-do members (Braga was one of them), together with friends of the Y, loaned the money to buy and adapt it to the needs of the Association. While in the States, the object of many of my husband's speaking tours was to raise money for this building. Now we were busy buying furniture for the building, and making preparations for the opening.

Besides my duties at home, I began to get ready for a *kermese. Kermeses* and auctions kept us busy, as this was a good way to raise money. I had received gifts from missionary societies and friends to be sold for the benefit of the building, and I made neckties to sell to the clerks in English and American firms who spent Sunday afternoons in our house. Neckties were expensive in those days, all imported. I bought imported material and made out of a yard quite a few neckties. Each one was sold for the price I paid for the material. The building was inaugurated on November 1st, 1898, with 500 people attending. How I love to remember those early busy days! Yet they were days when we both worked to the limit of our strength. Remember—in those days in Brazil there were no gas stoves; wood was used for cooking and heating water, and in the

---

44. A district in Rio.

bathroom there was just a cold shower.

And the evening passed and so did the morning and another year came. There was sickness and lots of work, and lots of houseguests, not always expected. Because Myron spent most of his days and evenings at the Association, one of his superiors advised him to take one day in the week to be home all day. He chose Thursdays, and believe me we were together all day long except when he took a nap—a very regular feature of that day's program.

If this were a movie you would find me now without a maid, very tired and worn out telling my husband the secret reason for my feeling that way. But as this is a true story, he knew just as much as I did that our family was going to be increased again. Argentina, who we began calling "Baby" when we were in the States, was going to be two years old on the 18th of June, and on the 15th, a big boy, looking very much like a foreigner—an American—was born. When I was informed that the child was a boy, I said, "His name will be Henry Parker Clark, after dear Uncle Henry." Dr. Henrique Baptista, who had been with me when Orton and Argentina came, presided again at this event.

So time came and passed with some of the sicknesses one has with children: teething, fevers and colds, measles, whooping cough, and stomach troubles. In the city there were sometimes cases of yellow fever and even bubonic plague. And there was pleasure and friction at home and in the work, and lots of company to stay, on days when it was convenient and when it was not. But our guests were always welcomed.

On the last of the year an entertainment was given at the Y with stereopticon[45] views, ending with a prayer meeting to see the old year out and the New Year in. This Magic Lantern was one of the more popular means of entertainment at the Association, to which members of all churches and outsiders came. It was accompanied by a good lecture that was translated into Portuguese by my husband.

The New Year, contrary to what happens here in Ohio, comes to Brazil wrapped up in hot weather. All of the family needed a change to a cooler

---

45. The Magic Lantern was an early slide projector with a small oil lamp. Magic Lanterns with two lamps were called stereopticons.

place We decided that a few months on the lovely beach of Copacabana on the wide ocean where we could have sea baths would be a very good thing for us all. We rented a house planted in the sand at Rua Tonaleiro, 23, not very far from the tunnel and the streetcar worked by mule power, the only and very infrequent means of transportation that brought you to that beach. We called it *Quinta do Pão d'Alho* (Garlic Bread Farm). The tunnel poked through a hill covered with vegetation and shaped like a closed hand with the thumb sticking up.

This hill brought us shade very early in the afternoon, and the little palm trees scattered here and there were a delight to our eyes. On the main street, there was a row of one-story buildings: the grocery, the butchery, and the house where the owner of these stores lived. We saw only sea, sand, and sky in front of us. Behind us were high peaks where the *quaresmeiras*, so called because they bloom at Lent (*Quaresma*), and the palm trees reigned supreme, and vegetation grew undisturbed.

Rua Toneleiro, 23, Copacabana, where
Daddy (on Vovo's lap) was born, 1903.

Early next morning, to the beach for sea bathing we went. What a struggle between sea and sand! The waves came one, two, three—up they went forming a high, light blue-green wall all along the shore, then curving and falling over themselves and we had to *furar* (tunnel under the waves) before they came roaring like thunder in foam that disappeared gradually on the white sand. Then little waves came and spread out in several white fringes on the beach. The bathing was wonderful, but rather dangerous. Many times we could not get into the ocean; every summer that beach claimed some victims. But how we loved to see the Queen of the Night come up from the water, spreading a silver path over the waves! And from the silent lighthouse, spinning its red and white lights, a trail from its island to the wet sand.

We had two delightful months there and when we were getting ready to leave, the owner of the stores said to me, "I should think you would stay here always. The day you arrived I said to the people in the store: 'Here is another skeleton coming to Copacabana!' You look like a different person now!"

We did a very good piece of business while at Copacabana, which was very special to me. As I told you before, when Orton was born, the physician, Dr. Henrique Baptista, suggested that we buy a lot by the sea. This being the first time that my husband was around at such an event, he was too nervous and excitable to pay much attention; he heard what was mentioned but didn't give it another thought. Such was not the case with me—to live by the sea—what a dream! Two years later our dear doctor mentioned it again when Argentina came to enrich our home—again there was no response from my husband. Then came the fourth child, Henry, and again he advised us to buy a lot there saying that someday another tunnel was going to be opened and that beach was going to be the best residential section of the city, and it was worth a little sacrifice to get it now as the price was going up quickly!

Well, I gave no rest to my husband after that, so that he called at the office of *Empreza Construcçoes Civis* for information about the sale of lots in Copacabana. Two days later he consulted our friend Senhor Braga, who said, "Do it." We went to see the lot, measured and chose it, and paid the first installment on the lot in Leme![46] There was not one house on that beach then. Cactus and wild flowers that grow in the sand, seagulls, and crabs were the only inhabitants of that beach. For several years the only sign that we owned a piece of land was the mark made by two iron bars. In 1904 the tunnel was built, and houses, *palacetes* (mansions), and villas began to spring up like the leaves and the flowers in the spring and when the time comes I will tell about ours.

We went back to Rua Henrique de Sá from our first experience by the sea. My husband was glad to get back nearer the city, as so much time had to be spent on the slow streetcar. The work was growing, and he had no help. Many times when my husband came home for dinner (he often didn't) he brought one or more unexpected guests with whom he wanted to talk about the work. At home things moved sometimes smoothly and again in a not very encouraging way, as could be expected with four children, the oldest one being only six years old.

By the end of the year, the heat was terrible and we were missing our house by the sea. Besides his work as the Secretary of the Association, he was Superintendent of the Sunday school, and I had a class also. The needs were many in those days and there were very few who could do the work. I was about exhausted with the work and the heat, so I accepted another invitation from my sister Cacilda to go to São Paulo. I took only the baby, who was a little over one year old. When I returned to Rio the heat was terrible yet, so we decided to look for a house by the sea again.

We two went on a beautiful morning to Copacabana and the beach. How beautiful the sea was! Three big waves would pile up and then break with a big stampede over the long curved beach, which ended near a rocky hill where a very modest Church of the Fishermen attracted many picnickers. There was only the one street where the grocery, the butcher, and the bakery were. In this last one we inquired about a house. The storekeeper thought there was one up on the hill.

We followed the directions given and arrived at an old rusty iron gate. Inside the stone wall there were banana, *caju* (cashew), and *goiaba* (guava)

---

46. The beach at the far northeast side of Copacabana, on the ocean side of Pão de Açúcar. Leme means rudder.

trees, almost suffocated by the weeds. There was a little trail winding up the hill but we couldn't see any vestige of habitation! My husband said, "Wait here. I will go up and if there is anything worthwhile I will call you." I sat inside the gate under a beautiful Flamboyant tree. Soon after he turned on the trail up the hill he came back where he could see me and waved for me to come up, and his smile encouraged me to do it quickly.

There sitting against the hill was a square, one-story house. Three wide doors opened to a very wide tiled *varanda* (porch) and what a view! The sea was indigo blue and so was the sky; there was not one house on the beach——just a wee island straight ahead, ten miles away, just big enough for the lighthouse and the abode of its keepers. Hills marked either side of the entrance to the most beautiful bay in the world! We sat there on the steps speechless before the magnificence of nature. Myron had one arm around me. I said, "I have no hopes to live here; the place must be rented already." I didn't see how such a place could be empty.

After a while we explored around the house; there were five rooms with big windows with iron bars. We could see inside; all the rooms were whitewashed. We could not see the kitchen, but there was a big door in the back of the house and a small window way up near the roof. This door we thought must be to the kitchen. The hill and the woods began right from this door. We noticed a cave on one side of the hill: it seemed to be a spring. While we were in the middle of our explorations we heard some footsteps and a boy about twelve appeared and handed to my husband a very large heavy key very much like the key of the Bastille at George Washington's house.[47] The boy, Maximiano, told us that his mother lived on the grounds with a sister and a little brother.

The kitchen had a red tiled floor that made it nice and cool. There was an old rusted stove in a corner, and no faucet to be seen anywhere although there was a big zinc (tin) box on the roof for water. This precious beverage was to be carried from down near the iron gate where the only faucet on the premises was. A little "fireless cooker" (metal outhouse,

---

47. A key to the Bastille, presented by Lafayette to George Washington in 1790, is now in the museum of George Washington's home at Mount Vernon. See Mount Vernon Ladies' Association, "Bastille Key."

probably very hot inside) behind the house served as a bathroom but there was no old Sears Roebuck catalogue behind its door.

The view was interrupted on one side by two little hills near the beach. On the top of one there was a rather dilapidated tree and on the other a *palmeirinha*, (a small palm) then the sea again and some hills marking either side of the entrance to the bay. On the way home my husband stopped at the proprietor's residence and I went on home on the streetcar. I had to wait until night to find out if we could have the house. My, what a joy!

We rented it for the summer of 1901. After some cleaning and scrubbing for which we needed our friends the beachcombers—Antônio Gibraltar this time—we moved in, bringing our two roomers, Dominges and Mr. Hodgekiss (a Portuguese and an Englishman), who had asked us to take them, as they wanted to live with a family.

Tio Gerónimo, an old colored man who had been a slave and a soldier in our war with Paraguay, came to ask to cut the weeds which were as high as the many *goiaba* and *cajú* trees all over the place. As I was telling him what he ought to do, all of a sudden he said: "Senhora! Do not move your feet!" He said it in such a way that I became petrified and could not move if I had wanted to. There near my feet, twisted in several curls was sleeping one of the most dangerous snakes we have—*a jararaca preguiçosa* (which means lazy). He killed it just as if it were a job he was used to. We saw many snakes during the first months we were there, and a hen and several little chickies were killed by a kind of skunk. One morning another hen appeared with seven or eight newborn chickies! We kept her at night in a safe place, until her babies could fight for their lives.

All the time we were there Tio Gerónimo did any cleaning around the place when it was necessary, and when it was not he came just the same to get a big dish of black beans with salt pork and rice. Tio Gerónimo was one of the destitutes of Rio who lived in the hills around this marvelous city. They built their huts with mud and covered them with tin. The wooden box that brought kerosene—Standard Oil has been in Brazil as long as I have—served as furniture. They raised pigs and chickens and there was plenty of fish in the Big Pond, and bananas and *goiabas* all around. They needed very few clothes—it was so hot.

We were somewhat like them, but we had plenty of comfortable rocking chairs on our spacious *varanda*. We loved to see the fishermen's little boats whose white sails pointed to a beautiful blue sky, and the big ships coming in and out of the bay. We had no parlor. We spent most of the time on the big wide *varanda* enjoying the air, the view of the sea and the seagulls, and the little palm trees on top of the hills.

At night, while listening to the crickets and the frogs, we watched the little lights here and there in the hills and the light in the *pharol* (lighthouse) going around and around. In the first nights we were there, the children, lying down in the *varanda* after the sun went down behind the hill above our house, would wait to see who would be the first one to see the light appear in the *pharol* on Ilha Rasa. I can hear them screaming—"*Branco, branco branco …amarelo amarelo amarelo …vermelho vermelho vermelho*" ("White white white...yellow yellow yellow...red red red") as the light appeared and rotated, making a trail over the waves to the beach and disappearing out on the ocean to come back again, on and on through the night until early morning. My sisters Lydia and Manoelita, who were then teaching in Rio, and Noemi, who married from my house in 1900, enjoyed coming to see us and sometimes stayed overnight until Sunday.

On the days my husband stayed home I took my mending up the little hill on one side of the house where there was some level ground with *goiaba* trees and a big shady *jamelão*.[48] I kept all the mending and darning for that day and while he read out loud to me some good book on a special subject, an article, fiction, or some interesting literature, I kept my needle busy. He took a blanket, pillow, book, and a chair for me and while my needle made those old garments ready to be worn again he read to me until he dropped to sleep. It was up there that I got acquainted with *David Harum, Quo Vadis, The Man from Glengarry*[49] and others. What a nice rest he had on the bluff under the shade of the big tree, overlooking the ocean!

---

48. The Jambolan tree, *Syzygium cumini.*

49. *David Harum* was written in 1898 by E. N. Westcott; *Quo Vadis* is an 1895 novel by Henryk Sienkeiwicz, 1903 Nobel Laureate in literature; *The Man from Glengarry* is a 1901 novel by Ralph Connor that met international acclaim.

The sea was our everyday bathtub, and believe me it was not a sacrifice to use it, but a real relief from the heat. On Sunday afternoons many of our friends came to share with us this unique bathing spot. You are wondering how I kept those tender little knees clean for Sunday school? With the Saturday evening bath in our large round tin bathtub.

This brings back to me a memory of the way our mother got us ready for Sunday. Besides the tin bathing utensil which was used every night, there was a terrifically heavy wooden tub just the shape of bathtubs of today carved out of an enormous trunk of a tree, which must have been very, very old, judging by the size of it, and I am sure a very valuable kind of wood. It was smooth inside but left natural outside. There my mother put several of us at a time.

Summer was over and it was goodbye to Copacabana and to a delightful four-and-a-half months spent there.

The next year, we began to prepare for the new baby that we were expecting in March, the hottest month of the summer. We asked about the house upon the hill that we loved so much and as the owner had made some improvements—a bathroom with bathtub inside, and a new sleeping room to the house, we decided to move all our furniture there. We fixed up the place then to look like a home. Two lovely big pictures of Niagara Falls that Uncle Henry had given us, and some smaller paintings of flowers and country scenes looked very nice on the white-washed walls and attracted the attention of those friends who had never seen snow.

On Sundays we were never without two or three or many more guests, all the afternoon and for tea. How well I remember that hot Saturday, March 1st at six in the afternoon. I had baked my cake—really when I remember what people said about my cakes, I pat myself on the back thinking of the stoves where they were baked. When I was putting a chocolate frosting on it, I began to feel the first calls. My husband sent a messenger to get our doctor immediately as it would take at least four hours to get him. He came back saying that the doctor could not come then as he was gone somewhere all that night, but he brought back the card of another physician, a friend of his. He said too that Dr. Henrique would be available the next day at nine if nothing happened before. This was going to be the fourth time he presided at that kind of event, and such was my confidence in him and my fear of having somebody else, that I slept all through the night. Just about the time he said he could be available next morning, the call began again. The messenger had already gone for him in the morning.

Our fifth child, a fine boy, was born at ten minutes after two o'clock in the afternoon of March 2nd, 1902. We named him for my father, Manoel Pereira de Morães Clark. He was strong, hardy, and *manso* (gentle, good). Neco, as we called him, had convulsions during his teething, which scared me. It was marvelous that our children were never bitten by snakes. They had many bumps and sore feet since just as soon as they left the streetcar coming from school they pulled off their shoes and carried them home. Two of the children fell from the big tree under which we spent many of the hours on the day my husband stayed home.

So the year of 1902 passed. Lots of friends from the city visited us, always admiring the beauty of nature all around. Many who were leaving or arriving in Rio were met by us and brought to Copacabana to share what we had there that couldn't be bought: gorgeous scenery! We were visited not only by people but also by sickness and other cares. Myron was away twice to São Paulo, and even spent Christmas and New Year's there, and an Association was finally established there. And now for 1903: This year was very much like the one before. Friends visited us as usual and the children had their ups and downs. In this year, as in the past, there were lectures with lantern slides at the *ACM* and sometimes in the churches.

On October 6th, 1903, at nine p.m., our *caçula* (youngest) was born and slept peacefully in his little bed until noon the next day! He left there to have his bath with only a murmur. We named him George Williams for Sir George Williams, the British founder of the YMCA. He was a perfect mixture even in his talk. Once, playing alone, upon hearing someone talking about age, he said, "I *fazi* three *anos!*" He was the strongest and most mischievous of all.

My grandmother, for whom I was named, was visiting us, and we celebrated her seventy-third birthday on November 13, 1903. My! In two weeks I will be that old and I thought my grandmother was very, very old then. We never dreamed that she could be moving around doing things that I do now. She did lots of handwork and was very fond of reading.

We were now to have another furlough year. Remembering my experience seven years before, I wanted to have a good rest that night to be ready to face my woes! I knew I would miss this very cozy place with the sea in front, hills, rocks and woods behind, and above, the blue sky by day and by night millions of stars winking at us. On the 2nd of May, late in the afternoon, in a big steam launch full of friends, we went on board the *Tennyson*, which sailed the next day.

# IV. Sentimental Journeys

Chiquita's second visit to the United States in 1904 and her visit to Europe in 1905 came at a time when the United States had ascended to first place among the world's manufacturing countries. The industrial age was in full swing; mass production had brought prices to all-time lows. The Ford Motor Company had been incorporated in 1903. Sears, Roebuck and Montgomery Ward catalogs were read more than any other book besides the Bible. It was the beginning of materialism and consumerism. There was also a boom in agriculture made possible by the railroads, and it was a time of mass immigration to the States, mostly from eastern and southern Europe. In the United States people had been moving west since the 1860s, but the American West was still a wild and violent place.[50]

The Louisiana Purchase Exposition opened in St. Louis in 1904. It was to be a "living, working university of man—his work and his world, his progress to that day and the meaning and potential of all this for humanity."[51] People came from all over the world to see it. Palaces of Art, Education, Electricity, and others were arranged along lagoons with gondolas and water vessels of many kinds. A daily crowd of 100,000 people "came down the Pike",or midway, with 125 restaurants and 80 lunch stands, where they could taste new treats like ice cream cones, iced tea, and hot dogs. There were concerts, animals, entertainment and scenes such as representations of the Alps, "Ancient Rome," "Mysterious Asia," and the "Cliff Dwellers of the Far West." A popular show called "Shoot the Chutes" had elephants sliding down a ramp into a pool of water below. In another Pike exhibit, boats took spectators past depictions of each day of creation. There was even a statue of President Theodore Roosevelt sculpted in butter, and one of a bear made entirely of prunes![52]

---

50. Much of the background information for this section was derived from Adams, *Album of American History: Vol. 4, End of an Era*; Birk, *The World Came to St. Louis*; Griffin, *Four Years in Europe with Buffalo Bill*; and Wimmel, *Theodore Roosevelt and the Great White Fleet*.

51. Birk, *The World Came to St. Louis*, 12.

52. Birk, *The World Came to St. Louis*, 45–95.

In 1905 when Chiquita traveled to Europe, France was in the middle of what has come to be known as the *Belle Epoque*, a golden time of peace with its neighbors. New inventions were making life easier for all classes. The cinema was born. By March of that year, a new group of artists were making a big splash in Paris—*Les Fauves*, or "the Wild Beasts"—the group of artists led by Matisse. Picasso was in the early stages of his Rose Period. It was also a time of rising working-class militancy and organized socialist movements.

William F. Cody, or Buffalo Bill as he called himself, exploited the world's interest in the American Wild West by taking a troupe of cowboys, Indians, and buffaloes on tour in the United States and abroad. It was the sensation of Europe. In Paris in 1905, he appeared at the Champs de Mars, an army parade ground with seats on three sides, sheltered by a huge tent. It was a combination rodeo and gigantic circus, a spectacle with fancy riding, sharpshooting, and theatrical depictions of scenes of the conquest of the West, including Custer's Battle of the Little Big Horn.

From 1907 to 1909, the "Great White Fleet," manned by 14,000 sailors, was sent around the world by President Theodore Roosevelt to show American muscle and to promote "gunboat diplomacy" after the success of the Spanish-American War. A great pageant of American sea power, the fleet consisted of sixteen battleships painted white with gilded scrollwork on their bows, accompanied by destroyers and other vessels. The ships were in Guanabara Bay, Rio de Janeiro, from January 12th to January 21st, 1908. This visit was the impetus for the Bureau of Information for the visiting sailors that my grandfather established in Rio. The fleet was just for show; the single-hulled battleships were structurally obsolete and in poor repair. As soon as the ships returned, they were stripped of their beautiful fancywork and painted gray. Most were decommissioned and scrapped at the end of the First World War.

In a story about the Great White Fleet and an intoxicated sailor and a burro, Chiquita observes that alcohol has different effects in different cultures. Since alcohol tends to release inhibitions, this suggests that what is repressed in American culture is playfulness—that sounds right— and in Brazilian culture, sadness and hostility—well, I'm not so sure about that. Probably someone has studied this phenomenon—if it is one. Sadly, we have heard and seen a lot of gunboat diplomacy since the Great White Fleet.

The optimism of the Kubitschek years in the 1950s was short lived. Brazil fell once more  into the hands of the military. The next president, Jânio Quadros, resigned without explanation after seven months while his vice president, João Goulart, was out of the country. The speaker of the Chamber of Deputies was installed as interim president, which gave rise to a dispute between supporters and opponents of Goulart. The impasse threatened the stability of the nation. A creative compromise between opposing forces was made by means of a constitutional amendment, which changed the form of government to parliamentary rule, making the president little more than a figurehead. The vice president, João Goulart, then took office. The parliamentary experiment had little support except as a means to end the impasse, and was rejected in a vote of the people; Goulart was then elected in his own right in 1963. He was unable to complete his term because another military uprising toppled his presidency the following year. The leader of the coup, General Humberto de Alencar Castello Branco, was elected president by congress in 1964, ushering in twenty years of military dictatorship and harsh repression.

In 1983, when I returned to Brazil after an absence of twenty-seven years, high-rise hotels and apartments had replaced homes, not only along the beaches of Ipanema and Leblon but on the side streets as well. Traffic and pollution had increased along with the pace of life of the once-leisurely *cariocas*. The *lotações* I used to ride to work and all the *bondes* (streetcars) except the one to Santa Teresa had disappeared. The president was yet another military dictator, João Baptista de Oliveira Figueiredo.

Brazilians, who had not been allowed to vote for president since 1964, were about to demand the return of the democracy.

# 23. *Carnaval* in Rio, 1983

 *Rio de Janeiro, February, 1983*

After a long struggle with emphysema, Mother died in 1981. When she had been honored by her friends and relatives, and they had brought their love and comfort to us, when all the business of death was taken care of, and we were alone with our loss, we three sisters scattered her ashes in the woods near the same lake where we had strewn our father's twenty-two years before. As we held each other and wept, we knew in our bones that our mother lived within us forever. I kept a small piece of bone from the body that had brought me into the world, and on my way out of Athens I planted it under an elm tree in the yard of the house on Highland Avenue where I had lived the first thirteen years of my life.

Twenty-five years had passed since I had lived with Uncle Neco and his family in Rio and with the de Paula family in Vitória, and I was longing to return. In those years I had married, raised two children, and divorced. I suggested to my sisters that we use part of our inheritance to take a trip to Brazil together, reminding them that Daddy had waited to take Mother to his birthplace, and it had never happened. Jan declined, but Sydney and I began planning a six-week trip. We decided to spend half of the time on a Brasil Airpass, the other three weeks in Rio, and we decided to be there for *Carnaval*.

Sydney and I are greeted at Galeão Airport in Rio by Sima and Saúl, Brazilian friends I met in Berkeley. It is my first arrival at this airport, which is located on an artificial island in the bay far from downtown Rio. It is not nearly as dramatic as the approach to Santos Dumont, the older, domestic airport downtown. They take us to their apartment right across the street from Arpoador Beach, where Ipanema begins.

The view of the Atlantic from Sima and Saúl's living room is truly *maravilhosa!* They live in one of two apartments on the eighth floor of a ten-story building near the corner of Rua Joaquim Nabuco and Avenida Viera Souto, which runs along the beaches of Ipanema. The entire front of the apartment is glass, with sliding doors off the living room to a standing-room-only balcony from which you can see, hear, and smell the open ocean. The apartment is spacious and graciously furnished with lots of books, classical records, and paintings by Brazilian artists. The parquet floors are polished daily; everything is spotless.

Syd and I go right to the beach. We swim and walk to the rocks at Arpoador, where I said goodbye to Brazil so long ago. Sima takes us for a little drive. We go down Afrânio de Melo Franco, but I can't even find the place where Uncle Neco and Aunt Ginger's house had been among all the high-rise apartment buildings that have replaced it and the others on the street. That night they take us to dinner at a *churrascaria*.

A *churrasco* is a Brazilian-style barbeque. You start with a salad bar, and then servers bring all kinds of meat to your table. The meat is pierced by a long skewer; the waiter takes a long sword-like knife and whacks off a slice or hunk onto your plate. There is beef of many different cuts and pork, lamb, sausage, chicken, fish, and variety meats. Waiters bring onion salsa, rice, *farofa* (manioc flour cooked with onions, bacon, and eggs), fried bananas, and collard greens to the table in large serving dishes. The waiters just keep coming and offering various meats until you tell them to quit.

Back in our room in the apartment with shades drawn, we sort, count, and hide from possible intruders our big pile of *cruzeiros* that Saúl has changed for us. This currency is going to be tricky; we are not used to denominations in the tens of thousands.

The next day Syd and I go downtown on the bus to arrange an itinerary for our Brasil Airpass, good for 21 days of flights anywhere in Brazil. In the years since I left here, much has changed, and I have come with some trepidation because I loved it so much when I was young. I wondered if I would be disappointed, but it still excites me, and it is wonderful to be showing it to Sydney. We arrange our trip; we will go to Manaus first, and then wing it from there. It's wonderful to be walking around downtown!

We take a *bonde* over the *Lapa* arches (the old aqueduct built in the early 1800s) and up the hill to Santa Teresa, where we stroll through the cobblestone streets lined with flowering trees and colonial houses covered with bougainvillea. From here we have a breathtaking view of Corcovado and the city. Then we catch a bus and another *bonde*, the one that goes straight up Corcovado. As we look down from the top of the mountain, clouds float below us, partly obscuring the panoramic view of the city, the bay, the outline of the ragged shoreline. As they shift and shrink we peek through the veil to see here a scene of bustling metropolis, there a piece of velvet green rainforest, and again a sight of the Atlantic looking smooth and static.

We come home on the bus through Flamengo, Botofogo, Copacabana; all the while I'm pointing out landmarks and sharing memories. Everything is familiar; everything has changed. The language is difficult, but I'm listening and speaking. The air pollution is terrible—that is the worst change—and the drivers in Rio are reckless and inconsiderate. Everyone is in a hurry. These are not the relaxed, good-natured *cariocas* that I remember from before. But pedestrians are friendly and helpful, always warning us (unnecessarily, we think) of thieves—they point at our purses and say, "Teef, teef!" Back home, we sit by the beach for a while then we come in and Saúl puts on a violin record "to relax us." We listen; we go to bed exhausted. Next day after breakfast we go to Pão de Açúcar for a spectacular view of the *Cidade Maravilhosa*. Another day we're up early and off to the beach. I swim to Arpoador and back; it feels wonderful.

After another swim at sunset, we have dinner at home with Sima and Saúl, then take a walk and have mango juice at a fruit stand. I want to try to connect with Renato, my shipboard romance a quarter century ago, but I am too shy and too insecure to attempt Portuguese on the telephone. Sima calls at random one of the four Renato Coutinhos in the phone book—and a woman tells her that he is dead. We have no way of knowing whether this was *my* Renato, but the news upsets us both, and we give up trying to find him while hoping he is still alive. I fall into bed exhausted.

Today I'm feeling tired and achy—jet lag catching up to me, I guess. We're taking it easy today; we walk around for a couple of hours in the Jardin Botânico, established by Don João in 1808 when he was regent. It is badly neglected, but we see some interesting trees, including the famous Royal Palms and the monkey's apricot, and we see lots of birds. Afterwards we go to Rua Senador Vergueiro looking for the *IBEU*, but we can't find it—I guess it's gone.

Sydney is really fun to be with—she is getting a huge charge out of everything. She doesn't mind, and even seems to enjoy, my hunt-and-peck method of getting around. We are always on the same wavelength it seems, and we both enjoy spontaneous discoveries. I think Sima and Saúl are enjoying her very much too. They are perfect hosts—leaving us lots of freedom to go on our adventures, but still so gracious and warm. One evening, we watch my old pupil Jardel Filho on a TV *novela*, the prime-time soap operas that are so popular here, and then go for a walk for *sorvete*, the Brazilian ice cream that comes in delicious tropical fruit flavors and is sold in stands all over the city. Time is going fast, but we are seeing a lot.

Sima and Saúl will be going to their mountain home in Teresópolis tomorrow, Sunday, to get away from the madness of *Carnaval*. Syd and I will be alone for two days in this fabulous apartment—the maid has *Carnaval* off. We spend today with our hosts on a drive through the Tijuca Forest. The roads are narrow and winding, and although their car has seat belts in the front, they don't use them because, as Sima explains, "It's not the fashion here." Syd and I shudder and keep our eyes off the road, awed by the emerald kingdom that surrounds us. Under the canopy of green, there is more green underbrush, with tangles of vines lacing everything together, and rays of light filtering through, focusing our gaze first on one, then another vignette of the shady forest. Here and there a waterfall stumbles over rocks and sprays the air. It's cool up here; the air is soft and refreshing. Birds and butterflies and the occasional monkey fly among the trees. We stop for a view of the lagoon at the *Mesa do Imperador* (the Emperor's Table), the huge granite rock where legend says Dom Pedro II had picnics with his family, then we get views of Corcovado and Pão de Açucar from *Vista Chinesa* (Chinese View—for some reason there is a pagoda here!) and the Dona Marta Belvedere, another overlook just below the summit of Corcovado.

Returning this evening, we hear *Carnaval* rhythms on the Avenida and hurry to the window to see the transvestites' parade go by just as the sun is setting behind *Dois Irmãos*, the mountain called "Two Brothers," and the sea is smooth and pink. Syd and I hurry outside to watch. The parade passes by on the Avenida in front of Ipanema beach, and the mood is wild and exuberant—the air sizzles with hilarity at the outrageous caricatures of female sexuality and mannerisms. A hairy-chested Lady Godiva dressed in black bra and garter belt and a man's hat rides by on a fake donkey. Red Riding Hood and Orphan Annie strut and wiggle their huge breasts and buttocks, throwing kisses to the crowd. It's over-the-top vulgar, but lighthearted, gay in both senses of the word.

We follow along, dancing The parade ends in front of a bar, *Garota de Ipanema*, supposedly where Tom Jobim wrote the song that made the "Girl from Ipanema" famous. A band is playing and people are dancing in the streets. Now Syd and I join performers and other spectators in the street outside the bar, jumping wildly and swinging our hips to the samba beat. No policemen in sight; no one is bothering anyone else. The men preen like peacocks, pose, and invite us to take pictures

We have been in Rio for a week, and already are familiar with the many *Carnaval* songs that play incessantly on radios all over the city. Tonight is the all-night parade, so we must take it easy today. We wait until Sima and Saúl leave for Teresópolis, then hop on a bus to the end of the line at Jacarepaguá, just to see another part of the city. On the way back we see many floats and people in costume.

The excitement last night was so intense; I can't imagine what tonight will be like. Syd and I are both whirling with wonder and pleasure. *Carnaval* has changed a lot since my first visit. There are still parades down Av. Rio Branco, but the main competition now takes place on Av. Presidente Vargas. The big parade—it is really a parade of parades—is now sponsored by Riotur (the official promoter of tourism in Rio) and the best seats cost more than 100 dollars, but there are lots of cheaper places in open sections high in the stands, and Saúl has given us tickets for two of these.

At four or so we hop on the *Integração*, the bus that connects to the subway station in Botofogo, then we go underground on the *metrô* to our destination. We find our section and choose our place. To our surprise there are no benches, just concrete tiers wide enough to dance in place on, or on which we can sit if the person in front happens to be sitting too. Excitement charges the air as before a thunderstorm. As soon as the *bateria* (drum corps) of the first *escola* is heard, all leap to their feet and begin dancing in the stands. Then the familiar song begins, and the crowd goes wild.

Each *escola* is led by its baton-twirling *Mestre Sala*, the Dance Master dressed in 18th century costume, and his partner, the *Porta Bandeira*, the Flag Bearer; she bears the flag with the colors of the *escola*, strutting to the rhythm of the *bateria*. We know that each *escola* has an *enrêdo*, or theme, that is carried out in the song, costumes, and floats, and each *escola* is divided into many *alas*, or wings, of perhaps a hundred dancers each. Each *ala* will be costumed to elaborate one aspect of the *enrêdo*. Sandwiched in between the *alas* are the elaborately decorated, many-tiered floats with actors, musicians, and *fútebol* (soccer) heroes riding on them, hanging onto poles for support, dancing in place, waving to the crowd.

Tradition demands that one *ala* be of *Baianas*, middle-aged black women dressed in the typical costume of Bahia, long hoop-skirts, turbans, beads—a contrast to the mostly young, scantily-dressed dancers who make up the other *alas*. The *Baianas* do a graceful twirling dance, also in contrast to the frenetic, sexy dancing of the other *sambistas*. And scattered among the floats are more drum major/majorette teams, more *baterías*. They get a big cheer from the crowd.

It takes a little over an hour for the first *escola de samba* to go past us, then there is a 30- to 45-minute wait until it gets far enough up the street so that the next *escola* can begin without the two songs competing. We are happy to sit and rest in between. During the third *escola's* parade, it begins to rain; the lights on our end of the street go out and we sit for half an hour at least in darkness. No one moves; no one comments on the sudden darkness, the *sambistas* keep on dancing. We run for shelter under the roof at the top of the stadium, and we watch the parade from there. It is the best so far, but we are wet and uncomfortable. We know we have at least a half-hour wait for the next *escola* without any place to sit down, then an hour of jumping and getting shoved by other dancers and people moving around. We have been here four-and-a-half hours and the parade is only a quarter over.

*Carnavaleiros, 1983.*

We know we can't possibly last all night, so we decide to go home.
We walk through a sea of mud, garbage, and human bodies, dancing,
jumping, calling out their wares, past the costumed *sambistas* and
elaborate floats waiting in line for their turn. We push our way through
this happy, dirty, hot, muddy, smelly, crazy crowd of people to the *metrô*.
Inside, coming towards us is a group of costumed, singing people dancing
their way off the train. One man grabs my hand and we do a happy
turn. For the first time I feel a part of the spectacle. When we get to the

apartment, we discover we have only missed one-and-a-half *escolas* in transit. We watch it on TV until we fall asleep around 3:30.

On TV, we have a close-up look at the fantastic costumes and floats. Even more unbelievable are the people in the stands who never sit down but keep dancing all night long. When we wake up around six we find that once again we have missed only one-and-a-half *escolas*. Now they are really getting elaborate in costume, with more professional-looking floats and better choreography. Our favorite is one with an ecological theme about the destruction of the rainforest, the spoiling of indigenous cultures by the Europeans, and the re-conquering of the jungle. The white man arrives on a bird-like plane (or plane-like bird) spewing smoke from its beak, with an old car on top and beer cans hanging down. We watch the parade until it ends at 12:30 in the afternoon, about 18 hours after it had started, by which time the temperature downtown is over 40° Celsius (104° Fahrenheit) and people are still in the stands, and still dancing. We are flabbergasted!

Next day we are to leave Rio and start our Brasil Airpass tour. I wake with a raspy throat from the air pollution. I go for a brief swim and then rush to get off on time for the flight to Manaus.

# 24. The Amazon

 *Manaus, Amazonas, February 1983*

Sydney and I are both hot and tired when we arrive at the Hotel Tropical outside of Manaus. The hotel is very large and elegant, but here we meet only other tourists. The air conditioner doesn't seem to be functioning, and there is a musty smell in the room—maybe all over this very humid city. I prefer to be nearer the heartbeat of each city I visit. We want to see the Amazon, but we don't want to share a big tour boat with a lot of people. I call Moacir Pereira, a guide who takes people on individual tours in his motorized canoe. I want to see if we can arrange something, and I make a date to meet him tomorrow evening at our hotel.

The next day in Manaus is extremely hot and humid, but we do our tourist duty, seeing the Indian Museum and the city's pride, the *Teatro Amazonas*, the Victorian opera house built in 1896 in the middle of the jungle during the rubber boom, where legend says Enrico Caruso sang. That evening, we meet Moacir for a drink by the pool and tell him we want to see wildlife, and also something of the social and commercial life on the river. Over a couple of *caipirinhas*, a Brazilian cocktail made of limes, sugar, and *cachaça* (a rum made from sugar cane), it is all arranged for tomorrow. Moacir tells us to dress in our bathing suits, bring shorts, tops, and cover-ups, our toothbrushes, soap, and mosquito repellant.

Next morning Moacir is here early; we jump in his car and go to a supermarket for supplies. We buy beer, cokes, a frozen duck, cheese, mortadella, and candy for the children we are sure to meet on the trip. (Mo's insistence—I would rather give them something healthy!) Mo says we will fish and buy produce from farmers along the way. Another stop for ice and bread, then we go to the place where Mo's canoe is docked: a bustling pier with lots of garbage floating in water that smells like an open sewer. We load the boat and take off. I am full of misgivings, but I have some kind of trust in our ability to survive. I know Syd and I are to have a great adventure.

We pass the port of Manaus with all its shacks on stilts at water's edge; we stop for gas, and then take off across the Amazon. We have to cross this wide river and it is *very* choppy, with huge waves, unusual for February. One wave explodes over our bow, and Mo yells to us to move back in the boat. Fearing we will capsize, he decides to get us out of the center of the river. We get to a bank on the leeward side of an island, tie up to a floating log used to keep other lumber from escaping, and wait there for calmer waters.

The Amazon is a system of many rivers, and near Manaus two of the largest tributaries, the Solimões and the Rio Negro, join at the famous tourist destination called the Meeting of the Waters. The Solimões is reddish brown, carrying lots of mud, and very fecund; the Rio Negro is dark and clear, containing lots of tannic acid, and the two ribbons of water flow in the same channel for 6 kilometers before merging. We are going upriver in the opposite direction from the meeting of the two rivers, but it is possible to go from one river to the other through *igarapés*, those seasonal waterways in the forest that small boats can navigate.

While we wait for smoother waters, we swim in the Rio Negro, which Mo assures us is safe, without the seven deadly perils of the Solimões. He lists them: a large fish that pulls one down to the depths to drown, a very small fish that swims up the urethra into the bladder and wreaks some sort of havoc there, the electric eel, the *jacaré* (an alligator, or caiman), the anaconda, the piranha, and the mosquito, which can carry malaria or yellow fever. The water of the Rio Negro is the color of dark tea, and very transparent; our skin through the water appears quite red.

Back in the boat, the waves calm down and Mo says it is safe, so we cross to the south side of the river and motor down a tributary to a fishing village where we stop to rest because it is too hot to be on the river. There is a young woman there with two children, her niece and nephew. I talk with her a little but she is shy, and so am I. The shack, built on stilts over the water, is cooler than outside; bare except for benches, a table, and a big shrine with religious and family pictures and candles. There are several calendars on the wall including a cartoon of a couple in bed with a caption that translates, "I don't care if you're poor, as long as you're hard."

We fish, and Syd catches a piranha, which Mo assures us is very good to eat. When Mo decides it is cool enough, we leave and motor to a wonderful spot under the trees where we have our lunch; Mo fishes for bait and naps. Syd and I read a little, gaze at the wonders around us, and slap at mosquitoes. Mo wakes up and we take off again through *igarapés*, seeing giant kingfishers, terns, snow herons, and butterfly birds (Wattled Jacana). These are particularly beautiful, with dark, red-brown bodies, green-black necks and heads, wings that are yellow in flight. We see numerous other colorful birds—red and black, yellow and black, the lugubrious vultures called *urubu* (lots of them), and hawks.

We row silently through a protected area and see huge iguanas in trees full of noisy parakeets. As we take turns rowing, Mo tells us about life on the river and about Indian villages farther upriver. He himself speaks several Indian languages, as well as Portuguese, Spanish, English, French, and German. His knowledge of the river is prodigious, and we are learning about the river itself, the amazing seasonal flooding of the forest, and how the flora and fauna have adapted to that.

Around five, we stop near a farmhouse, follow Mo up the steep bank and find two thatched-roof shacks connected by a plank. The houses are on stilts, protection from the annual rise of the river. On the ground, zinnias and marigolds protrude from sun-baked soil. A little apart from the dwellings there is a rubber tree grove, and a man is repairing a fishing boat under the trees. He is friendly and curious. He tells me nine people live in the two houses—he and his wife, two daughters, four grandchildren, and a son-in-law. He asks where we live, how old we are, and he's amazed that I still have my teeth at age fifty. He and Mo show us rubber seeds, and demonstrate how they cut the bark of the tree to get rubber. Mo arranges for us to sleep there and we leave for an exploration, telling them we'll be back about eight.

The sun is setting as we zip down the river through floating islands and *Victória Regia* water lilies with their gigantic pads, between 4 and 6 feet across. He steers the boat close enough for us to see and smell the blossoms as they open. Soon we come to a place where the *boitos*, pink river dolphins, are playfully, gracefully, leaping from the water—magical! I want to swim with them, but Mo says there'll be time later, and slyly reminds me that according to Indian folklore, they are responsible for getting maidens pregnant! As it darkens, fireflies come out and we hear the mating calls of crickets and frogs. Mo shines his flashlight on the water's edge, and we see the red eyes of several alligators. Suddenly, Mo turns the boat, guiding it into a small stream almost completely covered by water hyacinths. Fireflies on the water's surface look like fallen stars. Tall trees on both banks arch overhead, cathedral-like. Vines and moss cascade from trees. The waxing moon hovers in the heavy, warm, perfumed air.

Mo turns off the motor and we glide in awed silence. We are in a very sacred place. The sounds are a perfect harmony of jungle voices; besides crickets and frogs we hear owls, monkeys, the swooshing of wings, the soft staccato plinking made by unseen animals breaking the surface of the still water, the syncopated cadences of insect songs, and many melodies impossible to identify. Just as in an orchestra, the tones and rhythms of each, heard individually, blend perfectly in the whole. But unlike a symphony concert, there is no coughing; in fact there are no extraneous sounds at all, no sounds of civilization. We are in the Garden of Eden, yet I know the struggle of life and death is all around us. A few stars shine above the canopy of trees. Sydney and I hold each other and silently weep.

We arrive back at the farm about nine. The shack is about 8 feet above ground level, now many feet above the river. A ladder leads to the opening of the house; there is no door. At the height of the flooding of the forest, the family will be able to take their boat nearly to their house. Inside the door, there is a big room with a table at one end and some crude benches along the other walls. On the wall above the table is a sort of collage of magazine pictures and political posters. Under the house live chickens, pigs, and a dog. The family also has a parrot named Rosita. Mo hands the grandmother our duck, which he has cut up on a paddle, and we get acquainted while she cooks it. The family is hospitable, friendly.

Behind the front room where we hang our hammocks, there are two enclosed sleeping rooms for the two couples with a passageway outside them leading to the kitchen in back. This is a small open room with a table holding two big bowls of water and some cooking utensils. On the floor are some gourds full of more water. On one side of the room is a place where the fire is built. Upon this is a big kettle where the duck is cooked with rice, garlic, onions—I don't know what else, but it is delicious!

On the wall common to the kitchen and bedroom are some shelves with a few cups, glasses, bowls, and spoons. In front of this is the table at which we eat. Although we invite everyone to join us, no one will sit with us except the grandfather. All the others stand around watching and talking, Mo telling jokes that I don't understand, but that all the family think very funny. Right after dinner, exhausted, we fall into our hammocks, covered with a canopy of mosquito netting, and we fall asleep happy. Next morning after coffee we boil some eggs and set off in the direction we had come. We see more dolphins, and then we attempt to cross the wide Amazon.

Mo wants to do it at just the right time so we won't run into difficulty like before, and he seems to know when that is. We start off across this huge expanse of water. It is choppy, and I enjoy riding the waves, feeling the spray. Suddenly waves are spilling into the boat, and Mo tells us to start bailing. I don't realize that we are in danger again until he begins praying out loud, *"Mãe de Deus, ajuda-me!"* ("Mother of God, help me!") We bail as fast as we can; even Mo is bailing while steering. It is precarious, but we make it to a huge island. Mo says in all his years on the river (thirty-five or so, I imagine) he has never seen such waves—not only big, but also chaotic, coming from all directions. He tells us one more wave would have capsized the boat. Syd is terrified; but somehow I don't feel afraid. At the time, I did think we might go over, but I knew we wouldn't drown, and I didn't even consider the possibility that we would be prey for any of the seven deadly scourges of the Amazon.

It is strange how safe and trusting I feel in this totally foreign environment. We are completely in Mo's hands, and I trust his ability and his judgment. We round the island and continue upriver before attempting the rest of the crossing. We see men harvesting jute and many women putting clothes in the water to soak, then soaping and slapping their laundry on the rocks. The crossing on the other side of the island is calm and uneventful.

We stop at a river store in a fishing village. These villages are becoming very familiar to us now—they are usually located in a cove with four to six houses on stilts built right over the river. Mo, who always asks the people what they grow and what they have to sell and what the river is like ahead, finds out they are making *farinha*, manioc flour, in a nearby hut. We take a little girl in the boat with us to show us the way, and then climb out of the boat and up a long ladder of tree limbs that leans against the bank to a thatched hut where a woman is toasting *farinha* in a round, shallow, flat pan, five feet in diameter, built over a roaring fire. She stirs the *farinha*, flipping it in the air with a long-handled wooden spatula. It is extremely hot in the shack. The ubiquitous skinny, mangy-looking dog drags himself about. There are several children, all curious, excited, and shy. Another woman is straining the liquid from the mass of the ground-up manioc that will become tapioca in a *tipiti*, a long, elastic tube woven of reeds, which she twists to get the liquid out. We are off again after leaving our little gifts, saying our thanks and goodbyes.

There is more cruising in the afternoon, enjoying the sounds and now-familiar sights, feeling lazy, contented, somehow at home in this exotic, overabundant place. We tie up to a tree on the side of a hill for lunch. Mo fishes, hoping to get us something to eat, but keeps catching the same small piranha over and over. After lunch, Mo says he will sleep under a tree for fourteen and a half minutes. Sydney sleeps, too, and I try but can't. The mosquitoes are biting—I want to get moving. Finally we do; when we leave this place it is late in the day.

We pass several homes and small farms along the riverbanks, and soon turn off on another waterway and see many birds, including the *hoatzin*, a large bird perched proudly high up in a tree, showing off his blue face, his long, skinny neck, and his small head with its impressive, peacock-like crest. We see lots of weaverbirds' nests and some monkeys, but we can't get close enough to get a really good look. I tell Mo I'd like to see some of those iridescent blue Morpho butterflies, whose wings appear on plates, trays, and jewelry in souvenir shops in Rio, and he says we will. Half an hour later, the forest is dancing with them. Mo, it seems, is a magician who can make anything appear!

We take turns rowing through lots of *igarapés* clogged with tall grass, water hyacinths, and lily pads. Sometimes Mo revs up the motor and charges right through. Always in these swampy places there are lots of giant kingfishers and butterfly birds. Around sunset, we see hundreds of snow herons having a meeting. The president is standing on the bare branch of a small, dead tree, with the sergeant-at-arms at his feet. All the rest, except for one or two rebels, are standing on a sandy beach facing these two, apparently listening attentively, or possibly just bored and faking it.

Sometime during the afternoon we pass from the muddy Amazon into the black waters of a tributary. Mo wants to have dinner in the boat before dark, and when the sun sets here it is almost immediately dark. But we aren't hungry, and we want to swim in the safer waters, so we keep going. Mo has forgotten to put Syd's piranha on ice, and is unsuccessful in catching anything else except small ones, which he throws back, so we're going to have to make do with what we've brought. Back on the Rio Negro, Mo finds a place in a wide bay. We're in the middle of a large lagoon with dark waters, smooth as glass—a black mirror reflecting the almost-full moon.

We let the boat drift while we swim. It's wonderful to cool our sticky, itchy bodies. We decide it is light enough by moonlight to eat in the boat. We eat hard-boiled eggs, cucumbers that we bought from a farmer along the way, mortadella sandwiches, and for dessert, *Romeu e Juliete: goiabada* (guava paste with Minas cheese). Afterwards we take off our clothes, slide out of the boat, soap ourselves, and swim again. Now we are really creatures of the river. It is marvelous to be in the warm air and water, in the moonlight, with the silhouettes of the trees encircling us and the night sounds chorusing. Sydney and I are ecstatic.

Mo begins to look for a place to sleep. He finds a fisherman's hut, makes the arrangements, and we scurry up the bank. I think it's eleven or so. Two men leave the large shack to sleep in a smaller one beside it. Our hut is much cruder than the one we slept in the night before; Mo says it's because fishermen are more or less nomadic. It is also on stilts, but not so high, and there is a big hole in the middle of the floor where they build their fire. There are no sides, just a thatched roof. There are chickens underneath, probably a dog. We hang our hammocks; the space is tight and our hammocks are almost touching one another. In the middle of the night some bats attack and kill a chicken and Mo and the fishermen get up. Sometime in the early morning, unable to sleep, I get up and go outside. I am too afraid of snakes to sit down, so I can't stay long, but it is lovely. The moon has set and the stars are bright and near. The *Cruzeiro do Sul* (Southern Cross) shines in the sky, a sign that all is well.

Sydney and I are up early, but Mo is already out fishing. He soon returns, without fish. He finds a coconut on the ground, cracks it open, and we have that, and coffee, for breakfast. We cruise down waterways, Mo always looking, directing our attention from one wonder to another. He seems to be looking for specific animals, and will suddenly shout, "Look!" or "There!" And we squint and try with naked eyes and binoculars to see whatever it is. We are constantly being reminded of how much sharper his powers of observation are than ours. This time it is a sloth lumbering down a branch high in the trees. Later, Mo points out a carnivorous water plant that traps fish and roe in its roots. It has a small yellow flower, like a buttercup. I lift it up out of the water to see its roots, which break. Moacir winces, saying the plant is very sensitive, and I should be careful not to hurt it. I feel terrible.

We are almost out of food, so we try fishing in several different places. Syd catches a black piranha, the only catch of the day. Mo is frustrated, but remembering a small farm we have passed, he suggests we go back there to see if the people will sell us a kid (a baby goat, not a child!). He climbs out of the boat and up the bank and disappears. Sydney and I sit in the boat, feeling squeamish and suddenly vegetarian. While we are sitting there, hoping the farmer will refuse, we see the little goats scampering out of the forest, and Mo comes down and tells us to go up to the house, where a woman greets us, offers us chairs—this is the most prosperous looking place we have been in—and we talk as well as we can with me as interpreter. Mo is off with the men, butchering.

These river/forest people are called *caboclos*. They are civilized Indians or people of mixed Indian and European descent—the word also means backwoodsman—and their accents and many of their words are difficult for me, as are mine for them. It is awkward for us all, but they are pleasant. They offer us a drink made from *cupuaçu*, a brown fruit related to cacao. It's delicious, but the texture is strange; large lumps like the inside of grapes that you have to suck, and seeds you have to spit out. The women and children laugh at our ignorance of the fruit, so commonplace to them. Then we go to a wooded place where Mo builds a fire, roasts the kid, rests, and fishes. No luck, but we have to admit, the kid is delicious, and so is the piranha that Sydney provided.

We have been three days winding our way through narrow *igarapés* where the roots of trees and vines dig unseen somewhere beneath the caramel-colored water; we have drifted in the clear, tea-colored water of the Rio Negro and crossed the wide and turbulent Amazon, not knowing or caring where we were in relation to the rest of the world. Now we realize that the trip is nearing its end, and we are sad.

Just before sunset, we leave for Manaus; Moacir assures us that the crossing will be calm. It is. The full moon rises. It's warm, balmy. We are relaxing, sometimes singing. Mo flashes his light on the banks, either to see alligators or to find his way—it doesn't matter to us—we trust him completely now. Mo begins to shine his light around the boat, and suddenly a fish leaps out of the water, bounces off the oar, hits Syd in the head, and falls into the boat. Then it begins raining fish—we can't believe

Annita roasting a kid in the Amazon rainforest.

it—we all laugh with surprise and happiness. He tells us they are sardines; more than ten of them leap into the boat before we are back. After an unsuccessful day of fishing and the sacrifice of the kid, now we have fish vying with each other to get into our boat!

We make a brief stop at Mo's house where we meet his wife and his little daughter. He offers to cook the sardines for us, but we have only a short time before we have to catch the midnight plane for Recife. It is hard to believe we have been together for only three days; they have been so full of new and rich experiences, and we know each other so well now.

Sydney's piranha—good catch!

# 25. Netas do Fundador

Sydney and I arrive at the hotel in Recife exhausted and still feeling grungy from the river. We take a long time bathing and grooming, have a short nap, lunch, and go to bed early to make up for lost sleep. After a couple of days of quick sightseeing, including a spin on a *jangada* (a raft of logs lashed together with a single mast and sail, used by fishermen of the northeast coast) followed by beer, shrimp, and some *umbu* (a plum-like fruit) with the fishermen, we are on the plane again bound for Salvador da Bahia.

It's not easy to be a tourist in Bahia; it is very hot; the spicy smells and exotic flavors of the unique Afro-Brazilian cuisine are intense, as are the vibrant colors of handiwork displayed everywhere, and the fervor of the unique Bahian brand of music. My body twangs with the overdose of sensation. We spend a few days in Bahia, a city on two levels connected by an elevator. The heart is the *Cidade Alta* (High City) adorned with gilded colonial churches built in the time of the sugar barons, and the *Cidade Baixa*, or Lower City, is where the port and markets are located. Short distances away, sugar-white beaches are shaded by palm trees rasping in the ocean breezes. Everywhere *Baianas* in their long white dresses, brilliant in the pulsing sunlight, sell spicy *acarajé* from their carts.

All over the city, groups of young men and sometimes young boys entertain us, playfully showing off their *capoeira* skills and collecting money in their gourds. *Capoeira* is a kicking martial art/dance form of African origin performed by two men (lately, occasionally by women), always accompanied by the *berimbao*, a musical instrument made out of a gourd, and drums. It was originally developed by slaves to disguise their battles from their masters, but is now an art form widely practiced in Bahia. Nearby Ilheus is the birthplace of Jorge Amado, the author of *Dona Flor and her Two Husbands* and many other historical novels of the colonial period, and the books seem to come alive here in Bahia, as does the music of Caetano Veloso, his sister Maria Bethânia, Gilberto Gil, and many other *Baianos*.

*Candomblé* is the Bahian equivalent of the spiritual practices of *Macumba* and *Umbanda* in Rio. All are derived from African religions brought to Brazil by the slaves. *Candomblé* is very strong here, and although it has been synthesized with Catholicism it seems to be truer to its African origin in this place. At the same time it has permeated the whole culture, so that many devout Catholics in Bahia also practice *Candomblé*. We go to the Afro-Brazilian museum where we see gorgeous carved wood panels, many with embedded cowrie shells, depicting the many divinities (*orixás*) of *Candomblé*, each with his and her unique characteristics and accoutrements.

And then we board a plane again and fly south. I want to see Vitória again and Sydney agrees, provided we include Iguaçu Falls on our trip. Since my stay here in 1955, Vitória has increased its population from 60,000 to half a million. It's a big disappointment to me—nothing is familiar. I can't find the street where I used to live with the de Paula family, the University, or the *Instituto*.

Back at the hotel, I study the phone book and a map I bought. I look for the Pastor's phone number; can't find it. Sydney says she thinks I dreamed my stay here, as it seems impossible that I don't recognize anything at all. She urges me to call Moacyr Cabral, my old friend. I find his number but I fear he won't remember me, or his wife might answer and be jealous, and I remember when Sima tried to call Renato and a woman told her he was dead. I go to bed feeling frustrated and bewildered and sleep poorly, dreaming that I've returned to the hotel to find many messages from people who have learned I'm here and want to see me.

The next day we are up early and we walk around looking for familiar sights, using the map. We find Parque Moscoso, but it is now dirty, uninteresting. Couples are necking on the benches in contrast to the quaint courting which took place twenty-five years earlier, when boys and girls in pairs circled the meticulously groomed park in opposite directions, speaking volumes with their eyes. We are discouraged and decide to leave today for Belo Horizonte, but there is no flight so we book one for tomorrow. Today we will go to Guarapari, the beach of black sand where my students had given me a *despedida*; we will spend the night there and return tomorrow for our flight to Belo Horizonte.

We return to the hotel, pack our bags, shower, and remembering my dream, I decide to screw up my courage and call Moacyr. He just happens to be home for lunch, and we arrange to meet at the bank where he works. What a pleasure to meet my old friend after all these years! He looks at me and, smiling, says to Sydney, "We are both older." He tells me the Pastor and Dona Orlinda are now living in Vila Velha, on the mainland. He calls them for me, and it is arranged for Syd and me to go to there right away to see them. We decide to forget about going to Guarapari.

Moacyr gives us instructions for the bus. We are watching for our stop when suddenly a young man seated behind us, who was not even born when I was last in Vitória, offers in English to help. I show him the address, and he says, "That is my grandfather's house!" I ask whose son he is, and he says, "Ruth's." Syd and I nearly faint with surprise. We just can't believe that in this city of half a million people, Ruth de Paula's son would be sitting in the seat behind us on the bus. Truly, this was a real coeencidence, as Vovó would say!

When the three of us get off the bus together, the Pastor is waiting. He hugs me, and then bursts out laughing when he hears the incredible story. We go to the house, where Dona Orlinda is waiting with *cafezinhos*. She also hugs me, saying, "*Minha filha—pensei que nunca mais que vê-la.*" ("My daughter—I thought I never would see you again.") All cheeks are damp. They had made quick arrangements while waiting for us; the Pastor tells me we are going to Guarapari that afternoon to spend the night at their apartment there. Syd and I are going to Guarapari after all!

I remember Praia Prêta, the beach with the radioactive black sand.[53] We have a swim there and that evening and the next day many family members appear, including Ruth and her husband Júlio, and many young people born since I left. They all greet us warmly, and seem to be delighted with the coincidence of our bus meeting.

---

53. The sands of old beaches along a roughly 500-mile portion of Brazil's Atlantic coast are naturally radioactive.

We say goodbye to the Pastor and Dona Orlinda in Guarapari; he blesses us, and Ruth and Júlio take us to the airport and wave as we board for the flight to Belo Horizonte. We are running out of time on the Airpass, so on arriving there, we immediately arrange a car and driver to take us to the colonial towns of Congonhas where we see Aleijadinho's[54] statues of the Prophets at the Igreja de Bom Jesus de Matosinhos, and the beautiful Ouro Preto, now an International Heritage Site, where the *Inconfidência Mineira* (Conspiracy of Minas Gerais) ended in betrayal and martyrdom.

We enjoy a good lunch of *comida mineira* (cuisine of the state) then return to Belo Horizonte, where we make arrangements for an early morning flight to Brasilia, and after a day-and-a-half of architectural feasts there—the government buildings, monuments, the magnificent Cathedral, sculptures, fountains, and memorials spread far apart and very consciously arranged on this wide plateau of red dirt—we are in the air again for Iguaçu Falls.

The falls are breathtaking. Each turn of the path down a bank on the Brazilian side offers a new view of falling, muddy water; we keep walking, ending at a place where you walk way out on a long path cantilevered over the chasm. We get soaking wet. The falls are impressive, but I am most surprised by the tiny yellow butterflies somehow able to flutter around flowers that cling to the mossy cliff behind the hurtling cataracts, defying gravity, wind, and the steep plunge of water. The lunch beside the pool at the hotel is dreadful; even the gadabout emu who snatches a piece off my plate can't eat it, but that night the *Cruzeiro do Sul* blesses us as we enjoy our dinner in the garden of our hotel, listening to live Paraguayan music and hearing the sound of roaring water. And then, to Rio de Janeiro!

Back in Rio, we have five days left; we check into a hotel on the beach at Arpoador, take walks on the beach, swim, do easy things. Once in the early morning, we see a whole school of dolphins close to shore. Sydney wants to visit the cemetery where our grandfather is buried, but we don't know which one it is. She points out that the YMCA—the *ACM*

54. Antônio Francisco Lisboa (1738–1814), called "Aleijadinho" (little cripple) was a major influence on Brazilian baroque art and architecture. The son of a Portuguese architect and his slave, he was severely handicapped, and worked by means of tools tied to hands. His work can be seen in the churches of old mining towns in Minas Gerais (Mann, *12 Prophets of Aleijadinho*).

here—probably knows, and wants me to call them. I don't want to—I don't like making phone calls in Brazil; I have trouble understanding people on the phone. "Besides," I tell her, "They may think they have to make a fuss over us, and then we will spend our last day in Rio with me trying to interpret and respond to everything, and you forcing smiles and nodding without having a clue what is going on." My sister is persistent; so, feeling a little foolish, finally I agree to call, explaining to a receptionist that we are *netas do fundador* (the founder's granddaughters) and that we want to find out where our grandfather is buried. We go out, and upon returning to the hotel we find a message saying they will send a driver for us tomorrow at ten to take us there.

That night, our last, dressed in our best, we go with Sima and Saúl to an elegant Portuguese restaurant where I have delicious *bacalhau* (codfish) and we listen to two *fadistas*—singers of *fado*, the traditional Portuguese songs of fate. The restaurant on the *lagoa*, the beautiful lagoon that lies at the base of Corcovado, serves delicious food, and the *fadistas* are plaintive, authentic. Sima and Saúl sing operatic arias on the way home, telling us that's how he had courted her.

On our last day in Rio we are up at five to see the sun rise from the beach. At a little after ten, a car and driver, with a staff member from the *ACM*, arrive at the hotel to take us to the Cemetério de São Franciso Xavier where we see the tombstone with the name and dates of our grandfather, Myron Clark, along with those of Uncle Neco and our cousin Jim, who died in São Paulo shortly after I left Brazil. From there they take us to the *ACM* in Lapa and tell us that after a stop there we are to be taken to lunch. We are greeted by the General Secretary, Sr. Civitate. He seems very excited to meet us and takes us on a tour of the building, snapping our picture beneath one of our grandfather, which is hanging in a conference room.

During the tour, Sr. Civitate steers us to a little gift shop in the building and asks if we want to select a remembrance. We choose T-shirts, and then he asks if we would like tote bags as well, which we accept. Suddenly, as if we had just won a contest without even knowing we had entered, we have a new identity. We are introduced to everyone very respectfully, as the "*Netas do Fundador*." Afterwards, in the General Secretary's office, we meet Tasso da Silveira who is waiting for us. He's about seventy years old, with lots of energy. He is writing a history of the *ACM* in Brazil, and wants to talk with us about our impressions of our grandfather, not realizing that he died in 1920, a decade before I was born.

Before leaving for lunch, Sr. Civitate presents me with an orchid (because I am older), and Sydney with a bunch of roses; then Tasso kisses our hands, and we are joined by two other directors and go to lunch at a *churrascaria* in Botofogo, facing Pão de Açucar. We have a delicious lunch and pleasant conversation. My predictions are playing out on an even grander scale than I had imagined, but instead of being perturbed, we are touched by the courtesies shown to us and by the esteem in which our grandfather is held ninety years after the founding. They return us to our hotel with gracious goodbyes.

We spend the rest of the day on the beach, feeling very sad to leave Brazil. Sydney and I watch the sun set behind Dois Irmãos from the beach. We stay until dark and then go to Sima and Saúl's for dinner. Their sons are all here, and they are all very warm and gracious. On the way to the airport, I realize that we are leaving a part of ourselves behind in Brazil. This time, I know I will return.

# 26. Broader Horizons

We were a big family aboard the *Tennyson* in 1904. Just think, six children from 7 months to 10 years old! The ships that joined the States and South America were not palaces like now. The rails around the deck didn't have a wire net to protect the children from falling overboard, and as they were so used to lots of space and climbing, it was a worry all the time to me and for my husband a constant watching. I was seasick, although it was not as bad as the first time, and some of the children were too, so Myron had considerable work with them.

Passing near the islands of the West Indies we could see the lava flows, the destruction of St. Pierre, and the smoke and cinders shooting skyward from Mt. Pelée.[55] The cinders landed in the water, creating opal-like spots on the emerald Caribbean. On the eve of May 20th we anchored by the Statue of Liberty for the night. What a grand sight!

After seeing dear Uncle Henry and the other dear relatives in Buffalo we went to Minneapolis where we were welcomed by the family who were no longer strangers to me. We had not been in Minneapolis very long when Baby (Argentina) was taken ill with Scarlet Fever. Two of the other children had very mild cases. When we arrived, there was so much excitement over these Brazilian children that many times we counted thirty and forty children playing with them around our house, but right after the quarantine sign appeared on the front door, you couldn't see a person for blocks and blocks around. And that was not all—just a little before the quarantine was over we were visited by the tail of a tornado, which knocked down the steeples of several churches!

As the children were not used to being kept in the house, and there was no fence around the yard, we were facing a hard situation, but my

---

55. Mt. Pelée, a volcano in Martinique, erupted on May 8, 1902, destroying the colonial city of St. Pierre, which had been known to European tourists as the Paris of the Antilles (Zebrowski, *Last Days of St. Pierre*, 31).

husband and I made it so serious that we had no trouble; they never disobeyed. One of the neighbors told us that our little two-year-old Neco appeared on the porch one morning with a little rubber elephant and, as a child would do, was making it walk the porch rail back and forth, when suddenly it fell outside. The rules were for them not to step out from the porch. He stayed there looking at his elephant for some time. Then she noticed that he had made a decision. He looked all around and quickly as a flash went down the steps, got the animal, and ran to the porch as quickly as he had gone down, always looking to see if there was anybody watching him.

We were not yet out of quarantine when my husband left for a speaking tour, and when he returned, he immediately announced to me his resolution—he and I were going to the World's Fair in St. Louis, the Louisiana Purchase Centennial. He wrote to his brother's wife Nan, a fine, intelligent, and unselfish girl, asking her to come and stay with the children. We also had very good help; a cook and the maid who helped with the children. Nan came immediately and so we were off to the Fair. It was the first time we ever left all the children to go away together! We saw all those things one sees in fairs

We made the Brazilian building our headquarters. A replica of this building stands now at the entrance of our principal avenue Rio Branco, which was opened that year of 1904. At the fair, I met a very distinguished Brazilian couple who had traveled around the world, and were then visiting the United States for the first time. Anyone familiar with the restrictions placed upon women in Europe and South America, who was coming to this country when the bicycle fever was at its height, would be either shocked or delighted with women's freedom. This lady was delighted, and on going back to Brazil she published in a little book her traveling experiences. Among other things that she wrote I remember this: "If I were to be born again and had the privilege to choose what I wanted to be, I would like to be a dog in France, a soldier in Germany, and a woman, by all means, in the United States." If I were to be born again, I would let the Lord choose my birthplace, and as He makes no mistakes I am sure He would choose South America again! We did enjoy every minute of those ten days away, but we were very glad to get back to our babies on the 30th of September.

While away, Myron had decided to spend the winter nearer New York, so after farewells in Minneapolis, we moved to East Aurora, New York, on the 21st of October, at the invitation of one of his cousins whose wife promised to arrange a furnished house for us. Her mother and sister lived right next door to us in an old-fashioned house in an apple orchard and the old lady herself was old-fashioned, but her daughter was a very up-to-date and fine young lady.

When we arrived in the house there was a bushel of apples in the cellar and a big pan of applesauce in the kitchen from this next-door neighbor, Gramma Lyles. We had not been there many hours when she came in dressed very neatly in old-fashioned garments and said, "I am so tickled to have a large family next door to me. There has not been one as large around me since I raised my nine children. I want you to let them come to my place any time they want." My, what a relief! My six children were not a problem anymore, but a pleasure! We were near Buffalo, and our dear Uncle Henry came to see us very frequently and on Christmas he was a regular Santa Claus. While in East Aurora, we visited the Roycroft community[56] where quality, not quantity, was emphasized.

My husband was very anxious for me to have a chance to see historical places in Philadelphia and the seat of the government of this land of freedom, so as I had a fine maid and the dear old lady Mrs. Lyles and her daughter were very near, everything was arranged for me to go with him to these places. In Washington we were taken to the White House, where we met the new President, Theodore Roosevelt, and the Secretary of War, Mr. Taft. Knowing that my husband was in YMCA work Roosevelt said, "I just signed, a few minutes ago, permission for barracks to be built in Panama for headquarters for a YMCA for the soldiers there." We visited Washington's monument and saw there the stone sent by the Brazilian Emperor, Dom Pedro II, with the arms of the Empire carved into it.

This reminds me of a little true story about Dom Pedro that came to me

---

56. The Roycroft Press and community of craft workers and artists were influential in the Arts and Crafts Movement in the United States at the turn of the twentieth century. The emphasis on quality craftsmanship was a reaction to the dehumanizing effects of mass production. The Roycroft began to decline after Hubbard and his wife died in the sinking of the *Lusitania* in 1915.

first-hand from Orton who heard it right from Alexander Graham Bell
who was speaking at Mt. Hermon School in Massachusetts. As Orton
tells it, in 1876 the Emperor of Brazil, who was a guest of honor at the
Centennial Exposition in Philadelphia, met Mr. Bell in Boston at the
Institute for the Deaf and Mute where Bell taught and worked with his
invention. Mr. Bell spoke about it to the Emperor, and later took his
"little machine" to the exposition to demonstrate it, but did not succeed
in attracting the attention of the judges. Suddenly, in the last days of the
exposition he saw the Emperor, who, recognizing him asked, "How is
it going with the deaf-mute and your invention?" Mr. Bell then invited
the Emperor and the judges who then almost begged to be included, to
attend his demonstration. He took the transmitter, gave the receiver to
Dom Pedro, and read a poem. The Emperor, quite moved, exclaimed,
"*My God, it talks!*" The judges, until then uninterested in his invention,
took the receiver in turn and marveled at the discovery. It was thus that
before leaving Philadelphia, Alexander Graham Bell received the patent
for his invention, in great part owing to the interest Dom Pedro II
showed in it.

We were back to East Aurora on the 8th of February to a warm
reception from the children, and on the 15th of that same month, Myron
was on the road again. The end of the vacation was nearing. There were
going to be big YMCA Conventions in Paris, Holland, and Portugal. Our
dear old friend José Braga, being a Portuguese, was very anxious for my
husband to be present at this one, so he offered to pay the extra fare in
order that we might go to Europe! I could hardly believe that this dream
was going to come true! I was going to Paris, where every Brazilian who
could afford to, would surely visit. Paris where the Eiffel Tower and the
Ferris Wheel had made such a sensation! Paris, the scene of the novels
that my well-read grandmother had told us about: Paris of the Bastille,
Notre Dame, the Bois de Boulogne, Napoleon, and more than anything
else, the Paris of Victor Hugo who I knew from my own reading. Paris,
the capital of the world! Whenever I am over the waves, I am sick and
disgusted with myself; but this time, I went with great expectations!
London was not so familiar to me, because the adventures of Sherlock
Holmes were not yet in the language of Camões.

Preparations began. Relatives came from Minneapolis, Kansas City, and Buffalo at different times to say goodbye. In New York City the Association gave a reception in our honor and presented us with two cups; inside them was fifty dollars! Many friends including one of my oldest and dearest teachers, Mrs. Magalhães, now living in Brooklyn, came on board to see us off on the *Minnetonka* bound for London. My new friends from East Aurora gave me a package of letters—one for every day on board. It was such a surprise and a pleasure.

George, the baby, was fine, and there were many children on board for ours to play with. One day one of the deck stewards came to us with a smile on his face and Neco, our three-year-old boy in his arms, and said, "This boy fell in the cattle pen; he was not hurt; he is just scared!" So were we when we heard that! The steward explained that there was an open place on deck with a rail around it where you could see the cattle. He couldn't explain how Neco got over the rail, but he saw him when he landed in the pen. This boat had first class passengers and cattle! I don't think cattle sail to foreign countries anymore; they go through the packinghouses.

We docked at Tilbury, took a train to Liverpool Station, then to a Missionary Home in Tottenham. The fine house with a lovely garden and beautiful shady trees was given by some devoted woman to be used as a hotel for passing-through missionaries. It happened that there was nobody else there but our family, and the managers of the place were very willing to keep the younger children so we could go sightseeing. Our oldest boy, Orton, celebrated his tenth birthday in London on April the 4th.

We spent two weeks sightseeing there, including visiting St. Paul's Cathedral, Trafalgar Square, and Madame Tussaud's wax works. The children were spellbound by the Tuppenny Tube and the red-coated guards at Buckingham Palace. In Westminster Abbey the guide asked Ruth if she wanted to sit in the chair where all the English Kings and Queens had been crowned. My, would she? She talked about that for a long time. We went to the British Museum where we saw a Codex of the Bible and the Rosetta Stone. Myron took me to the Houses of Parliament where we heard Dillon and Balfour[57] speak in the House of Commons. We went to the Tower of London where we saw the Jewels of the Crown that we had seen before at the St. Louis Exposition.

Just as we were planning to leave for Paris, Miss Woods, one of the managers of the missionary home, said, "Why don't you leave the children here and you two go alone, so that you can have an opportunity to see Paris well? Then you can come back and get the children. We decided to accept the proposition. We left London to take the boat to Boulogne, now known by the entire world for that heroic retreat.[58] To say that I was very seasick does not describe my condition! The crossing was a bad one and most everybody was sick. I was in agony and probably would have welcomed a Nazi bomb! Ordinarily I felt all right when my feet were on land but even after we took the train to Paris my misery continued, and only after a good night's rest did I feel like myself. My courageous husband said that when the time came, he would go back alone and bring the children! What a relief!

Next day we started seeing Paris: the Trocadero Palace,[59] the Louvre, the Tuilleries Gardens, the Champs Elysées, Notre Dame, the Luxemburg Gardens, the Pantheon—I think it is here that we saw the great Victor Hugo's tomb. On Tiradentes Day, April 21, when in Brazil we honor the martyred hero of the first movement for independence of Brazil from Portugal, we saw the Place de la Bastille. Remembering those novels where this famous prison appeared frequently, I thought there would be a part of it, a wall or something of the Reign of Terror but no, just a monument to indicate the place!

From the top of the Eiffel Tower—I think it was the tallest construction in the world then—we could see at a distance a show going on; it was

---

57. John Dillon, leader of the Irish Parliamentary Party in the House of Commons before independence, and Arthur Balfour, author of the Balfour Declaration in 1917 to establish in Palestine a national home for the Jews.

58. On May 26, 1940, the evacuation of British, French and Belgian troops from Dunkirk was begun. Called Operation Dynamo, 251,000 troops were evacuated to England between May 28 and June 1. See Gardner, *Evacuation from Dunkirk*, 33.

59. Constructed for the 1878 *Exposition Universelle* (World's Fair), it was demolished to make way for the Palais de Chaillot at the 1937 exposition (Sutcliff, *Paris: An Architectural History*, 110–11).

Buffalo Bill! That night, we went to another performance of his show at eight o'clock at the Champs de Mars.

We visited Magdaleine Church and saw Good Friday service there. I shall never forget the enormous cross of flowers brought by the pious multitude. The windows were marvelous, especially the big one with Christ in Gethsemane. I wonder; what do these French people think now of all those saints that didn't save them from the Germans? And what about those Germans who had reformed their church because they wanted a purer Christianity?

Myron went back to England to get the children, crossing the channel from Calais to Dover. These place names were not written with blood on the pages of history as they are now! Another YMCA secretary and his wife, friends of ours, also coming to the convention in Paris, were on the return boat and they helped Myron with the six children.

The convention opened, with many important people in attendance, including Count Bernstorff[60] and the founder of the YMCA, Sir George Williams. The biggest affair I have ever attended was the reception given by the American Ambassador in Paris, General Horace Porter. At the door of the reception room we were received by two men in the uniform of the time of Marie Antoinette, white wigs and all. The next second, I heard one of the men announce at the top of his voice; "Madame Clark!" Before I had time to think too much about my importance or to show my embarrassment, another Madame was announced, followed by many others, and I came down to earth.

From Paris, my husband was going to Holland to attend a meeting; the children and I went to Porto, Portugal, to wait for him. We went by train to La Pallice, the seaport, and we were settled in four spacious cabins on the *SS Victoria*. My husband had a nice talk with the room steward and I am sure the talk was accompanied by something more substantial as Myron knew the reputation of the Bay of Biscay. We were all rather sad to have our family separated again. The cabins were on deck but I never left mine. It was two wretched days for me and even the children were not very well. This was better as I didn't have to worry about them.

---

60. German ambassador to the US from 1908 to 1917, when he was recalled to Berlin.

In Porto several friends whom we knew and several that we didn't came on board and suggested that I stay with them to wait for my husband. Hospitality is one of the characteristics of the Portuguese people and the Brazilians, I am bold enough to say. Myron returned from Holland by train to join us, and on the 19th of May we were off to Lisbon by train. We visited the Museo Archaeológico, saw Dom Pedro II, ex-emperor of Brazil, at the São Vicente Church, and went to the Igreja dos Jerónymos, built in 1100, where we saw the great writer Alexandre Herculano's[61] ivory tomb.

The Portuguese people were very kind and hospitable; the food was delicious and abundant. The little country was all cultivated but there seemed to be lots of poverty and ignorance: old churches and convents everywhere and not many schools. Lots of the wealth that was in the walls and altars of the churches ought to have been in buildings and books to educate the people. But at that time already, new ideas were taking hold of the educated young generation, laying the foundation for a new form of government which came in 1910—the Republic. Separation of church and state was made immediately and drastic changes took place.

We left Portugal for home on the boat *Oussa* on May 31st, down the Tejo river with a beautiful view of the city and the *Torre de Belem*,[62] from which Pedro Álvares Cabral sailed on that trip to the Indies when Fate carried his boat to a land they called *Terra da Santa Cruz*,[63] which later became known as Brazil. There were very few passengers. My meals were brought on deck and as the cabins were then always downstairs, some nights I slept on deck as well, as I was in agony below in the cabin. But even with all these discouraging circumstances, my husband kept high spirits, writing, "Beautiful evening on deck, moonlight." Yes, many times I have seen the moon go down in the water at dawn, and before Apollo brought Aurora in his beautiful carriage, the sailors came up to scrub the deck and moved me around as they did it! They were always very kind, and

---

61. Alexandre Herculano, 1810–1877, Portuguese historian and first mayor of Belém, now a suburb of Lisbon.

62. Tower of Belém, or Bethlehem Tower, a fortress built in 1515–1521 in the middle of the Tagus River as a starting point for Portuguese navigators searching for trade routes.

63. Land of the Holy Cross.

sometimes they told me some gripping sea stories. In one of my recent voyages, the captain told me they were fish stories!

We entered our beautiful bay on June 14th, and were met by many friends and relatives and by the *ACM* people who had a launch to take us to shore; there were still no docks. We stayed with my sister, Noemi. We had not forgotten the House upon the Hill, as the owner had promised to keep it for me.

# 27. The House on the Hill, 1904-1908

 *USA, 1942*

My husband went to see the owner of the House on the Hill, who remembered his promise to me. Houses were scarce then, because the beautiful *avenida* that now goes along the beach[64] was being opened, and hundreds of homes in the way, some of which were just going up, were being torn down. Passos[65] was the name of the engineer and *prefeito* (mayor) who had the courage to face wealthy owners who were serious obstacles to the implementation of this plan. We had to pay more rent than we did before but I reminded my husband that the International Committee never had a man who tried to live as cheaply as he did.

We took the house and our beachcomber, Antônio Gibralter, scrubbed it, and again we were settled in this place that would seem very modest for anybody else, but to us was a palace, because we had the sea in the front and the hills as our backyard! We moved on Friday, and Sunday our friends, the ornaments of a home, immediately found the way to ours.

The days at the Association and those at home were very busy. A month hardly passed that we did not meet some missionary arriving from or going to the States, and we usually brought them home for a day or two. Mrs. Kyle, one of those missionaries who was coming back from home leave, visited us and she loved to sew. She took note of the meagerness of the children's wardrobes, made a pattern for each one of them, and afterwards filled her own order. Many times they were made over from her own garments and the children gained from this, for the material was better than what we could afford if we were to buy it in Rio.

One night, I went to call on some friends, leaving the children with another visitor, and when I got home very late that night with my husband—I always stopped at the Y to come home with him—we found

---

64. Avenida Atlântica.

65. Pereira Passos (Bello, *A History of Modern Brazil*, 177, 180).

that the children, trying to kill mosquitoes, had set fire to the mosquito netting, scaring the poor old lady like everything. You see, candles, kerosene, and a wood fire were the things that gave us light in this house. I have gone through almost all scares that can come to a growing family. Children were lost, nearly drowned, nearly burned, they suffered falls and broken heads, all this in addition to all the sicknesses that children had to have in those days and that you can prevent today.

We never were alone Sunday afternoons and evenings; this was our informal "at home" when our friends called. We had some ladies, relatives or friends, but men were our main visitors on Sundays. They were always welcomed and there was always plenty to eat without any fuss. As my maid left right after our midday meal on Saturday, that afternoon I baked the bread and cake for Sunday. Although we didn't have a refrigerator, we had good salad and tea. Those afternoons and my husband's day at home are very bright spots in my life-size memory quilt. He read for me *Little Lord Fauntleroy*, *Ralph Marlowe*, *Outline of World History*, *Ben-Hur*, Camões's *Os Lusiadas*, and *The Doctorate*. On one of our blessed Thursdays we went to Leme to see our lot and tunnel. Oh, my!

Our children were well and prospering in school. Our family circle was broken up for the first time in 1907 when Ruth went to São Paulo to boarding school at the American School where I had studied and taught—she had the same French teacher who had taught me. The next year, while Ruth was celebrating her fourteenth birthday in São Paulo, we were getting Orton ready to go to a Methodist boarding school in Minas, because one school was the best for girls and the other the best for boys. We ordered a tailor-made suit for Orton; it was cheaper to have it made than to buy readymade. On the 27th of March, Orton was off to Juiz de Fora, happy and content. Myron wrote in his diary, "Finished reading with him *What a Young Boy Ought to Know*. Had several talks with him. May God keep him from evil."

Christmas of 1907 brought Ruth and María Ovidia home from São Paulo for vacation, and Myron, too, who had been visiting the *ACM* in São Paulo and Rio Grande do Sul. How well I remember on Christmas Day the boat passing by Copacabana on her way to the entrance of the Bay. We waved a sheet from our house to welcome them, which was seen by all on the boat. Myron found me with guests and no servant. This happened very frequently as I probably mentioned before. They couldn't stand me and I couldn't stand them, or they did not like the wilderness around us!

New Year's Day of 1908 found me in the kitchen baking cakes and pies, as my cook had left me. A member of the *ACM* who was a friend of ours came to help me prepare a turkey, a present from my sister Noemi and her husband, Henrique, who had come to spend the day with us. That evening the American colony met at the Y to discuss the coming visit of the American Navy. Many ships on their way to San Francisco were going to stop several days in Rio. The American community, much smaller than that of today, wanted to make plans to entertain the sailors. The officers were guests of the Brazilian government, and of course receptions of all sorts were given to them.

An American colonel had deposited some money in a bank for the expenses of a "Bureau of Information" for the American Fleet sailors, so they would not be cheated by profiteers. There the sailors could change the dollar to Brazilian currency by fixed exchange, and buy tickets at reasonable prices for meals in well-known restaurants. At my husband's request, the Visconde de Morães, owner of the ferryboats in our lovely bay, gave permission for the use of the new Ferry Boat Station as the location of the Bureau. Excursions were arranged to places of interest, and Brazilian curios were sold. These were twelve days of real excitement for the Rio population! Sailors everywhere, always surrounded by Brazilians. They left the impression of happy and well-behaved men of the seas! They had plenty of money and they spent it seeing the city and buying curios. Lots of tales were told about them that I cannot swear were true, but I venture to pass one on to you.

A happy gob went around one of the poor sections of Rio and met a man with his burro, probably going home after having sold whatever he had to sell. The sailor showed by pulling out from his pockets a bunch of bills, that he meant to buy the burro. The man was amazed and just laughed at the big joke. Well, the transaction was done; the gob jumped on the back of the burro after the amount was safe in the pockets of the peddler and with just an ordinary rein to guide the animal, the sailor saw

Rio from the burro's back, furnishing à gratis entertainment wherever he passed. When he, with hundreds of others, was due at the docks to go on his ship, he was there on his burro, and after saying goodbye to him and arousing much laughter from the multitudes who were around the sailors always, he let the poor beast loose, saying; "Go and enjoy your freedom!" Please don't ask me anything further; I said I heard this tale and I could not verify whether it was really the truth.

Lots of drunken sailors were seen around but it did not make them quarrelsome or sad, as it seems to affect people in my country; it made them laugh. The American fleet in Guanabara Bay for twelve days was an event never to be forgotten. From then on, every time a warship of any nation stopped in Rio, the Bureau of Information, located now at the *ACM* building, resumed functioning, but I don't think we ever had such a big visit of the American Navy as the one in January of 1908.

Not very long ago I read that Dr. Lee DeForest[66], who had been stalled in his wireless enterprise, had the opportunity to resume its development after he sold tubes for the wireless telephone to the American fleet in 1908, when it went around the world. Well, my babies, when the Fleet was in Rio, I was taken to one of the telephone operating rooms where the chief put earphones on my head, and I heard messages which were being transmitted by the wireless telephone in those tubes.

Myron worked at the Information Bureau every day from 6:30 in the morning until 11 at night with half an hour for lunch and the same for dinner, answering questions, exchanging money, and arranging tours; and he found me still in the kitchen when he got home. On the 22nd of January, we, along with many friends, saw the fleet pass in front of our place. It was a grand sight: sixteen battleships and the Brazilian fleet also.

After all the work at the Bureau, all the wrapping up, and straightening up of the affairs at the *ACM* that had been neglected, Myron was ready to drop, but his wife was right there with a plan to rest him up. Ruth, who had been spending her vacation with us, was going back to school. My sister Noemi and her two sisters-in-law, good friends of mine,

---

66. Dr. Lee DeForest was the inventor of the triode vacuum tube, a key element in voice radio transmission.

invited the children to stay at their houses. The children were packed off to them, and Ruth and I, after some sewing and other preparations, went to São Paulo; she to the school and I to my sister Cacilda's to wait for my husband who was straightening up the accounts and making arrangements for a vacation.

Your grandfather arrived in São Paulo on the 8th of February 1908, and on the 10th we two started for our greatest adventure all by ourselves, with all our cares left behind and our children being looked after by our relatives and friends. I had not been back home to Caldas since the vacation before the one when my future was united to that of my Moço Louro. Now that he was my faithful husband he decided to take me back home.

# 28. *Janelas*

 *Berkeley, April 1984*

After six weeks in Brazil, I could make myself understood in Portuguese, and get the drift of what was going on. But now, back at home, I realize that I want to regain my fluency so that I can live in Brazil and know it from the inside rather than see it as a tourist. So while Sydney and I were saying goodbye to Brazil and to each other, I was already thinking about how I could manage to go back on my own.

The thought of leaving my family, friends, and the life I have built in Berkeley to go alone to try to make a different life in the now-familiar but still exotic culture of Brazil excites and scares me. I have always been haunted by the idea that in another culture I would be somebody else, and I want to explore that idea in reality. I don't know whether I have the courage to actually do it, so I allow it to live in my heart as a fantasy. I intend to find out whether it would be possible, without making a decision.

Meanwhile, my cousin Sylvia has copied the thirty-five typewritten pages that she found, along with the airmail tablets, in the curly maple bureau and sent them to her cousins, including me. These pages reveal Vovó's early life in Caldas from her birth in 1868 to 1879. I am fascinated and eager to see the tablets.

Sylvia and I have many telephone conversations; I tell her about my tentative plans to go to Brazil, and she tells me more about the content of the tablets. Now I am flooded with excitement, and I'm beginning to see a connection between our grandmother's accounts and my purpose in going to Brazil for an extended stay. These pages are my *janelas*—the windows through which I may understand and assimilate my heritage. Sylvia and I are tugging on a long thread going far back in time; I am so thankful these memories were preserved, and I wonder where they will lead me.

Things fall easily into place; my fantasy is becoming reality. I rent my flat in Berkeley for a year; with this income I can live in Brazil. I will stay with Aunt Ginger in Rio until I find a place of my own. My visa will allow me six months; after that I can renew by leaving and re-entering Brazil. I'm going with the intention to stay at least nine months, and to build a life on a *tabula rasa*, without the overlays of North American culture and the expectations and opinions of everyone who knows me here. I want to travel all over Brazil, eventually arriving in Caldas, and I know somehow that something wonderful is waiting for me there.

As I am preparing to leave, the package from Sylvia arrives containing the three writing tablets, each one with a picture of a TWA airplane on a blue cover. Along with these come a big pile of loose papers, including letters. All of it is yellow and brittle with age and obviously written on different tablets, but in no particular order.

This is daunting, to say the least. Luckily for me, Sydney is visiting. We spread the loose pages all over the dining room table and sort them according to the way the pages look—the size, color, width of lines, etc. This results in six separate piles, each with a different numbering system; reading them, we are able to put the separate groups more or less in chronological order. There are also many photographs including one of the house where Vovó was born, taken by Uncle Henry in 1920.

Except for some dated letters, there is no indication on any of the papers when they were written, but the pictures of the airplanes and the captions on the fronts of the tablets are the clues, dating the tablets prior to the Second World War. Quaint reminders of a time when flying was a rare and glamorous mode of travel, they read: "Luxurious TWA Skyclubs by day, Skysleepers at night, travel from coast to coast at 3 miles a minute," "TWA Stratoliner above the clouds," and "Giant of the Airways—TWA's Stratoliner! 107 foot wing span; 75 foot overall length; 17 foot overall height."

The pages of the tablets are numbered eccentrically; Vovó did not identify the tablets or their contents in any way, and when she came to the end of one tablet, she began another wherever she left off. Since the last tablet ends in mid-sentence, I am reasonably sure there had been at least one more. The manuscript is addressed to her grandchildren, and is obviously a first draft. There is a gap in the narrative, which coincides with missing page numbers. The questions haunt me: were the pages simply lost, or possibly destroyed? Could they be lying incognito in someone else's house? And, most important, where was the page that finished that last sentence, and how far did she go with the story?

Holding the pages in my hands, I am overcome by a strange sensation of eternity—the same feeling I had with Mother's ashes in my hand. But these pages will reveal what bones cannot; my grandmother as a young woman, in a time and place unknown to me. I am filled with awe and gratitude for this marvelous gift, and I realize that if they are to be enjoyed by my sisters and cousins and preserved for our descendants, they will have to be transcribed, and that I am the one who has the time and the interest to do it.

The pages are fragile and very difficult to read. Sentences meander all over the pages; there are insertions between the lines, in the margins, on the backs of the pages. It is hard to follow the narrative; sometimes there seems to be at least two stories going on at once, weaving around each other on front and back of the same page; sometimes written upside down, sending me to previous or following pages. I know I can't work directly from the labyrinth of the page, so I begin to read them into a tape recorder, switching it off and on as I struggle to read.

Despite the difficulty, it is a great pleasure to read them, although I am disappointed to find little about my father, the last-born. There are some accounts of incidents involving my Aunt Argy and Uncle Henry, but Aunt Ruth as Helen of Troy, Uncle Orton as Horatio Alger, and Uncle Neco as Huck Finn are the stars of the drama.

When I was a girl, Vovó told me many stories of her early life; about her father; his hunting trips with his horse, Condor; about her mother and grandmother, and their conversion to Protestantism; about her seven sisters and one brother. And she also told me about her family's slaves, Eva and her son João, and how she persuaded her father to grant them their freedom even before Princess Isabel issued the doctrine of the free womb, which decreed that the children of all slaves born after May 13,1888 were free. But a lot of what I read is new; there are many surprises.

She certainly got the wish of her childhood dreaming. Here she is, a village girl of Caldas seeing the sights of London, and especially Paris, that Brazilians then—maybe still—regard the center of civilization. Not only that, but living every woman's dream of having a happy marriage and healthy attractive children. But I know her life was not easy.

Vovó never told me that besides her six children, she raised her niece, Maria Ovídia, after Vovó's sister Josefina died, and was responsible for her sisters Cacilda and Manoelita and brother Argentino at the American School in São Paulo, all of whom would only be names to us were it not for these *reminiscências* and my travels to Brazil. Not only that, but her house was always full of visitors—missionaries, boarders, and visiting relatives. How hard it must have been for her, coping with all the illnesses of six children in a foreign land without the support of her own family.

I wonder if her Moço Louro realized? I wish I had asked my father about him; I have so little impression of my grandfather outside of his dedication to his work. I never knew my grandfather, who died ten years before I was born, but he looks stern in all his photographs, and everyone seemed to think him a very serious, earnest, dedicated man. I do have his love letters to Vovó, the ones she saved anyway, and some of fatherly counsel to the children, which show tenderness, encouragement, and exhortation. Here it is wonderful to see him young and in love! Vovó has given us all a treasure, and I am so grateful to her, and to him, too!

How strange, and how wonderful this is! Vovó's decision to write her *Reminiscências* was made in my father's house, shortly before Mother and Daddy met, and I wonder—when she visited us in the '30s and '40s was she writing? It is strange that no one seems to remember; was she keeping it a secret? Someone typed those thirty-five pages, so someone knew. Was she still writing in her late eighties when we both lived with Uncle Neco, Aunt Ginger, Dolly, and Paulinho? Perhaps she did tell us, and we weren't even interested enough to remember. I know she was writing for us, her

23

In fact we can say that the door of his home was always opened (not only to my people but) to any body that needed a shelter. From then on most of the english speaking people who arrived in Rio for the first time were met by him and those sailors from cargo boats (each members of those days came to the "Y") for some help and sometimes he would send them to me to give them work as house cleaners, floor washers and they were wonderful. Little did I know then that my fate was going to be acquainted not only with sailors but with many captains who always did everything to make me comfortable. Lately I have been the oldest on board so in my last trip (?!) my son wrote from Brownsville this: "I heard that you were the belle of the boat..." Anybody that sees me knows that it was not of my phisic that he was speaking... It was the way I was treated.

The author's first challenge—reading!

One of the activities or entertainments on the Social Department were the picnics for which the families were invited. And they may have some pictures of them at them (I have one) that showed that the women wore their best hats and clothes. The conduct & transportation was most always given or provided very cheap or by companies or have locations on the others. The city and touring orchestra afforded they did that more than those that could afford that more than that...

Myron Clark was very active always and walked very fast. The streets down town in old Rio were very narrow, and the Gamas and José Braga our very dear friends in actives in the work always looked, when we were together, saying that some times one would see far away in the street in the center of the city a coat flying and only when it stopped in front of an office one realised that it was Clark! Sandade!.. Yes, stopping to ask subscriptions for the Revista Cristã de Moços! Sandade!...

Then the time came for his much

She writes about picnics, and Myron's coat
flying down the narrow streets of downtown Rio.

grandchildren, and she probably meant to make it more accessible to us; and then what happened? Did it become too much for her, or did she just put it away one day and forget about it? This I know: a treasure that comes from beyond the grave somehow carries more meaning. I hope that the answers to the puzzle will emerge from the writings, but I am glad they weren't found until fifty years after her death, when I am the age she was when she began writing.

These paper tablets are incomplete, unfinished, disorganized, but they are windows into another time, another culture. Through them, I am able to know my grandmother as a young girl; and not only my grandmother, but also her grandmother, and her great-grandparents. It was a time and a culture very different from mine, but it is my history, and I know I must preserve it for future generations. As I work with the papers over the years, I come to realize that what I am learning is changing the way I look at life and the way I see the culture of my native land.

# 29. Home Again, 1908

Sixteen years had passed since I had been in Caldas. Since then, I had been to the States twice and even to Europe, but there had never been time to return to this place where I began my journey. Finally, I would be able to *matar saudades* (put to rest—literally "kill"—the longings) for the poetical town of my birth! Really this trip to Caldas was like a dream of which I was afraid I would awake any minute! The railroad was the same one, the Mogyana, that twice a year for eight years [1883–1891] I had taken, combined with two days on horseback, to get to and from school in São Paulo.

How glad I was to get back to Minas, the land of my childhood where for fifteen years I lived without knowing that Caldas was not the center around which the rest of the world turned. I felt enormous pleasure seeing those green mountains, and those pastures where the cattle satisfied themselves on grass, and the creeks and cascades where they quenched their thirst.

The train ride was not a bad one; the dust had been laid by rain. The ride over the *serra* was beautiful, through rolling hills and cultivated fields. Myron said it reminded him of the rides to Curitiba in Paraná and to Porto over the Spanish frontier, but to me it just felt like going home again. We arrived at Poços in the afternoon and went to the Hotel Globo. After dinner the rain came up but we went out just the same to call on my old friend, Eduardo Westin, and another, Reinaldo Amarante, both about my age. They were very surprised to see me, and greeted Myron very graciously.

From our window at the hotel we had a beautiful view of the *serra*. The next morning after our *culto* (worship) we went for a walk in the invigorating air, to the Pedro Botelho, a wonderful hot spring with sulfuric water at 43° centigrade [104° Fahrenheit], in the Hotel

Empressa.[67] After breakfast and a nap, we had calls from friends, including Dr. Pedro Sanches, an old friend of my father's in Caldas, now principal physician at the place. We had a fine *mineiro* dinner at the home of Senhor Reinaldo. He showed us all over his wonderfully commodious house with all modern conveniences, and his *quintal* (backyard) with peaches, grapes, and other fruits. We had a delightful time there, and after dinner we had a long talk while walking through the town. We met several acquaintances on the street—Myron was amazed that I remembered so many people. I was elated to be showing all this to Myron, but I was aching to get to Caldas.

We woke at five a.m. for the trip to Caldas, but Chico Bretas, a mail carrier who was to be our *camarada* (groom), did not come with the animals until 7:30. We started at eight, a party of five. Besides Chico there was a man to look after the suitcases and another to help us on the road. We had very good horses and enjoyed the ride very much: over hills and plains, through valleys and woods, on a constantly winding road full of gullies and stony ridges. We made the trip of five leagues in five hours, arriving shortly after one o'clock.

An hour before reaching it, we could see the poetical town of my birth. It was a struggle to keep my composure, but I controlled myself until we were alone in the hotel, when I gave way to weeping. We stayed at a hotel owned by Dona Maria Madalena,[68] an old friend of my mother's. We had only a little bit of a room with a narrow bed, but Dona Maria was as good and kind as she could be.

Now it was Myron's turn to experience the strange sensation of walking the streets in the town where I had lived as a girl, as I had done with him in his hometown of Buffalo. There, time seemed to speed up, but here it slowed down and I felt as if I were dreaming. I showed him the house where I was born, the cemetery where my parents, Dr. André, and other old friends were buried.

It was wonderful to see old friends of my family, my godfather's wife,

---

67. It was still there in 1988, when I was there—Annita.

68. I found a reference to Maria Madalena de Paula (1821–1915) in *Famila Franco*. I assume this to be the woman referred to here. See Junqueira Franco and Franco Junqueira, *Família Franco*, 29; picture on 31.

and prominent people of old days. Then João, son of Eva, my father's slave, came to see us with his two little daughters, María and Ana. Dr. Gabriel Pio da Silva, godfather of two of my sisters (and one of the sons of the rich old lady of Capivary where we stayed when I was ten years old), was in town from his big coffee plantation, as was the Baron of Campo Místico, a very interesting old man who had been decorated by the Emperor because of service to his party.

In the afternoon, callers came in and kept us busy until late at night. One of the callers was Senhor Honório, an old man now, who had been a clerk in my father's pharmacy when I was a child. Some time after he left my father's employment, he was accused of murder, of which he was innocent. He was condemned to life imprisonment, but he escaped with the help of friends and lived twenty years hidden in the woods and farms until the murderer confessed his crime. Senhor Honório could appear now; though he was feeble and weak and would not live very long. He came with a dish for me that he had prepared himself.

In the evening we went to dinner with João's family and it was a good one too. Myron wrote in his diary, "He seemed so happy to have us there at his table; it seemed so queer to think of his having been a slave. He was white." João's mother, Eva, was a *mulata*, and João was probably the grandson of a former master.

The week that we were there was so full of reminiscences for me, and of surprises and pleasure to my beloved and to myself, that it would take too many pages to write them all. We spent a day with some friends whose *chácara* (country place) used to belong to my father when I was a child. We visited the *Juiz de Direito* (District Judge) who lived in the house where I was born. Can you imagine what was going on in my heart from the minute I arrived in the little town that had been my world until I was fifteen?

There was very little change. The same old houses with the same dark red paint on the windows and doors, and the same whitewashed walls. There were a few new houses, not half a dozen, which had different colors. But I noticed that everything had shrunk. That spacious *largo* now seemed much smaller. Those vast *salões* where we danced were now of

ordinary size, and that far horizon seen from our bedroom that gave me
love for views and panoramas had shortened also! Of course all this was
imaginary, but one change was real, and I could weep when I noticed that
those little forests of *pinheiros* all around the town had been replaced by
vineyards.

And the last day came on the 24th of February, ten days spent here as
a mother, as Chiquita Clark, and not Chiquita Pereira. We were up at
6:30 to finish packing. João insisted that he would take us back to Poços
where we had to take the train. He turned up with the horses and soon
everything was secure. Dona María prepared a lunch, as did João's wife
who came with all the children to say goodbye. Dr. Pimenta, Dona Cota,
Anabal, and others came and by 8:30 goodbyes were said and presents of
peach preserves, grape juice, and baskets of fruits to eat on the way were
given. Alfredo, João's son, accompanied us to do the job that his father,
as a slave, did when we went to school. Halfway we stopped to eat the
delicious lunch: chicken, pork, sirloin, and fruit.

After an excellent trip we arrived at the hotel in Poços, not nearly so tired
as before, because João had seen to it that we had better horses. The next
day we were off to São Paulo, all our acquaintances being at the station to
say goodbye. We stayed with my sister Cacilda, and how we lived our past
and talked about Caldas! Ruth was there in the boarding school so she
visited with us after school the three days we were there. Then the long,
dusty trip to Rio, our home. My sister Noemi had gathered the children
and was there waiting for us, on the 29th of February. I think this was the
most perfect vacation my husband and I ever had.

And now, my grandchildren, clouds are gathering in different spots of
Vovó's blue sky! Troubles and more troubles are approaching our happy
home!

# V. Sunshine and Shadows

In 1910, after a brief period of relative stability, Brazil was once again in political turmoil. The "Civilianists," supporters of presidential candidate Rui Barbosa, often demonstrated in the streets against the government candidate, Hermes da Fonseca. Fonseca won the election thanks to the political machines of the state governments, especially those of Minas Gerais and the northern states, in spite of Barbosa's enormous support in Rio and all the other big cities of the south.

A week after Hermes da Fonseca took power, sailors protesting against corporal punishment staged a rebellion called the *Revolta da Chibata* (Revolt of the Whip) on the battleships *Minas Gerais* and *São Paulo*. The government bowed to their demands to end the practice, and agreed to amnesty for the sailors. A few days later, another warship and a barracks on Cobras Island in the bay rebelled, and this time the government, fearing that insubordination could grow, bombed the island and subdued the rebel vessel. The second group of rebels, instead of receiving amnesty, were banished to the outposts of Amazonia to pay for their crimes.[69]

From 1910 to 1920, Brazil went through dramatic social and economic changes. Large numbers of Italian immigrants settled in the state of São Paulo, providing a new source of cheap labor, and coffee became the dominant export. The resulting economic growth increased the political power of the states of São Paulo and Minas Gerais, which took turns controlling the presidency.

The outbreak of war in Europe in 1914 turned the attention of Brazilians away from domestic problems and squabbles. Brazil entered on the side of the Allies, contributing mainly by providing raw materials and foodstuffs. By necessity, Brazil had to fend for herself in the manufacturing of goods it had been importing. Rapid growth of manufacturing resulted in a rise of the political influence of the cities, and the beginning of unrest in the urban working classes. The rise in economic prosperity brought on by war could not last, however. As exports fell off, public unrest increased, and the precarious republican state was

---

69. Bello, *A History of Modern Brazil*, 214–17.

falling into bitter regionalism and open opposition between the state governments. It was in this milieu that Getúlio Vargas rose to power, and held it until mid-century.[70]

After a brief period of democracy in the 1950s under Juscelino Kubitschek, a briefer experiment with parliamentary rule, and 21 years of military dictatorship beginning with a 1964 military coup, democracy was restored with the election of Tancredo Neves in 1985. Brazilians called it the New Republic.

The 21st century would see the election of a woman president, Dilma Rousseff, of the Workers' Party.

---

70. The last two paragraphs were gleaned from my reading of Bello, *A History of Modern Brazil*. xviii, 190, and 230-2–55.

# 30. Culture Shock

 *Rio, September 1984*

Ginger welcomes me back to Rio—she was in the States when Sydney and I were here—but it's time to make the transition from tourist to resident, and I've found a furnished apartment and rented it for one month; I can extend it if I wish. The basic furniture is here—except for the TV, which the agent says will be here tomorrow—along with dishes, bed and bath linens, everything I will need. The main difficulty I've had in renting a *temporado* (short term apartment) was that none of them had phones. Neither does this one, but the agent says that when I provide a huge deposit, the owner will install one for me within a couple of days. That was the main reason I took this apartment, although it is also bright (many I saw were very dark) and quiet, because it is in the back of the building away from street noise.

So I pay the rent and the deposit that will be worth probably ten percent less when I get it back on account of the high rate of economic inflation, and I return the next day to move in. There is still no TV, which is important to me since it is my teacher. Also missing are hangers and pillows, although the bed is made and there is a pillowcase on top. There is plenty of drawer space, but one drawer is broken and two sliding doors don't work. In the kitchen there are four new pans, two plates, two knives, two forks, two spoons, four glasses, one paring knife and a slotted spoon. No cups, bowls, pitchers; nothing to start cooking; not even salt. In the bathroom there are three squares of toilet paper and two chips of soap. Ginger loans me various things for the apartment.

I go to Sima's for lunch, and while there I call the agent who had assured me I could call him at any time if there were any problems. I leave messages at his home and office, and wait all afternoon at Sima's for him to return my call. While we wait, we talk about cultural differences and the problems they create.

When Sima and Saúl were living in Berkeley I was the one to interpret and help out. One day Sima called to tell me that a neighbor had "invited" her to a garage sale the following Saturday. She was completely baffled and wanted to know what she should wear, what time she should go, how long she should stay, should she take something, what should she expect. I tried to explain the custom, but she was incredulous and very reluctant to go. However, she felt because she had accepted an invitation, she had to show up. When she returned home, she called again. "Oh, Annita, I was so embarrassed! How could they put out for display and sale all those personal items—even used clothes—for all the neighbors to see? I felt like I had to buy something, but felt so ashamed and sorry for her!" Saúl loved it; he thought it was funny, wonderful, practical—and so American.

Now in Rio, Sima and I wait all afternoon in vain for the call from my agent, so that night I ask Saúl to call him. I've learned by now that men get results when women don't. Sr. Vasconcellos assures him that the TV and list of things I have requested (except serving bowls; these are not regularly included) will arrive tomorrow and be left with the doorman, so I don't have to stay home and wait.

So today, Friday, I go shopping for food and other essentials like clothespins and matches and toilet paper and soap. Tonight, as I am leaving for the ballet with Sima and Saúl, a young woman appears with two dish towels, five hangers, a coffee cone and filters, and a cup and saucer. She says the TV will arrive tomorrow. It doesn't. Saúl calls again, this time is told I will get a color TV on Tuesday, and the phone should arrive in a week. This is all so frustrating, but typical, I'm afraid. I realize that I should have paid only half of the rent.

Finally, in order to get my phone and the other promised things, I stage a sit-in at my agent's office. Sima and Saúl are shocked, and probably embarrassed that I am connected to them—this is not the way to do things here, but enough of "when in Rome." Ginger is surprised, but amused. Sr. Vasconcellos is "out," but three young men are in his office reading the newspaper. They say the boss will be back *daquí a pouco*, which literally means "in a little while" but actually means nothing. When he finally emerges, he sends one of them to get some of my items, and tells me to go back to the apartment to wait for him. I give him the key to my apartment and say I will wait in his office, and also that I will move on Saturday if I don't get the phone. He wants me to leave, of course, and says they have to close the office to go to lunch. I say that I have brought mine, and that I will just stay here until they return. While I wait (I have a book), the errand boy delivers some stuff to my apartment and helps himself to a T-shirt. Ginger tells me later that I never should have turned over my key to him, and I'll be lucky if that is all that is missing, but I can't bear waiting helplessly for some turkey who, for all I know, has no intention of ever coming.

I finally get the phone, but I am pretty disillusioned with Rio. It was different being a tourist; especially with such a compatible person as Sydney. I guess there were a lot of things I didn't see. There is the pollution, the excruciating poverty, the unnecessary filth—dog shit all over the beautiful mosaic sidewalks. The drivers honk and zoom out of driveways, around corners; even when it is pouring and you are waiting to cross, they zoom and honk. Pedestrians don't count. You have to walk around parked and moving cars on the sidewalk. One night Ginger and I see a bus just miss a man in a wheelchair. Even blind people are not given right-of-way. There are lots of distressing sights. Yesterday as I was coming back from an open-air antiques fair, I saw naked children in a pedestrian street full of debris. Some of the adults were sorting through the debris; others were sleeping in the street, and beggars were displaying their deformities. It was awful.

And this business of promising and not delivering, of the *cariocas'* propensity for giving directions when they really don't know—Saúl explains it as a psychology of fantasy that things will work out, which he equates with a love that has nothing to do with time. Other Brazilians I have talked to say it's nothing but laziness, and blame it on their Portuguese heritage! I say that Brazilians are the world's biggest hedonists, and truthfulness, unfortunately, often brings pain. To me, it seems a lack of respect, not a quaint national trait. I ask Saúl how a Brazilian man would communicate a commitment if by chance he wanted to. In that case, Saúl says, he would say, "I swear by God's beard" or "on my dear mother's grave" or "on the cape of the Virgin" or some such. This is hard for a person like me, who was brought up to believe that one's word is sacred, but I want to learn how to cope, in my own way, in this culture. I'm going to stick it out for at least six months, travel as much as I can during that time, do something with Vovó's journals (I haven't even started that project yet), perhaps come back in future years to Brazil, but not—the way I'm feeling now—to Rio. Pity.

Shopping for my needs is also very difficult and frustrating, but I need to learn how to do it, and the sooner the better. This is my project now—just learning how to cope. I have to learn where to go for everything I need, what to call it, and then deal with paying with *cruzeiros*. The exchange rate changes so fast, and so much, that you don't know how much anything costs—not even postage. The last time I changed money, I got 2,667 *cruzeiros* to the dollar. Tomorrow it will be close to 2,800, and it is always going up, so I don't exchange very much at a time. There is an "official" and an "open" exchange rate. No one except a tourist who doesn't know better would use the official bank rate, because the open rates are published daily in the paper. Currency exchanges can be transacted in exchange houses all over town and usually in a back room at travel agencies.

The coins are 1, 5, 10, 20, and 50 *cruzeiros*. Bills are in denominations of 100, 200, 500, 1,000, and 5,000, the largest bill, worth at this time about 2 dollars. No one will accept a 5,000 bill unless the change will be 1,000 or less. Prices are usually quoted without zeros, so when someone says "twenty-seven," I have to figure out which multiple of ten I should use. I can't seem to think in *cruzeiros*, so I have to convert these prices in my mind to an equivalent in dollars or cents. All the while, I'm concentrating on the language, which does not flow in an unconscious stream from my ears to my brain, but instead must be processed with rapt attention. And when prices are quoted in millions, I get nervous and my mind just goes blank!

My apartment is on Rua Joaquim Nabuco, down the street from Sima and Saúl's, half a block from the beach; Ginger lives on the next street, Rua Elizabeth, and we are in almost daily contact. We are having a real renewal of our relationship, becoming closer. It is a great benefit of my presence here. The apartment has a *sala* (a combination living-dining room), with a round, white, glass-topped table and six caned chairs, two with arms, and two with broken seats. Sr. Vasconcellos said they'd be taken out to be fixed, but I don't believe him; anyway, why would I need six chairs when I only have two plates? In the opposite corner there is a little round table where I have my radio/tape-recorder. I put the two armchairs on either side of the small table to make a little conversation space, and today at the hippie fair[71] I bought a cushion for one of them and a plant for the table. There is a built-in cupboard with some open space in it for my books and a bowl of fruit. Then there is a tiny kitchen with a two-burner gas stove and oven, and under the sink, a tank of gas (called a *bujão*), which feeds the stove. There is also a refrigerator and a couple of shelves.

My bedroom has a built-in *armário*—closet and drawers—a double bed with a mattress about three-quarters of an inch thick—if I lean on my elbow I can feel the plywood underneath—and outside the sliding windows which open into the air well, a hanging rack for drying clothes. They have to be pinned tightly to the rack, or they will fall seven floors to the bottom of the shaft that brings air to the interior of the building. Off the bedroom is my bathroom with its bidet, toilet, shower, and a tiny sink, which leaks at the base and doesn't drain very well. Inside the shower stall is another sink with a washboard front for washing clothes. The only hot water in the apartment is in the shower. There is an electric water heater built into the showerhead, which you turn on when you want it.

I have to learn how to do everything; but I am enjoying the apartment now, especially since I have put in a few touches of my own, like fresh flowers. There is a newsstand on every block, and all kinds of services—shoe repair, laundries, and restaurants—close at hand. I like that; I am getting familiar with my neighborhood and beginning to feel at home in it.

What the Brazilians call supermarkets are located on nearly every other block. These markets are much smaller than ours, they are not as clean, and the aisles are narrower; but to me they are more inviting somehow. No canned music, and no overwhelming variety of choices—no aisles and aisles of packaging, screaming, "Buy *me*!" But I prefer the *feira*. The *feira*, or farmer's market, is wonderful. It occurs on Tuesday morning in one *praça*, on Friday in another. Gorgeous vegetables, fruits, fish, chicken, flowers, cookies, spices (ground to order and wrapped in pink paper). I went with Sima the first time, and felt overwhelmed and intimidated. I got her to leave me, and after walking around until I was familiar, I

---

71. A local weekly arts and crafts fair held in an open square in Ipanema.

began to answer when vendors shouted at me, "*Fala, freguêsa!*" ("Speak, customer!"). I bought oranges and bananas and pineapple (I'm learning which varieties I like best), *jabuticaba*, the national fruit of Brazil, spinach, tomatoes, and carrots. So now I'm going to the *feira* three times a week.

I have been told I must not eat raw vegetables; so I don't have salads. I can't think of any fruit or vegetable I know that wasn't at the *feira*, plus lots I have never seen before, yet none of them seem to find their way to restaurants, or if they do they taste as if they had been boiled in a pot for days. Later I learn to wash my vegetables in potassium permanganate so I can eat them raw in salads. After I wash everything and dry it all in my spinner I am just about set. I have my daily rice and black beans, just like all Brazilians.

Today I wait for what seems like hours at the butcher counter to get some hamburger to make stuffed peppers for Ginger, who is coming to dinner. No organization for turns; you have to be aggressive. I don't like to do it—you have to make a whistling noise with your lips and shout "*Moço! Moço!*" The butchers work slowly, and they do what ever else they have to do before waiting on customers. While I am waiting patiently, because I can't bring myself to enter the elbow-jabbing, whistling throng, one of the butchers comes around to the front of the counter and rolls up a cart next to where I'm standing. A butcher behind the counter begins throwing sides of beef over the counter (and the heads of waiting customers) to the first butcher, who catches them, putting them in the cart. A perfectly logical way to get the meat across the counter, and the flying beef doesn't come close to hitting anyone, but to my ultra-fastidious eyes the scene looks like something out of Monty Python's Flying Circus. The other customers don't seem to notice. Can you imagine this happening at Safeway?

The weather has finally gotten into the mid-70s, occasionally even into the 80s, and the sun is out. As I learn how to do things, I'm sure I will feel better about Rio. Everyone is always warning me about being careful—not wearing jewelry or carrying a large purse, which I don't do, but I feel very safe here, even at night, as there are doormen in front of every building and lots of people on the street. I walk home at midnight from Ginger's without any apprehension.

Something besides my grandmother's story calls me here—roots, maybe, or perhaps the climate. I am definitely a tropical person. The culture is still new enough, different enough, so that I am still surprised and amused, sometimes horrified, disgusted, or appalled; but I am interested in the everyday dramas I see around me. Amazing, but I still seem to be Uncle Wiggly, with a new adventure every day. I accept experiences that would drive me crazy at home because it feels as if there is something unreal about them, as if I'm in a play or something—a play in which I improvise my lines and have no idea where the story is going. Or a dream in which bizarre surprises keep happening, and I'm a participant as well as an observer. Most of the time, it's fun.

I seem to be getting over my feelings of stupidity, confusion, incompetence, and powerlessness. When I look back on the month I have spent here, I realize I have learned a lot about this language and culture, and myself. There is another thing, harder to explain: Brazil seems a magical place to me; I think and dream differently. I don't know what the culture shock will be like on the other end. Maybe it will be like waking up. Now, feeling much more confident about my language and coping skills, I'm off on another Brasil Airpass, starting out in Belém to see the *Círio de Nazaré*, Brazil's largest religious festival.[72] Then I will explore the cities of the north and northeast coast, ending in Ilhéus where I will switch to buses to wend my way slowly to Caldas, my grandmother's town.

It is presidential election time in both the United States and Brazil, and as I travel along the northern and eastern coasts I pay attention to both. In the United States it is Ronald Reagan vs. Walter Mondale; in Brazil it is Paulo Maluf vs. Tancredo Neves. Here, as in the States the people will vote, but the election here will be decided not by an electoral college, but by the Congress. Still it is very important, because it is the first election

---

72. Círio de Nazaré is one of the largest Catholic processions in Brazil and in the world. According to legend, a small image of the Virgin sculpted in Nazareth performed many miracles in medieval Portugal before somehow arriving in Brazil, getting lost and then found in what is now Belém do Pará around 1700. The procession in Belém attracts pilgrims who carry symbols of parts of the body and other icons representing divine healings, intercessions, and petitions. (Lonely Planet., "Círio de Nazaré").

after more than twenty years of military dictatorship. Both candidates want popular support to influence the electors.

Everywhere I go there is excitement about the election. Flags, green and yellow streamers, political posters, slogans on walls, and even bumper stickers, which are not so common here, decorate all the cities. Maluf is the military candidate (he is always called by his last name, which is pronounced "Maloofy") and the liberal candidate, always called by his first name, Tancredo, is favored to win. He looks like everybody's favorite uncle, and he has promised direct elections next time if he is elected. He is a *Mineiro* who is respected and very popular, and carries on his shoulders the people's hope for democracy. There have been some rumors of a *golpe* (coup) if Maluf doesn't win, but the consensus seems to be that whoever wins will be inaugurated. I watch the news on TV, read the papers some, and talk to everyone I can.

My last flight is a two-minute hop from Bahia to Ilhéus, the cacao town made famous by the novels of Jorge Amado. I have a hotel reservation tonight in Porto Seguro, 282 kilometers down the coast. I love to travel by bus; it's the best way to see this vast, varied, and beautiful country, but it is hard to make all the connections and to manage my heavy suitcase. While I wait in the airport for my puddle-jumper, I'm trying to figure out how to get by bus from Ilhéus to Porto Seguro. There are scores of bus lines with offices in the airport, but in Brazil you can only buy a ticket from your city of departure for the next leg of the trip, and it seems it is impossible to get information about bus schedules until I arrive at Ilhéus. Obviously, no one expects a traveler to go from city to city, as I am doing.

I go to the booth of every bus line with service to Porto Seguro, and am told in each that they don't have the information that I need. I ask how to get it, and they look at me like I'm nuts or repeat that they don't have that information. Then they say, *"Fique tranquila"* ("Remain tranquil"; I am nowhere near tranquil), "don't be worried, you can find out when you get to Ilhéus." I am frustrated. It seems so unnecessary and inefficient, but I know they look with amusement at me, and other *gringos*, who are so anxious, demanding, and impatient.

I finally find a woman in the airport who will make a call for me—too many steps for me to do it myself, and my language facility, which is about 80% (I think) of a native's, becomes 40% on the telephone. She finds out that the last bus for Porto Seguro leaves twenty minutes before I get to Ilhéus, but I can go from Ilhéus to Itabuna, then get another bus to Eunápolis, from where I will be able to get another to Porto Seguro. I am assured it will work. I hope so.

It is only 33 kilometers from Ilhéus to Itabuna, so when I arrive in Ilhéus I get a taxi. From there, supposedly, buses leave every twenty minutes for Porto Seguro. Hope so. I buy a ticket for Eunápolis on a bus leaving in an hour. An old, frail man comes over to me as soon as I have my ticket and picks up the suitcase, carrying it on his head down a double flight of stairs. I point out that it has wheels, but there is no response. We arrive on the street, with an hour to wait. I can't face going up and down the stairs with an old man carrying my very heavy suitcase on his head, and I'd feel like a real cheapskate if I tried to do it myself. (I wouldn't attempt the head-hold, of course!) So I stay here, surrounded by flies and bad smells, my butt sore from sitting on the handle of my suitcase, until the bus comes. The bus ride is lovely—rolling hills with *fazendas* of cacao groves and an occasional sleepy village; lush, green vegetation; clear, deep blue skies. The twilight lingers because I'm going south, and the sun on these hills is gorgeous.

After it gets dark though, I begin to get nervous about the connection I have to make before arriving at my hotel. But then a couple gets on the bus, and I hear them say they are going to Eunápolis too, and I begin a conversation with them. Then I know I'll be OK, that they'll be there for me if I need them. I don't. I decide to pay the equivalent of 13 dollars for a taxi to take me sixty-five kilometers to the coast and deliver me to my hotel in Porto Seguro, rather than wait for another bus.

This morning brings a wonderful surprise. When I arrived at my hotel in Porto Seguro it was very dark; I could hear and smell the ocean, but could not see anything around me. But now I can see: this place is paradise! I'm lying in a gently swinging hammock on my veranda in a very modest, small hotel overlooking the Atlantic. I am very near the spot where Pedro Álvares Cabral landed almost 500 years ago and claimed the land for Portugal. It is so simple, peaceful, and quiet here—and beautiful. Coconut palms; hibiscus with the largest flowers I've ever seen; the historic city on the hill with its ruins, churches, and modest houses.

At a coconut stand, I buy a chilled whole coconut with the end cut off and a straw inserted to drink the coconut milk. It is delicious and refreshing. The owner's son is peeling the fiber off the coconuts to make something, I don't know what. His eyes are clear light green, beautiful with his dark brown skin. I ask the father where his son got those beautiful strange green eyes, the color of a Coke bottle. He replies, "From the Dutch." There I also get acquainted with their pet sloth, a really sweet and lazy creature, the man says. Later I stop at another place and drink the juice of the cacao fruit. It is delicious, but has no trace of chocolate flavor, which comes from the seeds.

*Porto Seguro*—safe harbor—a respite from my travels and my difficulties. I have the time and space to reflect on why I came to Brazil, where I'm going, and who I am now, this middle-aged woman swaying lazily in a hammock, drinking in the ocean air. I know I am not the same person I left behind in the States, and will become again I suppose, when I return. Being alone and a stranger, I have left behind shyness and self-consciousness. Here in this sensuous country I am more keenly attuned to pleasure and playfulness, and I am recapturing the spontaneity of my youth.

After a restful stay in Porto Seguro, I leave the coast and resume my bus travels, heading west into Minas Gerais. I'm getting closer to Vovó's territory now, exploring a little in Brazilian colonial towns full of baroque churches, narrow, cobblestone streets, fountains, and sacred art. Finally, I arrive in Poços de Caldas, the larger spa town near the village where my grandmother was born. The setting, nestled in the mountains, is spectacular, and the city has beautiful gardens and parks. I get to know the town a little, visit the baths, the library, and the museum where I find a picture of Maria Ovídia Junqueira, my father's first cousin, who was adopted by Vovó when her mother died.

And now I'm going to my grandmother's birthplace: the place that she called "the poetical little town of Caldas."

# 31. Cloudy Skies, 1908–1909

Poor Orton had been in the boarding school in Juiz de Fora less than half a year when he was sent home from school very weak, thin, and with a fever. After examining him, the doctor said one of his heart valves did not work due to a congenital lesion, and warned he must always be careful to avoid running and violent exercises. Later, he had pneumonia and then pleurisy. He was very patient through it all. When he began to improve a bit, very slowly, he had callers every day. Pardon me if I blow my own horn, but the doctor told me that the boy's recovery from this sickness was in a great part because of my being so exacting in doing what he told me to do.

At about the same time, I went to see Dr. Henrique about a lump in my breast we feared might be cancer. The doctor prescribed something to rub on the lump, knowing all the time what had to be done. When I went back to him several days later, he said it was better to operate, and added that it was nothing serious then. I could not decide to do it, and at the same time I was getting very nervous. Then I received a letter from my Dr. Lane who had heard about the lump and said, "*Minha filha*, have the operation immediately. It is nothing now but it may be very serious later." Well, that settled it. I could read on the faces of my relatives and friends that my condition was serious. We had constant company, all of whom wanted to be with me and who would add little words of advice, and all my friends and relatives who were physicians advised me to have it done right away.

The children, four of them, were sent to my sister Noemi and our dear friends, the Tuckers. Ruth was in São Paulo and Orton refused to go far away—he went to the only neighbor we had, who was very near. The operation was done on November 18th, 1908. Doctor Henrique came with his son, Renato. Doctor Mattogrosso, my brother-in-law, came also. Other relatives and neighbors also came.

I was taken to the kitchen table where Doctor Henrique administered chloroform. The operation took over one hour, Doctor Mattogrosso holding my pulse all the time, and Renato the chloroform. The doctor came every day. The first Sunday after the operation I continued to improve and had many callers during the day. On the 24th, Dr. Henrique took the stitches out and said everything was going fine. By December 21st I was up, but Orton was down in bed, feverish. We had the doctor who said we had to be very careful with him on account of his heart.

At about the same time, my husband received the news that the Secretary in Recife, Pernambuco, had been very sick—I am not sure if it was yellow fever, but I guess it was—and then his wife also came down with the same thing. The family was ordered to go immediately to the States, as it was about time for their home leave. The National Committee decided that the Secretary in São Paulo was the man to take his place; but he refused to obey, saying that his work in São Paulo was just as important.

My husband then asked the National Committee to let him go. The Directors of the Association in Rio met and agreed under protest to his going. I certainly made it more difficult for him to leave as I saw that it was not his duty, because of sickness in our family and selfishness on the part of the person who ought to have gone. How little did I know then that these frequent absences were going to bring me a world of comfort some day when I could not hear from his lips what flowed so freely from his pen! His letters are a *Cântico dos Cânticos* (Song of Songs) to soothe my lonely days! I say lonely because there is nothing and nobody that could fill his place! I have not seen anybody among my acquaintances that kept the flame of love burning bright for twenty-seven years of married life as we did!! We loved to tell each other what we felt.

But when my husband brought me the resolution, I was furious! Maybe if I had wept it would have been better. There I was with a big sore yet, the results of an operation not healed, and responsible for five children at home. Orton, the oldest, not quite thirteen, was in such condition that the doctors said he could not go to school for a while, and was not allowed to play roughly! Well, I said to my husband, "All right, then I'm going to Caldas with the children. It will be easier for me there to be away from you. We can rent our house to pay for the trip, and living expenses there are nothing compared to Rio." I wrote to my friends in Caldas that if they could get me a furnished house I would go there for four months.

My husband decided to take us to Caldas and have a few weeks there with us as he was very tired, and was going to a very debilitating climate. We seven—father, mother, and five children—were on the train to São Paulo from seven in the morning until six in the afternoon, and it was a very dusty trip. Ruth and Maria Ovídia were at the American School where we visited them before leaving on the train at 6:45 the next morning, arriving at 4:45 in the afternoon in Poços de Caldas. We went to my friends the Westins for the night. In the morning, our ex-slave João and his son Alfredo were there to meet us with the horses for the trip to Caldas.

The children went in a *caleça*, which looks like a little house carried by two mules, one in the front and the other in the back. It wobbled quite a bit, so the children got sick, and once in a while they got out and walked a little. I have an idea that Orton went on horseback like we two. This *caleça* was an antique and the only one in existence then. It had belonged to the old ladies at Capivary where I spent one night when I was ten years old. I remember many times seeing one of those ladies arrive in Caldas in a *caleça* to visit her daughter, the mother of Eduardo Westin, at whose home we now stayed.

It was a good day: cloudy, so not too hot. We had lunch by a babbling brook at about two o'clock in the afternoon, and reached Caldas at four under heavy rain. We went to Sr. Liberato's house. He and his wife, Dona Tereza, who was very kind and attentive, were great friends of my family. We stayed with them until everything was ready in the house we had rented. We took only bedding, towels, and so on; everybody there brought furniture, china, kitchenware, silver, and all the most necessary things. People were coming all the time to see us, even before we went to our house.

João arrived every day with his children to see if we needed anything. He felt that we belonged to him. Slaves had no family name. All the men, ex-slaves, had the family name of their masters attached to theirs. His was João Pereira. My father bought him and his mother when he was two years old and, as I said before, he was supposed to be a son of his mother's master's son.

Before we left Rio I had news that my oldest sister Mariquinha, with whom I had spent that vacation when I became engaged, was very sick with lung trouble in a hospital in São Paulo. Caldas was the best climate for that, so I wrote to her to come and stay with me there. Her daughter Henedina, a teacher, gave up her position to come with her mother. While we were waiting for them, we in Caldas were having the time of our lives, eating, visiting, and sleeping. Everybody sent us grapes of different varieties, peaches, and other things. We went out almost every day and again we had visitors, my old acquaintances, every day.

On the south side of the city rises quite a *serra* and in one part of it there is a big rock called *Pedra do Coração* (Heart Rock) because of its shape. This place is chosen for picnics but one has to climb all the way. Well, João planned a picnic at the place; a fine lunch was prepared, and we went at six in the morning. It was a beautiful view, unsurpassed, but it was a little bit too much for me—the walking and the excitement. I had to have the doctor next day, and stay in bed for five days.

Then came *Carnaval*. The celebration was very inoffensive here. People threw confetti and fruits made of wax of different colors and filled with perfumed water. Then there was a parade of masked men on horseback carrying flowers to exchange with the ladies, who waited at their windows, also holding flowers. How I do remember when in my teens I held a bouquet and waited by my window for Joãosinho, who was one of the masked horsemen.

The time came for my husband to leave. It was a good day for riding; he went with Chico Breitas and reached Poços de Caldas at three. There he met Mariquinha, Henedina, and Cacilda, my other sister from São Paulo, who arrived that afternoon in Poços. He wrote that Mariquinha was very low, that even the good climate of Caldas could hardly restore her.

I was preparing for her. Eduardo Westin and his family were all coming to Caldas where they had a family home, so they were coming together, and they made quite a caravan. Eduardo arranged the *bangué*,

João on Pedra Branca or Pedra do Coração.

(stretcher) and the *caleça*—the same one that had taken the children—for Mariquinha. They took the seat out and put in a mattress so she could lie down all through the journey. So for the first time since the summer of 1889, just before my father died, we three sisters were there together. My sister Cacilda had been a widow with five children since 1905. It was a very unusual experience I was having. I was really not living! I was floating in the past, in the present, and in the future.

The whole population of the town was just as kind as they could be, and João acted as if it were his duty to look after these three women whom, in his younger days, he had to wait on without even a thank you! My sister was failing every minute. Doctor Pimenta, the physician, and Pedrinho, the pharmacist, hardly left the house, always giving her some drug to minimize her sufferings.

Mariquinha passed away on the 8th of March. Again I was facing the

Harvester of Lives here, where I had seen it pluck the precious life of our mother when I was only sixteen. That generation of mothers was almost all gone now. The adults now, who were children with us, were all there comforting us. João, as sad as any of us, moved around doing things that were supposed to be done. He brought candles that, when night came, he lit and put all around. Then he told me he had ordered a kilo of coffee, because lots of people would stay there all through the night, and they had to have coffee. You didn't buy coffee in a store; you had somebody roast it when you needed it.

Procópio, the son of a dear colored woman who had been a slave of Westins', now was a coffin-maker, and he got busy immediately. Almost everybody went to the funeral. The band of the town, sons, most of them, of the bandleaders of our time came voluntarily to accompany the funeral, playing a *marche funebre* of one of the masters. Henedina and my sister Cacilda left a few days later and I felt terribly lonesome. Josephina, the sister who died at my house in Rio, had not had such a demonstration of love because we had not been in Rio very long and very few people knew her there when she passed away in 1895. The only two relatives to mourn her had been her daughter Maria Ovídia and myself. The rainy days brought me memories of my childhood when I could see the rain approaching through the mountains and fields. And then the water pounding on the roof making each tile a pipe carrying heavy streams; and in their falling, that sound so monotonous and so familiar to me. At night the light of lamps and candles also carried me back to the last century.

The public primary teacher for girls was the daughter of a very good friend of my family. This friend had always been known as *João Mestre* (John the Teacher). João Mestre's daughter was slightly younger than I was. She stopped at our place almost every day and we went for walks in the part of the country that I used to see from the back window of our room. On our walks, I could see that window, just as it had been in the past. It has always been easy to let my imagination run wild, and once, when I went there just with my children, although there was a bench there, I sat on the ground as of old, facing that window, and in the twinkle of an eye, I brought to life all those dear ones who had been dead for so many years; and left to oblivion those precious lives who were playing nearby as I wept. All of a sudden the children appeared and with them came the present.

There was not much for the children to do in Caldas, but they had a good time, as they were the center of everybody's attention. Orton, thirteen years old, had the great pleasure almost every day to take a big coffee pot to the jail on the first floor of the courthouse where there were two or three prisoners. I remember how nice the public attorney was to Orton, taking him to the courthouse when they had any case going on there. Argentina had a friend about her age to play with. Henry, Neco, and George played in front of the house in that *largo* where their mother had played on moonlight nights.

Let me leave Caldas and float around my husband for a while. In Recife, Myron was riding on a streetcar to Madalena, a suburb, in the moonlight, wishing I were with him. He decided to try to arrange to bring the family there. You see, he saw that he probably would have to stay about six months. How about the other half, so far away south? When he wrote to ask me what I thought about picking up the family, six of us, to ride horseback for one day, then two days by train, then three or four in some small boat, after all I had gone through, I said "Nothing doing." The last part of the trip scared me.

Then I received a letter from José Braga, saying that the *Directoria* had decided to ask Myron to come for the General Assembly of the *Associação* in Rio in June, and as they were needing him badly in Rio, they were going to do everything possible not to let him go back. Myron's assistant in Rio, Pereira, who had taken his place, was very sick and the doctors had not been able to diagnose his case. José Braga advised me to come back to Rio.

When it was known that we were leaving Caldas, a picnic in my honor was planned at Pedra do Coração. The eats were prepared, and sandwiches were never part of lunch! Oh, no; there were roast chickens, fresh ham and tenderloin, and *tutu de feijão*—reddish beans mixed with *farinha* making it somewhat like baked beans. Also sweets, fruits, and wine. I didn't drink that, because there was plenty of fruit from which the nectar had been taken. We did not start back until we saw the sunset on the horizon, as the sunset from there was famous, and one of the reasons people went there.

When the day arrived, that big crowd gathered in front of the house, and *Vivas* were proclaimed. I think there were a good deal more than sixty people. Then we started, and at the outskirts of the town there was a horse ready for me. The people around me sang, they danced, they shouted, and with glasses we could see people walking in that *largo* far below. Picture in your mind your Vovó on horseback and all around her this crowd of friends. But my joy has to be always mixed with sorrow; even while I was honored and tried to show appreciation for kind actions toward me, I could not help but think of that procession in front of my house taking my oldest sister to her last abode!

Chiquita with children; in mourning for Mariquinha, 1909.

# 32. Dona Ana

 *Caldas, Minas Gerais, Brazil, November 13, 1984*

My new friend Denise, whom I've just met on the bus trip into Caldas, leaves me to get settled at the Hotel Itacor Fazenda, on the *Morro do Coquerinho* (Hill of the Little Coconut Tree) overlooking Caldas, promising to return tomorrow. There is only one other guest at the hotel. I unpack just the necessary things and walk the grounds of the hotel overlooking the *praça* way down below. From this perspective, any rough edges disappear; all is dreamlike calm. The air is still and soft; a perfect place to do nothing. Tamar, the young receptionist, shows me all around and tells me to make myself at home.

On the veranda at the entrance to the hotel, there is a pool table and a place to relax and enjoy the view of the city below. Near the reception desk is a *bar da consciência* (honor system refrigerator) from which you choose what you want from a selection of beer and soft drinks, and make a note of it in the book provided. On weekends a local musician plays the guitar and sings Brazilian popular music and folk songs in a *salão* (large living room) with a fireplace.

Further back is a game room with chess and checkers and on the other side of the long hall, a TV room where I can watch the *novelas* (my daily Portuguese lesson) before dinner. My room has three single beds, a bathroom with shower (with an attached heater), and a tall window with lacy curtains and folding shutters that looks out on a rose garden to the north. In the evening, stars and flickering fireflies wink at me.

The hotel has eighteen rooms, and there is one other semi-permanent guest, Dona Jorgina, an old Portuguese lady, mother of the owner, who is here for her health. It is run by a family—Dona Emília, the mother, cooks; her daughter Maílde is manager; and Maílde's young twin brothers help out around the grounds. It is all so different from the life I am used to, and yet I feel at home here. I am floating on the waves of this new life as effortlessly as I do on the ocean, supported by people who don't know me, yet who accept me graciously, as if they had expected me.

At the end of the building is a big dining room where I have all my meals; there is no other restaurant in town. The food is good, but heavy; I will have to watch my diet here. They want to know what I like to eat so they can plan the meals for me! I tell them I want lots of fresh vegetables—not generally appreciated in Brazil. Dona Emília says, "*A gringa só come mata!*" ("The American eats only weeds!") I breathe a long sigh, sloughing off all my mind's questions about what I'm doing here.

On my second day in Caldas, Denise comes to the hotel for me. We walk down the hill on the dirt road lined with eucalyptus to her house to meet her mother, children, and sister. I can hardly believe it—at last I am here, in Vovó's poetical town of Caldas! Almost one hundred years after she was born, it is still a quiet hilly garden town of flowers and trees, and all around, the mountains she so lovingly described. People are strolling (no one is in a hurry here) and chatting in the long, wide *praça* with a church at either end, that has replaced the fearsome largo of her childhood. The *chafariz* has been moved out of town, but I am told it is still a source of water for the Caldenses.

It is thrilling to be seeing the same sights, breathing the same crisp air, listening to the sounds, smelling the same scents that Vovó did when she was young enough to be my granddaughter. As we walk around town, Denise introduces me to everyone she knows, explaining that I'm here searching for my grandmother's past, and mine. The people I meet are curious about me, but reserved, polite. I silently thank my dear Vovó for bringing this to me.

The houses facing the *praça* look just like the one in the picture I have of the house where Vovó was born on Conde d'Eu; but the street name no longer exists, and no one remembers it. At some point during our walk, Denise arranges for us to visit this evening a former mayor and his wife who know a lot about the history of Caldas. At the post office, I send a telegram to my daughter, but don't have enough cash to pay for it; the postmaster tells me I can bring the rest tomorrow!

Returning up the hill to the hotel, I explore the grounds and meet a cow grazing on the lawn at the side of the hotel. There are turkeys, chickens, ducks, rabbits in cages, a goat and horses; and farther away, pigs. I see my laundry drying on a wooden fence, a small empty swimming pool, an orchard, flower and vegetable gardens, a shady patio. Not another of my species in sight. I take some pictures, weep, rest, write. I get a hammock and hang it under trees. A little sign identifies the spot as the *Recanto dos Amoreiras* (Nook of the Mulberry Trees). Lying in the hammock, I hear nothing but the sounds of summer—the warbling of many different bird voices, the soft humming of insects, the whir of hummingbird wings, the flutter of leaves, nothing else. No cars, motorcycles, radios. Suddenly, but without surprise, I hear in my mind my father's voice reciting:

> *"Minha terra tem palmeiras*
> *onde canta o Sabiá.*
> *As aves, que aquí gorjeiam*
> *não gorjeiam como lá."*[73]

Later, I look it up—it is the first stanza of the poem *Canção do Exílio* (Song of Exile) by Gonçalves Dias, which every Brazilian schoolchild learns. I feel like Emily Webb in *Our Town*, as if I had died and been granted one day to come back and re-live, and see for the first time the excruciating beauty of ordinary life.

The air is clean and fresh, no smell or sight of pollution. Bathed in stillness and peace, I am engulfed in a wave of feeling deeper than, but including, joy and sorrow and the absence of time. Above all, a peace unlike any I've ever felt. It's as if I've been lifted to a place where past and present meet and I am near to everyone, living and dead, whom I love. I embrace the presence of Vovó here, as if the past were opening up and I were walking right into it. In this lovely place I have found my spiritual home.

In the evening, as arranged, Denise takes me to visit Sergio Bellini, who

---

73. My homeland has many palm-trees
     and the thrush-song fills its air;
     no bird here can sing as well
     as the birds sing over there.

Gonçalves Dias, "Song of Exile," stanza 1; translation by Nelson Ascher. Gonçalves Dias wrote this poem expressing *saudades* for Brazil in 1843 while studying in Coimbra, Portugal. The last two lines of the second stanza ("we have woods more full of life / and a life more full of love") are incorporated in the national anthem.

Annita, Itacor, 1984.

she thinks might know something of my family. I think it unlikely since it must be sixty years since the last time Vovó visited here. He doesn't, but as we sip *cafezinhos*, I tell Sr. Sergio and his wife about finding the *Reminiscências*. They are familiar with the history of Caldas, and how it looked in the 1870s, and they enjoy hearing about her description of the town a century ago.

We talk about Dr. André with his one lung, and about the *largo*. When I say children were afraid to cross the *largo* because they might fall on top of a—he interrupts me with a hearty laugh and finishes my sentence with—"*cavalo*" (horse). I correct—"*vaca*" (cow), and we all laugh. I speak about the *cruzeiro* (cross) and Sr. Sergio tells me about an oil painting of the *largo* in 1875 that hangs in the courthouse, and then gives me a large framed photograph of the painting with the cross very prominent in the center of the *largo*, just as Vovó described it. I return to the Itacor blessed by the Southern Cross and Orion, here called *Três Marias*, seemingly within my grasp. I don't want to close my eyes. I do, though, and I sleep like a baby.

Next day, I walk slowly up and down the steep streets on both sides of the *praça* with my picture of the house where Vovó was born; looking for it, and other landmarks described in the *Reminiscências*. I think nothing remains of Padrinho's house, the grocery store, the chapel, or the house next door where Vovó's grandmother lived. I do not know where to look for them, but they are not on the *praça* or on nearby streets. I take lots of pictures, and make a copy of the photo Sr. Sergio gave me of the painting of the *largo*. Suddenly, in the copy place, I get teary.

Exploring the town on my own, I find the cemetery at the foot of the hill and see the huge obelisk marking Dr. André's grave. Everyone still speaks of Dr. André with his one lung—he is one of the town's luminaries along with the Westins and Dr. Vital Brasil of Butantã fame.[74] I think they all have streets named for them. Sadly, I could not find where my great-grandmother, great-grandfather, and great aunts were buried.

Another day, Denise takes me to the house of another *ex-prefeito* (just about every man in town must have been mayor at one time), Sr. João, the owner of a little private museum. It is not open to the public, but Denise persuades him to show it to us. There are many old and interesting things made of porcelain, crystal, and silver, including early pharmaceutical equipment, and I wonder, did any of these once belong to my great-grandfather?

It is not hard to feel I have entered a time warp as I dig like an archeologist for the past. I meet other people: old women who knew Vovó and Tia Noemi. People say, "You should talk to so and so," or they have some little piece of history to add. Everyone seems to remember my Uncle Henry, who was here with Vovó in 1908 and again in 1920 after his father died. They all say, "Such a handsome young man!"

Everywhere, I tell my story. Everyone is so kind to me, so welcoming and gracious. Vovó, and my father, too, would be so happy to see this. I haven't met anyone yet who remembers my family, but I have a feeling I will. Everyone here seems to be related; there are lots of Camargos, but I haven't met any Pereiras. It is easy to imagine everything as it was, except

---

74. Dr. Vital Brasil was the founder in 1888 of the Butanã Institute and Snake Farm in São Paulo, a research center for the study of venomous snakes and the development of snakebite serum.

for the slaves. I know some of their descendants must be here, but Caldas looks like a place of happy Brazilian miscegenation.

When I am not exploring or just drinking in the beauty of this place I begin to translate Vovó's story, so I can speak more easily about it. I continue the tedious chore of transcription from tape to paper, taking breaks to work on the translation. A cousin of Denise's, Maria Odete, a high school teacher of Portuguese, corrects my translation and little by little, it's getting done.

I am beginning to feel at home here at the Itacor. At first I had my own table by the window looking out on the rose garden, where I ate alone; now I eat with Dona Jorgina and Maílde. We are like a family. Often we are the only ones here. Sometimes there is a couple on their honeymoon or a family, and twice, whole *fútebol* teams that stayed a day or two and then went on to their matches. On the weekends there is more likely to be a couple or two from São Paulo, escaping the urban madness.

I have become good friends with Maílde, who has become interested in my quest. She tells me about an old woman who is the granddaughter of a slave of Capivari, a *fazenda* mentioned in the diary. As I am finishing lunch one day, the woman, Dona Bexuta, and her daughter, Maria Aparecida (called Cida), arrive to see me. Dona Bexuta is in her sixties, I guess, and has the most beautiful cherubic face and smile. They have heard that there is a North American at the hotel looking for people who might know of her ancestors, and they want to meet me. We have lunch, talk a while, and they say the person I should talk with is Dona Maria de Lourdes, that she might remember Vovó's family.

Maílde drives us to Dona Maria's house, the same one she lived in as a child. I imagine that the house is similar to Vovó's childhood home. You step up on a huge stone to the door, which is about ten feet tall. Inside are wood plank floors, high doors and windows, thinly painted walls. Dona Maria is eighty-eight years old, quite lucid, and truly happy to see me. It is thrilling to meet someone who knew not only my Vovó and Tia Noemi, who was a great friend of hers, but their parents! I am astonished to learn that she knows the names of all of Vovó's children, and also remembers when Vovó brought them to Caldas in 1909! What a thrill to hear about my father as a six-year-old boy!

We have *cafezinhos* and little cookies as she tells me how she, my father, Uncle Neco, and Aunt Argy were playing in the dining room while the adults visited in the *sala*. My father kept climbing up on a table and jumping off, making the girls hoot hysterically. She told me that Vovó came into the room to quiet the children—speaking to hers in English, which Maria did not understand. Daddy answered, also in English. Then, speaking to Maria in Portuguese, Vovó said, "*Brinque, sim, mas quietinho, para que os pais possam falar.*" ("Play quietly so that your parents can talk.")

The young Maria did not know, until Aunt Argy told her, that Daddy had told his mother that Maria was the one jumping; but Aunt Argy defended Maria, telling her mother the jumper was Daddy, who got a mild scolding—"Not for the jumping," Dona Maria says, "but for the lie." Shades of George Washington and his cherry tree, a frequent didactic tale in our house! Dona Maria says of all the children, he was the most *peralta* (mischievous). How delightful to see my loving but very authoritarian father as a *menino peralta*! Being with Dona Maria was a sweet, fantastic, moving experience. I had no idea that my father had ever been in Caldas— can it be that he never mentioned it?

Dona Maria is interested in the story I am writing and wants a copy of the translation, as well as the names and dates I have of my ancestors in Caldas and Machado. Many times I have to choke back the tears as I listen to her memories of my father as a boy, wondering if he had remembered her, as she did him. I tell her I have been unable to find Rua Conde D'Eu, the street where Vovó was born. She says the name was changed a long time ago to Rua Buena de Paiva, and tells Cida where the house had stood until it was torn down a year ago! How I would have liked to see it, maybe even to have gone inside for the same view that started Vovó on her longing! Dona Maria also tells me that my great-grandfather's pharmacy was sold to another pharmacist, who then moved it to the *praça*. He died, and the pharmacy is gone, but she says his daughter still has many of the furnishings from there.

After a wonderful visit there, Dona Bexuta and Cida invite me to their modest house where they show me lots of old things, including objects from Capivari—lamps, cooking utensils and bowls. Dona Bexuta tells me that her great-grandmother, a slave at Capivari, lived to be 102, and that her grandmother, also a slave there, made clothes for the other slaves on the plantation. Slaves, she tells me, built the cemetery in Caldas, and walls built by slaves can be seen in various places all around the town.

Dona Bexuta's husband was a dancer in the *Congadas*, the folklore dramatizations in song and dance depicting the crowning of a king in the Congo. She shows me some of the costumes. I tell her I have a letter written to Vovó from her sister Ophida shortly before she died telling how one of the singers drank pickle juice to make his voice falsetto for the *Congadas*. We laugh together, seeing the scene in our minds.

The next day I ask for and am given permission to pick some lilies from the garden to take to Dona Maria de Lourdes. We have a good visit; she tells me about her life as a young girl—about the pageantry of *Congadas*, the lamplighter making his rounds in the mornings and evenings until the coming of electricity in 1916, and the arrival of the first cars in Caldas. It is raining a little when I leave; I meet Cida, who walks me back to the hotel with her umbrella. Arriving there, we join a couple of people playing and singing at the piano. Cida has a very strong and interesting voice, and sings a haunting ballad about a romance between a Paraguayan girl and a Brazilian soldier during the war with Paraguay.

On the following day I go to meet Denise, and we stop at her grandmother's house. Over a *cafezinho*, her grandmother tells us about a João Pereira, who was called "Vô João" (Grandpa John), and could possibly have been the ex-slave mentioned in the journals. His daughter is still living, and she tells us where to find her. So my first clue in my search for João's descendants comes from the grandmother of my first friend in Caldas, whom I met on the bus on my way there. As Vovó would say, "What a coeencidence!"

Soon Denise and I are walking down a steep hill and stopping at a wooden gate, the entrance to a sloping garden of corn, yams, and manioc. The house we were told about is gone; only the garden remains, but Denise claps her hands towards a house in the back, and pretty soon a man about my age makes his way slowly to the gate, looking apprehensive. I let Denise do the talking for me. She explains that I am North American, that my grandmother was born in Caldas, and that I am looking for someone who might remember her. He says he doesn't know anything about my family. Denise asks him if we may talk with his mother who, he tells us, has been living with him in the back house ever since the front house was torn down two years ago. He tells us his mother is not feeling well; she is resting and, he thinks, asleep, but we may come back another time and talk with her. To my embarrassment, Denise keeps on talking, and pretty soon, looking very dubious, the man says he will check with his mother. Denise repeats my grandmother's name, Chiquita Pereira, and leaving us at the gate he goes down the path to the three-room adobe house below the corn patch.

He is back in an instant, inviting us to follow him to the house, a very modest cottage with a floor made of stone blocks covered with what looks like concrete. It is very uneven; globs of mortar protrude from between the bricks as if it were a wall. There is a *fogão* (hearth) in a corner, a table and four chairs, a cupboard with a basket of eggs on top, a small gas stove, a calendar on the wall, and some pictures. Besides this room, there are two bedrooms, separated by curtains. I don't know about plumbing.

The old woman is seated in a chair beside the *fogão*, the wood-burning fireplace that heats the house in the winter. Now, in November, it is not needed for heat, but this is where she always sits, her head tilted and slightly bowed, her eyes lightly closed because she is blind, her fingers picking lint off a blanket on her lap. She raises her head as Denise introduces herself and me, telling how we met on the bus. Her son Odair, called Ieiieí, pulls two chairs from the table, offering them to us. Denise sits at her side, I pull up a chair to face her, and her son sits on a chair by the table. Denise talks, explaining that I am the granddaughter of Chiquita Pereira de Morães Clark. Then the old woman begins to talk.

Her name is Ana, daughter of João, the son of Eva. She is eighty-three. She turns her ear towards me, and asks, "*A senhora é filha de quien?*" ("Whose daughter are you?") "*Sou filha do Jorge, filho caçulo da Dona*

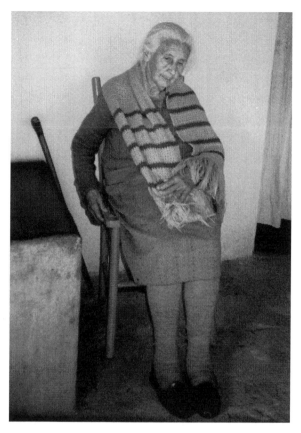

Dona Ana beside her fogão, 1984.

*Chiquita*." ("I am the daughter of George, Dona Chiquita's youngest.")
With a little sob, and with surprise in her voice, she softly cries,
"*Jorginho!*" Tears stream down both of our cheeks as she tells me how
they had played together on the floor the year Vovó brought her children
to Caldas to escape the summer heat in Rio. She seems to be seeing the
scene again, as she speaks in her raspy voice, with her twangy *mineiro*
accent:

> "*Dona Chiquita lived near the house of Capitão Amirantes. So
> there was myself, there was my sister Maria, Argentina, Arzila, the
> daughter of the Captain, Nequinho, and your father. We played hide
> and seek in the largo around the chafariz. Your father used to like to
> play around the chafariz; he liked to turn on the faucet and splash
> water on us. And another thing—we played with the rim of a wheel,
> rolling it around in front of the Rosário Church. There was a cross*

*in front of the door of the church—people put money there under a*
*rock, and your father pushed the rock away and took the money to*
*buy bananas for us. Bananas were very cheap in those days, but we*
*didn't have any money. My mother and Dona Chiquita were cross,*
*but we didn't pay any attention—we were just kids. Now your father*
*was a good boy, but he was mischievous—he threw water on me and*
*pulled my hair, but with all of this he was a wonderful little boy—*
*not impolite or bad-mouthed. And Dona Chiquita also and Sr. Clark*
*were good people."*

If my father ever told me about being in Caldas, I had forgotten; but that
does not diminish the sweetness of hearing of him now, seeing him as
a boy of six, chasing the girls around the *largo*, and daring them to run
through the cemetery at night. She knows the names of all of my father's
brothers and sisters, but Jorginho was her favorite. She asks Ieileí to fetch
a picture from her room, where it has been hanging on the wall. It is a
photograph of "some Protestant picnic" that Vovó gave to her. Among
a large group, I recognize my grandmother and grandfather, Daddy,
about six years old, Aunt Ruth, and Uncle Orton. I am amazed to hear
in Dona Ana's voice the esteem in which she holds her memories of my
grandmother. We are both flabbergasted. She says she can't believe that a
*filha do Jorge* would come all the way from the United States to sit beside
the *fogão* of an old poor woman, and I can't believe that I would find a
picture of my father and his family hanging in the house of a woman I
didn't know, until now, existed.

By this time, I am sitting on the hearth, holding her hand with my arm
around her. We are both weeping. Her son sits further away, silently
smiling. Whenever she says, as she often does, "I can't believe..." he says,
"*É assim, Mãe—a vida é assim.*" ("Yes, Mother—life is like this.") She gives
me the picture, and tells me where my ancestors are buried in unmarked
graves in the Protestant section on the hill of the cemetery. She and Ieiieí
say we may come back at any time. We say we'll come back soon with
camera and tape recorder. She says she regrets she cannot see my face,
but is very happy she lived long enough to "see" George's daughter. She
is also very happy that we have the same name, and that she and my
daughter Andrea have the same birthday. I kiss her; we leave.

It is raining today. Cida comes for me with her umbrella and as we walk down the hill, I tell her about yesterday's visit with Dona Ana. We walk to the street where Vovó was born, and find the place where the house had been. It is just a weedy sloping lot looking across a valley to the pastures and hills beyond, but it is not hard to imagine that I am a small girl, inside a house, looking out the back window to the forests and hills to the north, imagining that I would someday go beyond that horizon to far away places.

Among the weeds, the rubble of a fallen house can be seen; a house where I am told my grandmother, whose grandmother was then younger than I am now, played, laughed, cried, loved, and dreamed. I pick up a couple of shards of crumbling plaster. Later someone tells me—or did I dream it?—that one, a yellowish tan color, was from the outside of the house, the other, a light streaky blue, from the *sala*, the heart of the house. This is enough emotion for me for one day, but Cida has made plans. My head spinning, we go to Sr. Zuzú's house—most everyone here has a nickname; I don't get his real first or last name. His wife, Dona Geni, serves *cafezinhos* and he gives me some old postcards and an early photograph of the *praça*. He tells me Vovó was his mother's teacher! Then Sr. Zuzú performs a little puppet show for me with Cida and Dona Geni reading the parts. I don't really know what it's about, but it is sweet and ingenuous. I return to the hotel in pink light of sunset and mist–drizzle.

Today after lunch at the hotel, I stop for Denise, then buy a little present for Dona Ana. We are both excited as we descend the hill. When we get to her house, it is all *arrumada* (cleaned and tidied)—Ieiieí must have been busy—and coffee is ready. Dona Ana is seated in her chair, dressed in her best, a tan skirt and light blue sweater, with a long, hand-knit scarf around her neck. We talk; I tape, take pictures. She gives her permission before taping but I see she doesn't understand exactly what I am doing, so I ask her if she wants to hear the tape. When I put the earphones on her, she laughs and laughs with delight. She has a wonderful cackle, and it is great to see her so happy.

I visit Dona Ana once or twice daily. Each time she tells me more stories—

about herself, and about my family. She was born in Santa Casa da Misericórdia, the hospital founded by Dr. André and Father Trinidade, and where her mother worked for thirty-eight years. Dr. Pimenta was her godfather. Her grandmother, Eva, lived with them, but she doesn't remember her—she died when Ana was five. Dona Ana went to school from age seven until she was twelve when she left school to work in people's houses. When she was seventeen she married, but the union was not happy. She lived with her husband for twenty-five years and bore nine children, but she said she did not feel anything when he died, because he was not a good husband.

She raised her nine children and two grandchildren with little help from him. She worked in the houses of many women, including Vovó's niece Maria Ovídia, when she lived in Poços with her husband. (Maria O was the one who came to live with Vovó when her mother, Tia Josephina, died, and looked after my father when he was little.) Ana made many straw baskets to sell, going on foot. Dona Ana suffered a lot, went hungry—sometimes there was only broth from beans and corn meal. Sometimes she didn't have enough money to buy rice. But, she says, "Thanks to God, all of my children are strong, with good health. None have gone to jail, or been called a thief. I have worked hard in my life, and now here I sit, until God calls me. *Pois é, Annita, a vida é dura!* (Yes, Annita, life is hard!)"

She also talks about Vovó, Daddy, Argentina, Orton, Henry, and Neco, whom she calls Nequinho. She tells me stories she heard from her father, João, about my great-grandparents. I tell her that I knew about João from the *Reminiscências*. It is as hard to think of her as the daughter of a slave as it is to think of myself as the great-granddaughter of slave owners; in fact, when I read the translation to her, she insists that Eva and João were never slaves, but trusted servants of the family. Her love and respect for the family is genuine and amazing to me.

One day she tells me quite matter-of-factly that her father João was what is known in Brazil as the "natural son" of my great-grandfather, Manoel Pereira. I know this contradicts Vovó's story, which I believe she believed to be true. It is hard for me to reconcile the injustices of slavery with the affection that existed between the two families, yet I know that there was a connection between Dona Ana and Daddy during a few months of childhood, and remembered and renewed between Dona Ana and me. Whether we are related or not, I know in my relationship with Dona Ana the sense of belonging to one another—of common history.

The truth is not possible to know, and to me, it doesn't matter. Despite the inequality of station, despite poverty on one side and relative prosperity on the other, despite insensitivities, resentments, and all the other unpleasant emotions that inequality is bound to bring, in spite of the two different stories, Vovó and her sisters and Dona Ana's grandmother and father were all part of a family unit who looked after one another.

The stories about her grandmother Eva are very sad. She says that Vovó's mother (the first Maria Ovídia), upon discovering that Eva was pregnant, demanded to know who the father was, and Eva refused to tell. She tells me that when João was born, my great grandmother went to see the child in the *porão* (basement) where Eva lived, taking clothes for him. As he grew, she became jealous because my great-grandfather, Manoel, took João riding with him, instead of taking the girls. Dona Ana smiles as she tells me how he loved to take João on the back of his horse, and told him, "When we are with the girls you must call me '*patrão*' (boss, master) but when we are alone, you may call me '*Papai*'." She says that because of my great-grandmother's jealousy, João was sent to live with a family in a village six miles away; and on her day off, Eva would walk in her sandals the long way to visit her son.

And yet, Dona Ana has a wonderful sense of humor, this possible cousin of mine whose life is lived sitting in a chair in a simple house, listening to the radio. Her eyes see only shadows, but they have a sparkle; she has no bottom teeth, but she has a beautiful smile and a wonderful laugh. Because she is blind, and I try to be eyes for her, I see everything more precisely. She asks me what kind of a day it is, and I describe the sky and flowers and trees and birds and people I see on the walk down the hill from the hotel to her house, and she smiles, remembering, and I am grateful for the increased awareness she brings to my world.

She is so honest and genuine, she never fakes anything. When her daughter Ivone called for a priest to hear her confession because she had not been to church for such a long time, Dona Ana raised her head to the priest and said, "What do you suppose I have to confess? I sit here in this chair all day, unable to see or go anywhere!" The priest agreed and went away.

We have become very fond of each other. She tells me life is hard, but she never whines or complains, and she thanks me with grace and dignity for the little things I do for her and her family. She calls me *"Annita do céu"* (Annita from heaven) because to her, it is a miracle that I have come from a far-away country on an airplane, and dropped out of the sky to find her. She says what makes her most sad is that she can't see my face; I have her feel it. She repeats that one day when I bring Mailde, who says, "Dona Ana, I think she looks a lot like you," which makes us both happy. In truth, she looks a lot like Vovó.

And in that tiny house with its dirt floor, Dona Ana and I, with all the differences of age, education, culture, language, and material means that can divide people, understand and love each other's most essential selves.

# 33. Lost and Found, 1909–1911

*Athens, Ohio, 1943*

We were back together again in our picturesque little house with friends always calling on Sundays for afternoon tea. It was our At Home, and many times we had guests for dinner as well. On Christmas that year, 1909, we had fourteen with our family at table. On Thursdays, if the weather permitted, we carried the chair, the pillow, the mending, and the book to the hill and we went as before, enjoying friends in person and friends in books. We read aloud *Hiawatha* and *Rainier of the Last Frontier*, and all the authors, in English and in Portuguese, that we could get. It was a day of relaxation.

The New Year found Orton in bed for over a week with paratyphoid. He was feverish all through that month and the doctors advised us not to send him back to school. I was busy sewing to get Ruth ready for the MacKenzie College in São Paulo.

I remember that there were disorders on the Avenida Central because of the approaching election for president, and there was a revolt on board the *Minas Gerais* led by a sailor, João Candido. The sailors wanted abolition of corporal punishment and more men on board to lighten the excessive work. They killed the highest officer in command, put all the others in prison, left the bay, and drifted away to sea where they could not be reached by the guns of our three fortresses at the entrance of the bay. Other warships, the *São Paulo*, the *Bahia*, and the *Derdero*, joined the revolt, and were cruising around the bay and occasionally firing; a grenade even fell on the Sailors' Bureau, causing much damage. There was much sympathy for the men amongst the people. These men were out at sea for several days. In the evenings from our veranda we saw the searchlights of these boats. Admiral José Carlos de Carvalho ventured out to sea in a little launch with no other protection but a white flag hoisted where it could be clearly seen.

Ruth was back in São Paulo in the American school there, where I had studied and taught, and Myron had to visit the Association in São Paulo in November. He was staying with my sister and wrote, "Ruth came to Cacilda's. How she has grown, a fine looking girl, if I do say it." She was fifteen. In March I went there, leaving some of the children at home with Maria Ovídia, while the others went to my sister Noemi's.

While I was visiting in São Paulo, the Association received a cable saying that [U.S. statesman] William Jennings Bryan would arrive in Rio on March 12th for a lecture tour.[75] Myron met with the American Ambassador Dudley to arrange for meetings during Bryan's stay here and with the Minister of Foreign Affairs, the Barão de Rio Branco, who showed lots of interest, offered the Monroe Palace for one of Bryan's lectures, rooms at the Hotel dos Estrangeiros, and a special car from São Paulo.

When Mr. Bryan arrived, he accepted all the plans for the different lectures, but that was not all. He asked the Secretary of the Y to buy him a parrot for his wife! Well, not so very far from our house somebody had an *arara* (macaw) a most beautiful, colorful bird with the most annoying voice! More beautiful even than a parrot, but not so intelligent or as good an imitator. We could not see it, but we certainly could hear that cracked voice, so Myron told him about the *arara* and Mr. Bryan came to Copacabana, saw the bird, and paid the price, which for an American was nothing, but for this resident of a hut in the hills of Copacabana, was a fortune. I wonder if Mr. Bryan heard the *arara* before he bought it! I don't believe so. I heard many years later from Mr. Bryan himself that he gave the bird to the zoo in Nebraska. We were certainly delighted to be relieved of the annoying sounds of that now-aristocratic bird.

And now, my little posterity, on May 8th we had the privilege to see a thing whose arrival and departure were not controlled by men—the

---

75. William Jennings Bryan experienced religious conversion at a Presbyterian Church Revival when he was fourteen, and remained aligned with the Presbyterian Church and YMCA throughout his life. Bryan is best known to Americans for his 1925 debate with Clarence Darrow in the Scopes Trial, also called the "Monkey Trial," in which he argued against Darwin's "theory" of evolution.

comet Halley. In my teens I saw the Biela[76] which was not as long as Halley, but much more brilliant. We saw it at dawn; it was beautiful, but Halley turned out to be a disappointment.

The next year, 1911, opened with two happy events. Since the summer of 1909 when my sister Mariquinha died in Caldas, her daughter, Henedina, seventeen at the time and a teacher in Rio, had been living with us. She became engaged to one of our Sunday visitors, a fine Englishman, John Edward Anderson, and was married from our home. The other concerned some crumbs that we had cast upon the waters. They returned to us more like a rock, and we built our home upon it.

It happened like this: after my brother Argentino died in 1896, his best friend, Dominges, asked to stay with us as a paying guest. We were happy to have him, not on the basis of money but of friendship. Now he was the head of a shoe factory and doing fine. He came to my husband saying that because of what our home had meant to him, he wanted to loan us money free of interest to build our own home. We would just pay rent until we were paid up. He recommended the builder who had built his factory and would not accept "no" from my husband.

Oh, my dreams were coming true! There would not be anybody in front of us—just the Avenue and the sea! Several times my husband had been approached to sell the lot for two and three times more than we had put in it, but we wanted a home of our own. Minequinho was the oldest son of my sister Josephina, who died at my house when he was about nine; he was an engineer and offered to make the plans for it. Our vacation was nearing. Minequinho and Dominges advised my husband to have the house built while we were away so that we could move right into it on coming back. Minequinho and my niece Henedina, now Mrs. Anderson, offered to take charge of our home until we came back.

On Sunday, April 16th, we were on our way. After 19 days on board, we

---

76. The Biela comet was observed in 1846 to break in two, and in 1852, sixteen years before Chiquita was born, the fragments returned as twin comets that were never seen thereafter. Between 1880 and 1882, four bright comets were seen in the Southern Hemisphere: the Great Comet, Great Southern Comet, Great September Comet, and Wells Comet. One of these must have been the one she saw as a teenager ("Biela's Comet," *New York Times*; Bortle, "Bright-Comet Chronicles," paras. 21–24).

arrived in New York on the 5th of May. While we were there, we saw the New York Giants win over the Pittsburgh Pirates 4 to 3, and attended the cinema for 5 cents per person.

After seeing our very dear relatives in Buffalo, we continued on to Minneapolis. The next day we all went to Lake Minnetonka where we had rented a cottage for the summer.

My dear sister-in-law and her family came and spent several weeks at the Lake in their own cottage. We had a grand time that summer. My six children ranged from eight to seventeen-and-a-half and her three children from nine to eighteen years old. The bathing was grand, and we enjoyed fishing and boating on moonlit nights. Ruth took part in a vaudeville show, and one Sunday the Sunday school teachers gave an entertainment in which my husband took part. The children were the center of attraction as they could talk and sing in two languages perfectly. Really, we had a fine summer with relatives and friends

The day after we arrived at the lake, Myron took the night train to Columbus, Ohio, for a conference of the YMCA General Secretaries and Directors in the country, and there were many more trips after that. Once I got to go along, to a conference at Silver Bay.[77] The grandparents came from Minneapolis to stay at our cottage with the children, but they were big enough to take care of themselves now, and they ate at a restaurant.

On our way to Silver Bay we stopped in East Aurora to visit Grandma Tyler and Myron's cousin Ed. Ed's wife was away in some sanitarium with incipient consumption. He was anxious to rent his house furnished for the winter so they all could go to California. This was providential for both families, so we rented it. We loved East Aurora and its people but we loved most Grandma Tyler because she was not scared of a family of six children, and we loved to be near Uncle Henry.

We were back in Minneapolis on Myron's birthday, the 23rd of September, to spend our last week in Minneapolis at Winnie's. She had a birthday cake for him! There were luncheons and teas for us in Minneapolis, and we left on October 1st for our new home at East

77. On Lake George in New York. The Silver Bay Association was founded in 1902 as a YMCA conference and training center.

Aurora, New York. We decided to leave the two older children, Ruth and Orton, at Macalester College. Arriving in East Aurora, we arranged for the four other children to go to the public school. Soon my husband was on another speaking tour to raise money for the work in Brazil. I have letters and postal cards from most of the places he visited, as he was never too busy to send a word of love to his family.

## 1912

That winter we saw the hardest and heaviest snowstorm we had ever seen. One day I spoke at a missionary meeting in Buffalo; the thermometer registered 15 degrees below zero! A neighbor, a farmer, took charge of our furnace and was on hand always to see that these South Americans were comfortable. He was around very frequently to talk with us. One day he was praising our courage to cross the seas so many times facing so much danger. My husband told him that it was as safe as it was on land; that if a hole were made in the boat they could close that part until it got to some port to be repaired. In less than a month came the news that the unsinkable Titanic had gone down, and the farmer came with the paper to show my husband!

Myron continued his traveling, and while in New York the physicians advised him to have an operation for some old trouble, right there in New York. He was very homesick then; I sent him letters and a box of beautiful carnations. Soon after, when he could travel, he came home where he was in bed under the doctor's care, and mine, until the 11th of April. On the 13th he was on the road again, speaking and soliciting.

The children and I stayed in East Aurora until May 13th, with two trips to Buffalo for tonsillectomies for Henry, then thirteen, and me. Myron continued his trips; on one he saw the battlefields in Chattanooga. The children made many friends in East Aurora and there were parties for them before we left. On May the 30th, we left East Aurora to be with our Buffalo relatives until it was time to leave for New York. Ruth and Orton came by train to Buffalo to say goodbye. I was surprised at their growth. Ruth was a beautiful young lady, and Orton a handsome young man. On the 11th of June, we left for New York City.

Now, my grandchildren, it is going to be some fun to tell you this, but it was no fun at all to go through what I did that night and the day we sailed for home. My dear old teacher Mrs. Magalhães was living in Brooklyn then, so she invited me to spend a few days at her home with the two younger boys. Then Henry, the two girls, and I were invited by some friends for dinner in Montclair, New Jersey. It was arranged for Neco and George to stay with Mrs. Magalhães, who would bring them on board on June the 20th.

The other children were staying with our friends in New Jersey, and I was going back alone to New York to meet my husband. He explained what to do after I left the train to take a ferryboat. He would be there to meet me after I crossed the Hudson. After dinner my friends took me to the train and when I got to the ferryboats, instead of asking where that ferry was going to land, I forgot all my husband's instructions and took the first one, and landed in the opposite direction from where I ought to have landed in New York.

After waiting for half an hour, I called my husband at the hotel. After going to the ferry and seeing that I was not there, he waited for another one to come and as I was not on this one either, and as the hotel was not too far from the ferry station, he thought I was coming later and went back to the hotel. I told him I was there at the time he told me to be, and he told me he was going back there right away. I went outside, put myself where I could be seen and I waited and waited.

By this time the place was getting deserted and the few people around were probably wondering what I was doing there as ferryboats came and went and I seemed to be planted there. I had been there about one hour and was in my mind praying for help when one of the employees came to me and told me my husband was on the telephone. I am sure I praised Mr. Bell for his invention and went to the phone. He told me he had called up the different ferry stations and asked if there was a woman waiting there, and found out that I had taken one to the opposite side, so he was coming for me but it was going to take some time for him to get where I was, so I should go in where I could sit down. What a relief! It was after midnight when we got home.

This is nothing compared to what you are going to hear now, little ones.

I went back to Mrs. Magalhães's house the next day where the two boys were and from there she took us to the boat, the old *Voltaire*, not a first-class boat. Our friends from Montclair were supposed to bring Ruth, Baby, and Henry. Several friends came on board to say goodbye until the signal was given to all the passengers to go ashore.

After everybody had left the boat and we were as nervous as could be because there was no sign of our children or the folks with whom they had stayed, my husband came to me and said, "I am going on shore on the launch of the company to find out want happened. The captain is going to wait for a while; if they don't appear until the boat has to leave I will stay on shore and go with them on the next boat."

I was stunned. I felt paralyzed. Half an hour passed and the anchor came up and the boat began to move. I ran to the bridge where the captain was and told him that my husband and children were not on board yet. He said very nicely, "I have to leave the port now, but I will wait outside for a while." We were not quite out of the bay when we saw a tug following us and a chorus went around, "The missionary children are coming! Hurray!" The captain slowed down and the tug got to the boat and they attached a ladder and Myron and the children came up with the cheers of everybody. Neither the boat nor the tug stopped: they were going just slowly enough for that precious cargo to be put on board! This was the story: Somebody heard somebody say that the boat was always late so the friends wanted to let the children have a good time on land! What they did was to give a good story to a few newspapers, each one different, and to the parents, a few hours of agony!

From that day on the children had the Captain, the officers, and the crew at their orders as far as a good time was concerned. For once, I was not seasick. The steamer was very steady. We had a table all to ourselves. The Captain and Purser were very attentive. We anchored in Rio on July 9th, where Myron was to assume a new position as National Secretary.

# 34. Caldas in the Rain

 *Caldas, Minas Gerais, December, 1984*

It's December, and it has rained all day today. I am feeling a bit down, wondering what I'm doing here, out of place and out of touch with the rest of the world. Is it the constant rain or pre-Christmas blues? I need a plan; I feel I'm drifting. The idea of writing now seems absurd. I think that the excitement of Caldas is wearing off. Finding my place is hard. I miss my family, my friends.

Mailde, manager of the Itacor, and by now a good friend, takes me after dinner to a mass for her sister Silvana, whose graduation we then attend. It is very serious, very lovely. Each candidate is escorted to the front, walks across the stage, is kissed three times *mineiro* style from cheek to cheek to cheek by a teacher, shakes the hand of the person who gives the diploma, and is met and kissed three times by her escort. The singing of the many verses of the National Anthem is very serious, respectful. It is called the National Hymn, and it is sung like one. I sit with Cida, Dona Bexuta's daughter. She is so elegant! Afterwards I go with all of them to a dance. I dance with a boy who speaks English and who asks if I am here in Caldas without my parents! (I guess it must have been dark!) I leave with Mailde at three in the morning.

Tomorrow I go to Rio for a visit with Ginger. While there, I will mail Christmas packages, exchange money, and extend my visa for three more months; after that, I will have to go out of Brazil to get a new visa. I find twenty-two letters waiting for me at Ginger's in Rio! It is great to see her, and wonderful to read all these warm letters. Letters telling of trips to Europe, art openings, political meetings, concerts, hot tubs, and samadhi tanks—so far removed from the sweet, unsophisticated life I am living here. It seems impossible that I could be connected to both, but I am. I extend my visa for three more months.

Now back to Caldas, after a welcome respite in Rio. I feel happy, and don't know why. It has something to do with love, with the warmth, openness, and simplicity that I feel here; something to do with the way I perceive the world here—with involved curiosity, with trust, and without self-consciousness. I am seeing joy in others' eyes, and it makes me happy.

Dona Ana, who by day sees only shadows, dreams in color. Today she tells me, "*Nunca tinho sonho feio; só coisa bonita.*" ("I have never had a bad dream; only beautiful ones.") She dreamed she saw me returning after an absence, coming down the dirt path through the corn patch to her mud house, dressed in a maroon-and-white checked skirt and white blouse, bringing her flowers. She has never seen my face, but in her dream, she saw me smiling.

It has rained all day today; it's been raining forever.

Dona Ana and I have a good talk today. She laughs a lot. I am envious of the spontaneity, joy, and togetherness of Brazilians, and I miss my kids and my friends, Christmas trees, Christmas carols. It doesn't seem like Christmas in summer. A guest at the hotel, a *Paulista*, says even she feels like an outsider here. Every region in Brazil has its own slang, accent,

Rainy day in Caldas, 1984.

mannerisms, and I guess *Mineiros* are a special type—simple, sincere, warm, and accepting. I am discouraged; I don't fit in here. It rains a lot, almost every day—thunder and lightning, hard rain. When it is sunny, as it is now—I am typing on the pleasant veranda—there are always fluffy cumulus clouds, but the weather changes in an instant.

Saturday it rained during the day but ended in the evening, and the *praça* was full of people from the *roça* (countryside) walking around the new fountain with its gaudy red lights. The inauguration of the fountain was the big event a week or so ago. During the day the town is quiet—a few cars, men on horseback wearing big cowboy hats, families in horse-drawn carts, boys selling live chickens they carry upside down, their legs tied together. Yesterday, high in the bamboo close to the hotel, I saw a pair of toucans!

During a break in the rain, Dona Ana's daughter, Ivone, comes to the hotel for lunch. Afterwards we walk to the *vila*, which seems to be a sort of public housing for old people. She wants to show me the *chafariz* that used to be in the *largo*. We have trouble communicating—she is deaf and reads lips; my lips apparently don't move the way those of native speakers do, which I suppose accounts for the accent that I can't seem to lose. Her speech is guttural, and difficult for me. We both try hard, and use a lot of body language, and sometimes we write things down.

Another sunny day, and Denise's cousin Maria Odete, who is becoming a friend, arranges a trip for Denise and me to Capivari. A cousin of hers drives us there in a couple of hours, and I try to imagine the daylong trip Vovó made on the back of a mule. It is still a dirt road, and at one point we have to wait while a team of oxen fords a little river. I am surprised to see they still have wagons with wooden wheels that make deep tracks in the muddy road.

The remains of the *casa grande* are still here; the door is unlocked and we go inside. To my amazement, a couple of old portraits stare down from a crumbling wall. Foundations of other buildings are barely visible through the overgrown grasses. The *senzala* is gone, but we can see the place where it must have been. It is wonderful and eerie to be tracing my grandmother's footsteps like this. I wonder: had we spent the night,

Oxen teams fording a stream on the road from Caldas to Capivari, 1984.

would I have seen the ghosts?

The Itacor is being decorated for Christmas—someone has put a wreath on my door. I am invited to Denise's house for Christmas Eve. Everyone is friendly and very kind to me. I've decided to stay here until the first of the year, then I'll go to stay in Aunt Ginger's apartment in Rio sometime in early January, while she is in the States. I'll come back to Caldas at the end of the month for the Grape Festival. Vovó wouldn't like it, but Caldas is known, if it is known at all, not only for its *doces*, sweets made of fruit or milk, but increasingly, for its wine.

Tonight, Christmas Eve, I leave the hotel at 10:15 for Denise's house. Brazilians traditionally celebrate Christmas Eve with a *ceia* (supper) and then attend midnight mass. When I arrive at 10:30 the children are anxiously waiting for *Papai Noel*, and Denise's husband Eduardo is off somewhere getting into his red suit and white beard. People are milling all over the place; I don't know how many people are here. It is the whole extended family, grandparents, aunts and uncles, cousins, many children, much confusion.

*Papai Noel* arrives. The lights are put out so no one will recognize their daddy and uncle, and all is confusion. Names are called, gifts given and opened, all at once, not in the orderly way we do it at home (nothing is done in an orderly way in Brazil), paper flying all over the place, children running about, much noise. After the distribution of a doll to each girl, a toy truck to each boy, and an exchange of gifts between my hosts and me, we gather in the kitchen. The table is groaning with rice, potato salad, macaroni (Brazilians love starches), ham, roast suckling pig, roast chicken with dressing, *tutu à mineira* (a dish made of beans, pork, and manioc flour), and lots of beer.

While the girls are playing with their new dolls, and the boys with their trucks, a couple of men are playing guitars, and everyone is singing and laughing. There is not enough room at the table so some sit on a bench against the wall, some stand, some wait for others to finish. People are eating, singing, talking, laughing; children wandering in and out of the kitchen, jumping from lap to lap for food or affection. The adults want to sing something in English so I can sing, but the only song they know is *My Bonny Lies Over the Ocean*. I don't know where they learned it, but they have no idea what the words mean, so I have to translate, and we sing it a couple of times. Like all Brazilian *festas* (parties) this one is loud, with everyone talking at once, singing, laughing, children squealing and crying, adults telling jokes, most of them going over my head.

It is very joyful, warm; a great feeling. I can feel their acceptance of me, and it really touches me because they can't know me very well, since I still can't express myself the way I can in English. But it makes me sad, too, because as much as I want to belong, I just can't quite feel inside the group—it's not just the language, it's that all the customs are different, the common knowledge they all share, common experiences. Part of me remains an observer, trying to figure out what is going on, what will happen next.

And now it's Christmas Day, 1984, and I'm alone. After breakfast I hike to the *igrejinha* (chapel) on top of Pedra Coração, sing Christmas carols up here where I am really alone, feeling sad. Last night was wonderful and interesting, but I couldn't easily participate; it was hard to try to understand and respond to all that was happening.

At lunch it starts to rain; when it stops a little I go with Cida taking gifts to Dona Ana's, Dona Bexuta's, and Dona Maria de Lourdes's. All seem glad to see me. I come home soaked and cold, give gifts at the hotel, and talk to my kids via long distance.

Today, January 3, 1985, I go to Dona Maria de Lourdes's house to say goodbye and take pictures, then to Denise's house, and with her, to Dona Ana's to say goodbye to her, promising to return before going back to the States. And on my last day, I climb to the top of Pedra Coração again to see the sunrise, and stay there an hour or so. Then off to Rio.

# VI. Copacabana

Teddy Roosevelt's trip to Brazil in 1913–1914 is remembered for the Roosevelt–Rondon expedition sponsored by the American Museum of Natural History and the Brazilian government. The expedition was guided by Gen. Cândido Mariano da Silva Rondon, creator of Brazil's Indian Protection Service—now *FUNAI* (*Fundação Nacional do Indio*). The grandson of Indians, he was a Brazilian military engineer of great distinction and a national hero, for whom the state of Rondônia was later named.

Along with two trained naturalists from the United States and about twenty companions, including Teddy's son Kermit, Roosevelt and Rondon set out from the north of the state of Mato Grosso in December of 1913. They traveled through sparsely populated sugarcane fields and then through areas of unexplored Amazon rainforest. They explored the *Rio da Dúvida* (River of Doubt), so called because its route was unknown. From February 27th to April 27th, 1914, the expedition mapped the river, which was renamed Rio Teodoro Roosevelt. Though the trip made Roosevelt gravely ill, he later wrote, "I had to go. It was my last chance to be a boy."[78] Writing in the magazine *Outlook* in December 1913, Roosevelt said of a visit he made to the Rio YMCA,

> *There are very few institutions of any kind which do better work than the Young Men's Christian Association, and I was glad to go to the branch in Rio de Janeiro, expecting merely to say a word of greeting to the members themselves. However, I found the hall of meeting jammed with an audience for the most part composed of Brazilians, including members of the Government, judges, Senators, and Deputies. I had to make them a short speech. My audience was so obviously of a very high character. They represented a type both intellectual and forceful; they were men with whom we would be glad to associate in any movement for social betterment in the*

---

78. Wagenknecht, *Seven Worlds of Theodore Roosevelt*, 31.

*United States. Evidently the feelings to which I appealed, the ideals which I upheld, were the same in Rio de Janiero as in New York City.*[79]

This was the speech my grandfather Myron Clark translated, which we will soon hear about.

79. Roosevelt, "Rio de Janeiro: Third of a Series of Articles on South America," *The Outlook*, 838–39.

# 35. On the Avenida Atlântica, 1912, 1913

 *USA, 1943*

Three launches full of *ACM* members came to the ship to welcome us back to Rio. We went directly to my sister Noemi's house, and early next morning Myron and I went to Leme to see our new house, which was not quite ready. It was not the best thing to have had this house built while we were away—quite a few things were not done as stated in the contract and in the plans, but my husband thought it was the thing to do, and so did our friend Dominges, who was loaning us the money. Your grandfather would have left it as it was, but I insisted that the contract be followed.

The next day there was a reception for us at the Association, presided over by Gen. Serzedelo Correia[80] and attended by Ambassador Morgan and the general secretary of the YMCA World's Committee in Geneva. The *Grupo de Debates e Esperantistas* (Debate and Esperanto Group)[81] greeted us. Dr. Paranaguá, an ex-senator, made an address of welcome and offered a beautiful pocketbook to my husband in the name of the *ACM* of Brazil and friends. Inside it were a receipt for the first payment of our home, which was one-fourth of the loan, and a check for 1,000 *cruzeiros*, which then amounted to about 200 dollars, for some furniture. So, my little ones, the devotion without limit of Myron Clark to the young men of Brazil created among them the desire to make him comfortable by helping him to build his home. We had shared cups of tea on the hillside, and now our cup was running over.

Since our lot faced the sea on one side and the street on the other, our house had two fronts. Those parts of the house that ordinarily are in the back were in the middle. We began to clean up our old furniture, which

---

80. Serzedelo Correia was briefly the finance minister of Brazil during the presidency of Floriano Peixoto.

81. The Esperanto movement began in Brazil in 1907. I have no idea what the connection between it and the YMCA might have been. In more recent years, it has become linked both to the Baha'i faith and Spiritualism (Chuck, "Esperanto 101").

had been left in the basement of a church, and with the money that was given to us bought some furniture for the dining room and for our room. When we had the plan of our house made, a large porch, as big as the one on the house upon the hill where we entertained our Sunday guests, was the most important feature. We felt it was our duty to make a home for those young men who had no homes. Here on our spacious tile porch we had even more guests, as there were so many more attractions. We bought quite a few rough but comfortable porch chairs for it. We called our house Vila Caldas.

Moving day came, and we spent the day unpacking and straightening out things. We spent the first night in our new home at Gustavo Sampaio, 211, Leme, without the children, who stayed with my sister Noemi and her husband Henrique. And the morning passed, and Sunday evening came and our guests began to be the ornaments of our new home that we were enjoying very much. The lovely Avenida Atlântica was almost all built up now and its mosaic sidewalk with benches at short distances constituted a great attraction to the dwellers of other suburbs. It took some time for me to get used to the roar of the waves and the noise of the automobiles. Up on the hill we did not seem to be part of this noisy

Av. Atlântica, where the Clark's house was,
at Rua Gustavo Sampaio, 211, Leme. Early 20th century.

world. We were spectators; too far away to hear the struggle of living.

Among the regulars at our Sunday informal teas, two were very attentive to our *primogênita* (first born) Ruth—Mr. Meddley and Mr. Richardson. Well, there was hardly a Sunday when this Mr. Richardson did not come, and we seemed to be blind to his attention to our daughter. What blinded us was his awkwardness and his being quite a bit older than she was.

Autos were not common in those days, and our friend Mr. Richardson

Sunday afternoon "At Home" at Vila Caldas, Leme.
Ruth on step behind her parents..

invited us all for an auto ride *a la brasileira*—the whole family took part in the courting. We had a delightful day—Rio had so many places to visit if you had a way to get there. Then my husband received a most beautiful letter from him in which he asked permission to speak to our daughter about his deep love for her. Well, my beloved husband felt very sorry for the young man and said that we thought that our daughter did not care for him at all in that way. He replied, "But I'd like to do it if you allow me." So we had an agreement that the next Sunday he would stay until all the other guests had left, and then we would leave the porch and get any of the other children out of the way so that he could speak to her. My husband left me to be the last one, and when I thought that the time was ripe for me to say "Excuse me, please, for a minute or so," my daughter followed me. Mr. Richardson then said, "Ruth, wait, I want to speak to you." And of course it was "No, no, and no," and I am sure it was not only Richardson who made her say no; there were others, Americans and Brazilians.

All this time, my older sister Lydia had been very sick. One Saturday afternoon after the cake and the bread were made—my preparation for Sunday— I started to her house, taking with me my ten-year-old boy

Av. Rio Branco, c. 1910.

Neco. It was a very long ride in the streetcar from our house to the city, changing there in the Avenida Central to another streetcar line for another long stretch. I was going to leave my boy at José Braga's, our close friends, for him to play with their son who was about his age, and I would go on to my sister's and come back for him two hours later. When we got near the place, I said, "I am going to let you off here. You have to walk just a little ways and you will see the big iron gate." The house was way up on lovely grounds. He had been there before but not alone. He knew he could find it all right, of which I was sure too, because it was so easy. He was taking a loaf of special sweet bread to my friend, as she was very fond of it. Well, when the time came I stopped the car and I can still see his smiling face and eyes, waving to me in his white sailor suit as cute as he could be. The streetcar went on.

Two-and-a-half-hours later I stopped there to get him and, to my surprise, he had not been there. You cannot imagine the commotion. The telephone was connected to every ambulance station to find out if a boy about ten and all in white, carrying a loaf of bread, had been found. The police were called and the YMCA and all our friends. In almost every family that we knew there, a person was out, scouring the neighborhood. Even now, I am so moved and my eyes are so dimmed with tears that I can hardly write. I cannot think of that day without feeling the same way I did then.

As night was coming and no news came, I was thinking more clearly—I wanted to go the Y in the city where I could be reached by phone. We had no phone at home; we could not afford such luxury. So my friends the Bragas took me there. My husband was away but the secretary in his place, Sr. Manuel, and also the young men present, were kind to me. I had left Neco about two o'clock and it was about nine when the telephone at the YMCA rang with the news that he was home! Sr. Manuel said he wanted to see Neco, so he went with me. It took about half an hour for us to get home by streetcar. The streetcars in Rio roll on that track like a lazy *jararaca* (lancehead snake) and when I took hold of my son, lost for nine hours, my joy was beyond description and I was not the only one to weep—everybody did.

I had already discovered by this time that when I stopped the car we had already passed the gate, so I had pointed him in the wrong direction—what happened was all my fault. The street was like many in Rio. It wound around like a snail, so Neco got confused. After not finding the gate, he turned back with no success. Then he kept coming and going and finally he decided to follow the streetcar line downtown to the Avenida Central where the cars to Leme had a big station. There he would wait for some conductor that he knew and who he was sure would take him home. It took him several hours to walk to that place and everybody who heard about it marveled that he could find his way following the track because it was a long way and very confusing. But he did, and there at the station he was waiting for the car and the conductor to take him home. The poor child never dreamed that the conductor might not be working that day or at that time.

Well, this is not a movie, yet the rest of the story happened just as in the movies. My two daughters, together with some other girls, had been invited by some American and English boys for a ride to some of the many beautiful places we have and for tea in some fashionable hotel. They hired an automobile and chauffeur, of course—only very rich people had cars in Brazil then. After the tea, my daughters insisted on going back home in the streetcar because they thought the boys had spent enough. So they dismissed the car and went to that station and whom did they see there? Neco! They were astonished and asked, "*What are you doing here, Neco?*" Well, that was too much! He burst into tears and as he was one of those who talk very little, it took some time before he could tell what happened.

When Neco and the girls got home, they heard that I was at the *ACM* waiting for news, so they went to some place and phoned to tell me that he was home; that he had walked all the afternoon to the Avenida Station where they found him. That is why Sr. Manuel wanted to see him, the hero. So, my grandchildren, I have had worries and trouble enough in my lifetime. Fortunately, in most cases they turned out all right. Do you blame me for not wanting to have any responsibility with children now that I am seventy-three?

In the summer of 1913, there was a very heavy *ressaca* (heavy surf or undertow) on the beach in front of our house. The waves flooded

Avenida Atlântica, and in downtown Rio there was a lot of damage done and traffic interrupted. It was one of the greatest, most gorgeous, and most threatening sights I have ever seen! We watched it from our veranda, feeling that the next wave would surely get in our garden. It covered the beach and the wide avenue, but it was just a whisper when it got to our garden gate! There is a terrible undertow there, which has caused many accidents, but bathing was still going strong on that very dangerous beach. It was a great relief from the extreme heat.

My sister Lydia was very ill, and when I had to stay over at her house I worried like everything because a big crowd always gathered for bathing and they didn't seem to pay any attention to our warnings. Among those who did not pay any attention were our charming daughters who, in fact, were part of the reason for the gathering in front of our premises. Henedina, my niece, and her husband Mr. Anderson, a fine fellow, lived near and joined the crowd, so I was always asking him to keep an eye on the children until my husband got there.

One morning while my husband was shaving, Neco and George, who were not allowed to go to the beach before he did—especially that morning when the waves were breaking with the noise of a thousand cannons—called his attention to the commotion on the beach. Myron got to the porch in time to see Mr. Anderson put Baby on the sand with no other damage than a scare and a guilty conscience. This was what happened: the crowd was playing ball, a customary sport with the bathers. The waves took the suggestion and decided to play ball with them, and before they knew it, the sand began to melt under their feet and out they were, being tossed about with the waves. Baby was being pulled out into the ocean, and Mr. Anderson ran after her; holding her hand and warning her to be calm, he brought her on shore with great difficulty. The next morning, and for a few more in succession, the beach was left to the seagulls who peacefully dived for their food.

My poor sister Lydia, after living for many months with her illness, passed away peacefully on the 21st of February. As she lived quite far from us, I had been rather exhausted from going to see her; it took almost four hours to go and come back. Sometimes I had stayed two or three days. The heat was extreme also. So when scorching March came, with all the cares I had had the months before, it was decided that I would go to my sister Cacilda in São Paulo for a few weeks, not only to be relieved from the terrific heat but also to forget a little the troubles of that year. Just before I left, I remember that we had another *ressaca*, one of the worst we ever had.

Myron was busy traveling early in early 1913, but we were both home on April 4th, Orton's eighteenth birthday. He was still studying in the States, but we all drank coffee to his health. Our Thursday dates were not so regular on account of the work this year, yet I see that we read *O Guarani, Rebeca's Chronicles*,[82] etc.

All the children attended the Methodist school. Ruth was a teacher, and Henry, Baby, Neco, and George were students. Ruth was also taking singing lessons with an American singer who thought she had a marvelous voice, and offered to teach her *gratis*. We had had a piano in my home always and, of course, in the school, but when I was married my husband felt he could not afford one. I was too happy with him and too busy with home, Association, and church duties to miss it, except when I went places where there was a piano. I longed to play then, but I was not asked because people didn't know I could. Well, Ruth decided to buy one with the money she was earning, so just as soon as it was settled in our parlor I began to try to recollect those pieces I had played for my father and my friends in Caldas and those in the American school. My sister Lydia had persuaded me (not very easily!) to give not only the exercises but also every piece I ever had to the missionary school in the north of Brazil where she used to teach. So I had to call on my memory, and I noticed that in order for those pieces to come back to me I had to forget my surroundings and put myself in the past that belonged to each piece. A case of forgetting to remember. The whole family enjoyed singing around the piano.

August came, and Myron was calling on congressmen to talk about the suppression of obscene literature. In September he visited the YMCAs

---

82. *O Guarani* (The Guarani) was written in 1857 by José Martiniano de Alencar, called the patriarch of Brazilian literature. He was forefront in the romantic nationalism movement, also called Indianism, and is known for his deep feeling for the Brazilian landscape. The Guarani are indigenous people of South America. *The New Chronicles of Rebecca* is a novel by Kate Douglas Wiggin.

in São Paulo, Porto Alegre, Montevideo, and Buenos Aires. He also went
to a seaside camp in a eucalyptus grove given to the Association by a
Sr. Piria in Piriápolis, Uruguay. The delegates from Chile, Argentina,
Uruguay and Brazil stayed in over ninety tents loaned by the Uruguayan
War Department.

In November, Dominges, who had loaned us the money, saw the house
for the first time and was very pleased with it. Now we had to decide
about our monthly payments, which he had just left for us to determine.
So far, we had received for our rent less than any of the other secretaries
who lived in a large city. The couple that had arrived that year told my
husband that they could not live in a house that would rent for what we
Clarks got. It did not take much time for *me* to figure that statement out:
if a couple with no children has to have at least 300 [dollars?] for rent, a
family with five children (Orton stayed in the States) ought to have more
than that, much more; but as I was a Brazilian where the standard of
living was not so high, I would be willing to calm myself if my husband
got at least that much! Let me tell you that all this figuring passed
between husband and wife, and not very smoothly. We agreed to pay that
amount for rent to our friend— who would have accepted even less—
and the letter went to the International Committee of the YMCA asking
for that rent and it was given without any comment! Now, with just the
rent, we were paying for our house. Wasn't that some friendly business
arrangement?

Reading my husband's diary now, I notice a note: "Joe Cochman took
our whole family to cinema." Movies were rare then and I loved them
although I carried always with me the feeling that I was doing something
wrong as they did not have the approval of the Protestant churches,
and we looked to that approval as people nowadays look to Good
Housekeeping's Seal of Approval for their cosmetics. Oh! Believe it or
not, I read this, written on August 31, 1913: "Saw aeroplane this morning
in flight."

# 36. Men: Ys and Otherwise

 *Rio, January 1985*

It's good to be back to the excitement and warmth of Rio after the tranquil and cool repose of Caldas. What a wonderful balance they afford my soul! Ginger is vacationing in the States, and I'm playing *dona da casa* in her apartment on Rainha Elizabete. We have some time together when she gets back, and then I rent a furnished apartment in Copacabana, a block from the beach, on Rua Sousa Lima. It's the home of an American ex-patriot bridge-playing friend of Aunt Ginger's, who likes to escape from Rio's summer heat and *Carnaval* madness.

The apartment is tastefully decorated with Brazilian folk art. It has a telephone and TV. I resume my *carioca* life; going out with cousins and friends, working on Vovó's *Reminiscências*, swimming, and taking a beginning painting class in Barra da Tijuca. It's wonderful to be back in Rio, living in a comfortable and nicely furnished apartment. There is a little nook off the living room, where a hammock is hung, and from this vantage point I can look down the street and see a strip of Copacabana beach across Avenida Atlântica.

Tonight as my dinner of black beans, rice, and squash are cooking, Rio is blessed with a powerful thunderstorm, and I turn out the lights to watch. The lightning is gorgeous! It is like strobe lights, only the burst of light lasts a little longer and it throbs, flashes, and becomes more intense before the sky becomes dark, only to light up again in an instant. Each stroke is a slightly different translucent color—white, pink, lavender, yellowish, greenish, a kind of mushroom color—but pure light. I watch some pipes and antennas on the roof of a building across the street. The sudden light slams into them from different directions, making them sometimes white against a dark sky, sometimes black against a light color; off and on, changing. I've always loved the drama, smell, and charge of thunderstorms, but this is particularly tumultuous in its fury, awesome in its beauty. Mostly it is sheet lightning, but sometimes, jagged streaks radiate in all directions from a center. It takes my breath away; I feel my heart pounding in response. Now the rain is hard and heavy and I have to close the windows and turn on the fan, but I can still hear the thunder crash, rumble, and roar. Now the lightning makes gashes in the sky, and lights up the space outside my window, between my building and the next. It is worth coming here just for these almost nightly tropical storms.

Tasso da Silveira, whom Sydney and I met at the *ACM* in Rio, and who bowed and kissed our hands as we said goodbye, has introduced me to the Y's Men's Club, a social club to which more women than men belong, and has offered to be my tourist guide in Rio. The folks at the *ACM* are going overboard to welcome me back to Rio, especially the Y's Men's Club. Victor is the president, but Tasso seems to be in charge of me. They arrange lots of outings for me, including a rehearsal of a samba school revving up for *Carnaval*, a cocktail party at a very posh yacht club, and an evening at a nightclub.

On January 15th, 1985, Tancredo Neves is elected president, and the country goes wild. Tasso and I walk around the center of the city, where *Cariocas* are celebrating Tancredo's victory. A stage has been set up over the square; there is a band with a samba beat; people are singing, dancing, jumping, shouting, waving green and yellow streamers and balloons. Tasso takes me to an office of the Camping Club of Brazil, of which he is a member, and from the eighteenth floor we look down on the crowd filling the streets as far as the eye can see. But some are saying that Tancredo will never take office, that government forces will see to that.

On another day, my *ACM* friends take me to a *churrrasco* at the Myron Clark campground in the mountains near a town called Araras, which is near Petrópolis. It is a beautiful location, and even though it is raining the drive there is gorgeous. After having our *café da manhã*, we alternate between the sauna and a natural swimming pool, play a little volleyball, have drinks and the *churrasco*, and then have a meeting—where I am presented with a wood-burned plaque, which Victor made to honor my visit.

I have already renewed my three-month visa once, and to do it again I have to go out of the country. It happens that there is a Latin American convention of Y's Men's Clubs at Piriápolis, near Punta del Este in Uruguay in March; some members of the Rio Club group are going, and they invite me to join them. They even plan to leave a couple of days early so that I can renew my visa before it expires. We will be five days at the conference, but no one has the slightest idea of the program. Tasso says we will escape and investigate Montevideo, Punta del Este, and Buenos Aires. We are seven; two men, five women—Tasso is with Paula, Victor with Valda.

It is a thirty-six hour bus ride from Rio to Porto Alegre, the capital of Rio Grande do Sul, but the bus is comfortable with reclining seats, bathrooms, and a stewardess. We stay one day in Porto Alegre, then get another bus along the coastline of Rio Grande do Sul to Montevideo for a couple of days before going on to the conference grounds. It is really interesting to compare my impressions of Montevideo with those of my Brazilian friends, but Tasso and Victor are rather exasperating. Tasso is good-hearted, but somewhat petulant; and on this trip he is pig-headed and pouty, I guess, because of the competition with Victor. Victor is a large man: good-looking, optimistic, gregarious, and playful, but domineering in this Latin macho way; sort of a pompous porpoise.

Each of the men makes all the decisions for his *namorada*; both are constantly vying for control of the three of us (Vanda, Vandete, and me) who are unattached. It is a crazy game. The men decide where we will eat, where we will stay, how we will travel, etc. without consulting or even discussing it with us, and the idea of splitting up for any separate activities is apparently unthinkable. We'll be walking along the street; the men slightly ahead of us, each trying to lead the group in a different direction, the girlfriend of each sticking by her man. This has the unexpected result of leaving the three of us unattached women partially in control, as we can decide which of the two leaders to follow. Then the loser, along with his girlfriend, has to retreat and reluctantly follow the group.

I ask Vanda and Vandete, "What's the plan? Are we looking for a restaurant, just looking at the city, or what?" They never know; they just follow along passively and respectfully. Whatever Tasso suggests Victor dismisses, and vice versa. Tasso grumbles, pouts, and says, like a little boy, "Let him do what he wants, I'm not going to say anything." Victor, who seems to have won the battle for alpha male, chooses our hotel in Montevideo and tells the receptionist proudly, *"Son todas mis chicas!"* ("They are all my girls!") The couples pretend to be married so as not to shock anyone in Uruguay, but I don't know why it matters, because to save money all the women stay in a dormitory room, and the men together also. This gives me a chance to hear what the women really think of these guys when they aren't within earshot. When we are alone in the dormitory room we all laugh at the preening and prancing like peacocks around us. But they won't say anything to the men—that's just the way they are. My exasperation melts away—I'm enjoying the bonding with the women, the humor of it all. We are all—men and women—good friends.

But once Vanda and I sneak away from the group to explore Montevideo by ourselves; the men are upset not only about that, but because she also defies their authority and goes shopping by herself after dark (We are all over fifty!). Tasso demonstrates his annoyance at the others, but he won't say anything to me, because I'm *Dona Neta do Fundador*. He always introduces me that way, very reverently, as if it were a title of high rank. It is a whole different identity, which I accept as graciously as I can. I wonder, however, whether this *Neta do Fundador* stuff might be just a tad irritating to the rest of the group.

After a couple of days in Montevideo, we go to the conference grounds near Punta del Este. This Y campground, I learn later, is one that my grandfather had attended in 1913 for a Latin American Conference. Then, delegates stayed in over ninety tents loaned by the Uruguayan War Department. The tents in the eucalyptus grove have been replaced by rustic but comfortable cabins. It is woodsy, cool, and quiet; a nice place to relax.

Now, as then, there are delegates from Central and South America, so the official language is Spanish, spoken with many accents and dialects. There are only a handful of English-speaking people here. One night the group has a birthday party for the Y's Men's Club, and we sing "Happy Birthday" in Spanish (a couple of versions), Portuguese, English, and Quechua (a language of the indigenous people of Peru). Most are the same tune.

We all get together in the evenings and it is interesting to me to hear all the different Spanish accents, and to observe cultural differences, especially between the Spanish and Portuguese speakers—the Brazilians are a lot happier and noisier! Brazilians have little trouble understanding Spanish, so when we are all together, our group tries to speak Spanish because the reverse is not true; the others have a great deal of trouble understanding Portuguese and make no attempt to speak it. When off by ourselves the Brazilians imitate the others, repeating over and over the Spanish idiom, *sin embargo* (nevertheless). I don't get it, but it is funny to them and funny to watch.

There are some meetings, but I am not expected to attend any, and there is lots of free time to explore the beaches of Punta del Este. The ebullient Brazilians keep the energy level high—they are rowdy, noisy, and always laughing, singing, dancing. Everyone comments on the joyful Brazilians.

Coming back, the group separates; some go to Buenos Aries as planned, but Vanda and I decide to take a different way back to Rio through Curitiba, the capital of the state of Paraná. We want to visit Curitiba and the picturesque Bavarian-style towns of Gramado and Canela in the Serra Gaúcha of Rio Grande do Sul, to see their hydrangea gardens and chalets, and taste their wine. Curitiba, although it has a population of almost a million and a half, works on the human scale with efficient and varied means of public transportation, including bicycle and large pedestrian networks free of motorized vehicles. The city is remarkable for its urban planning, which began in 1965 when the city had a population of about half a million and wanted to preserve the character of the city despite inevitable growth. The resultant master plan for development, which included plans for education, health care, recreation facilities and a lot of green space as well as public transportation, still attracts worldwide attention and praise. The infrastructure works, it is clean, there is little traffic congestion or pollution. Brazilians are justifiably proud of Curitiba.

The city has a distinct European feel to it. In fact, the population is made up largely of people of European descent. After the abolition of slavery, immigrants from Europe, especially Italians and Germans, began to arrive in large numbers in southern Brazil. In the twentieth century there was another wave of immigrants, including Poles and Baltic

Russians—many of whom settled in Paraná. These peoples have left their mark in Curitiba, not only in the predominance of blonds that one sees everywhere, but also in the European aesthetic of cleanliness, order, and efficiency. To me it lacks the color, flavor, and rhythm of other Brazilian cities; its personality is pleasant but bland. Still, I have to admit that it is nice to be able to get around easily; not to hear the constant honking of cars and buses; and to breathe fresh, clean air. We see all there is to see in a day or two.

The highlight of our trip turns out to be our excursion through the Serra do Mar from Curitiba on the plateau to Paranaguá through the lush, dark rainforest. This is the same narrow gauge train my grandparents took in 1896—again, I am following in my grandmother's tracks. The train tracks are laid on a very steep gash through the rainforest, with a few stops along the way. There must be little villages at these stops, but all we can see is the tiny station, with a few people waiting for the train to sell food and drinks. The clearing for the tracks is so narrow I feel as if I were in the body of a long skinny snake, slithering through the teeming rainforest toward the sea. All we can see in the dense jungle are patterns of green and the graceful drapery of vines, with glimpses here and there of the coast so far below. Our eyes search in vain for the denizens of this primordial realm—they must be hiding from the snake! We have lunch, look around the port, and return to Curitiba the same day, seeing a whole new vista on the other side of the train, which moves much more slowly on the ascent.

Vanda and I are in Curitiba a couple of days before the inauguration of Tancredo Neves. Here, too, excitement in the streets about the coming of democracy is like the joy of *Carnaval* all over again. Then, on the day before the inauguration is to take place in Brasília, the shocking news comes—the president-elect has been admitted to a hospital with severe abdominal pains. There is no provision in the constitution for such a scenario, but somehow it is decided that the vice president-elect, José Sarney, who was chosen to balance the ticket rather than to agree with Tancredo's democratic views, will assume the post temporarily. I can't make it out from the media and ask everyone—what happened? There are conspiracy theories, but most people I talk with seem to think that he was sick all along, and didn't want the press to know until he made it through inauguration. He almost did.

Two weeks later, after seven surgeries, Tancredo is dead; Sarney is inaugurated and the country goes into mourning. And so do I. Etched in my memory, along with the picture of three-year-old John F. Kennedy Jr. saluting his father's funeral cortege, is the picture of the plane carrying Tancredo's body back to Minas, while Milton Nascimento's *Coraçao do Estudante*, the theme song of the Neves campaign, plays in the background.

Back in Rio, I'm still swimming daily in the ocean. Swimming keeps me sane; I get very cranky without it. I think it has to do with being weightless. It is so sensuous—the feel of the water, the sparkling of the sunlight on the water, the ease and grace with which I can move my body in the water. I finally find a pool and a Masters'[83] team (without a coach), and I manage, after the usual Brazilian fuss and flourishes and a little help from my friends, to get a temporary membership. The pool is at the Fluminense Futebol Clube, one of the two biggies in Rio. The other is the Flamengo, and the Fla/Flu *futebol* game is equal to Cal/Stanford in the ferocity of competition. Swimming is an afterthought at the club, but the Olympic-size pool is a beauty, and practically empty. Unlike Berkeley, where I usually share a lane with four or five other swimmers, here I have a lane to myself, with the *Cristo* atop Corcovado seemingly floating above me in the clouds.

I have only a week to prepare for a national meet that will take place in Rio, so I work out every day for at least an hour. At the meet I swim 50 meters in each of the four strokes, and win medals for third place in back and butterfly. A medal is a medal, and I'm not going to say how many women are competing in my age group—Masters is relatively new here, so it's not as well developed as in the States. There is lots of enthusiasm, though, and a couple of world-record holders at the club. I'll never get a medal in the States, so I'm enjoying my glory!

My latest visa is about to expire and I must leave Brazil again, and

---

83. An international organization of adult swimmers that provides organized workouts, competitions, clinics and workshops.

while I prepare to return to Berkeley, I'm already thinking of renting my apartment there for a year, selling my car, and coming back to Rio. I have finally succeeded in arranging a life here. I have activities, relatives, and friends I enjoy; I have learned the bus routes; belong to a swim team; and I know where and how to shop for my necessities. I also have pretty good language skills, but I want to improve and take some literature courses. I am at the stage to take advantage of the progress I have made.

I say my goodbyes in Rio and go back to Caldas to say goodbye to Dona Ana. This parting is harder than the first because I am going so far away, but I leave instructions with Maílde to look after her, and I promise to return the following year. I get together with a group of Rio cousins, and prepare to return to the States. Ginger's bridge partner Steve likes to leave Rio in January, when I like to arrive. So we agree that I will rent from him again when I return.

## Berkeley, July 1985

Back at home, I have happy reunions with family and friends, but I didn't expect the culture shock to be so strong in this direction. It is not at all like waking up; it's like a dream in which I don't know exactly where I am. Berkeley, which used to look so lively and diverse, looks strangely vacant—as if everyone knows something that I don't know, and is hiding somewhere: I am stunned by the space around me. It is almost ominously quiet, clean, and tidy. Traffic is orderly, and the sidewalks are bare of cars and pedestrians. I find myself drawing back a bit; I have to remember not to kiss everyone twice, from cheek to cheek. It's too staid, too formal, too quiet—is this the same Berkeley I left nine months ago? Living close to campus, it's easy to rent my furnished flat, so almost as soon as I am back, I'm planning my return to Rio. This life suits me, avoiding winter by alternating between Northern and Southern Hemispheres, and trying to assimilate the best aspects of two very different cultures.

I think I have it all worked out, balancing two lives and two cultures, and then I connect with Donn, a friend of mine for years. Suddenly, just like in the movies, the friendship blossoms into love! This is a man I know and can trust, a man who is not threatened by an independent woman. It is wonderful to find love again at age fifty-four, and yet I don't want to give up my peripatetic life. Donn is a sailor; when he retires, he wants to sail around the world. So we agree: we will marry, but we will not stand in the way of each other's dreams. We will live together, and apart. I will return to Brazil; he's saving his vacation and will come to Brazil to spend five weeks with me.

# 37. Teddy Roosevelt Meets His Match

 *Somewhere in the USA, 1941*

When we learned that Theodore Roosevelt, the ex-president of the United States, was coming to South America for a lecture tour and jungle expedition, Myron began calling on his friends in high places about the visit, even Ambassador Morgan. As a result, he met Roosevelt aboard his ship the *Van Dyke*, and got him to promise to speak at the *ACM* the following day. Myron spent the rest of day sending invitations and preparing for Roosevelt's appearance. On October 22, 1913, at five in the afternoon, the building was jammed with over a thousand people, including many prominent men. All the Ministries were represented. Myron interpreted, and it was a great success.

All the time that Roosevelt was speaking, I tried in my mind to translate his words, as if that would help my hero any. But before I could translate half of a sentence in my mind, my husband had given it all to the audience. One noticed immediately that Roosevelt's speech was a difficult one to interpret. At one point, Roosevelt said something that was impossible to translate, so my husband had to explain it, and his words were fewer than Roosevelt's. What do you think Teddy did? He turned to my husband and said, "Do you mean to say that all that I said you could put in those words?" My husband said, "Yes." He went on, "Did you translate this and this and that?" Let me add that Roosevelt's remarks here were not said in a joking way, as probably would have been the case if Franklin had said them. My husband was a little embarrassed but he went on magnificently. The next night the American colony gave a reception to Roosevelt and here is where, my grandchildren, your grandmother caused some embarrassment to your modest grandfather.

I had already had the honor of shaking hands with the guest of honor at the White House when he was leading his great nation. Again we were in line with the others, moving slowly toward this distinguished guest of Brazil. When he shook hands with me, Roosevelt said, holding my hands, "Do you know that I made your husband's reputation last night?" Now, have mercy upon me, my grandchildren, because you may be of the opinion that I disgraced myself then, but I am not sorry that as soon as he had finished his sentence I said, "Thank you very much, but he had it made before."

My poor husband was quite embarrassed and probably blushed. I know he was confused but soon he felt all right, seeing how all the Americans laughed heartily and thought it was a very good joke on Roosevelt. Well, teeth for teeth. Joke for joke. Perhaps I should have explained to Roosevelt that if my husband hadn't already made his reputation, he wouldn't have been invited to interpret for him, the man who led the Rough Riders in the Philippines and the American nation for four years.

Whether condemnation or praise, I don't know, but that answer I gave to Roosevelt that night hasn't been forgotten. In 1932 in Brazil, I was requested to be on one of the committees to raise funds for the *ACM* in Rio, and one of the names assigned to me was that of the head of a very important American firm. When I got to his office I tried to show him my credentials but he said very politely and with a smile all over his countenance, "It is not necessary, Mrs. Clark, I could never forget you after hearing what you said to Roosevelt. It was a very good joke on him!"

The next night Roosevelt was received as a member of the *Academia de Letras Brasileiras* (Academy of Brazilian Letters) which took place at the *Instituto Histórico e Geográphico*. This was *traje de rigor* (formal evening attire) we say, and we were there by invitation. Here Roosevelt made a special speech uninterrupted by an interpreter. One of the members of this very exclusive society, General Ramnis Galvato, aide of the ex-Emperor, read a translation of the speech prepared beforehand.

In those days the photographers used [for lighting] that stuff that not only scared you as if somebody had thrown a Bolshevik bomb, but the smoke induced by it nearly choked you. Well, when the shooting began on all sides and one could hardly see one's neighbor, Roosevelt turned to my husband and said, "Tell them not to do any more." So that was that.

Now, my grandchildren, I count this one of my greatest honors to have shaken hands with one of the Roosevelts. They are noble people.

Roosevelt's visit lasted from the 21st to the 25th of October, 1913. On his way down to Rio, Roosevelt did something that shows what kind of a man he was. Two American chorus girls were on the same boat, going to the same destination. There were rumors that what they were going down there for was not for their bettering. The positions they were going to have were rather suspicious. Well, he prevailed on them to return to their country. I may not have the details correct but I do have the facts. So here we leave that great American to go on with other reminiscences.

In 1936, Argy, as she was then called, and her family were visiting me in Rio. My granddaughter and namesake, Chiquita, was sick and a physician and old friend was called. Although the doctor had visited us many times in Leme, I had not seen him for many years. After the pulse and the temperature were taken, a tap here and there, he turned to Argentina. "One of you—he meant my children—ought to write a biography of your mother to mention what she said to Roosevelt." I felt rather cheap and said I didn't mean to be rude. It was a joke to reply to his joke. Then he said, "It was a very good joke" and almost forgot about the child, which did not please my daughter at all. As he left he said it was just a little stomach indisposition; Chiquita would be all right soon and did not need a prescription. And as far as my biography, it is not necessary: it has been told in these reminiscences.

# Note

Paul Vanorden Shaw, a columnist for the *Brazil Herald*, an English language newspaper published in Rio, upon learning of my grandmother's death the previous June, wrote in an obituary in the April 14, 1963 edition of the paper:

> *There is a true story which gives the stature of Dona Chiquita and her husband. When Theodore (Teddy) Roosevelt came to Brazil, Teddy was asked to make a speech in Rio's largest auditorium. Mr. Clark, who not only spoke Portuguese beautifully but also was a superb interpreter, was asked to interpret for the American ex-president. When Teddy realized that he had met his match in Mr. Clark, he threw in every slang phrase he could think of to make the interpreter's task even more difficult. In an extraordinary exhibition of virtuosity, Mr. Clark, without hesitation, turned Roosevelt's slang into its Portuguese equivalent. When Teddy finished his speech, it was difficult to know which had received more applause, he or his interpreter, whose performance Teddy himself realized was superb.*

> *After the meeting, at a reception attended by Roosevelt, many Brazilian and American VIPs, and the Clarks, Teddy was introduced to Dona Chiquita. After saying he was pleased to meet her, Teddy boasted, "You know, I made your husband's reputation tonight." Diminutive, soft-spoken Mrs. Clark looked the great American in the eye and without any hesitation whatsoever said, "Oh no, Mr. President, he had already made his reputation." To defend her American husband, she rebuked the mighty Teddy.*

Myron and Teddy facing off at the *ACM*, Rio, 1913.

# 38. A Brazilian State of Mind

 *Rio, January 1986*

Six months after leaving Steve's apartment on Rua Sousa Lima, I'm back, getting in the swing of my *carioca* life, swimming in the ocean and the Olympic-size pool at Fluminese, seeing friends and cousins. I'm also working at transcribing Vovó's reminiscences.

I have lost a bit of my speaking and coping skills, and I have more adjusting to do. I wonder, as I watch the water whirling the "wrong" way down the drain, if the change in magnetic fields doesn't do something weird to my bodily fluids and maybe the synapses in my brain?

The first time I went to the *feira*, I was overwhelmed, just like before, and sort of stood around; the beggars distress me, so I can't think. But gradually I get into it, the banter and all. *"Fala, freguêsa!"* ("Speak, customer!"). "The best here, the freshest, the best prices!" "Oh, limes, oh bananas." "Oh, Madame, at your service!" and so forth. The beggars are still upsetting; but the singing out of wares, the playfulness, I like. It reminds me of crowd scenes in opera—I can almost hear Puccini.

It all seems choreographed—the colors and shapes of the fruit and vegetables, the heady smells of fish and ripe fruit, the smiles of the vendors. I buy fresh collard greens for *feijoada*; tomatoes, okra, and squash; onions, lemons and garlic; luscious titian mangoes and ripe papaya, with its beautiful black spicy seeds; heart-shaped green figs for my breakfast; juicy sweet oranges; pineapple picked so ripe I can eat the core; custardy cherimoya and tiny sweet bananas—*banana d'ouro, banana de prata* (gold and silver).

My cousin Estefânia is helping me sort out the complex relationships and difficult names and nicknames of our mutual cousins and ancestors. She invites me to a play that another cousin, the actress Marieta Severo, is starring in—*Um Beijo, um Abraço um Apêrto da Mão* (A Kiss, a Hug, a Squeeze of the Hand) at the Teatro Villa-Lobos, a theater on Princesa

Isabel. I have seen her in many of the *novelas* I love to watch, but now, between acts, I get to meet my famous cousin that I didn't even know I was related to.

Copacabana is one of the most densely populated areas of the world, but as I read and transcribe Vovó's memoirs, I imagine my father's birthplace as it looked to him at the turn of the century when it was a small, remote, beach community. The air would have been clean, without the choking fumes from cars and buses that scratch my throat and water my eyes. Then, only horse-drawn streetcars linked it with the capital, Rio de Janeiro, which lay on the other side of the hills. From their rented house on the hill, surrounded by coastal rainforest, my father and his brothers and sisters could see, hear, and smell the ocean, and watch the lighthouse on the island far out to sea as the lights rotated white, yellow, red. They could see Pão de Açucar naked, without the cables and suspended cars in which tourists and *cariocas* alike ride to its summit for glorious sunset views. That was long before part of the shoreline was wrenched away to make the wide Avenida Atlântica that now sweeps along the beach, and the broad black, white, and red-brown mosaic sidewalks that lie between the *Avenida* and the beach, their design echoing the curving waves of the surf. And yet, the village of my father's childhood is still a neighborhood, and now it is mine. I am happy here, but I want to get back to Caldas and Dona Ana.

In February I get a flight to Poços de Caldas in a small plane seating fifteen passengers, flying low over Guanabara Bay past Sugar Loaf; south along the coast about halfway to São Paulo; then west, climbing over the mountains to Poços where Mailde is waiting for me. I have her drop me off near Dona Ana's. I take with me some rice to fulfill another dream she had of my returning, bearing rice. The floor is swept clean of dust and the droppings of the chickens that wander in and out. Dona Ana is dressed for me, I can tell. We have a joyful reunion, and then I climb the hill to the hotel, where everyone greets me with affection, as if I were a member of the family, and I hear all the news—Maria's baby, Silvana's wedding.

Once more I have entered a time warp in this enchanted place with something different in the air—I think it is the almost-forgotten smell of innocence. It's like a waterfall, sparkling in the sunlight, then splashing

Back of the Itacor, on a very *manso* horse.

into a clear, deep, silent pool. There is a perceptible sense of peace, of well being, of kindness, gentleness, good will, and my heart swells with love. I'm very much at home at the Itacor.

The *Festa da Uva* (Grape Festival) is on. I descend the hill, stop at Denise's house, meet several friends along the way, stop, hug, chat, and go with a friend to admire the displays. Like a small-town county fair in the States, the products of the labor of farmers and cooks are proudly presented and judged in a specially constructed straw hut. Outside, I listen to a brass band from some neighboring town play oompah music; the men are all working hard in ninety-degree heat, their red cheeks and big bellies distended by the effort of pushing sound out of the tubas, saxophones, and trombones.

The streets on both sides of the *praça* are lined with people from all over the area waiting for the grand climax of the festival—the parade— which is led by about twenty motorcycles and followed by a marching band playing, of all things, "Oh, Suzanna!" Next come ten tractors, and then decorated flatbed wagons pulled by tractors, carrying little girls in frilly dresses holding grapes and preserved fruit. Then come the floats of the hotels from the area: the Itacor's, which wins first prize, depicts the coat-of-arms of Caldas, which features two urns—one bearing water (the springs), the other wine; each being poured by a fetching young lady. Somewhere in between the floats are teams of oxen pulling carts bearing barrels laden with grapes, and last of all, a samba school from Poços de Caldas. I love it! It is very small-town; very authentic and wholesome to me. To the Caldenses, it is very beautiful and a source of great pride.

The Itacor is full: I have moved in with Mailde in her room at the back to free up my room for other guests. How strange, really, to be here— who would have thought just a few years ago that I'd be here, sharing this room, in this tiny town in the interior of Brazil. I am content. The other life seems so far away. I really don't miss it much—maybe because I know pretty much what's going on there. Here, I'm still discovering. I wish it would quit raining, though. It's summer, but today I got so chilled I can't seem to get warm. I long for Rio's balminess.

Another of Dona Ana's sons, Joãozinho, and his family have arrived from São Paulo and I am invited for lunch—thirteen people in all, including Ieiieí and Ivone. Joãozinho, named for his grandfather, is a familiar, hail-fellow-well-met type: backslapping and practical-joking; he piles his plate full of food, full of compliments and *carinhos* (expressions of affection). He's goodhearted and boisterous. He adores his new pregnant wife, who adores him back; she giggles at everything he says. Everyone is very open, expressive. No one knows me: because I am so adaptive, I blend in.

Today Dona Ana tells me a beautiful story:

> We were living in Santa Casa [the hospital, where her mother worked]. We were me, Papai, Mamãe, Alfredo, Maria, João, Targino, and Gilmar, the one that lives with Ivone. It was nine o'clock in the morning when the world became dark. All the stars came out and shone brilliantly. I was getting ready to go to school. A big star appeared—it was the most beautiful thing in the world! Papai filled a basin with water for us to see it. Then—it was hot so you couldn't touch it—so hot it broke a glass with the smoke that came from the star.
>
> It came from a great height, but I saw it perfectly! But where it came from, we didn't know—whether it came from the sky or from a city—

> *the city where Jesus was born—we didn't know, because it appeared when Jesus was born over there in Bethlehem, in a manger.*
>
> *I was just a girl, and I am old now, but if my eyesight weren't tired, I might see it again. They said that you could see it all over the world—even China—it came from a great distance. We could see it perfectly in the water in the basin, but I don't know if it was a saint that was in it, or a moon....You can believe it or not—it is still a mystery and I don't know what it was.*

Nor do I, and I wonder—was it a solar eclipse, a comet, a meteorite? Later, I look it up, and find the "Great Daylight Comet of 1910," which was first spotted from the Southern Hemisphere in the early morning of January 12.[84] It was brighter than Venus, visible to the naked eye in the daytime, and much brighter than Halley's comet, which appeared the same year.

Dona Ana's attitude of wonder, reverence, and joy are similar to the feelings I had with my father when we walked through the woods—he pointing out burrows and nests, identifying bird calls, teaching us about nature. Dona Ana has very little understanding of science, but she has another way of appreciating the world. She is not ashamed of her ignorance or her poverty. Seeing through her blind eyes is like watching a child experience snow or a rainbow for the first time.

February 13. I am not feeling well. I don't get better after a week, and Dr. João is summoned. It is only bronchitis, but I can't seem to shake it off. He puts me in the hospital just down the hill from the hotel, saying that I need medication that I can't get in the hotel. I agree: I know it is taxing the hotel staff to take care of me. Santa Casa da Misericórdia! I never thought I would arrive—in this shape, anyway—in the hospital referred to by Vovó and where Dona Ana's mother worked. I am scared—scared of being in a Brazilian hospital, scared of not being told the truth, of losing control of my life. I like and trust Dr. João, but he keeps telling me I have no fever, when I know I have.

---

84. The Daylight Comet of 1910 was spotted from the Southern Hemisphere in the morning twilight of January 12 and visible with the unaided eye from Jan. 12 until mid-February as a brilliant object of -1 magnitude. Dona Ana would have been eight-and-a-half-years old when this comet appeared. This must be what she saw (Bortle, "Bright-Comet Chronicles," para. 20).

It is a new experience, teaching me how spoiled I am. I have one of the few private rooms; there is a long ward down the hall with only a few patients. There is no bathroom in the room—only a toilet down the hall, generally full of urine. I didn't know you were supposed to bring your own towels, so I don't have any. I have them call the hotel, and Sr. Cassambo, the caretaker, brings me some. I ask for toilet paper; I am told someone will come to *arrumar* (tidy and stock) the room but no one appears. And when I go to the bathroom, not knowing I should call someone to hold the IV, the needle comes out and the nurse has a terrible time finding the vein.

I am bruised. I ask for a blanket—I am having chills—she says she'll have to ask the doctor. She comes back to give me a shot, which I refuse—I am afraid it is something to put me to sleep so I won't be so much trouble. She says the purpose of the shot is to bring down the fever and end the headache. I say I'd prefer fever, chills, and headache to a shot. She thinks I am afraid of the needle and looks as if she thinks I *really* need calming down. Maybe it is stupid, but at least I am acting on my own behalf. Whatever happens to me here, I want to be conscious. When I think of Vovó having a lumpectomy on the kitchen table, I feel very spoiled and weak; and when I think of how Mother suffered with emphysema...

I make a tape to Donn telling him I am in the hospital and wailing about my situation. I keep saying—only half kidding—that I don't want to die in a hospital in Brazil, and Dr. João laughs and tells me no one ever died of bronchitis. I know I am making much ado about nothing, but I feel alone and insecure. (Poor Donn—by the time he gets the tape, I will be out and fine, but he is ready to jump on the plane to rescue me.)

This afternoon I have a lot of visitors—Maria Odete, Ivone, Maílde, and her sister Martine; and Maria Antónia, the maid at the Itacor, who brings Jell-O. Denise and her mother, Dona Cedinha, call wanting to know if I need anything. Tonight, another woman whom I can't place, the quintessential Edith Bunker type, comes and tells hospital horror stories; and then another group arrives; more hotel maids with lively, wanna-see-my-scar kind of talk to cheer me up. They're all goodhearted.

Dr. João arrives later in the evening with Maílde. We all laugh about my fear of dying here. He says I probably will be here two or three more days. *"Tudo bem,"* I say—"OK." This time I want to get completely well. After five days, I am released. Maílde takes me to Dona Ana's, then back to the Itacor. She takes care of me all day.

Next day, when I go back to see Dona Ana, she is in bad shape. A bite on her lip is swollen and bruised, and she has abdominal pain. Ieiieí has called Dr. Lázaro, who has written out a prescription, but she also has been putting her home remedy—chewing tobacco—on her lip. She and Ieiieí are arguing—I am the outsider, but I can't stand by and do nothing. I get Dr. Ney, Dr. Lázaro's son, to examine her lips and belly: he prescribes for both—injections, salve, and pills. The pharmacist comes to the house to give her the shot. I think she is grateful.

Two days later, it's time to say good-bye again to Dona Ana. I'm going to Rio, but I'll be back in a couple of months with Donn. Back in Rio, I get a call from Maílde to say that Dona Ana had some angina on the day I left and had to be hospitalized for a few days. She is comfortable now at her daughter Ivone's. Fortunately, before I left Caldas I made some provisions for Maílde to look after her, but I think she would have anyway. She is a good, warm, wise person with a big heart.

Donn boards the plane in San Francisco at six o'clock on a foggy, 40-degree evening in March and arrives in Rio at seven the next morning when it's 90 degrees. I meet him at Galeão and lead him to the *Ar Condicionado*, a comfortable air-conditioned bus, for the ride through downtown Rio to Copacabana. Rio is a very romantic place, and it's wonderful to introduce him to it. We spend a couple of weeks in Rio, doing the usual sightseeing by day. At night, we walk along the beach breathing the balmy fishy air, feeling the spray of crashing waves, the wet sand on bare feet, or stroll along the mosaic sidewalks stopping for tiny stuffed crab and *caipirinhas*, those dangerously delicious Brazilian cocktails, in the sidewalk cafes of Copacabana on the wide Avenida Atlântica.

He wants to see Caldas, Brasília, and Iguaçu Falls, but first I take him to São Paulo to meet my cousins there, then Campinas, where Maílde is now

living with her husband René. We have a pleasant stay with them, and
then we go to Caldas, staying at the Itacor, by now home to me.

We came here mainly to see Dona Ana, but also to see Halley's comet
on its next swoop past our planet. There is not much interference from
lights here, so I thought Caldas would be a good place for viewing. It's a
big disappointment for us, too—just a fuzzy oblong ball in the sky, but we
know it is the same comet Vovó saw in 1910.

Dona Ana is happy again—when I introduce Donn to her, she asks what
he looks like. Ieiieí tells her he is handsome, with a beard. She says she is
sorry she can't see him, so he offers his face for her to feel it. She strokes
his beard, laughing. Donn sings for her; she listens attentively. She asks us
to sing together; we sing "You Are My Sunshine." She laughs and laughs.
We leave her happy.

Donn and I go to Brasília and Iguaçu Falls; then he has to go back to work
in the States, but I stay in Rio, working earnestly now with Vovó's papers.
I join him in Berkeley in July. The year ends as usual in the Northern
Hemisphere with winter. In only a day, I can have summer, and Rio, again.

## Rio, January 1987

Back in Rio, I go immediately to Caldas to visit Dona Ana. She is not well:
she is confined to bed and in pain. She laments, "I am not lazy, no, Annita;
I struggled hard during my life to raise my children. Took in laundry, made
baskets. Now that I am at the end of my life, I would like to walk, would
like to see your face; and I can't. I am worth nothing. I live in a dark hole:
day is the same as night to me. I am hungry and hunger hurts, but the
food I get is worth nothing. I need nourishing food, and the meat they
give me is tough and hard. My whole body hurts, my bones stick out all
over. Even the water is bitter, and when I urinate it feels like there are
bugs inside biting me, it burns so much. I am wasted; I could be thrown
on a pile of rubbish. But I will not cry, I will not pray. I don't care what
happens to me. If God wants to send me to a good place, fine; if I am
discarded in a hole, that's all right. Life is hard, unjust. Others can eat,
can laugh, can have fun, but not me. I don't want much. Just something
to eat—and such desire to walk! To sit up outside, feel a little breeze. Oh,
Annita, it is the lack of sight that causes all of this. I hear your voice, but

I don't know what you look like. If you break a leg, it mends, if you lose a finger, this is not important, but if you lose your sight.."

It is heartbreaking, and there doesn't seem to be anything I can do. She doesn't sleep well at night, and her daughter Aracy, who has come from Rio to take care of her, doesn't either. Aracy sleeps with her clothes on, ready to get up and turn Dona Ana or get her water or food, which she has trouble swallowing, or coffee, or the chamber pot. Dona Ana keeps saying, "I am tired, have no enthusiasm for life," and then she drifts off to sleep. I am always glad when she does and has a little relief from her suffering. I do what I can for her and for myself, and I don't think it makes much difference to her whether I'm here or not, so I'm returning to Rio; but if she is still alive in April, I will come back before leaving the country.

On my last visit before I go back to Rio, she tells me again how she longs to see the faces of her friends and relatives, to sit outside and feel a pleasant breeze, to walk about a little, and eat a little piece of nutritious food. She tells me she wants to escape from her suffering, and I tell her she will not have long to wait, and that she will always live in my heart. We say goodbye, knowing it is probably for the last time.

A couple of weeks later, someone from the Itacor phones me in Rio with the news of her death.

# 39. *Despedidas*, 1914

*Athens, Ohio, 1941*

Copacabana was growing fast and becoming the residence for American families of the big American concerns. Now, you know that where American men live, baseball thrives. Once when the *ACM* secretaries were visiting us, they decided to play baseball on the beach, and lacking one man, they seduced me into the game. The battlefield was sand, piles of it! Well, next morning when I woke I just could hardly move with pains in my muscles, and it took some time for me to discover the reason and then my reason whispered to me, "Served you right, an old lady running like a fool on the sand at forty-five!" But I think I was quite young at forty-five. After having some fun telling this, let us go on and face 1914.

I was teaching Portuguese to the wives of my husband's assistants and to the physical directors, and my husband was very irregularly teaching English to our son Henry as he was planning to send him to school in the States. We didn't have much time for our reading together but I see that we were reading *Pollyanna*[85] in January. Once in a while this year an airplane flew over Copacabana. It belonged to the only son of the pioneer builder of that region, our butcher and grocery man of 1902!

In February the missionary Methodist school that our children attended moved to Petrópolis. Ruth was teaching there even though she had had only one year of college. She and Baby went there as boarders, one teaching and the other studying. We also had to part with our son Henry, as my husband wanted him to have an American education, thus leaving me with just the two youngest boys, Neco and George.

The intellectual department of the *ACM* was prospering very much under an Englishman who dropped into Rio from one of the four corners of the British Empire. As his wife was not well, we took them

---

85. By Eleanor H. Porter.

into our home for a week or so, so that she could get stronger to go home. Poor woman, most of her suffering was not physical. It was caused by the gambling dens. The worst of it was that when money began to disappear at the Y, the suspicion fell on an innocent person. We were not the only ones who suffered because we trusted the man; others did too, and the YMCA much more!

Because of this trouble and the separation of my family, I was run down and very nervous, so my husband took me to one of the best physicians in Brazil. He gave me some tonic and assured me of thirty years more. I can assure you, if anyone ever reads these lines—which is not very probable—that his words were much more beneficial to my condition than the tonic. According to his prediction, I have two years and eight months yet to go to my goal...

Your grandfather was always a very active member of his church, and so we became unintentionally involved in an odd dispute among members. At this time some churches had introduced individual cups at the Lord's Supper, and one could be sure of the subject of the sermons in every church in those days. It was pro or con the common or individual cup. The pastor of the church in Rio to which we had belonged before we moved to the seaside, a fine preacher with an attractive personality, was very definitely against the change. The discussions became very hot and in many churches it became very personal. In one church it got so hot and some members were so unreasonable that they adopted both! Those that were for the common cup began slowly to change to the individual one until there was only one holdout. He could not see that the only difference then was the size of the cup! But he was an old man and had taken the wine from that cup for so long.

In July of 1914 members of the Protestant Church in Portugal asked Mr. J.R. Mott, the head of the Foreign Committee of the YMCA, to send Myron to Coimbra where there was a possibility for a YMCA among the students. Of course, we were reading the news. It looked as if war in Europe were inevitable. In August as we were preparing to leave, we received word from Mr. Mott that the war prevented Myron's going to Portugal then; possibly next year he could go. All through the rest of a very full year nothing more was said about the possible changes for us.

We continued to have Sunday guests, not all on our account: our daughters were home in December for vacation, and my dear roommate and one of my best friends, América, secretary in the American school now, visited us for the month. We all enjoyed sea baths together. While América was with us, we had great times remembering school days and our adventures, which to the girls of today would be common events. Several times we had our friends and whole families coming for sea baths from our house. Your grandfather did lots of translations of scientific lectures for stereopticon views and of the book *The Manhood of the Master*.[86] So the year 1914 ended in suspense for us, not knowing where would be our abode in the future, and for the rest of the world with the question: Where is this war leading us? We know the answer now in 1941: to another war.

## 1915

Our Sunday teas continued, always with new guests. I was much better fixed with help then. I got a woman from Minas, a daughter of an ex-slave, to cook and to wash the clothes, and a second one to do the ironing and the cleaning. This in Brazil is done every day. We had no washing machine or electric iron. White linen dresses and suits were used a good deal then and with all the company we had, we couldn't get along with just one maid. Besides, help was cheap.

Just when we were in the middle of meetings and controversies, each day with our dinner table full of guests, letters from Mr. Mott came, telling my husband to go to Portugal alone. The family—four children at home now, two girls and two boys—could come later if the war conditions permitted. Why such an emergency? It seems that a millionaire had given a large sum for buildings for YMCAs in different countries, and a certain amount could go to Coimbra for a student YMCA building, so that was why my husband was ordered to go. Well, I was then in suspense,

86. *The Manhood of the Master* was a devotional book based on the human character of Jesus Christ. The author, Harry Emerson Fosdick, was an outspoken critic of the fundamentalist movement that was sweeping the country. He was opposed by William Jennings Bryan, who succeeded in forcing him to leave his Presbyterian post as a result of a sermon Fosdick gave entitled "Shall the Fundamentalists Win?" Fosdick was rescued by John D. Rockefeller, who financed the Riverside Church, an interdenominational church in New York City famous for its history of social justice, and installed him as its first pastor (Miller, *Harry Emerson Fosdick*).

wondering what would come to us next. Europe did not then seem a very desirable place to go.

The next surprise came one night just before we went to bed. Orton, who we thought was in the United States, appeared at our door one night! He had been obliged to drop out of school in the States on account of his eyes and heart, so he had gone to appeal to one of our friends, a Sunday visitor who had been an American Consul in Brazil and who now was an agent for a Brazilian shipping company in New York, to get a job on board in order to come home, as he wasn't able to study. It happened that one of the company's boats was coming back to Brazil without passengers on account of some trouble with the boat, so a passage for him was easily arranged. He didn't realize that it would be at first a shock instead of a surprise. He had grown so! Of course, we were delighted to see him. My husband was very busy, so it was very nice to have his son around to help him get ready to leave, packing old papers, pamphlets, etc., in a box for storing. We celebrated Ruth's twenty-first birthday on March 11th with a party in the evening, a very pleasant affair. We gave her a pearl ring made with one of the pearls of my earrings.

On the first day of April, starting at eight in the morning and going into the night, we were making farewell calls to relatives and friends. Before Myron left we had to make plans about what to do in case we were to join him. Everything was unsettled then. Some thought the war would be over soon. Others were sure that it was going to be a long struggle. His work in Coimbra was going to be problematic, also. On one side, the very few Protestant or indifferent young men there were anxious to help, and on the other side the Catholics were suspicious of such altruism. He left home on April 3rd. The boat was of the Lloyd Brasileiro line.

After my husband left, I felt that the responsibilities that I was facing were more than I could carry. Ruth continued teaching her two young brothers and a few other children. Baby was in the boarding school in Petrópolis, and Henry in school in the States. Orton had arranged a summer job in the States in Silver Bay; a girl he was very interested in would be there also. Nothing would keep him from being there. He would take any job on board to pay for his trip. He went to see the steamship company every day to see if they could give him a job for his passage. One day I asked him, "Can you typewrite?" "Of course not," he answered. "That is a woman's job." Seeing that the days were passing and there was nothing in view, I suggested that he go to our dear friend Mr. Tucker; so he did. Mr. Tucker gave him a letter to Dr. José Carlos Rodrigues, the owner of the largest newspaper press in South America, *Journal de Comércio*, saying "This is to introduce to you Orton Clark, the son of our common friend, Mr. Myron Clark. He will tell you what he wants."

For several days my son went to see him with no success. He was very busy. Every day there was a big crowd to see him and when his office doors were closed, many were left for the next day. One day when the office boy was closing the door my son said, waving the letter, "I must see him and I know that he would see me if he read this." The boy did not budge, but while they were arguing, Dr. Rodriguez came out, so my son, giving him the note, mentioned Mr. Tucker's name and he immediately said, "Oh, come in. I am terribly busy because I am selling the *Journal de Comércio* and then will sail to Europe, but tell me quickly what you want."

Dr. Rodriquez wrote a little note to the director of Lloyd Brasileiro in these words: "This boy is the son of a friend of mine, and he wants to work his way to New York on one of your boats. Anything you will do for him I would appreciate very much." It took only a few minutes for this interview and my son was on his way to the office of Lloyd Brasileiro. After the director read the letter he said: "I am sure you have not had your lunch." My son began to answer, "Oh, no, but..." when his reply was interrupted by the director: "Well, you will be my guest and we will talk things over while we eat." If I remember well, his name was Dourado (Golden). If to Orton he was gilded, his following words were diamonds. He said, in a very friendly way, "In a few days the Brazilian Ambassador, Dr. Amaro Cavalcanti,[87] is leaving for the United States, and I think he is needing a secretary who has knowledge of both languages and has an attractive personality; I think you will fulfill the requirements."

87. Dr. Cavalcanti was not a Brazilian ambassador to the United States, but a retired Supreme Court justice on his way to a conference in the United States (Pan American Union, *Bulletin*, 379).

When he came home after the interview, this is what he told me. "One of the first things Dr. Cavalcanti asked was whether I could use a typewriting machine. I immediately thought of the hasty answer I had given you, Mother, and I answered his question like this: 'No, but I can learn very quickly before we sail.'" "I think so, too," Dr. Cavalcanti said, and added, "You can come to my office and practice right here."

Myron arrived safely in Lisbon on April 29. There was a letter from me waiting for my husband; it probably went on the same boat that he did! We had been a whole month in Portugal back in 1905, so there were many friends to meet him. Sr. Alfredo Silva, a preacher whom we knew from our first visit, was the man who had started the ball rolling about going to Portugal. He accompanied my husband to Coimbra where they had rented a room, which they called the *núcleo* (nucleus) for young men's meetings. Myron was settled in the Hotel Avenida by the Mandego River much sung by Camões in his *Lusiadas*. He cabled for us to join him. When Sr. Braga received the cable, he sent for me and told me about it, but said, "I think this is crazy. The *Lusitania* has just been sunk. I will send a cable to him to wait until the war is over."

I said, "We are going in a neutral boat; Dutch, Sr. Braga."

"So was the *Lusitania*," he said.

Nothing could convince me not to go to my husband, so we were getting ready. And so was another Englishman who was courting Ruth, preparing to get the "yes" from her.

Meanwhile, Orton was pounding a typewriter with his two forefingers in Dr. Amaro Cavalcanti's office in Rio. One day when it was nearing the time to leave for the States he came home sitting on the top of the world! Dr. Cavalcanti had asked him if he had a tuxedo. Since he was expecting a negative answer, when he got it, he handed Orton a certain amount to buy one and all the rest of the outfit for *traje de rigor*. The rest of his salary would be given to him on their arrival in New York. The next day he came home with a package and took it to his room, and when he came out I couldn't believe my eyes. There before me was a handsome young man—not Orton, but Mr. Clark! "This is not all, Mother, look here!" And he pulled from his pocket a little box with a small lovely diamond for the young lady he was hurrying to. (That diamond is not on her finger, but on the finger of the mother of my grandchildren: Phyllis, Virginia, Myron, and Patricia.)

More at ease now, with Orton's problems resolved, I began to try to rent the house. Everybody was very sympathetic, and agreed with me that I had an awful big burden to do this alone. I would have to leave with the children for Europe, which was boiling with war and worsening. Portugal, England's ally, could not help but enter the war soon. In fact some people said they were already in it, as they say now [1941] of the USA—there were rumors that armaments had gone to France from Portugal through Spain.

It is funny, but soon after Orton left and after I had rented the house and moved to my sister's while getting ready to leave, all that feeling of being a victim of circumstances left me, and I was anxious to be by my husband in that city immortalized by Camões, where the beloved Inêz de Castro was buried. It was a privilege, and we have to pay some way or other, for privileges! Now, my grandchildren, when we look to those peoples whose properties have been destroyed, whose sons have lost their lives defending their countries against these barbaric invaders, I am ashamed of myself for having felt so abused. It is true my husband had gone to one country and two sons to another, and now I was leaving my country, my sisters, relatives, and friends—but I was surrounded by all the comfort and all the help and love from those around me. Yes, I had been a coward: a self-centered, middle-aged woman.

The two girls were out almost every night and feeling very much abused to have to leave that gorgeous beach and their boyfriends. Coimbra did not appeal to them, as they never cared to read Camões. If it had been the United States it would have been another thing. All the allure came then from the land where movies were made. The night before we sailed, my daughters, together with the daughters of some other mothers, were out with some young men, when Mr. Meddley, our old friend who had lost his heart over my oldest daughter's countenance, appeared and asked about Ruth.

"Well, she is out with some boys and girls," I said. "I am going to wait for her, Mrs. Clark, because I want to ask her to marry me and I will come to Portugal later on; you know I have been in love with her." We certainly knew that, but I felt it was my duty to warn him that she was quite infatuated with the fellow she was out with that night. He thought that would pass, and if I didn't mind he would wait and speak to her. Why would I? That was his privilege. The girls appeared very late and their boyfriends left, seeing in the person of the Englishman a *Mouro na Costa* (a Moor on the Coast), a Portuguese phrase for such things as this. I went to bed, and after some time Ruth came into my room and said she was engaged. It made me cross because I was very fond of this young man, and I knew that my daughter would not keep her engagement. As fine a young man as he was, he was not her ideal.

The next afternoon, we were taken on board the *Gelria*[88] in a big steam launch among tears and roses by the hundreds. It was my birthday, June 2, 1915! My daughter's fiancé was with us and I noticed that she had a big button on her finger, the engagement ring from Mr. Meddley. Soon after we arrived on board, the other fellows began to flock. The future son-in-law invited all the boys to stay for dinner on board at his expense in honor of the engagement, which looked in every way more of a funeral than a festival.

The young fellow Ruth had been infatuated with, Dr. Houston—a dentist—took it very hard. After everybody had left and I was going to bed, I found under my pillow a little package and a letter from Dr. Houston. It was a lovely long *echarpe* (scarf) for my birthday. They all had been to our cabins, and he found my bed, quietly laid down a souvenir for me of my birthday, and wished me bon voyage. I never saw Dr. Houston again.

---

88. A ship of the Lloyd Amsterdam line built in 1913. Its length was 165 meters; its speed 16 knots.

# 40. Family Reunion, 1990

 *Wentworth, New Hampshire, July 1990*

We are thirty descendants of Chiquita and Myron Clark plus fifteen widows and spouses, gathering in July of 1990 for our second family reunion. The first occurred in my family home in Athens at Christmas of 1949, when all our parents were alive and my cousin Paul (Paulinho in my early Rio days) was not born yet. Two families were absent from that earlier reunion—Uncle Orton's and Aunt Ruth's. This time, there are children of all six siblings—four generations—three days of activities, and plenty of time for some to get acquainted and for others to relive old memories and catch up on family news. We have taken all the rooms in a bed-and-breakfast in New Hampshire, and rented a neighboring house as well.

My *Titia*, Aunt Ginger, is here, as well as her two children, Dolly and Paul, and Dolly's two children, Denise and John. Jan, Sydney, and I, who together organized this event, are here, and so is my son Clark. The spouses are patiently and tolerantly observing the clatter and chatter, flurry and ferment of the exuberant, ebullient Clarks. We have come from California, Illinois, Ohio, Florida, New York, Rhode Island, and the Virgin Islands.

Some of us at the reunion are meeting each other for the first time, but most of us first cousins are renewing relationships that began in childhood. Almost all of our children are meeting each other for the first time, but all of us recognize something familiar in each other that makes us feel immediately intimate. We three sisters congratulate ourselves enthusiastically for what we have accomplished in organizing the three-day affair. Sydney's contribution is particularly valuable—she gathered photographs from all the families and assembled them in a video that plays over and over in the lounge of the bed-and-breakfast that serves as our main lodging and meeting place. There is a big surprise for me: Sylvia contributed a photo of an *ACM* outing—it is the same one Dona Ana gave me in Caldas!

Jan has collected baby pictures of the spouses and made a little game of trying to match them with their aging selves—our attempt at providing some attention to the spouses. We have arranged for a local photographer, for meals, and for flowers for our matriarchs, Aunts Tuttie and Ginger, widows of Henry and Neco.

Naturally, we exchange memories, and after our Friday night dinner someone mentions the shoe game, a game Vovó taught us that we used to play on the floor when she visited us when we were children. Immediately and without a word, Aunt Tuttie, Enid, Dolly, Chiquita, Sylvia, Jan, Syd, and I are on the floor, arranging ourselves in a circle, each removing a shoe. The younger generation and the spouses are bug-eyed with surprise as we pass the shoes around the circle clockwise, while singing a song whose melody we know, but whose words we only vaguely remember—if we ever knew. Dolly helps us; it's a Brazilian children's game. We all know it, but have never played it together before. It goes:

> *Escravos de Jó*
> *Jogavam Caxangá*
> *Tira, põe, deixa ficar*
> *Guerreiros com guerreiros fazem Zig Zig Zá*

Like many childrens' ditties, it doesn't translate very well: "Job's slaves played *Caxangá*; (no one seems to know what this is). Take it, put it, leave it. Warriors with warriors did zig, zig, zag." Well, anyway...the point is to advance the shoes with each beat of the song, and reverse the direction of the shoes on the zig, zig, zá. We start slowly and with every repeat of the verse, the tempo increases, so that the shoes are finally flying around the circle. Each time one of us fails to place the shoe she receives in front of the person on her right, she has to drop out, taking her shoe with her, until only Dolly and Jan are left, wildly flinging the shoes about while everyone sings the ditty as fast as we can. Well, maybe you had to be there. We are all delighted to rediscover this forgotten bit of shared culture that we all thought endemic only to our own families.

Saturday is the traditional day in Rio for *feijoada completa*, the Brazilian national dish. Every restaurant in Brazil has its own version, and on Saturday we have ours. We have the use of a nearby house where some of us are staying, and Dolly takes charge of the preparation of an authentic *feijoada*, with rice, black beans cooked with meat (and a non-authentic vegetarian version for some of us), and the requisite accompaniments of julienned collard greens sautéed in olive oil and garlic and sprinkled with lemon juice; *farofa*, manioc flour sautéed with onions, garlic, bits of bacon or salt pork, and chopped hard boiled eggs; along with the traditional garnish of thinly sliced oranges. Incredibly to me, some are tasting *feijoada* for the first time, but no one is disappointed. No surprise there—it is delicious! There is Brazilian music, a little bit of samba, and much laughter.

On Sunday morning, we have a quiet memorial service on the top of a hill for our grandparents, our parents, and for two cousins—Neco's son Jim, and Henry's son Henricito. We exchange photographs and more stories: memories of long-ago happy times.

My mind is immersed in family history. I am still working on the transcription of the tablets, and have the story of meeting Dona Ana to tell. I have also begun tracking our genealogy, and have charts of the family going back many generations and sideways in long lists. This is necessary in order for me to place the many names I am encountering, and so I have become the *ad hoc* family historian. My cousins bring me letters, photographs, and miscellaneous papers—some in English, some in Portuguese, some written to or by our Vovó, but one gift is more important than the rest. Chiquita brings me something that I immediately recognize and value above all else: the missing pages of the second tablet, pages 609–723! It is the section on Vovó's trip to Caldas with her children, which I had learned of on my own trip to that "poetical little town."

Smiling, kissing, hugging, waving: we say our goodbyes and go our separate ways with happy memories, vowing to keep in touch. I now have pages 457 to 723, and 725 to 1076 of the tablets! Only page 724 of the tablet series is still missing. In addition, I have incomplete but various loose pages dealing with Vovó's early childhood, all with page numbers preceding page 457. Still missing are accounts of the years she spent as a student in the boarding school in São Paulo. The last page, 1076, ends mid-sentence, so she obviously wrote more. I don't have the complete story, but I have enough to keep me busy for a very long time.

# VII. Venus and Mars

In 1915, Myron A. Clark was sent to Portugal to establish a YMCA at the University of Coimbra, one of Europe's oldest universities. It was founded in Lisbon in the year 1290 by King Dinis and moved to Coimbra in 1537, where it has remained to this day. For my grandmother, it was stirring to be living in the place of legends known to her through Portugal's national epic *Os Lusíadas*, the masterpiece of Luiz de Camões published in 1572. Camões, who lived as a young man in Coimbra, celebrated in verse the voyage of Vasco da Gama to India and other events and legends in Portuguese history, including the love story of Inêz de Castro and Dom Pedro, the future king of Portugal.

This affair produced two sons, but ended badly. When Pedro's wife Constança died, he and Inêz were secretly married, but Dom Pedro's father, King Afonso—opposed to the liaison for political reasons—ordered Inêz de Castro murdered. Legend says that a spring arose from her tears on the spot where Inêz de Castro was stabbed to death, and that her blood can still be seen on a stone there. After the death of Afonso and his succession to the throne, Pedro ordered the hearts of two of her killers ripped out. He exhumed and crowned her body, declared her Queen of Portugal, paraded the corpse through the streets to the Monastery of Alcobaça, where he commissioned twin tombs, for himself and his beloved, and forced his court to kneel before her and kiss her decomposed hand. Venus-worship gone amok!

Portugal had become a republic in 1910, after a five-day revolution forced King Manuel II to abdicate and flee to England. With the Republic came the separation of Church and State, confiscation of church property, dissolution of religious congregations, and a strong anticlerical and antireligious sentiment among intellectuals. The ruling classes, who controlled the press, were contemptuous of traditional religious beliefs, often portraying them as mere superstitions in their newspapers and journals. Even rural areas normally immune to the views of cosmopolitan centers were affected by church closings and were cautious about any outward expression of religious belief.

Teófilo Braga became the first president of the Republic, and the political and economic problems were many. In March 1916, adhering to a long-standing treaty with England, Portugal entered the European war on the side of the Allies and sent 60,000 troops to the British front in France. In 1917 widespread food and fuel shortages fueled a wave of general strikes in Lisbon, and were aggravated by government attempts to repress them by force. The strikes began to spread throughout the country. By December there were revolts in Lisbon, Porto, and Coimbra, and an *estado de sítio* (state of siege, or martial law) was proclaimed in these cities.[89] Portugal was verging on totalitarianism, and Europe was bowing to Mars, the god of war. In Coimbra, my grandparents' family had its own encounters with Venus and Mars.

In 1917, the chairman of the Portuguese National YMCA, Don Alfredo da Silva, noting the work of the Y with the British troops in France, asked John R. Mott,[90] general secretary of the YMCA's National War Work Council, for American cooperation in service to the Portuguese troops. The Portuguese were welcomed in the British Y huts, but linguistic difficulties led to the request that Portuguese-speaking Y leaders enter the field. Because of his service in Brazil and Portugal and his knowledge of Portuguese, my grandfather was chosen by Mott to take charge of the work and was assigned to the Headquarters Staff of the British Y at Abbeville, France.

In February 1918, my grandfather went to France. The American Association provided funds, secured personnel, and plunged into the work with the Portuguese army at Brest, at the front in Flanders, and in the

---

89. Wheeler, *Republican Portugal*.

90. John R. Mott (1865–1955) was a major influence on the Y's missionary outreach in the first half of the twentieth century. The American YMCAs sent workers by the thousands overseas, both as missionary-like YMCA secretaries and as war workers. In 1946 the Nobel Peace Prize was awarded jointly to John R. Mott in recognition of the role the YMCA had played in increasing global understanding and for its humanitarian efforts, and to Emily Greene Balch, cofounder with Jane Addams of the Women's International League for Peace and Freedom, who also worked with the League of Nations and United Nations. See Taft, *Service with Fighting Men*, 359.

rest zone near the channel ports. There was also a Paris bureau at 29 Rue Montholon, with a dormitory and canteen to serve Portuguese officers and men as they passed through the city. The Association followed its regular athletic and social program and helped the Portuguese troops personally in many ways. By their acts of kindness, the secretaries endeared themselves to thousands of Portuguese soldiers who were very ill-at-ease to find themselves at war in a foreign land. Several of these secretaries were cited by the Portuguese command, and two, John Mott and Myron Clark, were made officers of the *Ordem de Cristo* (Order of Christ).[91]

The Y's efforts during World War I even inspired music. Irving Berlin, who was stationed at Fort Yaphank in 1918, wrote a song—"I Can Always Find A Little Sunshine in the Y.M.C.A.," which was performed in a revue he wrote titled *Yip, Yip, Yaphank*. Another song, "The Meaning of Y.M.C.A. (You Must Come Across)," written by Ed Rose and Abe Olman in 1918, had the lyric: "They've done their bit and more. To help us win the war....The Y is right there on the firing line."[92]

The soldiers made their own songs. The YMCA did not believe in distributing cigarettes, stationery, and other commodities free of charge to the soldiers, since they felt that men who paid their own way would have more dignity than those who accepted charity when it was not essential. The troops had a different point of view and added another to the countless verses of "Mademoiselle from Armentières": "The YMCA has very good times, parlez-vous....Cheating the soldiers of nickels and dimes! Hinky dinky parlez-vous!"[93]

91. Taft, *Service with Fighting Men*, 2:359–60.

92. Marshfield Area YMCA, "Wherever the Soldier Goes," para. 13.

93. From the diaries of Myron A. Clark, 1900–1920.

# 41. Coimbra

The ship bearing us to Portugal, the *Gelria*, was lovely, and one of the largest that then sailed in Brazilian waters. Next morning we began to meet the few first-class passengers; nobody was traveling unless, like us, they had to. Here are those that I remember: an English captain whose boat had been torpedoed—this was the rumor. He was a fine gentleman, a good deal older than I, always in uniform and his chair was most always by mine. There was an Argentine captain going to Spain, a German woman going back to Germany, an Englishman who rumor said had been down to Argentina buying horses for the English government, some Portuguese couples, and a very attractive Portuguese woman with her daughter and son. She did not mix very much with the other women, nor did we care to have her company. All the men, though, were like turkey cocks around a turkey hen.

My family (two daughters and two sons), both captains, and the German woman were at the captain's table. We were surprised when we got to the dining room to see the display of roses! Besides a big bouquet on our table, the table next to ours was full of vases of roses. Captain Napier, the Englishman, took a liking to my two boys. The Portuguese son began immediately to court Ruth. The Dutch captain of the ship, very good-naturedly, used to joke that he was keeping an eye on my daughters for me. We have a snapshot taken on board this boat, where my daughters and another young lady and the Portuguese young fellow posed.

One evening at sunset we saw on the horizon a boat flashing its lights and speeding toward us. Our captain happened to be sitting with the other captain near us, and they both immediately went up to the bridge while the passengers got all excited. Pretty soon the warship turned around and everybody calmed down.

My husband met us in Lisbon. Sometimes I think it is nice to be away from your beloved just for the happiness of the meeting again! We had forgotten all our woes. I don't know about my daughters, but I was perfectly satisfied, even though the older two boys were in the States. They would have been there even if I had been in Brazil. Lisbon is beautiful, and Portugal is full of interest for us, the Brazilians.

We began sightseeing as George, who was a baby when we were there in 1904, was twelve now. He and Neco, thirteen-and-a-half, were presented by the *garção* (waiter) of our table with a little caged cricket! Really, I could not see the point! I do love to hear from a veranda the crickets and the frogs when they are nested in the green grass and in the pools; it gives me a feeling of contentment. But on a table between candlesticks or hanging on the forefinger of your son, it is maddening!

Lisbon is surrounded by hills, and one of these is called Cintra. One of the king's palaces, the Palácio da Pena,[94] is there. We hired an automobile to go there but at the foot of the hill they had donkeys to hire for young people who cared to go up. Well, all the children wanted to ride on the donkeys. When we were all set to go, we noticed that the man who had rented the darling beasts had a whip in his hand and followed us. My husband told him it was not necessary for him to go up. "Oh yes, I have to go to make them go." Indeed he did: they moved only with the whip, and when the effects of this died out they would stick to the ground to start only with the whip. We had a very merry go-up, laughing all the way. Coming back, when my husband paid the man for the donkeys, the man said, "You have to pay me too, I am worth as much as the donkeys!" Those were happy days.

On June 25th, we left Lisbon for Coimbra—the city of traditions, the Oxford of Portugal and Brazil. Coimbra was the capital of Portugal in 1139, when Afonso Henriques declared himself Portugal's first king, and it is the seat of one of the oldest universities in the world. In that university many of the rulers of Portugal and Brazil learned all that Europe could teach in books. The only building, square and very large,

94. Now spelled Sintra. The palace was completed in 1885: it was built for Dom Fernando II, King Consort and husband of Maria II, on the ruins of a Hieronymite monastery founded in the fifteenth century on the site of the chapel of Nossa Senhora da Pena (Our Lady of Sorrows). See Jack, *Sintra: A Glorious Eden*.

was built as strong as a fortress, with solid iron gates. In the tower was the big old bell, nicknamed since the early days *a cabra*, which means "the goat." When it rang there were classes; when it didn't, there were not, so one of the students' tricks was to do something that prevented the man in charge of the bell from ringing it. History says that Coimbra was named after nearby Conimbriga, the largest site of the Roman Empire in Portugal, on the Roman road between Lisbon and Braga.

Myron had rented some rooms in a dilapidated old building and converted them into a simple recreation center that was called the *núcleo*, which he hoped would attract the students to play games such as Parcheesi, ping pong, Cue Roque,[95] Halma,[96] and croquinole,[97] that were popular with young men in the YMCA in the States. Another attraction they had was a very good gramophone. Later Myron inaugurated the educational program with the first evening class, the study of English. It was a success, so he soon announced the opening of a class dealing with social problems. No one came.

Coimbra was exclusively Catholic, and from the moment he had arrived, Myron was regarded with suspicion that grew into open hostility once his purpose became known. Since there was no Protestant church, we had family prayers and study of the Bible every Sunday, to which we invited anyone interested.

It was getting near one of the biggest events in the religious life of Coimbra—*A Festa da Rainha Santa*. My husband received a telegram from the secretary of the Brazilian Embassy asking him to reserve rooms at the Hotel Avenida for the ambassador and himself, as they wanted to see the festivities of the *Rainha Santa*, which would last several days. People came from all corners of Portugal and one could see them sleeping on sidewalks, in parks, and so on, since every room in the hotels and *pensões*

---

95. A game of croquet played on a billiard table. See "Says Cue Roque Is Not Like Pool," *Spartanburg Herald*, for argument that Cue Roque as played in YMCAs, unlike pool, is a healthy activity for boys.

96. Whitehill, "American Games," 125. A precursor of Chinese checkers invented in 1880. See Peterson, "Chinese Checkers."

97. A skill and action table game played on a round or octagonal wooden board. See Kelly, *The Crokinole Book*.

Students playing Que Roque; Myron looking tired
at the Núcleo, Coimbra, Portugal, 1915.

(boarding houses) was taken. Every night there were fireworks from the university tower and from the Mondego River.

The remains of a much-beloved queen lie in a coffin carved of solid silver in a church across the river, in a little town called Santa Clara. In that church, there is also a beautiful wooden image of her that is carried during her feast by prominent people and a long procession of brotherhoods with torches, sacred music, and imposing ceremonies from Santa Clara's church to a church in Coimbra.

Dr. Regis de Oliveira, the ambassador, and his secretary joined us in watching the festivities. Of course the papers had mentioned his arrival, so we were quite in evidence. The students have a way to honor people without a word. When they see you arriving they gracefully pull off their capes, and just as gracefully throw them on the sidewalks in front of you for you to walk over them. This was done continually those nights when we were parading the streets. From a window of the *núcleo*, along with some students, the ambassador, and his secretary, we saw the *Rainha Santa* pass.

The wooden image of the saint was dressed as any woman, simple and beautiful, and her hands held her apron in which one could see carved flowers. This was the legend: She was a very charitable and religious woman, and used to go about distributing money to the poor people around the country. Her husband very much disliked her charity and her religious inclinations, and prohibited her from going around exercising her charity. But whenever she could do it without his knowing, she did. Once when she was on one of these errands of mercy, she met him. She had the corners of her apron raised to form a bag, in which she had lots of coins. He asked her, "What do you have there in the apron?" "Flowers," she answered. He urged her to let him see them, and to her amazed eyes the coins had turned into flowers; so says the legend, and many believe this to be true. After the king died, she entered the Convent of Santa Clara, which she had founded, and there she died: her ashes are kept in the silver coffin. She was canonized by the Pope, and history says she was a very virtuous and wise queen.

Coimbra, like Lisbon, is hilly, and you lived in the *Baixa* (lower part of town) or *Alta* (upper part). The university was at the top of the *Alta*. We took rooms at the Hotel Avenida near the Chonpal, a forest of Lombardy poplars. The Mondego, which the citizens of Coimbra call *O Rio dos Poetas* (The River of Poets), ran in front of the hotel. This was downtown in the *Baixa*. On Sundays a band played in a *coreto* (bandstand) in front of the hotel.

Right here my worries began. I don't think Walter Winchell was on the map then, but the news flashed about the two attractive daughters and the rest of the family who were at the Avenida Hotel, and so began the promenade of the students in their uniforms, their Spanish capes moving gracefully and harmoniously with their steps! Students were the life of Coimbra. It was obligatory for them to wear a black Prince Albert coat and pants and a very graceful and wide cape that fitted very nicely on the shoulders and fell almost to the ground in graceful folds. Sometimes their cape, called a *batina*, was so worn out—even held together in places with safety pins, that to the newcomer it seemed ridiculous and pitiful, but soon it appeared very natural. It was considered to be a disgrace for a student to wear a new uniform in his last year. On their heads they wore little round caps in the winter, and nothing in the summer.

We were looking for a house, and Senhor Albino, a friend, and one of the men interested in the work but not at all in religion—especially Catholicism—was also looking for us. Some of the more daring students ventured inside the hotel. There were among these students some that met my husband at the *núcleo*, and they called on us with some others. One of them, a very bright fellow, was very anxious to speak English so he came every day and informed us of the things worth seeing.

We visited the *Quinta das Lágrimas*, which means "a country home where tears were shed." Here I have to tell of the romance of one of the kings of Portugal; familiar through the *Lusíadas* to Brazilians and Portuguese from the time they enter their teens. Now here I was in the scene where it happened! We all know that Cupid does not play a role when kings get married, except in that well-known transaction when a king gave up his kingdom for, in his words, "The woman I love."[98]

Well, Dom Pedro I of Portugal married according to the rules, and among the queen's *damas* (ladies-in-waiting) was a Spanish girl, Inêz de Castro. The king fell in love with this lovely girl and the queen noticed, too. Thinking that she could prevent something more than exchanges of woes from happening between the two, she made Inêz the godmother of her first child. According to the Catholic faith, the sin of having the godmother of your child as your mistress was more than a sin, it was a crime—almost unpardonable.

Her plan failed completely and Inêz de Castro ruled over the heart of Dom Pedro in that beautiful *quinta*, and had two children by him. My memory fails me now about some historic facts. It seems that the queen died and Dom Pedro's father or those ruling with him, being afraid now that his son would marry his beloved Inêz de Castro and that this would bring trouble for Portugal because she was a Spanish woman, had her assassinated. Don Pedro swore vengeance on the men who killed her, and even though she was dead, she was carried in a procession in the streets of Coimbra and proclaimed Queen of Portugal. All this is narrated in verses in the *Lusíadas*.

We climbed to the Penedo da Meditação, a big rock on which they say

---

98. A reference to Edward, Duke of Windsor.

that Dom Pedro was seen many times at sunset after his beloved was killed, and saw the little stream where the *cicerone* pointed out to us a red spot on a large, flat stone: the blood of Inês de Castro. Indeed we saw it and laughed. I wonder how often they painted the stone. But one almost believes it while in that place where centuries and kingdoms have passed by.

Coimbra began to seem deserted because vacations had started, and we were waiting for a house that had been promised. We received a letter from our friend Domingues in Brazil telling us to go to his *quinta* near the old city of Braga where he was born, which was kept now for friends from Brazil and Portugal when they needed rest. The name of the *quinta* was Rendufe. We thought it was a very good idea, as we were getting tired of life in the hotel. Besides, my husband could not do a thing about the Y while the students were away.

The place was kept by a family who lived on the premises. They raised corn and some wheat, but the principle product was wine. In Rendufe, we were living a lazy life without a care, as our treasures, the daughters, were away from the covetous eyes of the students. We saw many peasants' festivities there, among them the *Vira* and *Carnaval Verde* dances on moonlight nights at the *eira* (threshing floor), and we enjoyed an oxcart ride on a full-moon night. There was a *festa* given by the wife of the *caseiro* (the caretaker of the house). As was customary, she invited the women from other *quintas* to come and help her to prepare linen. The flax plant had been soaking for a day and they had to hit it on stone until it was all shredded, and only one-fifth the size it had been, and then put it to dry. This made very coarse cloth for them, and bedding. After the work, they made and served eats and wine at the *eira*. But we had to leave. We received a card saying that the house that had been promised to us would be ready by September 1st, so we said goodbye to this fine rustic family.

We bought nice furniture, rented a piano, and hired a maid. Our washing was done on the waters of the same Mondego sung by the muses. The ironing was always done by somebody else who came to the house to do it. Each maid did one thing. Our daughters were anxious to take music lessons, and we could afford this here. Ruth took voice and Baby piano, and as the curriculum of the *liceu* (secondary, preparatory school) was different and rather difficult for the boys, we hired a teacher to prepare them. And what could I do besides watching moonlight on the Mondego and sunsets from the *Penedo da Saudade*, but crocheting, crocheting, and again crocheting? Nothing else except reading, and this I did, enjoying immensely the Portuguese authors—and writing to my sons and friends. These activities wouldn't lower our social standing.

You may understand this better when I tell you that one day I told one of my boys to go to the *mercearia* (grocery store) to get something, and the servant immediately put aside what she was doing, put on her shawl and the handkerchief on her head, and said, "What do you think people will say about me, working in a house where the son carries groceries from the store?" It was *her* reputation, not mine, that would be at stake.

In Rio there was no winter at all. In Portugal houses were built very solidly and were nice for the hot weather, but in the cold rainy season, they were damp. There was no heating system, so we just sat around with our coats on and wrapped our feet with something, but this did not prevent us from having chilblain. We went to the pharmacy for some medicine for this, and there we were told, jokingly of course, that the only medicine was *pó de maio* (May dust). Then the students told us about *brazeiros*, fans where some embers were put, and we tried this on rainy days. They also had some bags to put your feet in, and I remember one rainy day going to the *núcleo* and your grandfather was sitting at his desk with his overcoat on, busy writing, with his feet in one of those bags. The picture was funny and pathetic.

The girls walked to their lessons alone. It was not far, and sometimes they did some shopping alone, too. One morning Sr. Albino, on whom my husband was depending for advice and suggestions so that we would not go too far away from local traditions, came to the *núcleo* and very politely said to my husband that Madame Clark ought to accompany *as meninas* (the girls) to their lessons and downtown. In fact, he added, both girls had been seen walking and talking with the students. My husband said he did not see any harm in that in the daytime, and in all probability they were some of the students we knew. Sr. Albino replied, "Oh, but this is not customary here."

The girls were furious, and to a certain extent they were right, because what harm could be done to them in plain daylight? At night it was entirely out of the question. So from that day on, I had to walk up to the lessons and sit there as the rest of the mothers did. This and many other incidents created a deep antagonism between the girls and us, and between them and the people who made it their business to watch them.

In Coimbra, students carried on flirtations in the church, in the theater, and in front of the loved one's house à la Romeo and Juliet; with the student in the street and the lady at a second-floor window or balcony. The students called this a *gargarejo*, a gargle, which I think was a very appropriate name. Our girls were, to these young men in Portugal, what movie stars are now for the young people of America and Brazil. Being half American and half Brazilian, they were very different from the Portuguese girls in their ways, and this seemed to lure the young Portuguese men—but it was not a student who made life for us in Coimbra very uncomfortable. Unknown to us, a dashing young fellow, who was not a student, found a way to talk to Ruth and confessed to her in verses the love of Escamillo for Carmen. He was an amateur *toureiro* (bullfighter)! Yes, away in my mind I am hearing The Toreador Song.

One day somebody brought my husband a small paper published I don't know where, with a lovely poem dedicated to Miss Ruth Clark. The poem was a sweet love story following the story of Ruth of the Bible, and to be sure, we named our Ruth after that fair lady of the Old Testament who once said, "Thy people shall be my people." Well, my daughter had a diamond on her third finger, which represented something, and this was why my husband was so upset. This whole affair started when we were still at the hotel. Everybody, even a *toreador*, had a right to go to a hotel.

We were there to deal with the students, the flower of Portugal, along with their fathers and grandfathers before them. The sons of working men, laborers and farmers, could not even read. Businessmen, however, were looked down on by the students and nicknamed *futricas* (troublemakers). Our Portuguese Escamillo was a *futrica* to the students, and they thought we ought not to allow any communication between our daughters and *futricas*. The girls were aware already that in Portugal, society would not allow even those ways that their father permitted. Well,

once upon a time an American in Brazil had paid very little attention to
the customs of that country regarding boys and girls, and this brought
heaven on earth to a certain girl that I know better than anyone else. But
that girl knew the kind of young man that American was and the kind of
work he was interested in, which was to help young men fight evil, and
not a bull.

One of our brothers in Christ was constantly visiting us from Lisbon
because he wanted to open evangelical work in Coimbra. He was the first
to suspect that Escamillo was very much enchanted with our Carmen,
and to warn my husband. Such a thing was a scandal there. (But a few
years ago, when in Brazil, I heard that because of more than a flirtation
this friend was called back home to Brazil and had to resign from the
ministry. *Gato ruivo, do que usa, disso cuida*, says the proverb.[99]

Well, my husband would not have a *toreador* for a son-in-law. And as far as
that was concerned, he would not want any of those students who visited
us to marry his daughters either, because the majority of them had no
religion and the moral standards for young men there were very loose,
so very unhealthy. The whole thing was so innocent compared with the
ways of the United States, even then. But in Rome, do as the Romans.
In fact, somebody even said that my husband had been chosen to go
there because of his handsome daughters, who would be sure to attract
the young men. This was pure gossip, but immediately their father took
action, and began to plan to send them to the States.

---

99. More or less: "Red cat, take care of your own reputation." This old Portuguese
proverb, much used in the family, means that if a person finds fault with others, it is
because he is guilty of the same fault, although he pretends innocence. A more modern
version still heard in Brazil is *"Quem usa, cuida."*

# 42. The Drumbeat of War

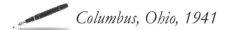 *Columbus, Ohio, 1941*

The atmosphere around our place was heavy. In Lisbon, rumors of Portugal joining England against Germany were thick, and on March 11, 1916, they were confirmed. On the 17th the merchant ship *Tubantia*, the Dutch sister ship of the *Gelria* that brought us to Portugal, was sunk by a mine in the North Sea before reaching Lisbon. Three of the boys who came frequently to the *núcleo* rooms and to our home had to leave for training camp. On April 4th we learned of Wilson's request of Congress for a declaration of a state of war with Germany. Then on the 24th of April came the decree of expulsion of Germans, Austrians, and other allies of Germany from Portugal.

The next day, Portugal began mobilization of part of the Twenty-Third Regiment. As Coimbra was the seat of the regiment, crowds of fellows who were recruited from the country and the neighborhood villages were coming. We heard the sounding of drums that night about ten, and it was getting nearer and nearer our place. Pretty soon we could hear the regular sound of the soldiers' footsteps, and then they began to appear at the Praça Santa Cruz where we lived, so we joined the crowd following them to the station. There was worry on their faces, and the mothers, wives, relatives, and sweethearts followed them weeping and screaming! It was a sad sight. Well, that night the full realization came to us that we were at war, and only a very few days from the battlefield. A few days later, four or five more of the students that had visited us and had joined the little *núcleo* were called. One morning right there in the *praça*, an officer was training a group of twenty or thirty boys in their civilian clothes with their guns. From that day on, training in the barracks and in the parks was going on all the time.

We had to be separated from our daughters. Life was miserable for them on account of the strain in which we lived. My husband noticed that the mail was constantly bringing local letters to the girls, so he told the janitor to deliver the mail to him or to Dona Chiquita; but the janitor was always willing to let the girls sort the letters and take them. The censor was working already with the government, and the girls were complaining that the home censor was worse than the government.

There was a cloud above the poetical Coimbra now, the only relief we had was a movie once in a while (silent yet), walks by the Mondego, and picnics by ourselves at the beautiful sites around Coimbra. We visited interesting cities like Valença, the old fortified city on our side of the river Minho in Portugal: on the other side was old Tuy in Spain. The fortifications in Valença seemed like playthings; the bridge that opened over the dry moat is there yet. We stopped in Porto (Oporto) where my husband bought 800 francs for passages for the girls on the Italian ship *Roma.*

The decision to send the girls to the States had been made for some time. Baby was going to college. We were waiting only for someone with whom they could make the trip safely. Our friend the American minister wrote to my husband that the American *attaché militaire* was going to the States and this was a good opportunity to send the girls with him, so everything was arranged. You can imagine how I felt when I said goodbye to them, who were going to travel on a ship of a belligerent country, Italy. But because there was a high authority of the then-neutral United States on board, the boat was going to fly the American flag.

Thus my daughters left the historic and romantic Coimbra, where they too had had their romances, with serenades under our windows by the students robed in their long, full, and graceful capes. To the music of their guitars they revealed their hopeless love in very melodious voices, under a starry sky or beneath the moon over the Santa Cruz Park near our house. Probably they could see the two shadows in another window, and they knew to whom these shadows belonged.

The International Committee of the YMCA was supposed to send us a cable just as soon as the girls arrived in New York, but even cables did not get through quickly; it was wartime. After the time passed when we ought to have had a cable and we didn't, the worry began. Finally, we received a telegram saying they had arrived in New York. Baby went to

Wooster, Ohio—where Henry was—as was arranged before, and he was delighted. Ruth was with my dear teacher and friend, Mrs. Magalhães, until something could be arranged for her. Later on, she went to Minneapolis to be with her grandparents.

My husband stayed home in the evenings and read, as of old, to me mostly Portuguese novels. I love some of them. Júlio Diniz's books made me think of Louisa May Alcott. We read some Eça de Queirós, but I don't care for him so much as he is like Emile Zola, and *America do Norte*, by Alfred Mesquita, a Brazilian. Myron gave some lessons to the boys too. He kept busy with his work and the building, and the boys were busy with their lessons with him and the private teacher. But we knew all the time that this was not a good way to give them their education, and they had no companionship of other boys. So we were worrying. By this time Portugal was thick at war and our friends the students were coming all the time to say goodbye to us.

The rest of the year of 1916 was full of anxiety about the building for the *Associação*, and the reduction of activities at the rooms due to the constant leaving of the students to training camps. The rainy season was delaying construction very much. My husband was worn out with the delay and slowness of everything connected with the building. Still, we had an open evening for visitors, especially young men, on Sundays in Coimbra—as we did all Sunday afternoon in Rio—and sometimes visitors came on weekdays when we played games with them (Parcheesi, Authors, etc.). This was entirely new to them, and how they enjoyed them! Before, they just played cards, and this always for money. Thus 1916 ended, and now to 1917.

January 1st was a beautiful, clear, springlike day. We took our lunch in a picnic basket to Penedo da Meditação. That evening several fellows called at home. When we saw that they came just the same after the girls left, we were very pleased. But of course as I said before, several of them had gone to war already. My husband continued his program of reading aloud for us—*When a Man's a Man; The Last of the Mohicans; Casa de Pais, Escola de Filhos* (House of Fathers, School of Sons). On the 5th we received photos of the girls, which I framed.

When Orton had come to Rio from the States just before we left for Portugal, he brought me a music book with popular music for piano and songs, easy classical pieces, as the radio would say today, melodies old and new that everybody would love to hear or play. He had heard that Ruth had bought a piano, and as all my music pieces were doing some missionary work in the north of Brazil, he had the bright idea to do this. Well, even before I had left our lovely home by the sea, I began to try to play these pieces, and my husband and the children sang while I accompanied them on the piano. But it was in those disquieting days in Portugal that this book became a source of pleasure and comfort. I spent many of those long hours in the winter pounding that piano, and pretty soon I was able to accompany my husband in some of those songs like "One Sweet Solemn Thought, Laddie"; also those sweet songs such as "Juanita," "Old Black Joe," and even a piece of the *Messiah*.

But of all of them, the one that made a chill of joy run all over me as I felt my husband's hands holding my shoulders and pulling my back toward his breast, was that sailor song, the melody of which I am singing in my mind, but cannot at present remember the words, except—"She is there waiting for me." I saw much more of my husband in those two years in Coimbra, because it was a small town where one could get everywhere in a short time. He could walk to the rooms in ten minutes. We had him home, too, for every meal.

Portuguese troops were leaving for France almost every week and believe me there was no enthusiasm in their faces; they didn't think they were going to defend their country. The work in the building was going very, very slowly on account of the constant rains, and there was a worker's strike. The workmen of our building didn't join them willingly, but the others came and made them leave the work.

At the same time, my husband was asking the International Committee to send a man to take his place, because he felt that our two boys' education was not what it ought to be. Besides, there was no social life for them at all. A man was found, but his surname was German. Although he was just as good an American as any American whose ancestors came on the Mayflower (or were there, as Will Rogers said about his, to welcome them), he could not enter Portugal. Brazil gained by that because he was sent there, and has done and is still doing fine work there.

Things were not very smooth with our daughters in the States, and so my husband had been trying to convince me to go to the States with the boys and keep house in Wooster, where Henry and Baby were already boarding; and Ruth could also come there. I would have five with me. It sounded pretty good, but for what price! My husband had to be left alone, and the crossing of the ocean was dangerous now, with the States at war also. As for my husband, he was sure that a man would be found soon and he would follow me. Considering it all, I reluctantly said, "Yes, I will go."

# 43. *Associação Cristã de Moços* Centennial

 *Rio, July 20, 1993*

Donn and I married in 1988. I have not been back to Brazil for six years so I practically fall out of my chair when I receive a phone call from the YMCA International Office for Latin America and the Caribbean. The Rio *ACM* has invited me to their Centennial with all expenses paid! I finally decide it is not a cruel joke—I have just won the lottery without even buying a ticket! The airline ticket is being sent to me; I am thrilled and terrified, but how can I refuse?

I have only ten days from the day I get the telephone call to get on the plane, but I can do it. I spread the word of my good fortune among my sisters and cousins: Mike, our grandfather's namesake, wants to send with me the framed medal—the *Ordem de Cristo* (Order of Christ) that our grandfather received from the Portuguese government for his service with their troops in the first World War. Mike mailed it; I wrapped and carefully packed it.

I write quick notes to two second cousins, Estefânia in Rio and Yedda in São Paulo, to tell them I'm coming. Then follows my usual pretrip panic about what to take, getting my visa and everything done on time—and this time, wondering what is expected of me. I assume that I will be expected to make some public remarks, and the thought of making a speech in Portuguese in front of so many people adds to my anxiety. I consult with my cousin Dolly about what to wear for the banquet; she says my light-blue beaded wedding dress would be perfect. I write the speech and read it to her on the phone for feedback before I leave. She says it too is perfect—that she is deeply moved by it. Everyone needs a cousin like that!

After a twenty-four hour trip, I arrive, exhausted, in Rio on Thursday morning, July 1st. I am met by Tasso, Paula, and Vanda, my friends from

the Y's Men's Club. We drive to the Othon Palace, a luxury hotel right
on Copacabana beach. It is almost noon when I get to my room on the
18th floor with a view to the ocean in front and a peek at the mountains
behind. The weather is gorgeous, midwinter and in the 80s. It is sunny,
with warm breezes off the ocean swaying the palms. Rio feels like home
to me, and I just hang over my little balcony and drink it all in, anxiety
fading away.

The entire U.S. delegation, nearly fifty people, is staying at the Othon,
but I have only met the two women from San Francisco who boarded
the plane with me at Los Angeles. We parted at the airport, so I don't
know what the plans are for getting together except that there is to be
a cocktail party tonight at the central subway station to celebrate the
publishing of the official book of the Rio Centennial/Historical Exposition.
My head is spinning with questions. "What is my role here?" "What do the
Brazilians want from me? What do the Americans think?" "How am I to
get to the opening?" "Will the Americans all be going together?" "Should I
just go on my own?" "Surely someone will call me" ...but they don't.

I shower, unpack, and rest a bit, but I can't sleep. I'm too excited. I leave
messages with the three contacts I have, go out and walk a bit in my old
neighborhood, exchange some money, return to the room, figure out
what to wear tonight, practice my speech, and wait. Finally a call comes
to meet in the lobby at six-thirty to go to the opening. A bus with guide is
waiting to take us to the Carioca *metrô* station.

There is a wide, open platform underground in the subway station,
where a photographic exhibition of the history of the *ACM* in Brazil has
been mounted. We seem to have the entire space to ourselves. I don't
see anyone scurrying to catch a train, or even hear any trains. Maybe I
am just tuning out any mundane activity. Coming down the wide stairs
to the platform, I see, on the first panel, an enlarged photograph of Sir
George Williams, the founder of the YMCA and the man for whom Daddy
was named. Next to it, smaller photos of our grandfather and of Vovó—a
beautiful image I have never seen before, when she was perhaps twenty
or so. I gasp at the sight of it—am I awake? Now not only have *I* walked
into her past, but it is opening up for all of Rio to see. I choke back tears
and swallow a huge lump in my throat.

There are other photographs, many familiar to me—Myron translating for Teddy Roosevelt, Myron in his World War I uniform, Myron and Chiquita's triumphant return to Rio after the war, Myron's funeral procession. There are also pictures I have not seen—Vovó cutting the ribbon opening a new *ACM* site in a *favela* (shantytown), and the opening of the Myron A. Clark campground.

The familiar quotation, which Vovó often repeated, from Myron's letter to his parents written on his first trip to Brazil, is prominently displayed:

> *"When I got up this morning and looked through the porthole, I saw for the first time in the distance on the horizon, the land of my adoption—Brazil."*

There is no way I could have prepared myself for the emotional impact of seeing the displays of photographs of my grandparents, and feeling the respect and admiration shown for them here in the center of modern Rio. I am treated like royalty, and I hope I do not disappoint. It is very exciting and moving, and I am basking in the warmth of this welcome. The exhibit traces the history of the Association in Rio from the beginning to the present day; the photographs become glossier and change from black-and-white to color, and all through the exhibit, as indeed through the whole five days of celebrations, there are references to my grandfather's vision and dedication. Through the *ACM*, I am finding connections to my grandfather that I had never felt before.

I am greeted warmly by Hector Civitate and Thex (pronounced "Tex") Correia, secretary general and president respectively, of the *ACM* in Rio. There are photographers wanting to take my picture alongside that of my grandfather. Several old friends from the Y's Men's Club take charge of me, and I am introduced to many people. When I first realized I was going to Rio for the centennial, I felt a little like an imposter. It still feels strange to be treated like a celebrity on the basis of my relationship to someone I never even knew, and yet I am beginning to feel very proud of my heritage.

The event is billed as a cocktail party, a bit of an irony. I remember Vovó's oft-told story of the first time she was offered a cocktail by someone on one of her many ship voyages. It was a new and—to her amusing—word, and she accepted, curious and not having any idea what it might be. Since she had never tasted an alcoholic drink, she choked, spilling the drink on her dress. The gentleman said "Oh, Madame, I think you do not want this," and quickly took it away.

After everyone has milled about for a while, looking at the exhibition and circulating, welcome speeches and prayers are made and translated, and the Y youth choir sings several songs. I am reluctant to leave, but my carriage has arrived! I am pulled along with the American delegation to dinner at a *churrascaria* in Ipanema, and then to Plataforma Uno.

I have never been here before. It's a tourist nightclub, with folkloric entertainment. In very lavish, Las Vegas-style costumes, men and women perform regional Brazilian dances and the martial arts dance form, *capoeira*. The main attraction consists of scantily clad *mulatas* dancing the samba more or less as it is done in the *Carnaval* parades. The irony is that my grandparents would not allow their children to attend, see, or participate in *Carnaval*, which they considered to be a pagan ritual. In those days, there wasn't so much nudity, and I kind of doubt they would have approved of that, either! So here we are in a nightclub, drinking beer or *caipirinhas*, those wonderful drinks made with sugar, limes, and *cachaça*, and watching what I and the other feminists among us consider to be an exploitative show.

The next day we Americans who don't have to go to meetings are divided into two sightseeing groups; mine will go to Petrópolis, the mountain summer home of the last Emperor, Dom Pedro Segundo. I am to translate when needed. But first, we have to make a stop at H. Stern, the BIG jeweler. So out to their factory and showroom in Ipanema, where the precious and semiprecious stones that Brazil is famous for are cut and set. We are given a tour of the factory, then the sales pitch, which many in our group succumb to—but not I. I remember how in years past when I was stranded downtown in the rain at rush hour, I would occasionally and larcenously take advantage of their free limousines. The limos wait at all the tourist sites to take tourists to the factory for the free tour, and then to their hotels or, in my case, to my apartment. Talk about exploitation! I have seen the tour and heard the pitch many times!

Then we are rounded up for a lovely trip up the mountains to the town of Petrópolis. Since we arrive late, it is decided to have lunch before the tour of the palace. Another *churrascaria*. I enjoy the tour of the palace very much. I have not been to Petrópolis since my first visit to Brazil, when I lived with the Neco Clarks. It's the usual kind of palace with beautiful inlaid wooden floors that you skate along in slippers, admiring china and silverware, chandeliers, paintings of kings and queens, furniture made out of beautiful tropical hardwoods, and tapestries. But what I like best is the refresher course in the history of Brazil during the Empire, which is so much the fascinating story of three men—grandfather, father, and son—and their tensions of loyalty between Portugal and Brazil, and each other.

After leaving the summer palace, we go to the cathedral where lie the remains of Pedro II and his wife Empress Teresa Cristina, their daughter Princess Isabel and her husband, the Conde d'Eu, grandson of Louis Philippe of France. It was Princess Isabel, acting as Regent in her father's temporary absence, who freed the slaves by issuing the doctrine of the "free womb." It was her husband whose name was given to the street in Caldas (since renamed) where Vovó was born. Near the marble mausoleum is a wonderful painting of the royal family and loyal friends leaving their palace in Rio for exile in Portugal on the day in November 1889 when they were expelled to make way for the Republic.

Back in my hotel room, every time I lie in bed sleepless with excitement in the wee hours of the morning, and every chance I get during the day, I practice my speech, often naked in front of the bathroom mirror. I decide if I can do it like that, I ought to be able to do it in front of a couple hundred people with my wedding dress on. And in spite of what Dolly told me, I keep revising it, because every day I hear from others new parts of the story I have to tell about the family. I keep trying to find out when the appropriate time would be to give the speech. Finally Jerry, the man who called me from St. Louis and who is coordinating everything for the Americans, tells me that the right time to present the medal would be at the awards ceremony Sunday night. So that's it. The speech and the medal are tied together.

Saturday night is the big night. There are sightseeing events during the day, but I elect to have lunch with my friends Paula and Tasso and have my nails done. Not having any responsibility, I am pretty calm as we arrive late, as usual, at the beautiful Glória Hotel, one of the most traditional in Brazil. Built in the 1920s, it has preserved its classic design with its original antique French furniture and art. We are ushered up the wide staircase where a cocktail party is in full swing in a huge Versailles-like hall. I learn there are 660 guests present.

I am met with an *abração* (big hug) by Paulão, an old friend from the Y's Men's Club who escorts me to the receiving line and then introduces me to the master of ceremonies, Sr. Enrique Irueta, who leads me into the banquet room which is totally empty of people. The tables are arranged in front of a rostrum flanked by the flags of Brazil, the United States, and ten other Latin American countries. Between the rows of tables, there is a large space for the dancing that is to take place later. Sr. Irueta seats me at the head table and leaves me alone in this enormous room. It is a strange feeling, like a dream, to be all alone in this banquet hall, but it gives me a chance to relax and collect myself. Pretty soon my tablemates are seated: Thex and his wife, Dayse; John Casey; the general secretary of the World Alliance; and other dignitaries. Soon all the other tables are filled. There are prayers and toasts and then I am introduced to the crowd. Again, there are many references to Myron and his vision and character.

We eat, and there are more speeches translated by Sr. Irueta. John Casey speaks about Thex, and I begin to understand how these people feel about the Y and about its founder in Brazil. Thex, he tells us, was one of many children of a single mother raised in one of the *favelas* of Rio. Through the *ACM*, Thex was able to escape from the poverty and crime of the slums, and eventually became president of the organization. I watch Thex's eyes fill with tears as John tells this story. Later someone tells me that there are many similar stories, which explains the loyalty that so many people have to the *ACM*. At some point, my own eyes fill with tears; it is just so moving to hear all this eulogy.

Then there is a show of *gaúcho* dancing—folklore dances of the cowboys and girls of the state of Rio Grande do Sul in southern Brazil. The costumes are bright and dashing; the energetic and intricate dances are accompanied by guitars. At midnight, the candles on the tables are lit, the electric lights extinguished, and everyone sings "Happy Birthday" to the Association. After that, there are more speeches, and then Thex is at the podium talking about Myron again and asking me to come forward. I thought my speech would be given the following night, at the awards dinner, and now I'm glad I didn't know I would be called upon tonight so that I was able to function normally during the dinner.

Thex holds my hand as he talks to me from the podium, and presents me with an engraved silver tray commemorating the event. He is very sweet, and it is without the slightest bit of nervousness that I speak to the crowd—the largest I have ever addressed—first in Portuguese, then in English. I know I am among friends. I can't give my prepared speech, since I don't have Mike's gift with me, so I just tell them what a great honor and privilege it is to be with my good friends in Rio, and with all the *ACM* people from Brazil, the rest of Latin America, and the States. I tell them that I am representing the descendants of Myron Augustus and Francisca Pereira de Moraes Clark, all of whom offer sincere congratulations and best wishes for success in their second century.

Then at one or so the music for dancing begins. Many people come to me, introducing themselves and inviting me to visit their Associations, and I am soon once again reluctantly pulled away to the waiting bus, with instructions to be ready to leave the next morning at 9:30 for church. No dancing for me!

The bus and churchgoers are on time, but unfortunately neither the driver nor the guide knows where the Presbyterian cathedral is located. Alas, neither do I. By now I am used to being chauffeured around, so I don't think to ascertain the address of our destination. We know it is in the center of the city, so here we are, driving around, asking people in the street—none of whom know, naturally. Finally we arrive, not too late, having found the cathedral by the hunt and peck method.

Arriving at the Presbyterian church, where my grandfather was an early member, I am ushered into a side room where I meet the ministers and where prayers are offered for the service. Then the processional music begins, and it is like a coronation march, with trumpets and all—and suddenly I notice John Casey and I are in it, walking two-by-two. When we get to the front of the church and the column divides I realize I am going right up to the altar with all the ministers in their robes, along with John, who goes to the right as I go to the left. The church is packed, and people are standing on the outside steps behind the open doors. The choir and congregation sing two hymns with lyrics that Myron had written or translated. Again I am introduced, and say a few words. The church service lasts over two hours, so there isn't time for the scheduled lunch. We Americans return to the hotel and have a quick bite on the roof beside the pool.

Then we are off to a "crusade" in the *praça* below the arches of Lapa. The arches support the remains of an aqueduct, dating from colonial times, that brought water down from the mountains to supply Rio. In 1896 the aqueduct became a viaduct, and trolley cars now run over the arches—still carrying residents and tourists to the charming old section of Santa Teresa, high on a hill overlooking downtown Rio. From the amphitheater below, which is fairly new and quite close to the central *ACM*, one sees not only the arches, but also the modern buildings of Rio—the Cathedral, the Banco do Brasil, and Petrobras, the oil company. A stage has been erected for the speakers and chairs for the choir and audience, but many are standing. I don't know what to expect.

There is a lot of high-power amplifying equipment, and lots of banners proclaiming the centennial. It is a colorful sight but the thrust is purely and simply a religious crusade put on by the Presbyterian Church. I am a little uncomfortable with this. I know there are historical evangelical ties between the YMCA and the Presbyterian Church and I am not offended by that—the *C* after all stands for Christian—but just as the Y now serves women, it also serves people regardless of their faith or philosophy. I think this crusade sends a confusing message. This was a controversy that my grandfather faced as well. Although he was conservative, even rigid in many ways, he was ecumenical in his thinking about the Y's mission. But I am a guest.

Rev. Guilhermino is on the stage, along with Thex and Hector Civitate, John Casey, and others. The two choirs are there, those of the Y and that of the church singing together; again, my grandfather's hymns. Thex's wife Dayse invites me to sit with her, and she makes sure I don't miss recognizing them. So it is kind of exciting for me, but the prayers and exhortations, all in Portuguese, go on way too long: the sun is very hot, and I feel sorry for the Americans who have to sit through hours of this without understanding what is being said, although I'm sure they get the drift.

Before it is over we are once again herded toward the bus, and this time I am not sorry. Once again we get back late with little time to rest up for the next activity, the awards cocktail party to be held in the auditorium at the *ACM*. There I finally present the medal representing the rank of knight in the Order of Christ, from cousin Mike, on behalf of all of Myron's descendants; congratulate them again for all of us; and thank them for their friendship and hospitality.

Afterward, an old man comes over to me to show me a picture of a young boy on an old *ACM* membership card. The boy was, of course, the old man, and the card was signed by Uncle Henry, who also once worked for the Y in Rio. I am so amazed that this man would save this card all these years, and then bring it here to show me! It is another touching example of the feelings the *acemistas* (members of the *ACM*) have about their organization. Again, before I have a chance to mingle very much—though it is already almost midnight—the Americans are off on the bus again to dinner at a wonderful seafood restaurant at the foot of Sugar Loaf. Thex and Dayse say goodnight to me at the door of the *ACM* and give me a triangular citrine pendant and a small wooden statue of Christ, a replica of the one that stands at the top of Corcovado.

The farewell dinner for the American delegation, a *churrasco*, is held the following night at the home of a wealthy member of the *ACM* in the section of Rio called Joá, on the side of the Two Brothers and Gávea mountains. This is a very posh neighborhood, and the house—which we do not enter since a real *churrasco* is held outside—is huge, with a swimming pool and a magnificent view of Leblon on one side and the Barra da Tijuca on the other. There is a full moon, the temperature is in the high 80s, a gentle breeze is blowing, and a wonderful aroma emanates from the grill. Senhor Melo does the grilling himself. It is a thrill to be here at this very pleasant party in a spectacular location, and at the end we all sing, "For

He's a Jolly Good Melo."

Next day, I move to the apartment of my friends, Sima and Saúl. Saúl shows me an article from the *Journal do Brasil*, Rio's main newspaper. The article tells how Myron and Chiquita met on a streetcar in St. Paul, Minnesota, where she invited him to hear a talk given by George Chamberlain. Chamberlain was going to speak at Macalester College about the urgent need of an organization for Brazilian youth, like the YMCA was for those of the United States and England. The account went on to say, "Come, dear reader, come and see the fortuitous meetings, the mysterious coincidences, the incredible and delicious happenstances that gently weave the web of time, the web subtly planned by Love, by Love which is greater than the sun and the stars," and so on. Saúl says what a beautiful story it is, to which I reply that it *may* be beautiful, but it is completely untrue: Chiquita had never been to the States before she was married, and she met Myron in São Paulo.

This story is not new to me. When Sydney and I first made contact with the Y about ten years ago, Tasso was writing a history of the *ACM*, and this story was part of it. Where it originated, I have no idea. We corrected him after much resistance on his part, because he liked it too. Now, on reading this in the paper, Tasso is ecstatic, because he was very unhappy about his work being "robbed." Now that it has been published in the newspaper, we have probably not heard the last of it.

I spend the next day with the help of my friend, Vanda, changing my return reservation to give myself ten more days. That done, I make plans to go to São Paulo on the following Tuesday. During my stay at the Othon, I had received telegrams from my cousins in São Paulo inviting me to visit, and now I look forward to seeing them again.

Yedda takes charge of me, hosting a gathering of many cousins. I get to enjoy another reunion—which has a lot of the feel of the one in New Hampshire, with much animated greeting, picture taking, laughter and joy. We have tea with lots of sandwiches and *salgadinhas* (savory bites), and cakes and cookies on Yedda's penthouse terrace, overlooking São Paulo as the sun is setting. I stay with Yedda, and she gives me her grandmother's (Tia Cacilda) *Historia Veradeira*, with some of the same stories as Vovó's, but including others as well. There are other gatherings in other homes, hosted by the offspring of Romilda (Tia Cacilda's daughter), and Yedda's son and his family. I am once again "*Neta do Fundador*" at a visit to the *ACM* in São Paulo.

My last evening in São Paulo is held at the house of my cousin Marila and her husband Sam. This is the house where Marila and her sisters and brother, grandchildren of Tia Cacilda, lived as children. There are seven young people here, and they seem just as happy as their parents to meet me. Some of them studied in the States as exchange students and speak English, so the gathering is bilingual and very lively. More picture taking, hugging, and laughter. It is impossible to convey in words the warmth of the welcome I receive everywhere, but especially in São Paulo. These cousins remember Vovó well, and we did much reminiscing about her. Marila is an accomplished pianist, and plays for us. Then, at midnight, Marila's son Roberto takes me to the bus. Yedda and Marila come along and make sure I am OK on the bus and wait for it to pull out, waving and blowing kisses. I am feeling very connected now to my Brazilian cousins, and I am sure the relationships will grow.

Back in a rainy Rio, I have five more days, which I spend visiting my Rio cousins, granddaughters of Vovó's sisters Josephina and Noemi. I have *feijoada* with Thex, Dayse, their daughter, and her husband at their apartment in Flamengo; I go on a drive with Vanda and her husband to the Recreio dos Bandeirantes[100] at the end of the Barra da Tijuca and sip beer with friends at sidewalk cafes. I stroll a bit in the Botanical Garden, and even catch a few waves at the beach, but not enough. The weather is still a little too cool for much swimming. I feel so grateful for this marvelous, unforgettable experience. It is a strange and wonderful feeling to find such compatibility in a culture so very different from my own, but to which I feel such a strong pull.

---

100. *Recreio* means a place of leisure, and *bandeirantes* were pioneer explorers, mainly from what is now the state of São Paulo, who carried the flag (*bandeira*) into the interior searching for gold, precious stones, and indigenous people to be sold as slaves. But why this beautiful beach is named the playground of the *Bandeirantes*, I do not know.

# 44. Crossing the Atlantic

 *Athens, Ohio, 1941*

Sailing from Portugal was out of the question due to the war, so we were booked on the Spanish ship *Alfonso* to sail August 9th from Vigo, Spain. Porto was not very far from Coimbra, and we had a standing invitation from friends there to stay with them whenever we needed to do any shopping. So to the city of port wine I went, to get what was absolutely necessary for the voyage.

On August 1st I was packing and in the evening making numerous calls of *despidida*. There was so much hurry, so much excitement and anxiety that I was really walking in a fog. On the 6th we took the train for Vigo, stopping at the old city we had visited before, Valença, and crossing the Minho River to Tuy. We had to attend to some business in the customhouse, and then on to Vigo, the beautiful bay and seaport. We put up at the Hotel Continental in front of the port where we could see the *Alfonso* and some Spanish warships. Next day we went to the American consul to get the passports and visas.

I was worrying a good deal about crossing the ocean at this time but the American consul said, "Do not worry, Mrs. Clark, this boat is of a Spanish company and they are for Germany." I still have among my souvenirs a letter bearing the American eagle and signed by Colonel Birch, asking protection and help in case of an emergency to the bearer of it, Mrs. Francisca P. Clark and children.

I also have a letter in which Myron tells me about his last moments on board. We went down to dinner while he stayed at the baggage room to see that everything was on board. While we were there, the bugle called all the visitors to leave, and when Myron heard the bugle notes—so well known to us—he could not hold back his sobs, which were loud enough to have been heard if anybody had been around! I was the worst guest of Neptune, feeling even the little movements of the boat caused perhaps by mermaids dancing over the waves. So I kept very much to my chair.

Reading his diary, I found out something that I had forgotten entirely. He knew that the boat had changed the route, which would take longer. It was going to Havana, Cuba, and not directly to New York, as was the itinerary. Before leaving Spain, the consul told my husband about a very important second-class passenger on board with his wife. He was traveling in the custody of the American police department, and his wife through the generosity of the American colony in Spain, but the consul asked us to act as if we didn't know and to get acquainted with his wife, if possible, for whom they were very sorry. My boys of course didn't know about this.

Neco was fifteen and George thirteen-and-a-half, and they seemed to always like to do the same thing, which now on board was reading. I was the only woman in first class, and as it was permitted for me to go to second class, I went and met the American lady. I don't remember their names at all, and I am glad of it. She was pleased and returned my call, which I really was not expecting nor wishing for, as I knew the rules.

The lady from New Orleans—I remember this about her—came to see me several times. Americans were persona non grata to the officers and crew of this boat, so one of the stewards told me to tell the lady not to come to first class. If I wanted, I could go to second. Well, this was true on every boat, but it seemed unnecessary on this one—there were just a few passengers. It was very hard for me to tell her, but I had to.

The gentleman (I think he was or at least had once been, even if he was brought back here by the police department), noticing that Neco and George were reading most of the time—there were no sports on board—began to talk to them about books and to furnish them with very good ones for boys, and they made frequent calls to second class. Once when I went on my errand of friendship, the man came to speak to me in the most polite manner and with tender words: "I would give anything I possess to have such nice boys as yours. I love to talk to them, and how interested they are in books."

When we arrived in Havana came the surprise for the passengers. Two policemen came on board to meet the man and accompany him back to the States. As the boat stayed there several days, everybody went

Neco and George, c. 1912.

on shore. Next day everybody that came back to the boat brought a newspaper with the big news that on board the *Alfonso* was an American who had stolen more than half a million dollars and had run away to Spain. Some young Spanish fellows, who were coming to the United States representing an exporting firm, came directly to me with the papers to show me what kind of man was so interested in the boys, and the type of woman I was seeing so much.

They did not know a thing against her, but for them she was guilty too. They were much more surprised when I told them that I had known when I came on board why this couple was coming back to the States; probably I too was worth less to them now. The man under arrest was a publisher and had misused money that didn't belong to him. I do not know the circumstances around the crime, but I would not be at all surprised if he were not as much at fault as it appeared. We did not see them any more from Havana to New York.

My how glad I was when I saw the Big Bronze Lady holding that torch, which I hope now will have real meaning. Soon we met the customs authorities, who were rather strict and were pretty *ríspidos* (rude), since that boat was coming from the war zone and from a neutral country. And so when I handed them the passport for my two boys and me I also gave them the letter from the American minister. The officer read the letter and immediately said, "We will be very glad to help you, Mrs. Clark."

The International Committee put us on the train to Wooster, Ohio, a city and state where we never had been before, although I had been in the USA three times. Henry and Baby and some of their friends were at the depot to meet us. What a big fellow Henry was! I had not seen him for three years! He was a boy when he left; now he was a young man like Orton. I had not seen my daughter, Baby, for over a year. There were tears in my eyes, but they were tears of joy. They took us to a furnished home right on the campus of Wooster College where we had everything we needed and the luxury of a piano.

We lived across from the dormitory of freshman girls, and it seemed that they liked our place, so some of them came and went any time they wanted. Henry and Baby had been in a dormitory for missionary children, so these boys and girls also came to see our children. Again I was among young people.

Life in a small college town was something new to me and I found it very interesting. Very soon, though, I found out that there was a division between young and old here in the USA. When the first Sunday afternoon came, I found myself alone, and how homesick I was at home! But several of the wives of the professors and missionaries on the campus called on me, and they treated me so nicely that I began to feel at home.

# 45. Triângulo Vermelho

We had sailed on August 10, 1917, leaving husband and father behind in Vigo, Spain. By the end of the month, he was beginning to feel concern as no word had come from us. Myron was very anxious and his heart full of *saudades* for his family. Finally, one month after we sailed from Vigo, the telegram of our safe arrival in New York arrived in Coimbra. Because of a strike of all post office and telegraph employees the cable had been in Lisbon since September 6th. On September 23, 1917, Myron's fifty-first birthday, he received the first letter from me. Mail was very slow.

In October there were assaults on grocery stores by laborers on account of the high cost of living. Soon there were revolutions in Coimbra, Lisbon, and Porto. About 100 people were killed, and 500 wounded in Lisbon. The President fled. A new government was in the process of forming. Meanwhile, the building was progressing, slowly.

A new *ACM* Secretary, Mr. Stallings, along with his wife, arrived in Coimbra from the States to be Myron's assistant. The plan was for Myron to stay there until the building was finished and the secretary could manage the language, and then for Mr. Stallings to be in charge of the work so that your grandfather could come to us for his much-needed vacation. In December it was very, very cold. Zero centigrade. There was no heating system, so I can see my poor husband going around the *núcleo* rooms and sitting at his desk with his overcoat on, and probably Joaquim bringing a *brazeiro* and putting it near his feet. This made clear to him that the new building to house the Association in Coimbra ought to have a heating plant.

While I was waiting for him in Wooster, what Myron called a "new thought" was unfolding in his brain. Fifty thousand dollars had been granted from the International Committee of the YMCA to start work among the Portuguese soldiers as had been provided for the English (The Red Triangle) and for the French (*Les Foyers du Soldat*). In October the Portuguese minister of war approved this service for the Portuguese troops. It was called *Triângulo Vermelho*. Myron received letters from Edward Clark Carter, general secretary of the American International Committee, and later chief secretary for the American Expeditionary Forces in France, and John R. Mott, general secretary of the National War Work Council, suggesting that he go to France to organize and direct it.

When I received Myron's letter saying that instead of coming to the States when his successor at Coimbra assumed his duties there, he was going to France to open this work for the Portuguese troops, I wrote saying that I didn't agree at all with that. We had already made plenty of sacrifices, and somebody else ought to go. What a fool I was to call that too great a sacrifice! Well, the same boat that took that letter carried another one telling him how sorry I was to have written the first one, and that for him not to pay attention at all to it, as I was sure now that he ought to go. When I wrote that letter I did not know that he had not only decided, but had already gone to France. It took a long time for mail to get through several censorships.

There was a lot of red tape connected with his new position, and thus after busy and tiresome days he left for France in February. Over sixty students were present at farewell meetings at the rooms, and many were at the station the next day to say goodbye. He left Lisbon by land, crossed Spain, and entered France. Here he had to go through lots of formalities and interviews until he got his English uniform, as the Portuguese were in an English sector. His assignment was to establish the *Triângulo Vermelho* posts throughout the front.

From February until June, he traveled all over the front setting up the huts, equipping them, serving the troops—many from the area surrounding Coimbra—and dodging the fire of the "dastardly Bosches."[101] On February 17, 1918, he writes, "Evening air raid threat. Saw many French planes: Boches driven off."

Myron went back to Portugal for the inauguration of the YMCA building in June 1918.

---

101. Derogatory French slang for Germans, especially soldiers.

His trips to Portugal from Paris and back were through Spain, officially neutral but pro-German, so it was necessary to go through lots of red tape. The American minister in Lisbon again came to help him, and said he would bring the diplomatic corps in Lisbon to the inauguration as his personal guests on a special train from Lisbon to Coimbra. This man was very rich. He paid for this privately, just to give prestige to the work.

The students gave a big welcome to the guests, but the Catholics were making every effort to prevent the inauguration. They thought that the YMCA had no other reason but to make those young men Protestant, and it is true that the Protestants in the country hoped that this would happen. The Catholics petitioned for the closing of the building and published articles warning the students against the YMCA, but the opening was successful in spite of the opposition. I have a fine picture of the group taken on the steps of the centuries-old university building.

A very uncharitable article about my husband and the *Associação Christã de Estudantes* (Christian Students' Association), as the Y was called here, had been published in a Catholic paper and signed by a priest warning the students about this Yankee institution. One day after my husband returned to headquarters in Paris, a priest came in and said he had been assigned as chaplain to a Portuguese division, and had not been able to get his papers through all the red tape. Somebody had advised him that my husband could arrange all that. He gave his name, and it was the author of the article. The priest seemed rather embarrassed, so Myron did all he could to avoid his knowing that Myron knew who he was. Myron got the papers through the bureaucratic tangle, and the priest, after telling him how thankful he was to him for all he had done, told him that he was very sorry he had written that article against the Association. So now, Myron was very glad to render some service for one he could not help but think was not a friend, and to realize he had made a friend. Knowing my man's heart thoroughly, I can say that the joy he got from rendering this service to this man and thus winning a friend compensated for all the pain that priest had caused him.

My husband's picture shows how tired and thin he was. I don't think he looked so bad even when he had yellow fever. When he was back in Paris after the inauguration, he was ready to drop with an old ailment that had gotten worse on account of having to stand on the train. The compartment was full and there were no accommodations for lying down. He suffered very much. He went to see Dr. Lord, an American physician, who advised him to enter the American hospital for an operation.

There were several young men from Portugal to help in the *Triângulo Vermelho*, and a few Americans who came from Brazil for this purpose too. The physical director of the *ACM* in Brazil took charge of the work, and my husband went to the hospital and was operated on. A Portuguese nurse was in charge of him. Here before me is a picture postcard of that hospital in Paris at rue Chauveau near rue Leon, in which I read this:

"July 6, 1918. My darling wife. Yesterday I sat up for the first time. I hope to be released in another week and then shall be heading home." Later on, a letter came from which I will copy a few lines:

*July 23rd, 1918. I expected fully to be by your side long before this, but complications have set in, showing that the operation was more serious than the doctor thought. How I have longed for your darling presence and your sweet face to be by my side during these days of sore trial and suffering! How I have missed your comforting ministries. But I know you have missed me too, and would have wished to be by my side. When I have seen something of the suffering of the poor soldier boys and have realized their heroism, I have choked down any complaining spirit, and prayed God for courage.*

Then another letter came, saying,

*My decline was so apparent Dr. Mitchell called a specialist in urinary disease, who advised another operation. There was abscess. Large numbers of American soldiers are in these wards, wounded; one sees them about the gardens. There are four large tents in the garden, fixed as a hospital for wounded soldiers. Dr. Mitchell has been working every night in other hospitals during the Château Thierry drive, helping operate on wounded soldiers. Of course his regular work suffers. I think in part, that is why I had my decline.*

The notes were written after he got better and was convalescing, since before that he was too sick to record anything. He suffered terribly, but he was always so sympathetic toward the wounded soldiers and he tried to conform, seeing their suffering. Finally, in September he was well enough to return. He said his farewells, sent a cable to inform me and at last, the *Leviathan*,[102] with two consorts and five destroyer escorts, sailed from Lisbon, bringing Myron and scores of returning war wounded who all wore life preservers until the danger zone was passed. At last, he was coming home!

---

102. The *Leviathan* was built by Germany in 1914 as the *Vaterland*, and was at that time the world's largest passenger liner. When World War I broke out, it was left in a New Jersey harbor. When the United States joined the war, the ship was confiscated, its name was changed to *Leviathan*, and it was used as a troop ship (Department of the Navy, Naval Historical Center, "*S. S. Leviathan*").

# 46. Going Home

When the boys and I got to Wooster in 1917 I wrote to Ruth, who was with her grandparents, to come home—so now five children were at home in Wooster. Orton was working in the YMCA in Dayton, engaged to the daughter of a United Brethren minister. They were married on Thanksgiving Day, the 29th of November; I went with son Henry, who was his best man. It was a lovely affair, and we were very sorry that his father could not be present. Thus the first nest was built by one of our children.

Those thirteen months here without my husband were troublesome days. I was entering on that crucial road which every woman has to go through at a very critical time. Henry and Baby were freshmen at Wooster College; Neco and George, juniors in High School. At home I was quite alone, as here in the States children's and students' parties were always by themselves; but the people of the city upon the hill, the college grounds, were marvelous to me. It did not take long for me to feel right at home here. On my fiftieth birthday on June 2nd, 1918, I had a great surprise when a cable came from Paris ordering some roses to be delivered to this little old lady who was keeping house for her children in Wooster College.

One Sunday during that earlier world war, I went for a walk by myself after church. I think it was the first time I was out alone for a walk in the countryside. My how beautiful the ripe wheat fields were! The breeze went over them and up and down, making them look like waves of gold. That day I remembered having read in one of my husband's letters about the restrictions on food, so I picked two sprigs of wheat and put them in a letter I wrote that evening, saying "Do not fear for the field, the United States are covered with golden wheat, and they will not let their allies suffer hunger." My children said to me, "Mother, the first censor will throw away those sprigs. Do you think they will be bothered with it?" Well, the sprigs got to their destination all right.

On the 15th of August the Wayne County Fair was going to take place in Wooster, and as I had never seen one, I was looking forward to it. The older children were away working in the Y camps; only Neco and George were at home. As good Boy Scouts, they were going to be active in the fair. A fine young man, Glen Kiester, who had been with them at the fair, brought them home for lunch. They had been guarding a military tank that was in an exhibition there in the fairgrounds. This was a very new weapon then. Just a little before they got home, I received another cable from France. When the messenger handed it to me, I couldn't help showing my excitement, joy, and even before I opened it I said, "I know what it is. My husband is coming home." But when I opened it, this is what I read: "Complications, not serious cause considerable delay. Keep up courage, Clark."

When Glen saw me and the cable, he said, "I am coming back here after I have my lunch, to take you and the boys out for a ride before we go back to the fair." I just could not convince him otherwise. After lunch he came back, and took us driving for two hours in beautiful rolling country. We went to a road called Lovers' Lane, a trail under lovely trees, and Glen said, "When Mr. Clark comes home, I'm going to bring you both to this place." Which he did, a month later.

What a happy homecoming it was, after our long separation and worry! Myron still needed a lot of rest, and wrote in his diary, "Many afternoons spent in reading old letters with Chiquita, enjoying again our old-time but ever-renewed romance."

On November 9th the report came that the Kaiser had abdicated, and German delegates were studying Foch's terms at Allied Headquarters. On the 11th, we were wakened by the firing of revolvers, etc. and learned of signing of Armistice. The war was over, praise God!

Early in 1919, Myron resumed his travels soliciting support for Y work in Brazil. During the next six months, he was home only for short visits. That summer all of us, including Orton and his wife Esther, vacationed at Lake Geneva in Wisconsin. Then throughout that fall and winter Myron was traveling again, until his vacation ended, and we prepared to return to Brazil—this time, just the two of us.

Myron and Chiquita, together again, 1918.

With four children established at Wooster College, we left Wooster together for the first and last time. We sailed from New York Harbor on April 12th. "Darling," he said to me with his beautiful blue eyes fixed on mine, and closing me in a tight circle with his arms, "We are on our second honeymoon!" To which I replied, laughing, "Second honeymoon—two old people!" He was almost fifty-four, and I almost fifty-two! This honeymoon was spent aboard the boat *Vestris*, where we celebrated our anniversary with a beautiful cake on which we read, "Congratulations to Mr. and Mrs. Myron A. Clark on the twenty-seventh anniversary of their marriage." I don't know when our life was not a honeymoon. His comings and goings were many, and this united us more!!

We arrived in Rio on April 29th, after an absence of five years. What joy to see Corcovado and the beautiful bay! Friends and relatives were at the docks to meet us. We were so happy to be together in our home by the sea, listening to the moaning and thundering of the waves, and watching a fisherman's boat with its snow-white sail in front of the lighthouse—its tower so white with the sun shining on it. At night, we loved to watch its light shining over the sea, and by day, on the other side of the house, white clouds sliding down the side of a hill made of solid rock covered with a green tapestry of grass.

Myron was pleased with the progress that the Rio Association had made in planning the new building while he had been gone. He was eager to assume his duties as secretary general of the Brazilian Federation of the *Associação Cristã de Moços*. We were honored at a picnic at Corcovado, and on Saturday night, eight days after our arrival, the Fernandes Braga hall of the *ACM*—named for our dear friend who had died the previous year—was decorated with flowers for a reception in our honor. It was a happy celebration with music, speeches, *abraços*, and congratulations. Speaking to the gathering Myron said, "I have two countries—the USA where I was born, and Brazil, the land of my adoption."

The next day, May 9th, in the same *salão*, I conducted a service dedicated to mothers—the second Mothers' Day to be celebrated in Brazil—and Myron appeared for the last time in public.

A week later on the 16th of May, the heart that guided your grandfather in the service of God and of young men, delivered him to his Master. Myron died on Sunday, the day he loved so well, the day of affirmation of faith. The following day, in the room that a week before rang with the joy of reunion and celebration, his body lay in eternal rest. Telegrams and letters came from everywhere, with huge, beautiful wreaths and bouquets. The fire department provided two enormous trucks to carry the wreaths. About seventy cars formed the procession to the cemetery. Those who spoke said the most beautiful things that could be said about a person, and this many times with tears flowing. The shock wasn't only to us;

the entire evangelical world, the American colony, and people of the government and high society found themselves dejected.

My world ended.

# 47. Laços da Família

 *Rio de Janeiro, August, 2000*

Most young women want a husband and babies or a head start on a career, or both.[103] At age twenty-three, my greatest desire was to know Brazil as my father, grandmother, aunts, and uncles had. I wanted adventure. I had a family there waiting to embrace me, and Rio was a magical place of unsurpassed natural beauty and unbridled joy. I dived into it and waves of emotion engulfed me; and I was swept away by the rhythm, the color, the warmth, the passion and playfulness growing in my heart.

And then I left Brazil to fulfill my desire for a family of my own. Like Vovó, I recognized in myself the tension of the two cultures—they try to co-exist in me, but one or the other must dominate. I left behind the playful, open, expressive, adventurous Brazilian part of myself that was full of wonder and curiosity; finding joy in learning another language, another way to experience life. Here in the States I was sensible, practical, organized—but maybe sometimes just a little bit too flamboyant. Now I think these two sides of myself are like lovers who are attracted to their opposites. The very traits that draw them together become the source of conflict; like allergic reactions to foreign objects in the body. If my American side is male, the Brazilian is female—perhaps that's why I feel my true nature is more Brazilian. So the resolution, if there is one, lies in a dance. If he is leading, he must not hold her so tightly that she can't move in her own way.

Twenty-four years had elapsed between my first trip to Brazil and the second when Sydney and I spent an enchanted six weeks together there, and she too felt the connection to a forgotten part of herself. Many visits followed, including two with Donn, and each time the ties to my Brazilian family, past and present, strengthened. But as they did, the gap between my two lives widened. And now I am having the immense pleasure of

---

103. The title of this chapter, *Laços da Família*, means Family Ties.

sharing Rio with my daughter, Andrea. I want to link these lives through her. I want her to meet our Brazilian cousins, and I hope that she will feel connected to them, and to this country that I love. She has only two weeks vacation. I will stay a bit longer.

Andrea and I arrive at our hotel in Rio around ten in the morning after a sleepless overnight flight from Los Angeles. I have chosen the small hotel in Leme for its proximity to Gustavo Sampaio, the street where my grandparents built their dream house by the sea. Our hotel room faces the ocean, too; if we ignore the traffic noise and the throngs of *cariocas* and tourists, Andrea and I can feel that we are seeing the same view her grandfather saw almost a century ago. A high-rise apartment building now covers the site where their home, Vila Caldas, once stood. As we walk there I tell Andrea about the Sunday at-homes, the *ressacas*, the view of Pão de Açucar and the view of the lighthouse from the veranda.

There are calls waiting for us, and after a nap, our cousins Stila, Perla, and Ana come by the hotel to greet us, bubbling with warm greetings, and we make tentative plans—depending on the weather—to go to Corcovado or Pão de Açucar. The cousins are so pleased that I have brought my daughter here, and I can see Andrea is put at ease by their ebullience and affection. I show them my notebook with its genealogy charts and photographs. Stila, who lived several years in the States, speaks English very well, so she and Andrea can communicate directly. My friend Saúl comes by later; his wife Sima died a few years ago. Andrea and I end the day savoring a stuffed crab and a beer at a sidewalk café near the hotel, and then we sleep for eleven hours!

Stila is our guide at the fine arts museum, where there is an exhibition from the Prado, and at a wonderful small museum in a former residence in Gávea with photographs by Sebasião Salgado. In the garden is a pond with singing frogs and a tiled wall done by the Brazilian landscape architect and artist, Roberto Burle Marx. We three are having a wonderful time together—Stila is lively, fun, and easy to be with. I feel as though I've known her all my life. Andrea likes Stila very much: I am so pleased!

Our Rio cousins have planned a tea today in our honor. There are many cousins of Andrea's generation who speak English, as do a couple of mine, but still with so many conversations going on at once, mostly in Portuguese, I expect that this will be difficult for her—I remember how overwhelmed I felt when I first met my Brazilian cousins—but she sails through, speaking English and some words of Portuguese where she can, and using lots of body language. Gifts are exchanged; I share the charts I have made of each family. Pictures are taken; everyone struggles a little with language difficulties, but the communication of family ties is strong.

We return, giddy with the excitement of it, just in time to change and go out with Saúl to a *churrascaria* and then to the Bar do Vinícius to hear Maria Creusa, a singer of popular Brazilian music. The bar is packed and smoky, but we are thrilled to be here. We get back to the hotel at one-thirty, shower off the smoke, and chat like schoolgirls at a slumber party until three in the morning. It is marvelous to be sharing this with Andrea!

At the turn of the last century as now, the peak of Corcovado could be seen from all over Rio. My father, whose unrequited longing led me here, never saw the thirty-meter statue which now blesses the city from its summit and has become the city's signature; it was erected in 1931, the year I was born. Andrea and I have been waiting for a clear day to go up there, and at last we have one. A city bus takes us to Cosme Velho, where we board the cogwheel train that goes almost straight up the mountain through the thick underbrush of the Atlantic rainforest. If we look carefully, we can sometimes see the little resident monkeys springing from tree to tree, their tails curling like fuzzy question marks as they call playfully to each other in their squeaky voices. At the top, tourists from everywhere, bent with the weight of their cameras, spill from their sleek tour buses, their guides herding them in myriad languages to the base of the statue of Christ the Redeemer, emblem of Rio. It is impressive, but my daughter and I have come for the view of the city below.

Andrea is forty-one; it is her first trip to Brazil. I have brought her here to see the people and places that have become so important to me, hoping they will become important to her, too, and this is the place to start. Rio de Janeiro is no longer the capital, but it is the heart of Brazil, and from here the city is spread out beneath us. Along with hundreds of tourists we gaze in awe at the mountains—magnificent stone giants rising majestically out of the sea, dividing the city into neighborhoods.

My eyes move from one peak to another, like the hawks that soar around them. I introduce my old friends to Andrea: Pão de Açucar, Dois Irmãos, and *Gávea* (the Hawk's Nest), from which we see the rainbow colors of hang gliders' wings taking off for their descent to the beach below. The chattering tourists remind us of the monkeys as they point at the scene and take pictures of each other against the backdrop of the statue. I turn to Guanabara Bay with its green islands, delicate bridges, and busy boats, and I remember all the times I have arrived here by ship, and by airplanes large and small. I feel again the excitement of my first sight of these indestructible mountains, standing serenely above the *movimento*, the commercial and social activities, the noise and progress of the city. I do this at least once every time I am in Rio, and I have shared the experience with friends, cousins, my sister, my husband, and now my daughter, but only in imagination with my father, who loved his native city so.

Turning to leave, we see a wall display of our photographs on china plates. Our likenesses have been captured as we emerged from the narrow entrance at the base of the statue. Vendors scurry to identify each person, grab the right plate, wave it wildly, and appeal to each person in what they hope to be the appropriate language. They use all their charm and flattery to make the sale. What happens, I briefly wonder, to all the faces, including ours, on plates that are not bought? Then, somehow, I block it all out, gazing again at the scene below.

Picture-taking complete, the tourists are already lining up for their buses to take them back down the mountain as I turn my gaze to the *lagoa*, the serene lagoon that lies between Corcovado and the Atlantic, and then the beaches with melodic names that flow like the soft rhythms of bossa nova: Flamengo, Botafogo, Leme, Copacabana, Arpoador, Ipanema, Leblon, Barra da Tijuca. Finally, my eyes fall upon the city that flows around and between the silent granite hills, and then is kissed by the sea. Magically, everything here and below us is muted. The clear air smells green—not piney, like the *agua sanitária* (disinfectant) our noses are accustomed to below, but the soft, humid green of rain. The bustling cacophony of the city is now a pleasant hum, blending with the insect cadence of the forest. The traffic from this distance appears slow and orderly; even the waves that crash on the beaches are gentle ripples. From here, all is right with the world.

Next day, Sunday, we sleep late. Thanks to ECO 92, the Earth Summit held in Rio in 1992, the whole length of the palm-lined *avenida* is blocked to motor traffic on Sundays to make way for people. It is August, the weather is pleasant, and everywhere there are fleets of baby carriages. Vendors in tiny square shacks at the edge of the warm sand sell cool, fresh coconut milk for sipping out of the rough shell. This is new for Andrea: she loves it. A steady stream of joggers, cyclists and skaters winds around chic urban denizens coaxing tiny dogs along on slender leashes. In this mild winter month the pampered pets sport tiny, equally chic coats or sweaters. Tourists and residents amble along, taking the air, or mill about—gossiping, arguing, gesturing, watching each other. In the background, there is always a samba beat. I love walking along these beaches any day, but on Sundays it is a special treat to watch the *cariocas* stroll and strut and skate at leisure on the *Avenida* while others play volleyball or *fútebol* and display their dark bodies on the sand. My sandaled feet move lightly, my heart sings as I savor the scene, and at the same time, as I walk, I visualize the beach the way it looked to my father a century ago.

In the late afternoon, Andrea and I take the bus to Urca, a district at the foot of Pão de Açucar and wait in line for the cable car; then she clings to me in fear (I'm a veteran of this) as we dangle and sway on the thread that connects us with the ground, first to the top of the Morro da Urca and then on another car to the top of Pão de Açúcar for glorious views of the *Cidade Maravilhosa*—a total of 1,400 meters accomplished in six minutes. We have timed it to be here at sunset when, as the reds and golds and purples fade in the west, the lights along Botofogo Bay flash on and sparkle in reflection in the bay beneath the silhouette of Corcovado. Andrea and I watch in silence, our arms around each other.

We are going to São Paulo on Tuesday; today, Monday, we walk around the colonial part of old Rio, beginning at Praça XV (for the 15th of November, the day the first Republic was declared) and ending at the elegant Confeitaria Colombo on Rua Gonçalves Dias for lunch. The food at Columbo is fine, but the point is the place itself. The center of this restaurant is two stories high, with a balcony circling the perimeter. Built in 1894, the interior is all glass and white tile, dark wood, mirrors, and wrought iron. Andrea is thrilled—she says it is like stepping back into

Andrea, Copacabana, a Sunday afternoon in August, 2000.

nineteenth-century Vienna.

Next day we board the early morning bus to São Paulo to meet our cousins there. Yedda has planned an afternoon tea at her apartment. We arrive before the other guests, and Yedda gives us a tour of her apartment, showing us lots of old photographs. She is very chic and energetic, zipping up and down her open, rather tightly-wound metal spiral staircase flanked by graceful ferns. It is an extremely high-energy reunion, lasting from three in the afternoon until ten that night. Relatives come to greet us in droves throughout the afternoon and evening—about forty in all, some from out of town. I am dizzy trying to relate to everyone and translate here and there, not to mention the sugar rush from the many large, pastel colored cakes!! It is like being on an exhilarating tilt-a-whirl carnival ride. While there, we make arrangements to meet Stila's son Mário, an artist, in Campinas the following day. There we will connect with Maílde, whom I have invited to go with us to Caldas, and then to Ouro Preto, the colonial town in Minas that is now a World Cultural Heritage site.

Maílde and her husband René are at the bus to meet us, along with Mário. After a great lunch, we go to Mário's house and studio to see his paintings—abstracts with themes of Brazilian folklore that I like very much. I like him, too. Marío has lived in England and is bilingual. Andrea is an art historian—they have much to talk about. And then, Andrea, Mailde, and I leave for Caldas. We arrive in Caldas late at night after a long bus ride.

I came here for the first time, fifty-three years old, alone, a stranger, where no one spoke or understood my native tongue, and immediately felt awash in memories, dreams, spirits, joys and sorrows, and love of people long dead—even those I never knew except through the memories of others, and I became ageless. I seemed to pass through a shift in dimension into simplicity and truth, like the memory of the sound of children's laughter hanging in the long summer twilight of my native Ohio. Now I am here with my daughter and Mailde, the friend I made here. They are about the same age, and have somehow bridged the language gap.

We walk around the *praça*, so full of memories, and just as I come to Maria Odete's house, she comes out. She did not know I was coming, but she recognizes me instantly, as if she had seen me the day before. We visit; Odete suggests a drive tomorrow afternoon to see the cascades at the foot of Pedra Branca.

In the morning I take Andrea to meet Dona Bexuta and Cida, who welcome Andrea with quiet dignity. Cida accompanies us to the *praça* and we walk around town, showing Andrea Vovó's street, and Dona Ana's, and the cemetery. Ieiiei has since died, and Dona Ana's house is completely changed; the garden gone and the house improved.

That evening, on returning to Caldas from our excursion with Maria Odete, we stop at Ivone's and try to rouse her. We see the flickering light and hear the TV which fills the street with its noise, but she doesn't respond to our knocking at the gate, or our calling. Soon a neighbor hangs her head out a window, shouting to us, telling us that Ivone is deaf and telling us to throw stones at the house to get her attention. Of course, we know that Ivone is deaf, but we are reluctant to do this. We don't have to, because soon others appear at other windows, and people begin to gather, and then suddenly the street is full of people, everyone shouting at once—"*um, dois, três—Ivone!*" to no avail. Everyone is laughing, and someone climbs on the wall to knock on the window. It looks as if they will break into the house, so determined are they that we talk to her. I feel more than a little nervous to have instigated this, but then I realize that it is their project now: I am an amused observer. Andrea is incredulous. And then, out of nowhere it seems, a ladder materializes and someone climbs over the wall and bangs on her door. Ivone responds, the crowd disperses, satisfied, and we have a good visit.

Later, Andrea calls it "another Fellini moment." She says it was then that she understood a difference between Brazilians and Americans: here in the States, groups of people take a long time to accomplish anything, but we are efficient as individuals. Brazilians, by contrast, move more slowly as individuals, but once a critical mass forms then everything gets accomplished very fast, even though no one is in charge. I think she is on to something, and I think it has to do with playfulness—which Brazilians practice all their lives—and which we seem to forget or renounce when we become "grown up." It is like improvisation in drama or jazz, where one person plays a riff, and if it's good, another picks it up and expands on it. It also may have something to do with differing cultural emphases on competition and cooperation! Andrea observes that these people—at least here in this small town—trust each other in a way that is impossible for North Americans to understand.

Our visit here has been too rushed; there has not been time enough to be quiet enough to hear the voices of the past, and Dona Ana seems to have taken some of the magic with her. Andrea reminds me that the past is here for us to see, if we know it's here, but that the progeny of the past now occupies the past's place, waiting to become a memory of its own future. I take comfort in knowing that she and I are now both a part of that future memory.

Ready or not, arrangements have been made, and soon Andrea, Maílde, and I take leave of Caldas for Ouro Preto. I have reserved a room for us in a small hotel overlooking the *praça* dominated by the statue of Tiradentes with his back to the authority of the old governor's palace. We have only two days to explore the baroque beauty of the towns and churches of Ouro Preto and Mariana. I am sixty-nine, and feeling my age on the hills and cobblestone streets of these lovely colonial towns, so I am content to rest in the afternoon, and allow Maílde and Andrea to explore a bit on their own. I love these two women, and it is a pleasure to see them happy together.

Between Ouro Preto and Mariana, we visit an old gold mine. We are seated side by side on a narrow backless wooden bench—like a sideways teeter-totter, with only a small handle made of a length of narrow galvanized pipe to hold onto. It is a bone-rattling ride as the operator lets out the huge drum of cable on which the trolley rides. Bare bulbs strung on bare wires fly by as we descend 120 meters, ducking to avoid hitting our heads on the wires. We gaze at underground lakes and niches carved into the rocks, and are amazed to learn that slaves used the miles-long underground web of tunnels to escape their bondage, and wonder what system they had to keep from getting lost.

Instead of returning to Rio as planned, we decide to go back to São Paulo for an exhibition celebrating the 500th anniversary of the discovery of Brazil. We make plans to meet our cousin Mário there, and we get a reservation at a hotel near the beautiful Ibirapuera Park, designed by Oscar Niemeyer and Roberto Burle Marx, where the exhibition is held. On the way, in Belo Horizonte, we say a sad goodbye to Maílde, who is going back to Campinas.

Our cousin Marila takes us to the museum, where Mário joins us. There are five pavilions—each with a separate exhibit—Indigenous Art and Culture, Afro-Brazilian, Folk, Colonial, and Modern. The 500 Years of Brazil show, depicting five centuries of Brazilian history, seems a fitting way to end our trip retracing a big chunk of it in the family footsteps. The next day Yedda takes us to catch our plane for Rio. We fly into the downtown domestic airport, Santos Dumont. I am hoping for the spectacular view of Pão de Açucar for Andrea, but it is too cloudy to see anything. Saúl stops by the hotel to say goodbye, bearing gifts—a compact disk of Maria Creusa for me, and a Sebastião Salgado book for Andrea.

Back in Rio on Andrea's last day, we take a walk on the beach, share a delicious *feijoada completa* and a teary *despedida* at Galião, now called Tom Jobim Airport. On the way to the airport, Andrea tells me she knows me better now that she has been with me here, and on the way back, I reflect on the meaning of my journey. My daughter has given me a precious gift, and my heart is overflowing with gratitude.

I return to Copacabana by *frescão*, the air-conditioned bus, where I have a brief conversation with my seatmate, a sincere and earnest young Mormon missionary just arriving for his year of service. I seem to have come full circle, and I wonder—will my seatmate meet a *moça morena dos olhos pretos*[104] and begin a parallel story?

---

104. Brown girl with black eyes.

# Epilogue

A long time ago I heard one of those stories called *carochinha* (fairy tales), the gist of which was the following: A child ran away from home, and wandering through unknown places became lost. Tired of walking and overcome by drowsiness, she fell asleep. Upon wakening hours later, and not recognizing anything around her including herself, she began to cry, thinking that while she slept she had been changed into someone in a dirty and torn dress. Through her tears she said, "Is it really myself who is here, or am I some other little girl?"

The same sensation has taken hold of me in these last years upon waking in the morning. Where am I, I ask myself—in Minnesota, Ohio, New Jersey, Kentucky, or New York? Only one who has spent many years far from the motherland can understand the happiness that I feel now, when I can answer my morning's silent question with these words: "Yes, I am finally at the feet of Corcovado, on the shores of Guanabara, in my beloved Brazil!"

And now, turning my eyes to the past, I feel the most profound sensations: I gaze upon the Copacabana of today, and contrasting with that of old, note that the same beaches laced by the breaking of the waves are today bedecked with mansions and that fancy gardens replace the corner cashew and lush *pitanga* trees. I feel as if I were present at those happy *kermisses* and picturesque picnics of the *ACM* in the Canto do Rio, in Paquetá, and the Ilha d'Agua.

Then the scene grows darker with the call to Portugal. Crossing mine-laden seas, the stay in Coimbra, my husband's work there with its compensations, yes, but full of difficulties. With the participation of Portugal in the war we saw pass by our door one sad night 3,000 soldiers who marched to the front to the mournful sound of the drums, accompanied by the anguished cries of the afflicted hearts of mothers, wives, and sweethearts.

And everything passed, and everything changed; and climbing and descending the mountains of life, behold my baggage is reduced to that of a passenger, the sea always between me and mine: I, like that child, ask myself, "Am I myself, or not myself?"

*Francisca Pereira de Moraes Clark*

# Acknowledgements

My deepest gratitude rests with Francisca (Chiquita) Pereira de Moraes Clark, my paternal grandmother, who loved and valued her life enough to record her reminiscences, as she called them, for her grandchildren, and by doing so, enriched and changed my life. Ana Pereira, whom I sought and found in Caldas, shared with me stories from the slaves and servants who were an intimate part of family life, and whose identity was shaped by relationships with the family, but who lived apart. I will always be grateful for her acceptance of me, for her laughter, and her stories. None of these wonders would have happened without my cousin Sylvia's discovery of the tablets, so I'm most grateful to Sylvia Spencer Petrie for finding and entrusting them to me, and for her encouragement during thirty-plus years of writing and incubation.

My daughter Andrea Pappas suggested the inclusion of the story of my search for my grandmother's past as revealed in the people and places she knew, and the influences of Brazilian culture in my life. In this regard, she offered many of her observations and memories. She read the manuscript along the way several times and made useful suggestions. She has constantly encouraged me; this would simply not be in this form without her contributions.

Brazilian second cousins welcomed me into their very large and affectionate family and contributed greatly to my understanding and appreciation of Brazilian culture and family history. Estefânia Paixão and Stila Coelho da Sousa in Rio, Yedda Falzoni, Marila Kerr, and Virginia Amaral In São Paulo, and Mario Coelho de Sousa (Mario Gravem Borges) in Campinas, helped with genealogy and shared memories of my grandmother and theirs. Many other Brazilian cousins welcomed me into their hearts and homes; all with enthusiastic warmth, and encouraged me with the project; some of them also gently and patiently corrected my lapses in spoken Portuguese. To all my Brazilian cousins—*muitíssima obrigada!*

My cousin Dorothy (Dolly) Clark inspired me in so many ways—from our year together in Rio in the fifties to the present, she has shared her love for Brazilian music, food, humor, beauty, and vibrancy, all of which have influenced me so much. Her parents, Manoel (Neco) and Eleanor (Ginger) Clark took me into their home and guided me through my assimilation into Brazilian culture. Another cousin, Chiquita O'Leary, read early drafts as they were completed, and offered encouragement and suggestions. Both my sisters, Jan Horn and Sydney Hausrath added their memories to mine, shared my excitement, and read drafts. Sydney helped me sort through the piles of loose journal pages and notebooks to make some order out of the chaos of material. I owe much to my brother-in-law Don Hausrath for his many practical suggestions, including the organization of the chapters, and his guidance through the dry and thorny places of my discouragement.

In Caldas I found a second home at the Itacor Hotel Fazenda, and its manager, Maílde Jerónimo Tripoli became my guide and dear friend. Maílde also gave me source books of early Caldas history cited in the bibliography. I can't thank her enough for her friendship, understanding and support. It was through my first friend there, Denise Nicoletti Carvalho that I met Dona Ana, and her son and daughter, Odair and Ivone Pereira—all of whom welcomed me with Brazilian hospitality. In the home of Maria de Lourdes, I was transported back in time to the days of her childhood, and introduced to my father as a mischievous young boy who played with her while their parents visited. Dona Maria had many memories of the visits my father's family made to Caldas in the first decade of the twentieth century, and gave me a sense of what their life was like during that time. Maria Odete de Carvalho, too young to know my family's history, also became a good friend, and helped me with translations of the journals into Portuguese so that I could share them with Caldenses who were interested. She also took me to see what remained of the Fazenda Capivari that Vovó visited as a young girl.

I am also grateful to my friends Bexuta Mendes and her daughter, Maria Aparecida Mendes, descendants of slaves at Capivari, who told me stories handed down in their family, and showed me artifacts from the plantation. Sergio Bellini, a former mayor of Caldas, gave me the framed photograph of a painting of Caldas in 1875. Nilson Lemes da Silva, a historical researcher, sent me a copy of my great-grandfather's will that he had found in the archives of the city, and had bound for me. Olga Landi Guimarães da Silva, proprietor of a café in Caldas, received copies of my translation of part of my grandmother's journals and distributed them to interested parties, including a visual anthropologist who cited it in his studies. I thank all my friends in Caldas—*Obrigadíssima!*

The Rio branch of the *Associação Cristã de Moços*, welcomed me into their fellowship with open arms, invited me to their centennial, and showered me with loving attention. I would like to mention especially Tasso da Silveira, Paula Oliveira, and Vanda Magalhães of the Y's Men's Club; Hector Civitate, Thex and Dayse Correia, Enrique Irueta, and other staff members of the *ACM* who honored me with their kindnesses.

I wish to thank Matthew Restall of Penn State Press, Theresa May of University of Texas Press, and Candace Slater, Professor of Spanish and Portuguese at UC Berkeley, all of whom encouraged me at different stages of my work. Their belief in the value of this historical record kept me determined to persist in the face of many difficulties.

The Fuks family in Rio—Saúl, Sima, Hélio, Mário, and Maurício sheltered and fed me, and helped me over the bumps in the road of cultural difficulties. So many friends encouraged me through the decades—some read sections and gave feedback. I thank all of them: Amy Gorman, Betty Jane Snow, Beverlee McFadden, Anne Hannah-Roy, Eliene Bundy, Jacqueline Moser, Rose Hauer, Lou Hoblett, Michele Echenique, dj whelan, Judith Buist, Monica Meyer, Jaque Driggs, Jan Elster. My husband, Donn Weaver, never wavered in his belief that I would finally finish, and never complained about the time and energy it took to complete the book. Here's to you, Doninho!

Editors Laura Kennedy and Ken Sanderson gave valuable suggestions and found and corrected many errors. Martha McEvoy at Trumpet Vine Press and Anna Doherty, Laura Neil, and Leslie Peters of Together Editing and Design turned files full of words and folders full of rumpled old photographs into a printed book. My thanks to them for their patience, for the nitty-gritty, and the creative design work.

Memory is subjective, as are opinions; my observations and judgments are certainly not facts; I hope my account of events and the people I have encountered in my journey will not give offense to anyone, especially those who have given me so much.

# Glossary

Adjectives and nouns that change case are first listed in masculine form followed by the feminine ending and sometimes the plural after a slash. The list does not include verbs which are translated in the text, phrases, most proper names of people or places, or definitions given in footnotes.

| | |
|---|---|
| Abraços, abração | hugs, bear hug |
| Acarajé | croquette of cooked beans fried in *dendê* (palm oil) |
| Acemistas | members of the ACM (Associação Cristã de Moços), the YMCA in Brazil |
| Açúcar | sugar |
| Água | water |
| Água sanitária | disinfectant |
| Águamarinha | blue, aquamarine |
| Ala | aisle, flank, wing (but not of a bird, which is *asa*) |
| Amado/a | beloved, lover |
| Amazonas | horsewomen; also, a state in Brazil |
| Arara | macaw |
| Arpoador | harpooner, the name of a beach in Rio |
| Avó, vovó, vó (avô. vôvô, vô) | grandmother, grandma, granny (grandfather, grandpa) |
| Azul (pl. azuis) | blue |
| Baiano/a | a native of the state of Bahia |
| Baixo/a | low |
| Bandeira | flag |
| Bandeirantes | members of armed bands of early Brazilian explorers |
| Batería | drum corps |
| Batina | academic gown |
| Berimbao | string instrument made of a gourd |
| Boitos | pink river dolphins |
| Bom, boa | good |

| | |
|---|---|
| Bom dia | greeting, "good day" said in the morning only |
| Bonde | streetcar with outside fender for standees |
| Branco/a | white |
| Caboclos | backwoodsmen, usually of mixed indigenous and European descent |
| Cachaça | Brazilian rum made from sugar cane |
| Caçula | the youngest child in a family |
| Caducando/a | weak-minded, senile |
| Café, cafezinho | coffee, a small cup of coffee, demitasse |
| Café da manhã | breakfast |
| Caipirinha | a country girl; the name of a Brazilian cocktail |
| Caldas | hot springs |
| Caleça | a light carriage |
| Camarada | comrade, companion, hired hand; a servant for the road |
| Camareiro | room steward, steward, groom |
| Canção | song |
| Candomblé | religious or spiritual practice of African origin combining elements of many belief systems |
| Cantigas | ballads, songs |
| Capitania | a captaincy in colonial Brazil |
| Capoeira | martial arts practice/performance |
| Carioca | pertaining to, or a native of, Rio de Janeiro |
| Carnaval | Carnival, the pre-Lenten celebration |
| Casa; casa grande | house, home; big house, plantation owner's house |
| Cavalheiros | gentlemen, especially in dance |
| Cavalo | horse |
| Ceia | supper |
| Céu | sky, heaven |
| Chácara | a little country place |
| Chafariz | public faucet or fountain |

| | |
|---|---|
| Churrascaria; churrasco | restaurant featuring churrasco; Brazilian barbeque |
| Círio; Círio de Nazaré (Nazareth) | large candle used in churches; a religious ceremony in Belem, Pará |
| Colonos | tenant farmers |
| Congadas | folklore dramatizations in song and dance depicting the crowning of a king in the Congo |
| Coração | heart |
| Cruzeiro | large cross erected in a public square, also former Brazilian currency |
| Cruzeiro do Sul | the Southern Cross (constellation) |
| Curral | corral |
| Damas | ladies in ladies-in-waiting; the ladies in square dancing |
| Despachante | customs clerk, or one one who knows how to get through red tape bureaucracies |
| Despedida | leave-taking, a farewell party |
| Directora | head mistress |
| Directoria | board of directors |
| Doce; doce de leite | sweet; cooked sweetened milk |
| Dois, duas | two |
| Dom, dona | masculine and feminine titles of respect |
| Duro/a | hard, difficult |
| Dúvida | doubt |
| Echarpe | scarf |
| Eira | threshing floor |
| Escola | school |
| Escola de samba | samba club, each with its own colors and traditions |
| Espírito; Espírito Santo | spirit; Holy Spirit |
| Estado de sítio | state of siege or martial law |
| Estrangeiro/a | foreigner |
| Familia | family |

| | |
|---|---|
| Farinha | flour, usually ground up manioc root |
| Farofa | manioc flour fried with onions, bacon, and eggs |
| Favela | shantytown |
| Fazenda | plantation, ranch, farm |
| Fazendeiro/a/os | plantation owner/s |
| Feijão | beans |
| Feijoada | the Brazilian national dish of black beans, rice, collard greens, and sliced oranges |
| Feira | outdoor farmers' market |
| Feitor | administrator, foreman, overseer |
| Festa | party, celebration, feast, festival |
| Filho/a | daughter or son, also a term of affection |
| Fogão | hearth, stove, heater |
| Freguês/a | customer |
| Fundador/a | founder |
| Fútebol | soccer |
| Garção | waiter |
| Gargalhadas | boisterous laughter, guffaws |
| Gargarejo | gargle |
| Gaúcho | native of the state of Rio Grande do Sul in southern Brazil |
| Goiaba, goiabada | guava, guava paste |
| Golpe, golpista | a blow, coup d'etat (golpe de estado) |
| Gringa | female foreigner, especially a blonde North American |
| Guaraná | Brazilian soft drink |
| História | story, history |
| Hoatzin | the stinkbird, a large leaf eating bird |
| IBEU | Instituto Brasil-Estados Unidos, a bi-cultural arm of the US State Department |
| Idioma | language |
| Igarapés | seasonal waterways in the forest |
| Igrejinha | little church, chapel |

| | |
|---|---|
| Inconfidência Mineira | conspiracy in Minas Gerais in 1788–92 to overthrow the monarchy and establish a republic |
| Integração | integraton; the bus that connects to the subway station |
| Internato | boarding school |
| Jabuticaba | the fruit of the jabuticabeira, which grows directly on the trunk of the tree; national fruit of Brazil |
| Jacaré | alligator or caiman |
| Janela | window |
| Jangada | a raft of logs with a single mast and sail, used by fishermen of the northeast coast |
| Jararaca preguiçosa | a common lancehead pit viper, highly dangerous (*preguiçosa* means lazy) |
| Laço | loop, snare, lasso (*laços da família* – family ties) |
| Lagoa | lagoon |
| Lágrimas | tears |
| Lança perfume | perfumed ether in a spray canister |
| Largo | public square (noun); broad or wide (adj.) |
| Leme | rudder; name of a section of Rio |
| Liceu | secondary, preparatory school |
| Lotação (pl. lotações) | small bus or jitney that stops for riders when signaled |
| Louro/a | blond |
| Macumba | spiritual practices with many variations (related to Candomblé in Bahia) widely practiced in Brazil |
| Madrinha | godmother |
| Mãe, Mamãe | mother, mommy |
| Mamão | papaya |
| Manga | mango, also means sleeve |
| Manso/a | gentle, good, mild |
| Maravilhoso/a | wonderful, marvelous |
| Marcha funebre | funeral march |
| Menino/a/os/as | young boy (girl); also a term of affection, dear |

| | |
|---|---|
| Mercearia | grocery store |
| Metrô | subway |
| Meu (m.), minha (f.) | my |
| Mineiro/a | of or pertaining to, or an inhabitant of the state of Minas Gerais; also, a miner |
| Misericórdia | mercy, compassion |
| Moço/a | young man/girl |
| Morena | young woman of dark complexion |
| Morpheu | Morpheus, the Greek god of dreams |
| Morro | hill |
| Morte | death |
| Movimento | movement, bustle |
| Mulata | dark-skinned girl of mixed African and European descent |
| Namorado/a/os; namorando | boyfriend, girlfriend; sweethearts, dating |
| Neto/a | granddaughter, grandson |
| Ninho | nest, home |
| Noivo/a | fiancé |
| Novelas | prime-time dramatic television series |
| Novo/a | new |
| Núcleo | nucleus |
| Olho(s) | eye(s) |
| Orixá | spirit or deity |
| Ouro | gold |
| Papai; Papai do Ceu; Papai Noel | daddy; Father in Heaven; Santa Claus |
| Pai; pai de santo | father; the high priest of candombé or macumba |
| Palacetes | mansions |
| Palmatória | wooden paddle used on the hand of students in 19th century Brazil |
| Palmeira, Palmeirinha | palm tree, little palm tree |
| Pão | bread, loaf |

| | |
|---|---|
| Patrão | boss, master, employer |
| Patrício/a | compatriot |
| Paulista | a native or resident of the city of São Paulo |
| Pedra | rock, stone |
| Penedo | boulder or cliff |
| Pensão, pensões | boarding house(s) |
| Peralta | mischievous |
| Pharol | lighthouse (now spelled *farol*) |
| Pimenta | pepper |
| Pinheiros, pinhal | pine trees, especially the Brazilian pine or candelabra tree; *araucaria*; pine grove |
| Poços | wells |
| Porão | area under a house, basement |
| Praça | town square, usually with a church on one side |
| Praia | beach |
| Prata | silver |
| Prefeito | mayor |
| Primo/a/os | male cousin, female cousin, cousins |
| Preto/a | black |
| Professor/a | teacher |
| Quinta | rural residence, especially in Portugal |
| Quintal | backyard |
| Reminiscências | reminiscences |
| Ressaca | heavy surf or undertow; also colloquial for a hangover |
| Rua | street |
| Revolta | revolt, rebellion |
| Rio | river |
| Ríspido | rude, gruff |
| Roça | countryside |
| Sal; Salgadinhas | salt; savory bites |
| Sala, salão (pl. salões) | the main room of a house; a big parlor or ballroom |

| | |
|---|---|
| Samba, sambista | the rhythm of Brazil; a dance of African origin; one who dances the samba |
| Saudade | memory imbued with longing, sadness that you love to feel, poignant sweet/sad feelings |
| Segundo/a | ordinal number two; as a preposition, it means "according to" |
| Senhora; a Senhora | Mrs., Madam; with the definite article "a" it is the formal "you" for women |
| Senhor; o Senhor | Mr. Sir, the Lord; with the definite article "o" it is the formal "you" for men |
| Senzala | slave quarters on plantations |
| Serpentina | rolled paper streamers |
| Serra | mountain range |
| Sertão | the backlands of Brazil |
| Simpático | likeable, charming |
| Sonhos | dreams |
| Sorvete | ice cream |
| Temporado | short-term apartment |
| Terra | land, country, earth, world |
| Tio, tia, titia | uncle, aunt, auntie |
| Tipiti | a long, elastic tube woven of reeds used to squeeze poisonous juice from grated manioc root |
| Tiradentes | dentist (toothpuller); the Nickname for Joaquim José da Silva Xavier, a martyred Brazilian hero |
| Torre | tower |
| Toureiro | bullfighter |
| Traje de rigor | formal evening dress |
| Tranquilo/a | calm, tranquil |
| "Três Marias" | three Marys; the three stars in the constellation Orion's Belt |
| Tutu a mineira, tutu de feijão | red beans, pork, and manioc flour, a specialty in the cuisine of Minas Gerais |
| Turistas | tourists |
| Typografia | printers, now spelled tipografia |

| | |
|---|---|
| Umbu | plum-like fruit (also spelled *imbu*) |
| Urubu | black vulture |
| Vaca | cow |
| Varanda | porch, veranda |
| Vatapá | dish made of manioc flour and fish, a specialty of Bahia |
| Vermelho/a | red |
| Vida | life |
| Vila | cluster of houses, villiage |
| Vivas | cheers |
| Vovó, Vó | grandmother, grandma, granny (see *Avó*) |

# Genealogy Charts

Names are arranged alphabetically by first names or (nicknames). The second column shows each person's relationship to Chiquita; the third column indicates their location on Charts A–E, which follow.

| | | |
|---|---|---|
| Affonso Junqueira | Neice's husband | C7 |
| Ana | Great-great-grandniece | E9 |
| Andrea | Great-granddaughter | B23 |
| Annita | Granddaughter | B19 |
| Argentina (Argy, Baby) | Daughter | B5 |
| Argentino | Brother | A7 |
| Cacilda | Sister | A5 |
| Cacildinha | Niece | D2 |
| Carlos | Nephew-in-law | D |
| Chiquita | Granddaughter | B14 |
| Clark | Grandson | B24 |
| (Dolly) | Granddaughter | B17 |
| Donn | Grandson-in-law | B20 |
| Eduardo | Father's cousin | AA7 |
| Emília | Grandniece | E6 |
| Ernesto | Father's cousin | AA6 |
| Estafânia (Nona) | Grandniece | C8 |
| Esther | Daughter-in-law | B5 |
| Francisca | Niece | E3 |
| Francisca Carolina | Maternal grandmother | AA9 |
| **Francisca (Chiquita), Vovó** | **Self** | **A** |
| Francisco (Tio Francisco) | Father's uncle | AA3 |
| George (Jorginho) | Son | B10 |
| (Ginger) | Daughter-in-law | B9 |
| Godmother (Vovó's) | Great aunt | AA4 |
| Henedina | Niece | C2 |
| Henrique | Brother-in-law | E1 |
| Henry | Son | B7 |
| Jan | Granddaughter | B21 |

| | | |
|---|---|---|
| Jim | Grandson | B15 |
| João Sabino | Great-grandfather | AA8 |
| Joaquim Bueno de Camargo | Great-great-grandfather | N/A |
| John Anderson | Niece's husband | C3 |
| José de Aranjo Matto-Grosso (Dr.) | Brother-in-law | C2 |
| Josephina | Sister | A2 |
| Lia | Grandniece | E7 |
| Lydia | Sister | A3 |
| Lygia | Grandniece | N/A |
| Manoel de Paixão (Mineco) | Brother-in-law | C4 |
| Manoel Pereira de Moraes | Father | AA1 |
| Manoelita Oliveira | Niece | E2 |
| Manoelita Pereira de Moraes | Sister | A6 |
| Maria Ovidia da Paixão | Niece (lived with Chiquita) | C6 |
| Maria Ovídia Pereira de Camargo | Mother | AA2 |
| Maria (Mariquinha) | Sister | A1 |
| Marieta Severo | Great-grandniece | C9 |
| Marila | Grandniece | D4 |
| Mário Gravem Borges | Great-grandnephew | D7 |
| (Mike) Myron | Grandson | B13 |
| (Minequinho) | Nephew | C5 |
| Myron A. Clark (the Moço Louro) | Husband | B1 |
| (Nanny) | Son's mother-in-law | B11 |
| (Neco, Nequinho) | Son | B8 |
| Nell | Granddaughter-in-law | B16 |
| (Nina) Noemi | Niece | E4 |
| Noemi | Sister | A8 |
| Odila | Niece | D |
| Ophida | Sister | A4 |
| Orton | Son | B4 |
| (Paulinho) Paul | Grandson | B18 |
| Pedro Antônio de Silva (Padrinho) | Maternal great-grandfather | AA10 |
| Perla | Grandniece | E8 |
| Remígio | Brother-in-law | D1 |

| Romilda | Niece | D |
|---|---|---|
| Ruth | Daughter | B2 |
| Severo | Father's cousin | AA5 |
| Siá Tereza | Maternal great-step-grandmother | AA11 |
| Simão Antônio da Silva Teixeira | Maternal great-great-grandmother | AA12 |
| Stila | Grandniece | D5 |
| Sydney | Granddaughter | B22 |
| Sylvia | Granddaughter | B12 |
| Troy | Great-great-grandson | B25 |
| (Vida) | Niece | E5 |
| Virginia | Grandniece | D3 |
| **Vovó, Francisca (Chiquita)** | **Self** | **A** |
| Warren | Son-in-law | B3 |
| Yedda | Grand-niece | D6 |

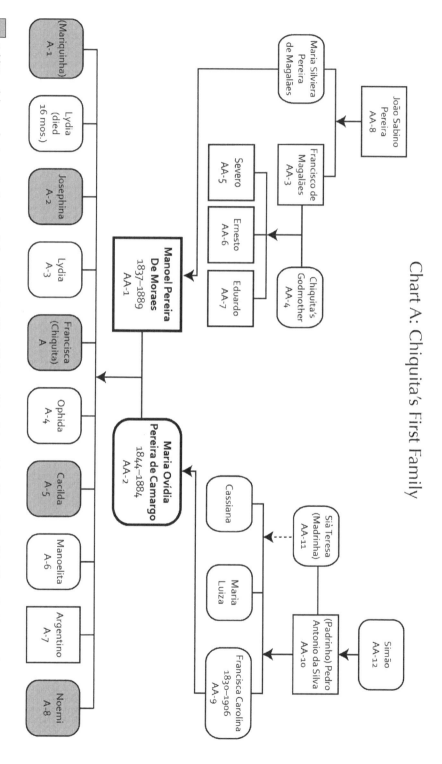

## Chart A: Chiquita's First Family

Additional descendants can be found as follows: Chiquita (Chart B), Marquihina & Josephina (Chart C); Cacilda (Chart D), Noemi (Chart E).

# Chart B: Chiquita & Myron's Family

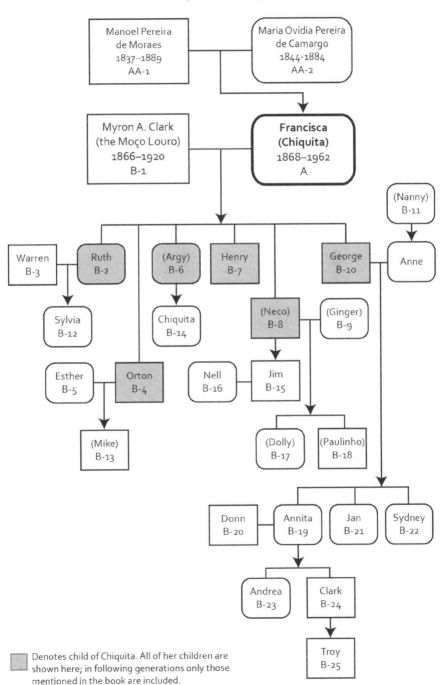

Denotes child of Chiquita. All of her children are shown here; in following generations only those mentioned in the book are included.

# Chart C:
## Mariquinha & Jose, Josephina & Mineco

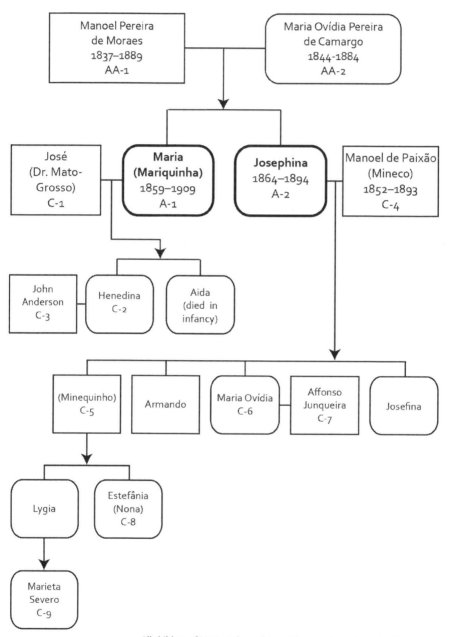

All children of Mariquinha and Josephina are shown here; in following generations only those mentioned in the book are included.

# Chart D: Cacilda & Remígio

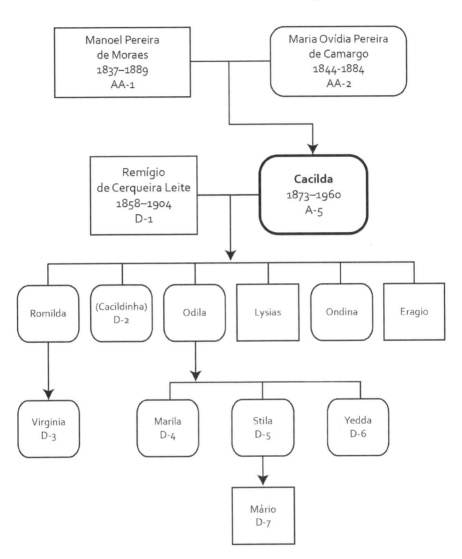

All children of Cacilda are shown here; in following generations
only those mentioned in the book are included.

# Chart E: Noemi & Enrique

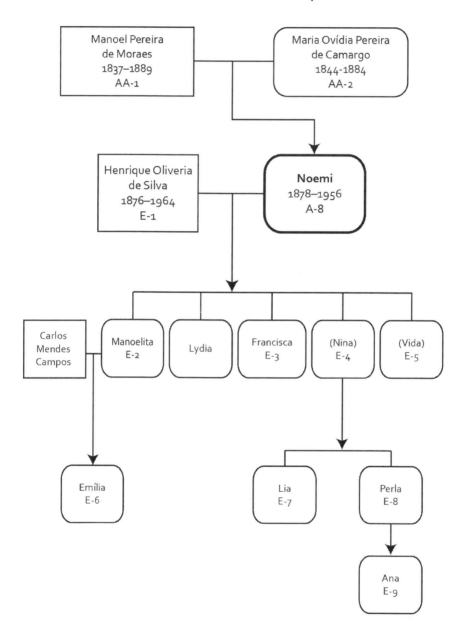

All children of Noemi are shown here; in following generations
only those mentioned in the book are included.

# References

## Works Cited

Ackerman, Diane. 1990. *A Natural History of the Senses*. New York: Random House.

Adams, James Truslow, ed. in chief. 1948. *Album of American History, Volume 4: End of an Era*. New York: Charles Scribner's Sons, 1944-[1961].

Alencar, José Martiano de, 1857. *O Guarani: Romance Brasileiro*. São Paolo: Comp. Melhoramentos de São Paolo.

Bello, José Maria. 1966. *A History of Modern Brazil, 1889–1964*. Translated by James L. Taylor. Palo Alto, CA: Stanford University Press.

Birk, Dorothy Daniels. 1997. *The World Came to St. Louis: A Visit to the 1904 World's Fair*. St. Louis, MO: Chalice.

Bortle, John E. 1998. "The Bright-Comet Chronicles." *International Comet Quarterly*. Accessed September 15, 2013. http://www.icq.eps.harvard.edu/bortle.html.

Buarque de Holanda, Sérgio. 1948. *Raízes do Brasil*, 2nd ed. Rio de Janeiro: J. Olympio.

Chuck. 2012. "Esperanto 101." *101 Languages*. Accessed September 15, 2013. http://www.101languages.net/esperanto/religion.html.

Clark, Chiquita Pereira de Moraes. 1930–1962. Unpublished tablets, letters, and miscellaneous writings; newspaper clippings, and calendar pages in the author's possession. See "About the Text."

———. 1900–1920. Unpublished diaries, private collection.

Department of the Navy, Naval Historical Center. 2004. "S. S. Leviathan." *Dictionary of American Fighting Ships*. Accessed September 15, 2013. http://www.history.navy.mil/danfs/l5/leviathan.htm.

Freidel, Frank. 2002. *The Splendid Little War*. Ithaca, NY: Burford.

Gardner, W. J. R., ed. 2000. *The Evacuation from Dunkirk: "Operation Dynamo" 26 May–4 June 1940*. Whitehall Histories: Naval Staff Histories, edited by Captain Christopher Page. London: Newbury House.

Gonçalves Dias, Antônio. [1843]. "The Song of Exile." Translated by Nelson Ascher. Originally published as "Canção do Exílio"(Coimbra, Portugal).

———. 1851. "I-Juca Pirama." In *Últimos Cantos: Poesias*, 12–35. Rio de Janeiro: Typographia de F. de Paula Brito.

Griffin, Charles Eldridge. 2010. *Four Years in Europe With Buffalo Bill*. University of Nebraska.

Haring, Clarence Henry. 1958. *Empire in Brazil: A New World Experiment with Monarchy*. Cambridge, MA: Harvard University Press.

Jack, Malcolm. 2003. *Sintra: A Glorious Eden*. Manchester, UK: Carcanet Press.

Junqueira Franco, Gabriel, and Luiz Alberto Franco Junqueira. 1983. *Família Franco: Genealogia e História*. Poços de Caldas, Minas Gerais: Escola Profissional Dom Bosco.

Kelly, Wayne. 1994. *The Crokinole Book*. Boston: Mills Press.

Lonely Planet. 2012. "Círio de Nazaré: A Guide to Brazil's Largest Religious Festival." *Lonely Planet*, July 25. Accessed September 15, 2013. http://www.lonelyplanet.com/brazil/the-north/belem/travel-tips-and-articles/77409#ixzz2eoN7aVES.

Mann, Graciela. 1967.*The 12 Prophets of Aleijadinho*. Austin: University of Texas Press.

Marshfield Area YMCA. 2013. "Wherever the Soldier Goes—YMCAs and the Military." Accessed August 2, 2013. http://www.mfldymca.org/about_us/history_national.php.

Miller, Robert Motes. 1985. *Harry Emerson Fosdick: Preacher, Pastor, Prophet*. New York: Oxford University Press.

Mount Vernon Ladies' Association. 2013. "Bastille Key." *George Washington's Mount Vernon Digital Encyclopedia*. Accessed September 16, 2013. http://www.mountvernon.org/educational-resources/encyclopedia/bastille-key.

Pan American Union. 1922. "Dr. Amaro Cavalcanti." *Bulletin of the Pan American Union* 54 (1–6), 378–79. Accessed September 25, 2013. http://books.google.com/books?id=cm8EAAAAIAAJ&printsec=frontcover#v=onepage&q&f=false.

Petersen, Vergard Krog. 2011. "Chinese Checkers: History of Halma." Accessed September 15, 2013. http://chinesecheckers.vegard2.no/history.html.

Pimenta, Reynaldo de Oliveira. 1998. *O Povoamento do Planalto da Pedra Branca—Caldas e Região*. São Paulo: RUMOGRAF.

Roosevelt, Theodore. 1913. "Rio de Janeiro: Third of a Series of Articles on South America." *The Outlook*, December 20. Theodore Roosevelt Center, Dickinson State University. Accessed September 16, 2013. http://www.theodorerooseveltcenter.org/Research/Digital-Library/Record/ImageViewer.aspx?libID=0279287&imageNo=1.

"Says Cue Roque Is Not Like Pool." 1915. *Spartanburg Herald* (South Carolina), April 2. Accessed September 16, 2013. http://news.google.com/newspapers?nid=1876&dat=19150402&id=-E8sAAAAIBAJ&sjid=28kEAAAAIBAJ&pg=2868,119145.

Spalding, Susan Marr. 1982. "Fate." In *Wings of Icarus*, 14–15. Boston: Roberts Brothers. Accessed August 19, 2013. http://archive.org/details/wingsoficarusoospal.

Sutcliffe, Anthony. 1996. *Paris: An Architectural History*. New Haven, CT: Yale University Press.

Taft, William Howard. ed. 1922. *Service with Fighting Men: An Account of the Work of the American Young Men's Christian Associations in the World War*. 2 vols. New York: Association Press.

Taylor, James L. 1980. *A Portuguese-English Dictionary*. Redwood City, CA: Stanford University Press.

Wagenknecht, Edward. 1958. *The Seven Worlds of Theodore Roosevelt*. New York: Longmans, Green.

Wheeler, Douglas L. 1978. *Republican Portugal: A Political History, 1910–1926*. Madison: University of Wisconsin Press.

Whitehill, Bruce. 1999. "American Games: A Historical Perspective." *Board Game Studies* 2, 116–41.

Wimmel, Kenneth. 1998. *Theodore Roosevelt and the Great White Fleet: American Sea Power Comes of Age*. Sterling VA: Potomac Books.

Zebrowski, Ernest. 2002. *The Last Days of St. Pierre: The Volcanic Disaster That Claimed 30,000 Lives*. Piscataway, NJ: Rutgers University Press.

# Interviews

Camargo, Maria de Lourdes. Oral history interviews with author, February 1985 and June 1986.

Clark, Chiquita Pereira de Moraes. Conversations with the author, her granddaughter in Athens, Ohio, 1940–1945; and Rio de Janeiro, 1955 and 1956.

Mendes, Bexuta. 1986. Oral history interview with the author, June 9.

Pereira, Ana. Oral history interviews with the author, June 7, 1985, and February 3, 13, and 14, 1986.

# Civll Regestry Archives Researched

Cartório do Registro Civil (Office of the Registrar). Caldas, Minas Gerais, Brazil.

Lemes da Silva, Nilson. Pesquisador Histórico (Historical Researcher) Caldas, M.G.

# Further Reading

## Brazil and Portugal

"Biela's Comet." 1865. *New York Times*, 3 September. Accessed September 15, 2013. http://www.nytimes.com/1865/09/03/news/biela-s-comet.html.

Coutinho, Afrânio. 1969. *An Introduction to Literature in Brazil*. Translated by GregoryRabassa. New York: Columbia University Press. Previously published as *Introdução à Literatura no Brasil* (Rio de Janeiro: Livraria São José, 1966).

Freyre, Gilberto. 1956. *The Masters and the Slaves: a Study in the Development of Brazilian Civilization*. 2nd ed., rev. ed. Translated by Samuel Putnam. New York: Alfred A. Knopf. Originally published as *Casa Grande e Senzala: Formação da Familia Brasileira sob o Regimen de Economia Patriarcal* (Rio de Janeiro: Maia & Schmidt, 1933).

———. 1963. *The Mansions and the Shanties: The Making of Modern Brazil*. Translated and edited by Harriet de Onís. New York: Alfred A. Knopf. Originally published as *Sobrados e Mucambos: Decadência do Patriacardo Rural e Desenvolvimento de Urbano* (São Paulo: Compania Editora Nacional, 1936).

———. 1970. *Order and Progress; Brazil from Monarchy to Republic.* Translated by Rod W. Horton. New York: Alfred A. Knopf. Originally published as *Ordem e Progresso: Processo de Desintegração das Sociedades Patriarcal e Semipatriarcal no Brasil sob o Regime de Trabalho Livre* (Rio de Janeiro: J. Olympio, 1959).

Gonzales Echeverria, Roberto, and Enrique Pupo-Walker, eds. 1996. *The Cambridge History of Latin American Literature.* Vol 3, *Brazilian Literature: Bibliographies.* New York: Cambridge University Press.

Levine, Robert M. and John J. Crocitti, eds. 1999. *The Brazil Reader: History, Culture, Politics.* Durham NC: Duke University Press.

Machado de Assis, Joaquim Maria. 1952. *Epitaph of a Small Winner.* Translated by William L. Grossman. New York: Noonday Press. Originally published as *Memórias Póstumas de Brás Cubas* (Rio de Janeiro, 1881).

———. 1998. *Dom Casmurro.* Translated by John A. Gledson. New York: Oxford University Press/Library of Latin America. Originally published in Rio de Janeiro, 1900.

Morley, Helena [Alice D. Brant]. 1995. *The Diary of* "Helena Morley." Translated by Elizabeth Bishop. New York: Farrar, Straus, Giroux. Originally published as *Minha Vida de Menina: Cadernos de uma Menina Provinciana nos Fins do Século XIX* (Rio de Janeiro: J. Olympio, 1942).

Ribeiro de Oliveira, Myriam Andrade. 1984. "Aleijadinho and Baroque Art in Brazil," in *Art and Architecture in Brazil, from Aleijadinho to Niemeyer.* New York: United Nations Headquarters.

Wagley, Charles. 1963. *An Introduction to Brazil.* New York: Columbia University Press.

Wheeler, Douglas L. 1978. *Republican Portugal: A Political History, 1910–1926.* Madison: University of Wisconsin Press.

## United States Culture, 1900–1910

Adams, James Truslow, and Joseph G. E. Hopkins, eds. 1944. *Album of American History.* Vol. 3, *1853–1893.* New York: C. Scribner's Sons.

———. 1944. *Album of American History.* Vol. 4, *End of an Era.* New York: C. Scribner's Sons.

Angel, Ann. 1995. *America in the 20th Century, Volume 1: 1900–1909*. Tarrytown, NY: Marshall Cavendish.

Bennitt, Mark, ed. 1905. *History of the Louisiana Purchase Exposition: Comprising the History of the Louisiana Territory, the Story of the Louisiana Purchase and a Full Account of the Great Exposition, Embracing the Participation of the States and Nations of the World, and Other Events of the St. Louis World's Fair of 1904*. Saint Louis, MO: Universal Exposition Publishing.

Johnson, Paul. 1998. *A History of the American People*. New York: Harper Collins.

Shifflett, Crandall A. 1996. *Victorian America, 1876–1913*. Almanacs of American Life, edited by Richard Balkin. New York: Facts on File.

## Foreign Missions

Clark, Myron Augustus. Unpublished diaries, 1900–1920; papers, 1877–1967. Records of YMCA International Work in Brazil, 1890–1989, box 34. Kautz Family YMCA Archives, University of Minnesota.

Hopkins, Charles Howard. 1951. *History of the YMCA in North America*. New York: Association Press.

Parker, Michael. 1998. *The Kingdom of Character: The Student Volunteer Movement for Foreign Missions (1886–1926)*. Lanham, MD: American Society of Missiology, University Press of America.

Made in the USA
Charleston, SC
04 March 2014